UWHARRIE LAKES REGION TRAIL GUIDE

SECOND EDITION

Don Childrey

Uwharrie Lakes Region Trail Guide
Second Edition
Don Childrey

ISBN-13 978-0-9915802-0-0

PUBLISHED BY:
Earthbound Sports, Inc.
Post Office Box 3312
Chapel Hill, NC 27515-3312

Printed and published in the United States of America

Proceed at your own risk.

"The use of cell phones has led to an enormous influx of people into the backcountry who come unprepared and then, faced with the reality of the wilderness, demand help immediately. There seems to be an increasing failure in our cultures' value system whereby self-indulgence is the norm, while self-discipline and personal courage are discarded as relics of the past." (Tom Vines, in Wall Street Journal April 1997).

In the October 1997 Register, a stewardship newsletter for the Appalachian Trail, Thomas McGinnis urged that we "restore the rightful place of self-reliance in the wilderness ethic." Too many of the "new breed of 'outdoorsmen' embrace the appearance but not the substance of adventure…" Backcountry visitors "must use mountains and trails by their own unaided efforts. If your personal values tend more toward self-indulgence than self-reliance, you will be at odds with the values of those you share the woods with: fellow 'adventurers', trail designers, trail maintainers, rescue personnel, and the bear behind that tree over there."

While I haven't seen the bears in the Uwharrie Lakes Region, I have seen lots of disoriented hikers and heard of several people unintentionally spending the night in the woods. Being familiar with this area and having spent a considerable amount of time in the backcountry, I worry that in writing this guidebook I will inadvertently convey the message that the backcountry is as safe as your living room. It is not.

You can have a safe and rewarding experience in the backcountry, if you take the time to learn the skills and gain the experience necessary to be self-reliant. That doesn't mean you have to know which plants and bugs to eat or how to use the stars as a compass. Self-reliance means you are aware of your limits (physical, mental, and gear) and are wise enough to turn around while you can still get yourself out of trouble. Thorough planning, proper preparation, and accumulated experience will allow you to go farther, do more, and enjoy the trip better.

This book is not intended to provide the reader with any knowledge regarding how to visit the backcountry safely. Rather, this book is intended to provide you with the information needed to get to the region and show where the trails are. It is your responsibility, as a visitor to the backcountry, to be prepared when you arrive.

The author and the publisher accept no responsibility for inaccuracies or for damages incurred while attempting any of the routes listed.

I'd like to extend my sincere thanks to several people:

My wife Sandy, whose assistance and support allowed me to complete this project, again,

My daughters Lainey and Lauren, who continue to be a source of inspiration and motivation for me,

Tom and Lorene, my parents, whose guidance and support started me out on the right foot and have always been there for me,

Pete Murphy, the Scoutmaster who first took me camping when I was eight and later introduced me to the Uwharries,

Crystal Cockman (aka Ivory Bill) and her LandTrust for Central NC colleagues whose efforts to protect these special lands have made great strides in reconnecting the historic Uwharrie Trail route.

Rebecca Schoonover (aka Hippie Longstocking) and her schoolmates who give us hope that younger generations still value wild lands and the wilderness experience enough to enthusiastically love and protect them.

All trail maintainers, volunteer and otherwise, whose efforts in building and maintaining trails provides us with an opportunity to experience the beauty of the backcountry.

Don Childrey
aka Infoman

Contents

Introduction

Welcome to the first revision of the first guidebook to cover mountain biking and hiking opportunities in the Uwharrie Lakes Region of central North Carolina.

This eight county region takes its name from a chain of lakes along the Yadkin and Pee Dee Rivers and the Uwharrie Mountains, a small range of mountains that many consider to be the oldest in North America. Three major trail areas offer a wealth of outdoor recreation opportunities to trail enthusiasts: the Uwharrie National Forest, the Birkhead Mountains Wilderness, and Morrow Mountain State Park. Together these areas provide nearly 60,000 acres of publicly owned land. Several smaller parks add even more trails.

Although mostly rural, the region is surrounded by major metropolitan areas: Raleigh, Durham, Greensboro, Winston-Salem, Charlotte, and Fayetteville. More than four million people live within a two hour drive. Some predict this region will become the Central Park of the future for North Carolina.

Very few hikers and mountain bikers have discovered the opportunities that abound in the Uwharrie Lakes Region. Instead mountain bikers frequently drive several hours to the western mountains in search of mountainous terrain and public lands where they are allowed to ride. If you've never visited the region, this guidebook will introduce you to a new destination to enjoy and insight into some of the lesser known spots and hidden treasures of the Uwharries.

I have always loved discovering and learning about new places, almost as much as I enjoy visiting them. Growing up in central NC, I spent many weekends with my Boy Scout troop hiking and learning the trails of the Uwharries. In the process of searching for and putting together the information for this guide, I still enjoyed the thrill of discovery on numerous occasions. Locating potential riding areas on maps and then exploring them on bike has provided me with plenty of anticipation and excitement over the past several years.

You now have the chance to enjoy hiking and riding some great routes, not knowing exactly what lies around the next bend but having the security of knowing where you'll eventually end up.

Hiking Opportunities in the Uwharries

Hiking trails in the Uwharrie Lakes Region are generally moderate in difficulty. Some sections present challenges such as steep grades, rocky tread, or difficult to follow routes, but these sections are relatively short. Several trails and trips in this guide are rated as Difficult simply due to their length.

You will find enough elevation change to make you realize you are in mountainous terrain, but you won't find thousands of feet of elevation change. The scenery is beautiful and varied enough to keep you interested.

Hikers should always take precautions to ensure that they have a safe and enjoyable trip.

The 20+ mile long Uwharrie Hiking Trail, a National Recreation Trail, is the longest. Several shorter hiking trails and woods roads connect to or cross the Uwharrie Trail. All of these trails are good for backpacking trips.

The Birkhead Mountains Wilderness contains several worthwhile trails. Portions of the Birkhead Mountain and Robbins Branch Trails were originally part of the much longer Uwharrie Trail. The Birkhead Mountains Wilderness trails are good for both dayhikes and backpacking.

Morrow Mountain State Park provides several trails which are suitable for dayhiking. There is only one location in the park where backpack camping is allowed.

The Wood Run Mountain Bike Trails are also open to hikers, as are any of the multitude of old roadbeds running throughout the region. Experienced and properly equipped hikers always have the additional option of striking out cross-country.

This guide also includes several smaller parks with trails that are suitable for partial-day trips. I've included them to acknowledge their contribution to the overall regional set of trail resources.

Mountain Biking Opportunities in the Uwharries
You'll find a wide variety of riding in the Uwharrie Lakes Region, from gentle gravel roads to steep rocky downhills to remote overgrown roadbeds.

By the 1930's, most of the land in what is now the Uwharrie National Forest had been logged heavily and poorly farmed. Little had been done to prepare for the future productivity of the land. The Federal government purchased a significant portion of these tracts between 1931 and 1934 under what was known as the Uwharrie Purchase Unit. The USFS began managing the land for timber production. Improvement of the timber stands was carried out with the help of Civilian Conservation Corps work crews.

In the early days of logging, small sawmills were set up in the forest to cut the logs into lumber. Simple roads were built through the forest in order to truck the lumber out. When the lumber industry switched to hauling the trees out of the forest to permanent sawmills in the mid 1900's, many of these sawmill roads were abandoned. However, quite a few of them have been used enough by hunters, horseback riders, and four-wheelers over the years to keep them passable. These old sawmill roads are perfect for mountain bike riding. Most of them were built on an easy grade and are sometimes wide enough for two to ride abreast.

The Uwharrie Lakes Region also has a bit of gold mining in its history, with over 200 sites producing gold at one time or another. Many of the creek bottoms and ridges were explored and mined in the search for gold. Numerous roadbeds still remain from the mining operations, adding to the multitude of potential riding routes in the Forest.

In addition to old sawmill and mining roads, US Forest Service properties also feature newer graveled access roads used for timber harvesting. After a tract of timber has been harvested, the access road usually remains in place. The Forest Service gates these roads and closes them to motorized traffic. These access roads are open to mountain bikes and provide riding routes free from the worry of vehicular traffic.

Horseback Riding Opportunties in the Uwharries
In 2000, a set of equestrian-built trails in the Badin Lake Area were numbered and signed, providing extensive riding opportunities for equestrians.

Off-Highway-Vehicle Riding Opportunties in the Uwharries
In the late 1970's the Forest Service established a network of trails for Off Road Vehicles (ORV) near Badin Lake. The ORV trails are quite challenging, with rocky treads and some extremely steep sections. Mountain bikes are allowed on the ORV trails.

In 1996, a group of mountain bikers organized the Uwharrie Mountain Bicycle Association and began developing a system of mountain bike trails in the Wood Run planning area of the Uwharrie National Forest. The Wood Run Mountain Bike Trails combine segments of old sawmill and mining roads, gravel access roads, and new singletrack trail to form a system of interconnected loop routes. This developing trail system promises to be as exciting as nationally known riding destinations such as the Tsali Trails near Lake Fontana.

I hope you will enjoy riding and hiking these trails as much as I have. Whether you visit for a day and get in a few hours on the trail, or if you come for the weekend and stay overnight, I'm sure you too will discover excitement on the trails in the Uwharrie Lakes Region.

Finding the Uwharrie Lakes Region

The Uwharrie Lakes Region lies almost in the middle of North Carolina. In fact, the midpoint of the state, from east to west and north to south, can be found in northeastern Montgomery County near the community of Star. Trail areas can be reached in about an hour from Charlotte, an hour from the Triad (Greensboro), and one and a half hours from the Triangle (Raleigh & Durham).

In order to simplify route finding, this guide provides directions to several landmarks or key intersections in this chapter. Later, in the chapter for each area, you'll find directions to the various trailheads from these landmarks.

Road Names Used in the Guidebook

Roads are referred to by their name and/or number. The NC Department of Transportation posts number signs for state-maintained roads at all of their intersections. State road numbers have a prefix of US, NC, or SR. US and NC routes are major primary roads. Roads with an SR prefix (for "secondary roads") are smaller two lane roads that may or may not be paved.

The USFS has its own system of roads that are listed with an FR prefix. Some of these are open to vehicular traffic.

Trail Areas in the Uwharrie Lakes Region

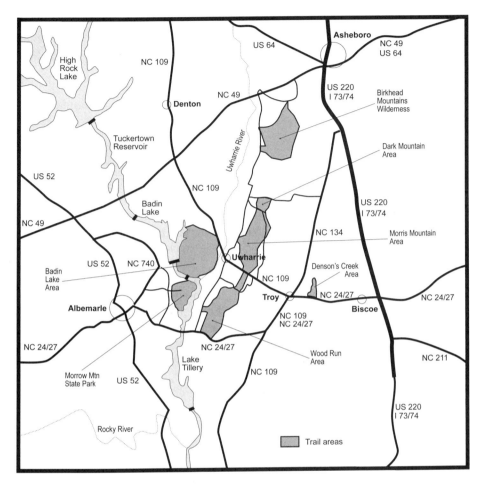

Some of the trails are referred to as "roads". These are backcountry routes that follow an old roadbed or a gated USFS road. Unless they are higher priority USFS roads, they may not have a number assigned to them. In some cases, I have not shown the FR number for such "trails", even though the road may have one.

Troy Courthouse

The Montgomery County Courthouse in Troy is a useful landmark for people coming from the north and east. Located on the southeast corner of the intersection of NC 24-27 and NC 134, the large stone courthouse is easy to identify. NC 24-27 runs from Charlotte through Troy and crosses US 1 just south of Sanford. NC 134 begins at NC 24-27 in Troy and runs north to end near US 220/Interstate 73-74 just south of Asheboro. The town of Troy, NC 24-27, and NC 134 are all shown on the publicly available NC State Transportation Map.

From the Troy Courthouse, you can follow NC 109 northwest to reach the Morris Mountain, and Badin Lake areas.

Follow NC 24-27 west to get to the Wood Run Area and Morrow Mountain State Park. The USFS District Ranger's Office is located on NC 24-27, 1.7 miles east of the Courthouse.

Tillery Bridges
A pair of bridges can be found where NC 24-27 crosses Lake Tillery/Pee Dee River at the west edge of Montgomery County. This landmark will be useful for people approaching from the west. Two large bridges span the lake at this location, one for each direction of travel, making it an easy landmark to recognize. NC 24-27 and Lake Tillery are both shown on the publicly available NC State Transportation Map.

From the Tillery Bridges, you're only two miles west of the Wood Run Area. One mile to the east is River Road (SR 1150), which you can follow north along the Wood Run Area to NC 109 (at Uwharrie, the third landmark) where you can easily reach the Morris Mountain and Badin Lake areas. About 3.6 miles west of the bridges on NC 24-27 is Valley Drive (SR 1720), which leads you north to Morrow Mountain State Park.

Also helpful for people coming from the west is the intersection of NC 24-27 and NC 740 in Albemarle. This stoplighted intersection is where NC 24-27 makes a right turn towards the east. You can follow NC 740 straight ahead to reach the beginning of Morrow Mountain Road (SR 1798), which will lead you straight into Morrow Mountain State Park. NC 740 is shown on the publicly available NC State Transportation Map.

Uwharrie
The community of Uwharrie is located on NC 109 about 8 miles north of Troy. Uwharrie only has a few houses, a gas station, a volunteer fire department, and a sign that says "Uwharrie" on both sides. Two roads connect to NC 109 in Uwharrie; River Road (SR 1150) which runs south along the Wood Run Area to NC 24-27, and Ophir Road (SR 1303) which leads north along the Morris Mountain Area. NC 109 runs from Winston-Salem to Troy.

Follow NC 109 north from Uwharrie to reach the Badin Lake Area. NC 109 and the community of Uwharrie are both shown on the publicly available NC State Transportation Map, however River Road and Ophir Road are not.

NC 49 & SR 1163

The western intersection of NC 49 and Tot Hill Farm Road (SR 1163) is located 6.3 miles west of US 220/Interstate 73 in Asheboro. Tot Hill Farm Road follows a U-shaped route that intersects with NC 49 in two places. Coming from the west on NC 49, the western intersection is 2.3 miles east of where NC 49 crosses the Uwharrie River or 4.1 miles past where NC 49 changes from 4 lanes back to 2 lanes. NC 49 runs from Charlotte through Asheboro to Burlington. US 220/Interstate 73-74 runs from Greensboro through the east side of Montgomery County to Rockingham, NC.

From this intersection you can easily reach the north and west sides of the Birkhead Mountains Wilderness Area. NC 49 and the Uwharrie River are shown on the publicly available NC State Transportation Map. Tot Hill Farm Road is not shown on this map.

How To Use This Guidebook

How the information is arranged
This guide book is divided into sections by geographical area. Each area consists of a tract of public land containing trails. The chapters are arranged alphabetically by name of the areas. The one exception to this organization approach is the Uwharrie Trail chapter. The Uwharrie Trail crosses several of the other areas, so it is presented in a chapter by itself.

Included for each area are access and parking details for each trailhead, items of geographical and historical interest, camping information, and a few notes about existing maps. A map detailing the roads surrounding each area, and how they relate to the area's trailheads and trails, is also included.

For each area there is a chapter containing details about the individual "trails". Each trail is described in the traditional manner: end to end, one named trail at a time. Individual trail descriptions include notes about background and highlights, a mileage chart, an elevation profile, and a map showing the trail and its surroundings.

Another chapter for each area contains route descriptions for the more obvious "trips" that follow sections of multiple trails. Trip information includes a map, mileage information, an elevation graph, and some statistics about the route. Every possible trip is not covered in this guide, leaving you the option to create your own unique trip routes.

Symbols are shown above each trail or trip map to indicate the uses allowed on that particular route. All trails and roads are open to hikers. Bike trails are open for mountain bikers and hikers. Horse trails are open for horseback riders, mountain bikers, and hikers. OHV trails are open for OHVs, horseback riders, mountain bikers, and hikers.

It would be impossible to include all the neat information about each trail or area or historical spot. I've tried to include enough information to get you interested, help you locate the trailheads, and find your way around the trails. It's up to you to come and discover the rest for yourself!

Summary Tables

The Trails and Trips chapters for each Area start with a Summary Table listing the trails or trips and providing a few details about each. The summary tables look like this:

Trail Name	Length (miles)	Elevation Gain/Loss	Difficulty Rating
Backpack	0.46	21' / 124'	Easy
Campground	0.60	37' / 82'	Easy
Duck Blind Spur	0.36	11' / 45'	Easy

Quick Reference Tables

In the back of the book you will find Quick Reference tables to help you find trips that meet certain criteria. Each Area chapter has a Summary table at the beginning listing the trails or trips in that area. Hopefully these tables will take some of the guesswork out of finding the right trip for you, leaving you with more time to enjoy the trails themselves.

Detail Tables

Each trail and trip in the book has a Detail Table which contains some of the important data about the route. The tables look like this:

Denson's Creek Trail

Map	page 288	**Difficulty**	Moderate
Length	2.22 miles	**Configuration**	Loop
Trailhead	Ranger Station	**Elev Gain/Loss**	320' / 320'

Start Coordinates N35.36210, W79.86276;   17 S 603318 3913793

Item explanations

The items of information found in the Detail Tables, as well as the Quick Reference tables, are as follows:

Map is the page on which the trail or trip map can be found.

Length is the length of the trail or trip in miles. This is listed to the hundredth of a mile, BUT your mileage reading will probably be different.

Trailhead is where the trip starts, if at a trailhead.

Difficulty is a rating of the overall challenge of the route. Unfortunately, difficulty ratings are very subjective. Additional details about specific challenges can be found in the background text for each trail. Mileage, elevation and descriptive information is provided for all trails and should be used to determine if a trail suits your abilities or desires. Overall, the ORV trails in the Badin Lake Area are much more demanding to ride than trails in the other parts of the Uwharries. Hiking trail difficulty usually arises from length rather than steepness or tread.

- *Easy* generally means the route is easy to follow and is fairly short.
- *Moderate* generally means the route presents some challenges in tread type, length, or with route-finding
- *Difficult* generally means the route contains significant challenges in the above categories
- *Difficult+* means the route offers extreme challenges

Elevation Gain and Loss are the total vertical feet of climbing and the total vertical feet of descending along the route.

Configuration describes the way the route runs through the area.
- *One way* routes start at one location and end at another
- *Out & back* routes go out and then retrace the route back to the start
- *Loop* routes forms a circle, ending at the starting point
- *Lollipop* routes backtrack at the end, but have a loop in the middle
- *Combined* routes may include a little of everything

Start Coordinates lists the Latitude and Longitude coordinates, followed by UTM coordinates, where the trail or trip starts. Lat/Lon coordinates are given in decimal degrees. UTM is another coordinate system often used in adventure racing and similar to the MGRS system used by the military. UTM coordinates are given in meters.

Lat/Lon: N35.36210, W79.86276 ;   UTM: 17 S 603318 3913793

Notes about mileage figures
You will notice the mileage figures are shown to the hundredth of a mile. The hundredth place figure is only worth its value to place one location before or after its neighbors. As an engineer-type, I had a hard time not being able to measure the trails *exactly*.

For the first edition of this guide book, I used a cyclo-computer which read to the hundredth of a mile, but in checking the calibration, I found that most such devices have inconsistencies due to internal rounding errors, among other things. I also learned that the little calibration charts that come with such devices, as well as the more involved circumference method of finding a calibration number, can both be inaccurate.

On top of all that, I watched the wheel bounce, slip, spin, etc down the trails enough to know that any trail distance measured with a wheel is somewhat suspect as far as accuracy goes. Despite those problems, the setup I used agreed almost exactly with Bob Finley's measurements of the hiking trails as found in his 1991 *Sportsman's Guide* book.

For this revision of the guide book, I used GPS technology to map and measure the routes. As fancy as that sounds, it's really just a different measuring technology with inconsistencies of its own.

GPS measuring consists of mathematically calculating the straight-line distance between a series of points in three dimensional space. You've probably noticed that there aren't many "straight lines" on a trail through the woods. I found trail distances calculated using the GPS method average 1% to 2% shorter than those calculated using the wheel method. This makes sense to me since the GPS isn't bouncing up and down over roots and curving around rocks in the trail like the measuring wheel.

Use these mileage and elevation figures as a guide, but don't be surprised if they vary a little from your cyclo-computer or GPS unit readings.

Symbols used on the maps

 Featured trails   Hike-only trails

 Other roads and trails   Bike-hike trails

 Streams   Horse-hike trails

 Named camp areas   Potential camp areas

Maps in this book
Trail and trip maps in this book were created using GPS technology. The scale may have been altered to make each map fit the page better, but the relative positions and lengths of the trails are accurate.

The benefits of GPS mapping are better accuracy in the two-dimensional representation of the trails on the maps, and better elevation data. My mapping method for the first edition of the guide book consisted of hand drawing the trail lines on a USGS topographic map and reading off the elevations at key points along the trails. That method produced better results than other guides available at the time. The GPS mapping method has allowed me to take the data accuracy to a higher level once again.

Having GPS data now makes it possible for this guidebook to include coordinates for the trailheads. That way, if you do get lost and you do have a GPS, you can use it to get back to where you started!

Other guidebooks and maps

Most of the previously published trail guides that mention trails in this region only cover certain trails and provide few maps, if any at all. Three of these guides are:

North Carolina Hiking Trails by Allen DeHart, 2005.

Sportsman's Guide to the Uwharrie Trail and the Birkhead Mountains Wilderness by Bob Finley, 1991. This guide is no longer in print.

G. Nicholas Hancock published a small guide book and map in 1983 titled *Guide To The Uwharrie Trail In The Uwharrie National Forest In Randolph And Montgomery Counties, North Carolina*. ISBN 0-89732-039-5. This guide is no longer in print.

Of the foldout maps that are currently available, several of them contain errors or don't show the "newer" trails. USGS topographic quad maps currently available also have some shortcomings. I have tried to provide information for each area to compensate for these inaccuracies and provide you with a more useful picture of the trails in this region.

The USFS Southern Region sells a 1:24,000 scale map of the Birkhead Mountains Wilderness, revised in 2011. This map only shows four of the named trails, most notably missing are the Camp Three Trail and Forrester Road. Those omissions make access from the north rather confusing. The map shows the southern end of the Birkhead Mountain Trail connecting to a public road, but the road is actually privately owned.

A larger, 1:63,360 scale map of the entire Uwharrie National Forest is also available from the USFS Southern Region. This map was also revised in 2011 and contains similar inaccuracies in the Birkhead Mountains Wilderness. The scale of the map makes the trail details difficult to see. There are several inaccuracies on this map with the Wood Run Bike Trails.

In the 1990's, Gemini Maps of NC, Inc sold a map of the Uwharrie National Forest that showed topographic information for most of the trail areas covered in this book. Although there were several inaccuracies in trail location, this map was probably the best map available for trail users at the time. Gemini maps were sold at many local stores. Gemini is no longer in business.

Elevation Profiles

The elevation profiles in this guide are a combined graph of the elevation and distance for a trail, overlaid with text information for significant points along the route. The texts are placed at the approximate mileage point along the graphed elevation line.

Elevation Profile: Uwharrie Trail: Section 1

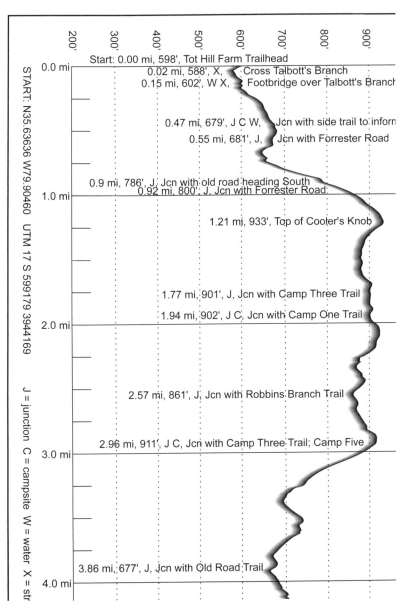

Responsible Use Guidelines

In the end
we will conserve
only what we love;

We will love only
what we understand;

And we will understand
only what we are taught.

Baba Dioum
Senegal

No book about the backcountry would be complete without stressing the importance of caring for the remote environments that we love so much. To that end I am including two sets of information on responsible use. LEAVE NO TRACE is a set of ethics for hikers and backcountry campers. IMBA's Rules of the Trail offer common sense guidance for mountain bikers and other trail users. Read this information, share it with your friends, and let's make sure our use of the trails preserves the backcountry so our children and their children can enjoy it as well.

The member-driven Leave No Trace Center for Outdoor Ethics teaches people how to enjoy the outdoors responsibly. This copyrighted information has been reprinted with permission from the Leave No Trace Center for Outdoor Ethics: www.LNT.org

The Leave No Trace Seven Principles

Plan Ahead and Prepare

Travel and Camp on Durable Surfaces

Dispose of Waste Properly

Leave What You Find

Minimize Campfire Impacts

Respect Wildlife

Be Considerate of Other Visitors

PLAN AHEAD AND PREPARE

Know the regulations and special concerns for the area you'll visit.

Prepare for extreme weather, hazards, and emergencies.

Schedule your trip to avoid times of high use.

Visit in small groups when possible. Consider splitting larger groups into smaller groups.

Repackage food to minimize waste.

Use a map and compass to eliminate the use of marking paint, rock cairns or flagging.

TRAVEL AND CAMP ON DURABLE SURFACES

Durable surfaces include established trails and campsites, rock, gravel, dry grasses or snow.

Protect riparian areas by camping at least 200 feet from lakes and streams.

Good campsites are found, not made. Altering a site is not necessary.

In popular areas:

Concentrate use on existing trails and campsites.

Walk single file in the middle of the trail, even when wet or muddy.

Keep campsites small. Focus activity in areas where vegetation is absent.

In pristine areas:

Disperse use to prevent the creation of campsites and trails.

Avoid places where impacts are just beginning.

DISPOSE OF WASTE PROPERLY

Pack it in, pack it out. Inspect your campsite and rest areas for trash or spilled foods. Pack out all trash, leftover food, and litter.

Deposit solid human waste in catholes dug 6 to 8 inches deep, at least 200 feet from water, camp, and trails. Cover and disguise the cathole when finished.

Pack out toilet paper and hygiene products.

To wash yourself or your dishes, carry water 200 feet away from streams or lakes and use small amounts of biodegradable soap. Scatter strained dishwater.

LEAVE WHAT YOU FIND

Preserve the past: examine, but do not touch, cultural or historic structures and artifacts.

Leave rocks, plants and other natural objects as you find them.

Avoid introducing or transporting non-native species.

Do not build structures, furniture, or dig trenches.

MINIMIZE CAMPFIRE IMPACTS

Campfires can cause lasting impacts to the backcountry. Use a lightweight stove for cooking and enjoy a candle lantern for light.

Where fires are permitted, use established fire rings, fire pans, or mound fires.

Keep fires small. Only use sticks from the ground that can be broken by hand.

Burn all wood and coals to ash, put out campfires completely, then scatter cool ashes.

RESPECT WILDLIFE

Observe wildlife from a distance. Do not follow or approach them.

Never feed animals. Feeding wildlife damages their health, alters natural behaviors, and exposes them to predators and other dangers.

Protect wildlife and your food by storing rations and trash securely.

Control pets at all times, or leave them at home.

Avoid wildlife during sensitive times: mating, nesting, raising young, or winter.

BE CONSIDERATE OF OTHER VISITORS

Respect other visitors and protect the quality of their experience.

Be courteous. Yield to other users on the trail.

Step to the downhill side of the trail when encountering pack stock.

Take breaks and camp away from trails and other visitors.

Let nature's sounds prevail. Avoid loud voices and noises.

International Mountain Bicycling Association

The mission of IMBA is to promote mountain bicycling opportunities through education in environmentally sound and socially responsible riding practices and land management policies.

IMBA is the only national or international organization devoted solely to responsible riding and land access for mountain bicyclists. Founded in 1986, IMBA has member clubs from all over America and several foreign nations. IMBA also has a wide ranging list of individual members, bicycle dealer members, and industry members.

IMBA aids its members to solve their local or regional problems and improve the sport of mountain bicycling. IMBA lobbies directly at the national level, and works with national land management agencies. IMBA organizes and distributes a library of information about managing mountain bicycling, political tactics, scientific studies, and environmental considerations.

IMBA participates in the national efforts to establish and maintain trail networks and to gain better recognition of bicycles as excellent transportation vehicles. Mountain bikes are a key toward achieving both the trails and transportation goals.

For more information about IMBA contact them at:
http://www.imba.com/

IMBA Rules of the Trail

IMBA developed the "Rules of the Trail" to promote responsible and courteous conduct on shared-use trails. Keep in mind that conventions for yielding and passing may vary in different locations, or with traffic conditions.

Ride Open Trails

Respect trail and road closures — ask a land manager for clarification if you are uncertain about the status of a trail. Do not trespass on private land. Obtain permits or other authorization as required. Be aware that bicycles are not permitted in areas protected as state or federal Wilderness.

Leave No Trace

Be sensitive to the dirt beneath you. Wet and muddy trails are more vulnerable to damage than dry ones. When the trail is soft, consider other riding options. This also means staying on existing trails and not creating new ones. Don't cut switchbacks. Be sure to pack out at least as much as you pack in.

Control Your Bicycle

Inattention for even a moment could put yourself and others at risk. Obey all bicycle speed regulations and recommendations, and ride within your limits.

Yield Appropriately

Do your utmost to let your fellow trail users know you're coming — a friendly greeting or bell ring are good methods. Try to anticipate other trail users as you ride around corners. Bicyclists should yield to other non-motorized trail users, unless the trail is clearly signed for bike-only travel. Bicyclists traveling downhill should yield to ones headed uphill, unless the trail is clearly signed for one-way or downhill-only traffic. In general, strive to make each pass a safe and courteous one.

Never Scare Animals

Animals are easily startled by an unannounced approach, a sudden movement or a loud noise. Give animals enough room and time to adjust to you. When passing horses, use special care and follow directions from the horseback riders (ask if uncertain). Running cattle and disturbing wildlife are serious offenses.

Plan Ahead

Know your equipment, your ability and the area in which you are riding and prepare accordingly. Strive to be self-sufficient: keep your equipment in good repair and carry necessary supplies for changes in weather or other conditions. Always wear a helmet and appropriate safety gear.

Safety and Security Concerns

Hunting Season
Deer hunting is extremely popular on public lands in this region, usually beginning in September and running through the first week in January. Bow and arrow season starts first, with gun seasons beginning sometime in early November. It is wise to wear bright colors, like blaze orange, and travel in groups when visiting at this time of year. Although there are no reports of hikers or bikers getting shot, several hunters usually get shot each year. Hunters also frequent these areas during the spring turkey season. The NC Wildlife Resources Commission website lists hunting season dates: http://www.ncwildlife.org/

Many privately owned properties bordering public land are posted with "No Trespassing" signs by hunting clubs. It's wise not to trespass on private land at any time, but it is especially smart not to provoke armed hunters during hunting season.

Ticks and Snakes and Flying Things
The Uwharries are home to insects and animals that don't mind biting you. During the summer months ticks are quite abundant. Insect repellent and frequent self-inspections can prevent most tick bites.

Rattlesnakes and copperheads (or 'pilots' as they are called locally) are also abundant in the region, although I have never encountered either on a trail. Many people have though, so it's a good idea to keep your eyes open. Do not kill or injure snakes, even poisonous ones. They are vital parts of the local ecosystem.

With the abundance of water and woods, mosquitoes are a nuisance found during the warmer months. Horseflies can also be part of the trail experience. I met some of these once that wouldn't slow down for bug spray or a shirt. When I tried to cover my neck with my hand, they just bit my hand - three at a time. My advice - run faster!

Vehicle Security
As with any remote area, you are better off not to leave any valuable items in your vehicle while out on the trail. If you have to leave something, make sure it is covered up. Why tempt someone if you don't have to?

Law Enforcement
In the event that something does happen either on or off the trail, you should contact local law enforcement officers. Even if they can't catch the person responsible or recover your belongings, making them aware of the incident might help prevent it from happening again in the future. The same goes for contacting the agency responsible for managing the area where the incident occurred. They can't work to correct a problem if they don't know it exists.

The Montgomery County Sheriff's Department can be reached at 910-572-1313 or by dialing 911. Their jurisdiction includes the Wood Run, Morris Mountain, Dark Mountain, and Badin Lake Areas.

The Randolph County Sheriff's Department can be reached at 336-318-6699 or by dialing 911. Their jurisdiction includes the Birkhead Mountains Wilderness Area.

The Stanly County Sheriff's Department can be reached at 704-986-3714 or by dialing 911. Their jurisdiction includes Morrow Mountain State Park.

The North Carolina Highway Patrol can be reached at 919-733-7952, by dialing *47 on a cell phone, or through each local Sheriff's Department.

The USFS also has its own law enforcement officer. He can be reached through the District Ranger's Office at 910-576-6391.

Morrow Mountain State Park has its own law enforcement officer. He can be reached through the Park Office at 704-982-4402.

911 Emergency
The 911 emergency call system is operable for all trail areas in this book.

Hospitals
Hopefully your visit to the trails of the Uwharrie Lakes Region will be a safe one, with no injuries. However, if you do require medical attention, there are hospitals in Albemarle, Troy, and Asheboro.

Stanly Memorial Hospital is located in Albemarle at 301 Yadkin Street, Albemarle NC 28002. You can follow the blue and white "H" signs west from the intersection of NC 24-27 and NC 740 into town and to the hospital. The phone number is 704-984-4000.

Montgomery Memorial Hospital is located in Troy at 520 Allen Street, Troy NC 27371. Follow the blue and white "H" signs from the Courthouse (NC 24-27 & NC 134). The phone number is 910-571-5000.

Randolph Hospital is located in Asheboro at 364 White Oak Street, Asheboro, NC 27203. You can follow the blue and white "H" signs from the intersection of NC 49 and US 64 into town and to the hospital. The number is 336-625-5151.

Water Source Quality
While most watercourses along the trails appear fairly clean, I would advise use of some form of treatment before drinking water from Uwharrie streams. I prefer to use a water filter, but iodine tablets or boiling will also protect you against most waterborne pathogens.

The USFS recommends that you boil any water you plan to consume for one full minute.

Albemarle City Lake Park

City Lake is a 112-acre impoundment on Long Creek. The lake served as the City of Albemarle water supply basin until the 1950's. The City opened a regional recreational park at the lake in 2003. This park consists of approximately 90 acres on the east side of the lake. The property is heavily wooded and provides beautiful vistas looking down on the lake.

The second phase of construction for the park was completed in November 2006. The park currently includes three picnic shelters (one with year-round restrooms) available for rental, two floating boat docks, approximately one-half mile of paved walking trail and one mile of non-paved trails, and an amphitheatre that is available for rental for weddings and special events. Fishing in the lake is permitted year-round (North Carolina Wildlife Resources Commission laws on licensing and limits apply). Fishing tackle is available for check out at the Parks and Recreation office at Rock Creek Park. Access to the lake is available for fishing, canoeing, and non-motorized boats.

In 2010, the Park worked with a local bike shop, Middle Ring Cycles, and SORBA/IMBA to build a mountain bike skills area and a purpose-built mountain bike trail - the Adventure Trail. This trail incorporated the latest sustainable trail design features as well as riding features for mountain bikers. The skills area included rock gardens, log rides, and a pump track.

Unless otherwise signed, the trails in the park are open to both hikers and bikers. The Eagle Trail is signed as a hike-only trail.

Hours for City Lake Park vary by season, and are posted at the park's entrance. City Lake Park is generally open to the public daily from 7:30 am to dusk. For more information, contact the City of Albemarle Parks and Recreation Department at 704-984-9560.

ACCESS

Entrance Trailhead

Just inside the entrance gate are paved parking spaces for four vehicles plus a handicap parking spot. There is also a trailhead kiosk. The Outdoor Discovery Trail begins across the park entrance road from this parking area. The street

UTM	17 S 570315 3912860
Lat/Lon	N35.35656 W80.22608

address of the park entrance is 900 Concord Road, Albemarle, NC.

Upper Amphitheater Trailhead

The Adventure Trail Connector can be accessed from the trailhead along the parking area above the amphitheater. There are paved, marked parking spots at this trailhead along the main road.

UTM	17 S 569883 3912656
Lat/Lon	N35.35475 W80.23084

Lower Amphitheater Trailhead

The lower end of the Adventure Trail can be accessed from the trailhead between the lake shore and the amphitheater. The closest parking is in the lot leading to the amphitheater. The trail starts at the treeline between the amphitheater and the lake.

UTM	17 S 569764 3912709
Lat/Lon	N35.35524 W80.23215

NOTES OF INTEREST

The trails in City Lake Park are not long, but they are great example of cooperative trail building. Local Scouts worked to establish the Eagle and Outdoor Discovery Trails. The Adventure MTB Trail and MTB skills area was a joint effort between the Parks and Recreation Department, the International Mountain Bike Association, and a local bike shop - Middle Ring Cycles.

An easy bike trip of just under 2 miles can be made by starting at the southeast corner of the picnic path loop. Follow the Mission Camp Trail to its end. Turn left on the Outdoor Discovery Trail and follow it to the MTB Skills Area. Next cross the main park road to the turnaround on the Adventure Trail. Go to the right on the Adventure Trail and follow to end at the Lower Amphitheater Trailhead.

CAMPING

There is no camping allowed in City Lake Park.

MAPS

A color photomap of the park was available on the City's website in 2013. It did not include the southern leg of the Adventure Trail. The missing trail segment is included in this guide as the first portion of the Adventure Trail.

Albemarle City Lake Park

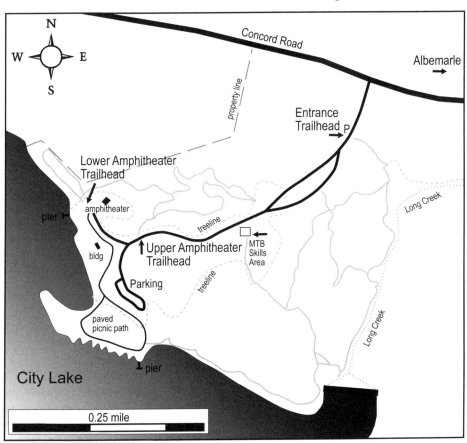

Albemarle City Lake Park Trails

Trail Name	Length (miles)	Elevation Gain/Loss	Difficulty Rating	Map (page)
Adventure Trail	0.74	107' / 213'	Moderate	38
Eagle Trail	0.20	21' / 80'	Moderate	40
Mission Camp Trail	0.62	71' / 71'	Moderate	42
Outdoor Discovery Trail	0.44	88' / 45'	Moderate	44

Adventure Trail

Map	page 38	**Difficulty**	Moderate
Length	0.74 miles	**Configuration**	One Way
Trailhead	Upper Amphitheater	**Elev Gain/Loss**	107' / 213'

Start Coordinates N35.35473, W80.23087 ; 17 S 569881 3912654

The construction of the Adventure Trail was a joint effort between the City of Albemarle Parks and Recreation Department, the International Mountain Bicycling Association, and a local bike shop - Middle Ring Cycles. Work was begun in 2008, with the initial trail running from the Skills Area North Trailhead to the Lower Amphitheater Trailhead. The loop along the lake shore was added later, as well as a new section running from the Skills Area North Trailhead to the Upper Amphitheater Trailhead. A 0.05 mile long connector trail in the middle ties the longer sections together and offers alternate routing options.

The Adventure Trail is open to bikers and hikers.

Eagle Trail

Map	page 40	**Difficulty**	Moderate
Length	0.20 miles	**Configuration**	One Way
Trailhead	N/A	**Elev Gain/Loss**	21' / 80'

Start Coordinates N35.35390, W80.22556 ;   17 S 570267 3912736

The Eagle Trail was built as an Eagle Scout project.

The Eagle Trail is only open to hikers.

Mission Camp Trail

Map	page 42	**Difficulty**	Moderate
Length	0.62 miles	**Configuration**	One Way
Trailhead	Picnic path	**Elev Gain/Loss**	71' / 71'

Start Coordinates N35.35258, W80.23045 ;   17 S 569921 3912416

The Mission Camp Trail starts near the picnic area beside the lake. It follows the shoreline to the dam, and then parallels Long Creek to near the entrance of the park. There it junctions with the Outdoor Discovery Trail.

Most of the Mission Camp Trail is singletrack trail, with a few parts following old roadbeds.

The Mission Camp Trail is open to bikers and hikers.

Outdoor Discovery Trail

Map	page 44	**Difficulty**	Moderate
Length	0.44 miles	**Configuration**	One Way
Trailhead	Entrance	**Elev Gain/Loss**	88' / 45'

Start Coordinates N35.35258, W80.23045 ;   17 S 570333 3912847

Most of the route of the Outdoor Discovery Trail follows old road beds that run through the property. They now serve as both trail and service roads for the park.

The Outdoor Discovery Trail ends at the Mountain Bike Skills Area next to the main park road. The Skills area includes a "pump track", "rock gardens", and "log rides". When I visited in the summer of 2012, the pump track was grassed over, but had been mowed. It did not appear to be getting much use.

An alternate leg of the Outdoor Discovery Trail leads to the base of the City Lake dam and connects to the Mission Camp Trail. This alternate leg is approximately 0.10 mile long.

Adventure Trail

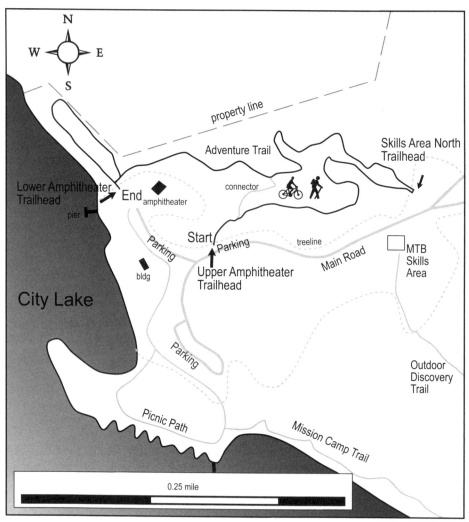

Elevation Profile: Adventure Trail

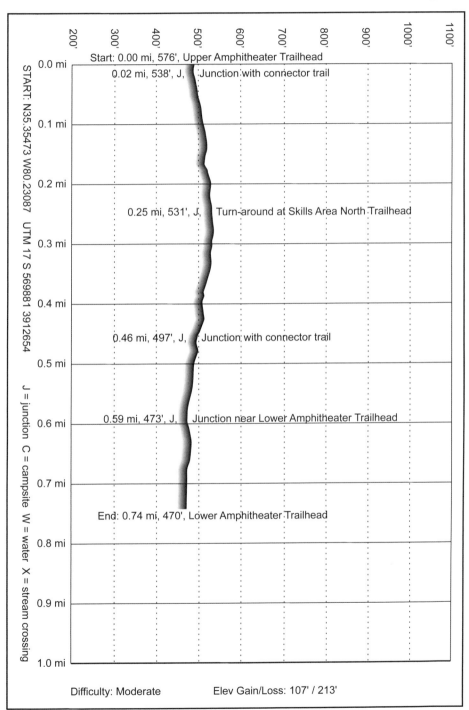

START: N35.35473 W80.23087   UTM 17 S 569881 3912654

J = junction   C = campsite   W = water   X = stream crossing

Start: 0.00 mi, 576', Upper Amphitheater Trailhead

0.02 mi, 538', J, Junction with connector trail

0.25 mi, 531', J, Turn-around at Skills Area North Trailhead

0.46 mi, 497', J, Junction with connector trail

0.59 mi, 473', J, Junction near Lower Amphitheater Trailhead

End: 0.74 mi, 470', Lower Amphitheater Trailhead

Difficulty: Moderate   Elev Gain/Loss: 107' / 213'

Eagle Trail

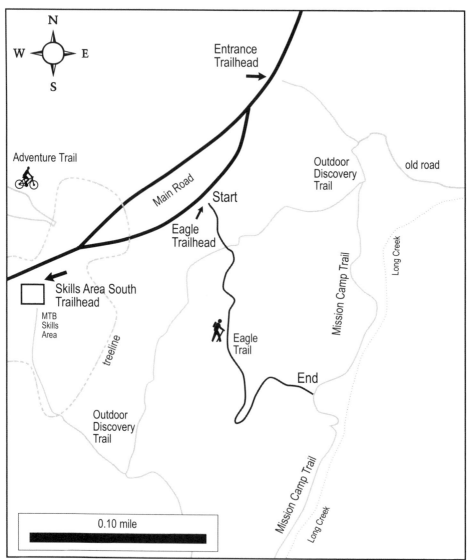

Elevation Profile: Eagle Trail

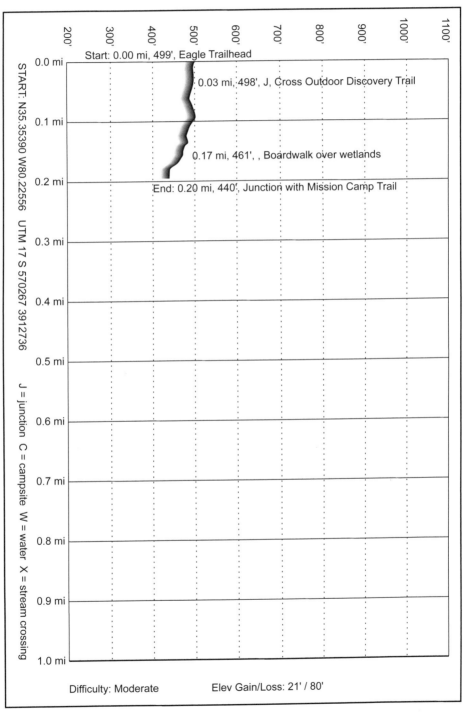

START: N35.35390 W80.22556 UTM 17 S 570267 3912736

J = junction C = campsite W = water X = stream crossing

Start: 0.00 mi, 499', Eagle Trailhead

0.03 mi, 498', J, Cross Outdoor Discovery Trail

0.17 mi, 461', , Boardwalk over wetlands

End: 0.20 mi, 440', Junction with Mission Camp Trail

Difficulty: Moderate   Elev Gain/Loss: 21' / 80'

Mission Camp Trail

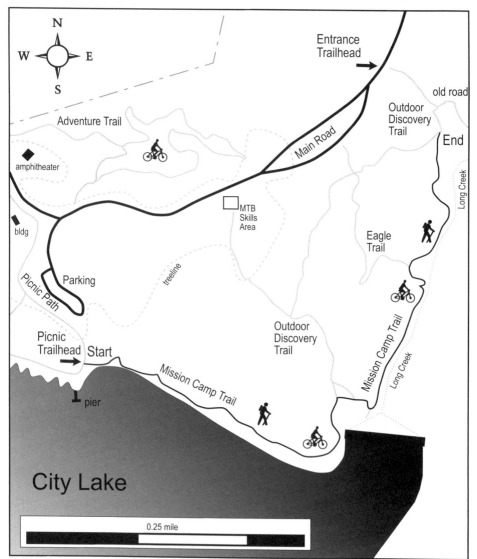

Elevation Profile: Mission Camp Trail

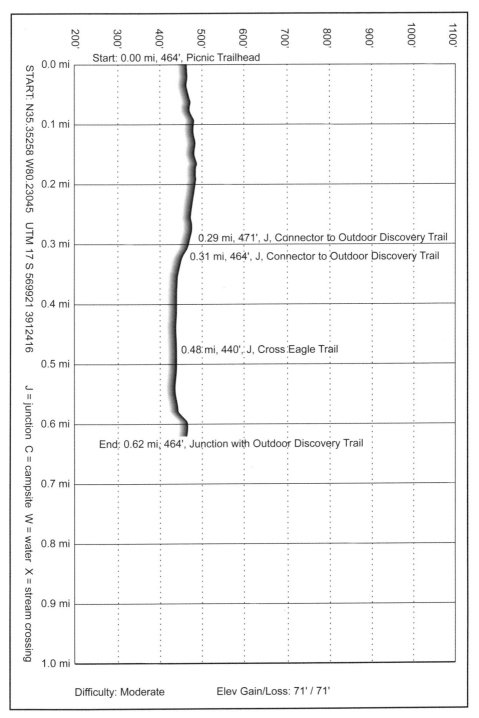

START: N35.35258 W80.23045 UTM 17 S 569921 3912416

J = junction C = campsite W = water X = stream crossing

Start: 0.00 mi, 464', Picnic Trailhead

0.29 mi, 471', J, Connector to Outdoor Discovery Trail

0.31 mi, 464', J, Connector to Outdoor Discovery Trail

0.48 mi, 440', J, Cross Eagle Trail

End: 0.62 mi, 464', Junction with Outdoor Discovery Trail

Difficulty: Moderate   Elev Gain/Loss: 71' / 71'

Outdoor Discovery Trail

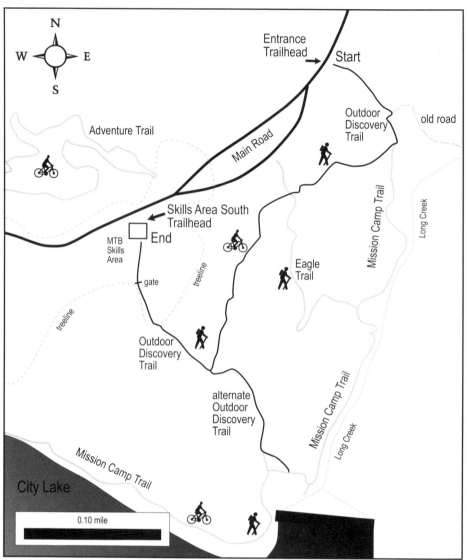

Elevation Profile: Outdoor Discovery Trail

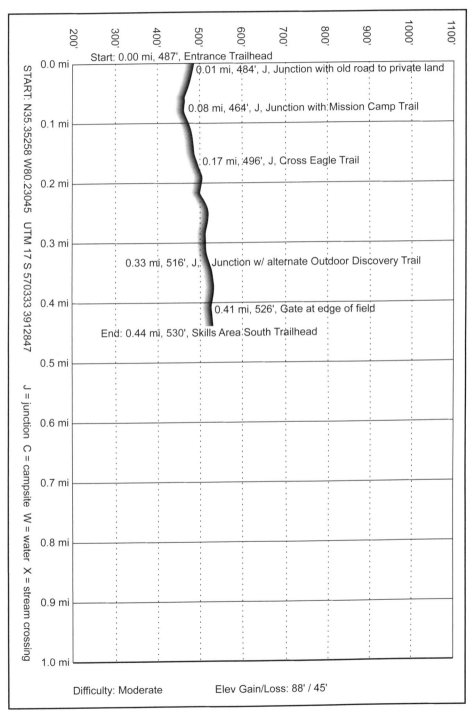

START: N35.35258 W80.23045 UTM 17 S 570333 3912847

J = junction C = campsite W = water X = stream crossing

Start: 0.00 mi, 487', Entrance Trailhead

0.01 mi, 484', J, Junction with old road to private land

0.08 mi, 464', J, Junction with Mission Camp Trail

0.17 mi, 496', J, Cross Eagle Trail

0.33 mi, 516', J, Junction w/ alternate Outdoor Discovery Trail

0.41 mi, 526', Gate at edge of field

End: 0.44 mi, 530', Skills Area South Trailhead

Difficulty: Moderate   Elev Gain/Loss: 88' / 45'

Badin Lake Recreation Area

The Badin Lake Recreation Area, situated along its namesake, hosts the only US Forest Service campgrounds in the Uwharrie Lakes Region with piped drinking water. Badin is pronounced BAY-den. This southern half of this area is home to the Off Highway Vehicle (OHV) trails, one of only three such trail systems on National Forest lands in North Carolina. The Equestrian Trail System, a fairly extensive set of horseback riding trails, also runs throughout this area, as well as the Badin Lake Trail (hiking only) which provides a scenic lakeshore walk.

The southern end of the area is bordered by two rivers; the Yadkin River on the west and the Uwharrie River on the east. The Yadkin and Uwharrie rivers come together at the south end of this area to form the Pee Dee River. Although there are some tracts of private land along each of these rivers, there are also several locations where public land extends to the water's edge.

Two hydroelectric dams on the Yadkin River lie adjacent to the Badin Lake Recreation Area; the Narrows Dam which holds back Badin Lake, and the Falls Dam which holds back Falls Reservoir. The Narrows Dam was the first dam in this area, built in 1917. The Falls Dam was built in 1919.

Before the dams were built on the Yadkin River, the river flowed through a narrow gorge and over a series of falls created by rocky ledges between the neighboring mountains. The gorge was known as the Narrows. Native Americans using the river as a highway were slowed by the Narrows. They spent a lot of time in the area hunting, fishing and gathering rhyolite to make their stone tools. They built stone fords and fish traps across the shallow rocky riverbed below the Narrows. When the level of Lake Tillery is dropped for maintenance of the dam, you can still see the rock walls of the fish traps near Morrow Mountain State Park. Archaeological studies have shown that this region was populated by Native American peoples for at least 10,000 years before the first Europeans began settling here.

The southern end of the Badin Lake Area is especially mountainous. Falls Mountain and Shingle Trap Mountain are two of the named mountains. Most of the mountain tops rise over 800 feet in elevation. Shingle Trap Mountain's four peaks are all over 900'.

Dutch John Creek and its tributaries drain most of the interior of this area while numerous smaller streams run off the outer slopes and directly into the two adjacent rivers.

Like most of the Uwharrie Lakes Region, past mining and logging activity resulted in a network of roadbeds. Most of the area was purchased by the government in 1931. These lands were transferred to the US Forest Service for administration in 1935. Not until 1961, during President Kennedy's term in office, did these properties become a National Forest. Prior to the 1960's, roads in this area were gated and closed to the public except during hunting season.

During the early 1900's, there were very few white tail deer in this region of the state. Efforts to reintroduce them were started in the late 1950's. As a large, undeveloped, forested tract of public land, the Badin Lake Area was ideally suited to be a release site for deer. Numerous fields throughout the property were planted and maintained to provide food for wildlife. Although no longer needed primarily for the deer, these fields are still maintained as wildlife food plots. The Badin Lake Area is known locally as the "Reservation", a name which most likely stems from its earlier use as a wild game reserve.

ACCESS

There are three main access routes into the Badin Lake Recreation Area. On the east side, Reservation Road and Mullinix Road lead in off of NC 109. Badin Lake Road leads in from the north side.

The southernmost access route from NC 109 is Reservation Road (SR 1153), located 1.7 miles north of the community of Uwharrie. Reservation Road is paved and runs by the Uwharrie Hunt Camp. An unpaved Forest System Road, Moccasin Creek Road (FR 576) starts on the right just past the camp. It runs across the area and goes by the Badin Dam before ending near Falls Reservoir.

The second access route from NC 109 is Mullinix Road (SR 1154), located 3.1 miles north of Uwharrie (1.4 miles north of Reservation Road). At the point where State Highway maintenance ends on Mullinix Road, the road becomes FR 554. A short distance further you will find the Badin Lake Horse Camp. FR 554 continues on to connect to another paved Forest System road, McLeans Creek Road (FR 544). Turning right on McLeans Creek Road will lead you towards the campgrounds on Badin Lake.

The northern access route is from Blaine Road (SR 1156), which connects to NC 109 at the community of Blaine (6.6 miles north of Uwharrie). Blaine Road runs from NC 109 westward towards NC 49. A half mile west of NC 109, Shamrock Road (SR 1179), leads southward from Blaine Road. After traveling 0.3 miles down Shamrock Road, you will see an unpaved road on the left. It is signed as Badin Lake Road (FR 597), when the sign isn't missing. Badin Lake Road passes by

Badin Lake Recreation Area

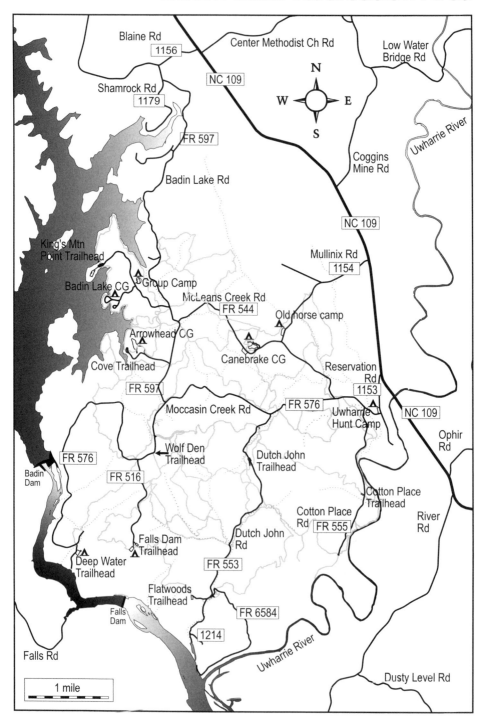

Holt's Cabin Picnic Area along the lake and by entrances to the campgrounds, eventually connecting to Moccasin Creek Road (FR 576).

Each of these three access routes connect with the Forest System roads running through the area, some of which are graveled and some are paved. Unlike other USFS properties in the Uwharrie Lake Region, several Forest System roads in the Badin Lake Area are open to public vehicular traffic. It can be a little confusing to navigate your way through the area, and the roads seem like they go on forever. However, a little care and attention will get you in to the various trailheads and back out again without any problem.

King's Mountain Point Trailhead

The King's Mountain Point Trailhead is located at the end of King's Mountain Point Road (FR 6551), beyond the campgrounds on FR 597A. The King's Mountain Point Day Use Area provides access to the Badin Lake Hiking Trail.

UTM	17 S 570127 3912716
Lat/Lon	N35.35527 W80.22816

This day use area offers paved parking, 34 picnic sites, a covered picnic pavilion, 4 handicapped accessible fishing piers, 4 vault toilets, and 2 flush toilets.

Cove Trailhead

Cove Trailhead is located at the parking lot for the Cove Boat Ramp, at the end of Cove Road (FR 597B). The beginning of Cove Road is 3.8 miles from NC 109 by way of the Mullinix Road (SR 1154), McLeans Creek Road (FR 544), and then

UTM	17 S 570127 3912716
Lat/Lon	N35.35527 W80.22816

Badin Lake Road (FR 597). The Badin Lake Hiking Trail is accessible from this trailhead. There is parking space for 20-30 vehicles and pit toilets. The full-service Arrowhead Campground is located on the right side of Cove Road, a short distance before you reach the boat ramp area.

Wolf Den Trailhead

Located on Moccasin Creek Road (FR 576), the Wolf Den OHV Trailhead lies on the northwest corner of the OHV trail system. This trailhead is 4.2 miles from NC 109 by way of Reservation Road (SR 1153) and Moccasin Creek Road (FR

UTM	17 S 570127 3912716
Lat/Lon	N35.35527 W80.22816

576). This trailhead is really just a wide graveled area in a bend along Moccasin Creek Road, with parking room for 10-15 vehicles. There is a bulletin board at this trailhead, but no other facilities. Wolf Den Trail leads southwest from the parking area.

Falls Dam Trailhead

The Falls Dam Trailhead is located midway along the Falls Dam Trail. To reach this trailhead, turn left off of Moccasin Creek Road (FR 576) 0.2 miles past the Wolf Den Trailhead. This road is actually FR 516, but there were no signs at the

UTM	17 S 570127 3912716
Lat/Lon	N35.35527 W80.22816

intersection as of September 2012. As you follow the road, it reaches the saddle where the Falls Dam Trail turns downhill to end at Wolf Den Trail. There is a sign in the saddle advising unlicensed OHV's not to continue back out to Moccasin Creek Road. From this point on to the trailhead, the road is shared between the Falls Dam Trail and public road traffic.

The trailhead parking lot is on the left. The Art Lilley Memorial Campground is on the right. Falls Dam Trail runs between the two, in a fenced corridor that routes OHV's through a big mud hole. There are alternate routes for OHV's through both the parking area and the campground to continue on the Falls Dam Trail beyond the trailhead area.

The Art Lilley Campground consists of a large graveled parking area with a vault toilet at the far end. Tent camping areas are located under the trees beyond the wooden fence surrounding the parking area.

When the campground was built in 2008, the trailhead parking area was graded and graveled. Prior to that, the spot had been an informal camping/gathering area along the Falls Dam Trail.

Before 2008, FR 516 was gated and closed where it intersects with Moccasin Creek Road. When the new Lake View Trail is opened, it will begin at this trailhead, at the south end of the Art Lilley Campground.

Dutch John Trailhead

Dutch John Trailhead is located on Dutch John Road (FR 553), 2.7 miles from NC 109 by way of Reservation Road (SR 1153), Moccasin Creek Road (FR 576), and Dutch John Road. This trailhead was called the Rocky Mount Trailhead in the first edition of this guidebook.

UTM	17 S 570127 3912716
Lat/Lon	N35.35527 W80.22816

This trailhead consists of two large graveled parking areas, one on either side of Dutch John Road. The Rocky Mountain Trail loop (OHV) crosses Dutch John Road just south of the parking areas. There is an OHV access trail connecting the parking lot and the trail. The Morgan Trail (equestrian) also passes close by. There is a bulletin board, loading ramp, and a vault toilet at this trailhead. Forty or more vehicles could park here.

Cotton Place Trailhead

The Cotton Place Trailhead is located along Cotton Place Road (FR 555), 1.1 miles from NC 109 by way of Reservation Road (SR 1153), Moccasin Creek Road (FR 576), and Cotton Place Road (FR 555). This trailhead was called Gold Mine Trailhead in the first edition of this guidebook.

UTM	17 S 570127 3912716
Lat/Lon	N35.35527 W80.22816

This trailhead serves the Daniel Trail. At one time, the Gold Mine Trail, another OHV trail, also connected to this trailhead. There is a graveled parking area with room for 20-30 vehicles at this trailhead, as well a bulletin board.

Flatwoods Trailhead

The Flatwoods Trailhead is located just beyond the end of Dutch John Road (FR 553). The end of Dutch John Road narrows to a single vehicle width and is shared between public traffic and the Dickey Bell Trail (OHV) traffic for the last

UTM	17 S 570127 3912716
Lat/Lon	N35.35527 W80.22816

hundred yards or so to the parking area. The parking area was established in 2009. There is a loading ramp in the fenced off parking area and a bulletin board, but no other facilities. The gravel parking area has room for 20-30 vehicles.

From this trailhead the Falls Dam Trail heads west and the Dickey Bell Trail heads east.

Deep Water Trailhead

The Deep Water Trailhead is located at the end of Moccasin Creek Road (FR 576). This trailhead provides access to one of the equestrian trails. Before reaching the end of FR 576, Deep Water Trail, a gravel road, turns off to the right

UTM	17 S 570127 3912716
Lat/Lon	N35.35527 W80.22816

and provides access to an open field maintained as a primitive camp. There are no facilities at this location. Beyond the Deep Water Campground, the road leads to the Falls Reservoir where you can find canoe access to the water.

NOTES OF INTEREST

A trial fee project was started in 1996 on the OHV trail system. User fees were channeled back into trail needs at the location where the fees are collected. Users were asked to pay $3 per day visit or $30 for a season pass. Roughly 90% of the fees collected remained in the Local USFS District. A few years later the "trail pass" system became more or less permanent. It is reviewed periodically and so far has been renewed each time. As of 2013, the "trail passes" are $5 per day. Season passes are still $30. Trail passes are required for all wheeled vehicles, including mountain bikes. Passes can be purchased at most local stores, like the Eldorado Outpost.

There is a local legend about a man who lived among these mountains many years ago, before the Yadkin was dammed and while the area was still considered to be wild. He was an expert hunter, fisher, woodsman, and moonshiner. The legend tells how he lived off the land and lived well. Perhaps he was the "Dutch John" the main creek drainage in the area was named after.

A group of large boulders stick up from a hilltop on the northwest side of this area, overlooking Badin Lake. Called Nifty Rocks by the Forest Service, the site is located off of Moccasin Creek Road (FR 576), 5.5 miles from NC 109 (1.4 miles past the Wolf Den Trailhead or 1.2 miles past FR 516). This spot has also been called the Boulder Field Overlook. Park at the Forest Service gate on the right side of the road, just before the top of the hill. Follow the overgrown road past some small rock outcroppings (10' high) and curve left toward the 20' boulders on top of the hill. The rocks offer several bouldering challenges for rock climbers. The overlook views are usually hidden by summer foliage.

Badin Lake Trail, the only hiking-only trail in this area, starts at the Cove Boat Ramp and makes a loop of about five and a half miles, following the shoreline around a peninsula and climbing up over some nearby ridges before leading back to the boat ramp.

Another hiking trail, known as the Dutch John Trail, once connected to the Badin Lake Trail but has now been abandoned. Part of it was incorporated into the OHV trails and other sections have become overgrown. While researching this area, I came across several maps that indicated a hiking trail running across the Badin Lake Area. I remember encountering an old section of hand-benched trail in the early 1990's as I was bushwhacking up Shingle Trap Mountain. This trail has been abandoned for so long now that little evidence of it remains, either on paper or on the ground.

A hiking trail called the River Trail once ran along the Uwharrie River. The route passed through several tracts of private property. This trail was eventually abandoned and has become overgrown.

Arrowhead Campground has a 0.75 mile paved trail circling the campsites. This trail is open to hikers and mountain bikes.

In the 1990's, a group of horseback riders began building a system of horse trails in the Badin Lake area. They hoped to provide horse trails free of the conflicts that often resulted between horses and motorized vehicles on the OHV trails. When the first edition of this guidebook was published, these horse trails were not yet marked or officially recognized by the USFS. In the late 1990's, the USFS worked with local horseback riding groups to close several of these trails that had severe erosion problems and put signage on the others. This edition of the guidebook includes a separate section covering these trails, which are open to horses, mountain bikes, and hikers.

CAMPING

The northern half of the Badin Lake Area hosts several Forest Service campgrounds. There are three campgrounds near or along the lake itself, three horse camps near FR 544 and 554, and a hunt camp at the Reservation Road (SR 1153) entrance to the area. Arrowhead Campground, opened in November 1996, is the flagship campground for the Uwharrie National Forest. Arrowhead features a rather nice bathhouse with shower facilities. This facility is located on Cove Road (FR 597B), off of Badin Lake Road (FR 597). The campground's interior roads and parking areas at each of its 54 sites are paved. Sites on the inside of the loop road have electrical hookups, those on the outside do not. Fees are $12 - $24 per site per day. The entrance gate to Arrowhead Campground is locked at night.

Badin Lake Campground and the Badin Lake Group Camp are both located on FR 597A, which is further north, off of Badin Lake Road (FR 597). The Badin Lake Campground has 34 sites and shared water sources and pit toilets, and showers. Fees at the campground are $12 per site per day. The Group Camp has 3 large sites for group tent camping, a shared water source, a shower house, and pit toilets. Reservations and a fee are required for sites in the Group Camp.

The Canebrake Horse Camp, opened in 2000, is located along McLeans Creek Road (FR 544). It has 29 sites and includes water spigots, showers, flush toilets, and a horse washing station. Fees at the campground are $12 per site per day.

Reservations for the campgrounds above can be made by going to www.recreation. gov or by calling 1-877-444-6777.

Below are several first-come, first-served camp locations with less facilities.

Uwharrie Hunt Camp, located on Reservation Road (SR 1153), has 8 tent sites, picnic tables, a vault toilet, and piped water. There is a camping fee at this site, and a pay station for honor system payments.

The Badin Horse Camp, or Old Horse Camp, is located near the Canebrake Horse Camp, along Marks Road (FR 554)/Mullinix Road (SR 1154). This was the first "horse camp" in the area. This camp has a pit toilet but no water source.

Just north of the Canebrake Horse Camp, on the opposite side of McLeans Creek Road, is a small field used for overflow horse camping. It is labeled Overflow Horse Camp on USFS maps. There are no facilities here.

The Deep Water Trail Camp is located near the end of Moccasin Creek Road (FR 576) on Deep Water Trail Road (FR 6560). There are no facilities here, just an open grassy field.

The Art Lilley Memorial Campground is located at the end of FR 516, on top of Falls Dam Mountain. It was developed in 2008. There is a pit toilet at the west end of the parking area. This "campground" consists mostly of a gravel parking area the size of a football field surrounded by a split rail fence.

Camping is legal anywhere in the Uwharrie National Forest, unless "No Camping" signs are posted. Other informal camping sites exist along the trails, usually close to the main gravel roads where OHV users have easy access for their vehicles and trailers. There are also numerous pull-off areas along the gravel forest roads in the Badin Lake area. It is legal to car-camp at these sites.

MAPS

The local USFS District Ranger's office occasionally produces simple maps covering the Badin Lake Area. One of these details the OHV trail system, drawn over a copy of the topo map for that area. The trail lines are generally accurate.

The USGS topographic map covering this area is the Badin quadrangle. The 1981 revision shows the main Forest Roads and some of the old roadbeds in the Falls Dam Mountain area, but none of the other trails. A 1994 revision shows the Badin Lake Trail and some of the OHV trails.

The USFS produces a color map titled Badin Lake Trail Map. It is available online. This map shows the trails, roads, and major creeks in the area, along with the trailheads, campgrounds, and a few scenic features.

Several user groups, such as NC4X4.com, have published maps of the trails they use.

Gemini Maps of NC, Inc. published a 1997 revision of its Uwharrie National Forest map. This large fold-out map includes the Badin Lake Area. This map does not show the Badin Lake Trail or the Rudolph Trail, but it does include the other OHV trails. Although the map has topo lines, the trail lines are only a rough approximation of the trail locations. The campgrounds that existed at that time are indicated on the map.

Badin Lake Hiking Trails

Trail Name	Length (miles)	Elevation Gain/Loss	Difficulty Rating	Map (page)
Badin Lake Trail	5.64	651' / 624'	Easy	56
Short Loop Trail	1.86	248' / 221'	Easy	58

Badin Lake Trail

Map   page 56   **Difficulty**   Easy
Length   5.64 miles   **Configuration**   Loop
Trailhead Cove Boat Ramp   **Elev Gain/Loss**   651' / 624'
Start Coordinates N35.43945, W80.07463;   17 S 583989 3922171

The Badin Lake Trail (USFS Trail #94) is the only hiking-only trail in the Badin Lake Recreation Area rated "Easy". The trail was built around 1979 or 1980 by the Youth Conservation Corps, shortly after the Badin Lake Campground was established. The Badin Lake Trail was renumbered from #90 to #94 in 2012. You may find references to the earlier number on older maps.

White paint blazes are used to mark the route of the Badin Lake Trail. Over the years, the trail route has been relocated several times in numerous places, resulting in quite a few white blazes on trees that are no longer along the trail. Some of these blazes are still visible and may confuse hikers.

Short Loop Trail

Map   page 58   **Difficulty**   Easy
Length   5.64 miles   **Configuration**   Loop
Trailhead Cove Boat Ramp   **Elev Gain/Loss**   651' / 624'
Start Coordinates N35.43945, W80.07463;   17 S 583989 3922171

The Short Loop option cuts across the middle of the larger loop formed by the Badin Lake Trail. The Short Loop is also blazed in white and shares its route with the green-blazed Lake Trail, one of the equestrian trails. The indistinct junction of these trails near the lake shore can be confusing.

A relocation of the ridge top section of the trail in the mid 1990's moved the trail away from its junction with the now-abandoned Dutch John hiking trail and relocated it along part of the paved trail around the Arrowhead Campground.

Badin Lake Trail

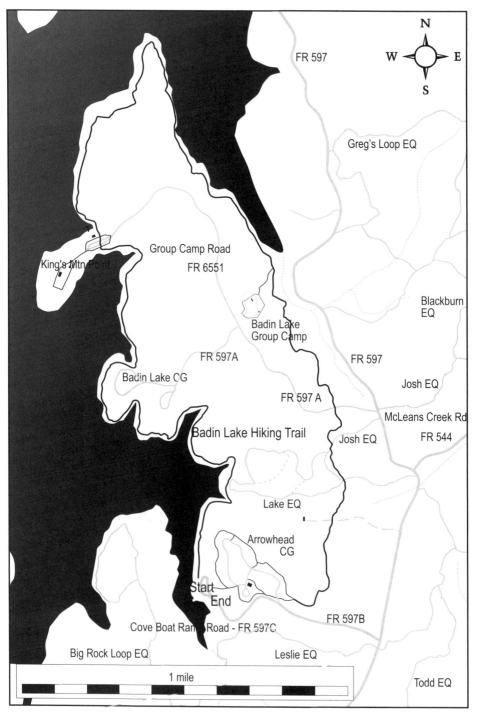

FR 597

N
W — E
S

Greg's Loop EQ

Group Camp Road
FR 6551

King's Mtn. Point

Blackburn EQ

Badin Lake Group Camp

FR 597A

FR 597

Badin Lake CG

Josh EQ

FR 597 A

McLeans Creek Rd

Badin Lake Hiking Trail

Josh EQ

FR 544

Lake EQ

Arrowhead CG

Start
End

Cove Boat Ramp Road - FR 597C

FR 597B

Big Rock Loop EQ

Leslie EQ

1 mile

Todd EQ

Elevation Profile: Badin Lake Trail (BLRA Trip B)

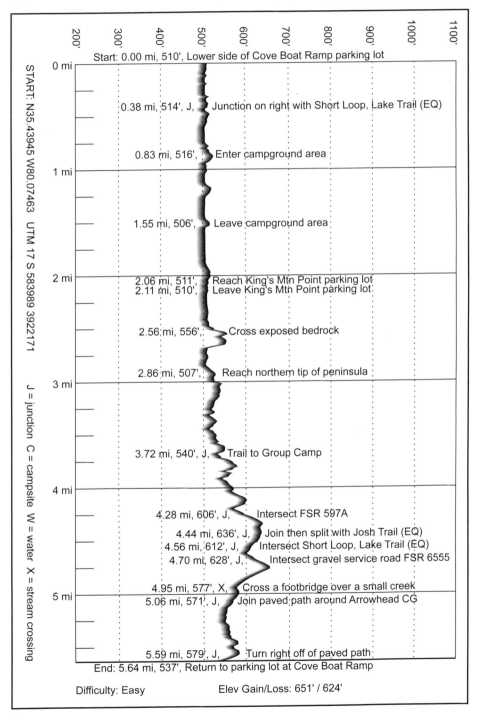

START: N35.43945 W80.07463   UTM 17 S 583989 3922171

J = junction C = campsite W = water X = stream crossing

200'   300'   400'   500'   600'   700'   800'   900'   1000'   1100'

Start: 0.00 mi, 510', Lower side of Cove Boat Ramp parking lot

0 mi

0.38 mi, 514', J,   Junction on right with Short Loop, Lake Trail (EQ)

0.83 mi, 516',   Enter campground area

1 mi

1.55 mi, 506',   Leave campground area

2 mi

2.06 mi, 511',   Reach King's Mtn Point parking lot
2.11 mi, 510',   Leave King's Mtn Point parking lot

2.56 mi, 556',   Cross exposed bedrock

2.86 mi, 507',   Reach northern tip of peninsula

3 mi

3.72 mi, 540', J,   Trail to Group Camp

4 mi

4.28 mi, 606', J,   Intersect FSR 597A

4.44 mi, 636', J,   Join then split with Josh Trail (EQ)
4.56 mi, 612', J,   Intersect Short Loop, Lake Trail (EQ)
4.70 mi, 628', J,   Intersect gravel service road FSR 6555

4.95 mi, 577', X,   Cross a footbridge over a small creek
5.06 mi, 571', J,   Join paved path around Arrowhead CG

5 mi

5.59 mi, 579', J,   Turn right off of paved path

End: 5.64 mi, 537', Return to parking lot at Cove Boat Ramp

Difficulty: Easy   Elev Gain/Loss: 651' / 624'

Badin Lake Short Loop Trail

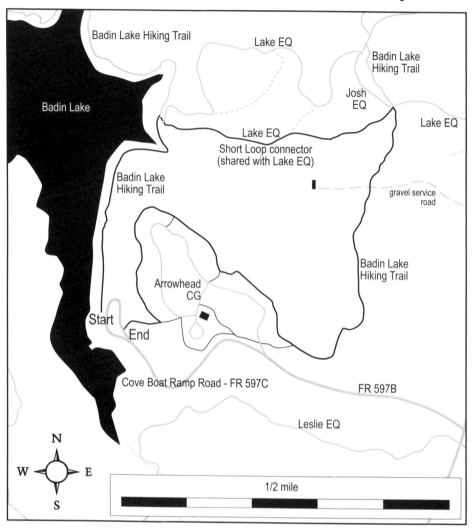

Elevation Profile: Badin Lake Short Loop Trail (BLRA Trip A)

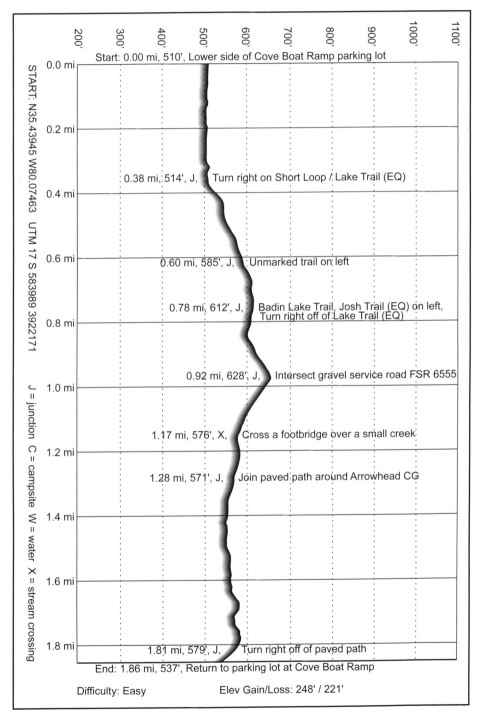

START: N35.43945 W80.07463 UTM 17 S 583989 3922171

J = junction C = campsite W = water X = stream crossing

Start: 0.00 mi, 510', Lower side of Cove Boat Ramp parking lot

0.38 mi, 514', J, Turn right on Short Loop / Lake Trail (EQ)

0.60 mi, 585', J, Unmarked trail on left

0.78 mi, 612', J, Badin Lake Trail, Josh Trail (EQ) on left,
Turn right off of Lake Trail (EQ)

0.92 mi, 628', J, Intersect gravel service road FSR 6555

1.17 mi, 576', X, Cross a footbridge over a small creek

1.28 mi, 571', J, Join paved path around Arrowhead CG

1.81 mi, 579', J, Turn right off of paved path

End: 1.86 mi, 537', Return to parking lot at Cove Boat Ramp

Difficulty: Easy   Elev Gain/Loss: 248' / 221'

Badin Lake Trail starts at the lower side of the Boat Ramp parking lot at the Cove Trailhead. The route runs along the water's edge in and out of small coves. The route is paralleled by the Lake Trail (equestrian) for a short distance. The Short Loop option follows the Lake Trail as it cuts across the loop formed by the full Badin Lake Hiking Trail.

The route then passes between the lake and the Badin Lake Campground campsites for about half a mile. The trail route is somewhat indistinct through this section due the heavy use of the area by campers.

The route crosses the paved parking area in the King's Mountain Point day-use area. The road from the parking lot leads to unpaved FR 597A, which runs by the Badin Lake Group Camp and the Badin Lake Campground.

Heading north along the shore, the trail reaches a unique rock outcropping that slopes down to the edge of the lake. The route crosses the rock and climbs away from the shore, crossing several small ravines and passing by a few old mine pits. The trail then returns to the water's edge and passes around the end of a large peninsula with beautiful views across the lake.

As the trail follows the shoreline into the cove, it occasionally climbs away from the edge of the lake for short distances. The trail passes a junction with a side trail leading to the group camp area near the head of the cove.

The trail crosses graveled FR 597A and then passes by several wildlife food plots before reaching an old gravel road and the Josh Trail (equestrian). The route follows the Josh Trail for a short distance before splitting off and then paralleling it. The route eventually crosses the Lake Trail (equestrian).

From this point the trail climbs over a small, thickly overgrown mountain. The trail eventually reaches a grassy utility clearing, crosses a small footbridge and then turns left onto a small graveled road. The graveled road is followed until it reaches the paved Arrowhead Campground Trail. The route turns right on the paved trail and follows the white blazes most of the way around the campground.

The route eventually turns right off the paved trail and descends on a dirt path to end at the Cove Boat Ramp parking lot.

Badin Lake Equestrian Trails

Trail Name	Length (miles)	Elevation Gain/Loss	Difficulty Rating	Map (page)
Bates Trail	1.92	262' / 609'	Moderate	84
Berner Trail	0.53	6' / 58'	Easy	86
Big Rock Trail	1.05	133 / 184'	Moderate	88
Blackburn Trail	2.12	560' / 452'	Easy	90
Burl Tree Way	1.56	251' / 342'	Easy	92
Buttermilk Trail	0.92	201' / 460'	Moderate	94
Fraley Trail	2.16	389' / 655'	Difficult	96
Greg's Loop	1.29	246' / 249'	Easy	98
Hang Glider Trail	1.30	524' / 120'	Difficult	100
Helen's Loop	2.11	286' / 286'	Easy	102
Home Trail	2.35	460' / 431'	Easy	104
Indian Trail	1.14	293' / 1445'	Easy	106
Josh Trail	1.81	389' / 300'	Easy	108
Lake Trail	1.48	217' / 213'	Easy	110
Larry Trail	1.42	310' / 185'	Easy	112
Leslie Trail	1.26	257' / 231'	Moderate	114
Megan Trail	1.65	244' / 468'	Easy	116
Morgan Trail	1.59	333' / 312'	Easy	118
River Trail	3.59	533' / 501'	Moderate	120
Robbins Trail	1.65	213' / 455'	Easy	122
Rudolph Trail	0.26	58' / 17'	Easy	124
Tanager Trail	0.70	135' / 117'	Easy	126
Todd Trail	2.04	372' / 319'	Moderate	128
Tony Trail	1.75	396' / 314'	Moderate	130
Wren Trail	0.28	43' / 51'	Easy	132

Equestrian Trail System

In addition to the OHV Trail System, the Badin Lake Area is also home to 40-50 miles of equestrian trails. These trails are open to horseback riders, mountain bikers, and hikers, but are primarily used by horseback riders.

When the first edition of this guidebook went to press in 1998, the equestrian trails existed, but were unsigned and for the most part unmapped. In 1999 and 2000, the USFS worked with the local equestrian groups to review these trails. They identified several sections that had severe erosion problems and worked together to close those trails off. The better trails were then named and numbered. Name signs were erected on the trails.

In 2007, Elizabeth Earnhardt self-published a ring-bound, 48-page Trail Guide covering the equestrian trail system. Her guide was no longer in print in 2012.

The USFS-produced "Badin Lake Trail Map" lists the trail numbers, names, and blaze color. The trail blazes are typically placed 5-7 feet off the ground and on both sides of the trail. This USFS map was last updated in 2012 and is available as a PDF on the USFS website.

Mountain bikers who ride the equestrian trails can expect to find generally challenging conditions. The challenge will come partly from the rocky, mountainous terrain through which they run, but will also come from the way horse trails wear and are maintained. Horses easily step over logs that would normally be considered a hindrance to hikers or bikers. In stepping over logs, horse hoof traffic tends to create depressions before and after the log. This pattern is the exact opposite of the log and rock ramps that are usually built up around logs on bike trails. Horse traffic tends to expand wet areas in the trail and leave them churned up with deep hoof prints. There are a few spots where erosion has resulted in a trenched in trail tread that is deeper than it is wide. There will also be some piles of horse-processed oats and hay in the trail. As bad as this description sounds, there are many miles of equestrian trail that "flow" as well as any bike-specific trail.

Mountain bikers should follow proper etiquette when meeting or overtaking horses on the trail. Announcing your presence, approaching slowly, and yielding the trail are key to avoiding conflicts and preserving bike access to these trails.

If you bring your bike to these trails expecting a typical "flowy" bike trail experience, based on the fact that the trails can be legally ridden, you will probably be disappointed. If you are excited by the prospect of 40-50 miles of trail to explore in a remote, forested area, then you're headed in the right direction. If you're ok with sometimes pushing your bike up a hill that you can't ride, and you're ok with some dust, rocks, a little horse poop, and red mud, then you're ready to ride Uwharrie!

For horseback riders, the equestrian trails are generally considered to be rockier and more mountainous than most other trail systems in central North Carolina. Easier and better maintained sections of trail can be found closer to the horse camps. Rougher and steeper trails can be found farther out in the trail system. In some places, the trail will be quite wide. In other spots the trail is narrow and must be traveled single file.

Equestrian Trail System Color Sections
In order to organize this extensive trail system, the trails were divided into five color-coded groups, based on their geographic location within the Badin Lake Recreation Area. The different areas also group trails with somewhat similar difficulty levels, helping visitors chose an area that may better suit their riding abilities or desires. The blazes along the trails match the color group to which the trail belongs. The numbers assigned to the trails run sequentially through the color groups.

Green - The Green trails are located in the northwest corner of the trail system. These trails are all rated Easy, but the intersection signage can be a little confusing to follow on Greg's Loop and Blackburn. Lake Trail is the only trail in the system that runs along the shore of Badin Lake.

- Blackburn Trail
- Greg's Loop
- Josh Trail
- Lake Trail

Dark Green - The Dark Green trails are located on the west side of the area. These trails are all rated Moderate.

- Big Rock Trail
- Leslie Trail
- Todd Trail
- Tony Trail

Magenta - The Magenta trails are located on the northeast corner of the trail system. These trails are all rated Easy. These trails are the closest ones to the horse campgrounds.

- Helen's Loop
- Home Trail
- Indian Trail
- Larry Trail
- Megan Trail

Salmon - The Salmon (pink) trails are located in the southeast corner of the trail system. Most of these trails are rated Easy, but there are two Moderate rated trails and one short trail rated Difficult.

- Burl Tree Way
- Buttermilk Trail
- Hang Glider Trail
- Morgan Trail
- River Trail
- Rudolph Trail
- Tanager Trail
- Wren Trail

Yellow - The Yellow trails are located on the southern side of the trail system. Two of these trails are rate Easy, but the other two are rated Moderate and Difficult. Robbins Trail starts at the Deep Water Trail Camp and connects to the other trails with a long, but easy, out and back run.

- Bates Trail
- Berner Trail
- Fraley Trail
- Robbins Trail

Bates Trail

Map	page 84	**Difficulty**	Moderate
Length	1.92 miles	**Configuration**	One Way
Trailhead	NA	**Elev Gain/Loss**	262' / 609'

Start Coordinates N35.42037, W80.07223;   17 S 584227 3920058

Bates Trail (USFS Trail #723) is one of the equestrian trails in the southwestern section of the equestrian trail system. It is part of the Yellow blazed group of trails.

Bates Trail starts at an intersection with Todd Trail (EQ), Tony Trail (EQ), and Robbins Trail (EQ) just north of Moccasin Creek Road (FR 576), near its intersection with FR 516. The route for Bates and Robbins run together as they head southward and cross FR 576, following the graveled road FR 516. About 150 feet down FR 516, Robbins Trail turns off to the right. The Bates Trail route continues following FR 516 another 0.3 miles before it turns off to the left.

From there the Bates Trail route drops to cross a small creek and then begins climbing. The route crosses the Wolf Den Trail (OHV) three times before topping out near the summit of an unnamed mountain. It then begins descending the mountain and intersects the Dutch John Trail (OHV). The trail continues a gentler rate of descent along tributaries of Dutch John Creek. Shortly before it ends at Dutch John Road FR 553, it passes a junction with the FraleyTrail (EQ).

EQ Tips: Much of the Bates Trail is relatively close to OHV trails, so expect to hear loud noises from ATV's and dirt bikes that could spook sensitive horses.

MTB Tips: The northern half of the Bates Trail, north of its intersection with Dutch John Trail (OHV), consists of parts that are either unremarkable gravel road or are unpleasantly steep trail covered with large loose rocks. I would recommend simply avoiding this section of the trail and ride the nearby OHV trails instead. The southernmost half of the trail that descends more gently beside a creek is pleasant to ride in either direction.

Berner Trail

Map	page 86	**Difficulty**	Easy
Length	0.53 miles	**Configuration**	One Way
Trailhead	NA	**Elev Gain/Loss**	6' / 58'
Start Coordinates	N35.41053, W80.04723;	17 S 586506 3918988	

Berner Trail (USFS Trail #721) is an equestrian trail in the middle of the equestrian trail system that ties together the Salmon and Yellow sides of the trail system. It is part of the Yellow blazed group of trails.

Berner Trail starts at an intersection with Morgan Trail (EQ) and Hang Glider Trail (EQ), not far from Dutch John Road (FR 553). The route follows a small creek as it heads southwestward, paralleling the gravel road FR 553. The route crosses the small creek several times and at one point runs up onto the shoulder of the gravel road for a short distance. The trail ends near a large metal culvert under FR 576 and across the road from the end of the Bates Trail (EQ).

EQ Tips: The numerous creek crossings make this a great trail to teach a horse to cross water.

MTB Tips: This trail has a number of wet creek crossings, but it also has a number of logs across the trail that aren't very rideable. The presence of the gravel road less than 100' away for nearly the entire length of the trail prompted my riding buddy to declare that he saw no reason to ever try to ride this trail again.

Big Rock Loop Trail

Map	page 88	**Difficulty**	Moderate
Length	1.05 miles	**Configuration**	Lollipop
Trailhead	NA	**Elev Gain/Loss**	133 / 184'

Start Coordinates N35.43388, W80.07599;   17 S 583871 3921553

Big Rock Loop Trail (USFS Trail #705) is an equestrian trail on the west side of the equestrian trail system that runs along the edge of Badin Lake. It is part of the Dark Green blazed group of trails. See map on page 88.

Big Rock Loop Trail starts at an intersection with Tony Trail (EQ) and Leslie Trail (EQ). The route heads northward to the lake shore, then turns left and follows the shoreline. It eventually heads back away from the lake and ends at a junction with itself, forming a lollipop shape.

The views of the lake from the shoreline section are a special feature of this trail.

Blackburn Trail

Map	page 90	**Difficulty**	Easy
Length	2.12 miles	**Configuration**	One Way
Trailhead	NA	**Elev Gain/Loss**	560' / 452'

Start Coordinates N35.44745, W80.05680;   17 S 585599 3923075

Blackburn Trail (USFS Trail #701) is an easy-rated equestrian trail on the north side of the equestrian trail system. It is part of the Green blazed group of trails.

Blackburn Trail starts at its junction with McLeans Creek Road FR 544. A few yards west of this junction, the Josh Trail (EQ) crosses FR 544.

The route heads northeast from the road and soon crosses a small creek. From there it generally follows the small creek, going up and down over small ridges on the hillside. It eventually reaches a larger creek, then turns left and follows that creek for a short distance. The route then heads back uphill along an old road. Look closely in this section and you may spot a small waterfall in the small valley to the left of the trail.

After reaching a broad saddle, the route passes a junction with the beginning of Greg's Loop Trail (EQ), on the right. Not far from there it passes a junction with the end of Greg's Loop Trail, also on the right. The route then turns sharply and climbs up and over a small mountain. The route ends at a junction with the Josh Trail (EQ).

EQ Tips: The section of trail on the small mountain has a lot of loose rocks in the trail tread.

Burl Tree Way Trail

Map	page 92	**Difficulty**	Easy
Length	1.56 miles	**Configuration**	One Way
Trailhead	NA	**Elev Gain/Loss**	251' / 342'

Start Coordinates N35.42899, W80.04122;   17 S 587033 3921040

Burl Tree Way Trail (USFS Trail #717) is an easy-rated equestrian trail on the east side of the equestrian trail system. It is part of the Salmon blazed group of trails.

Burl Tree Way Trail starts on the south side of Moccasin Creek Road - FR 576, across from the end of the Home Trail (EQ).

The route generally runs eastward along the lower northern slopes of Daniel Mountain, going up and down over small ridges. Along the way it passes junctions with the Rudolph Trail (EQ) and Tanager Trail (EQ), as well as couple of unmarked trails.

The junction with Rudolph Trail can be a little confusing. In this area, Burl Tree Way first tees into an old roadbed. To the right, the old road leads up the mountain. This old road was once an ORV trail, but was closed to ORV use in 1994. From this junction, the Burl Tree Way route turns left and follows the old road for less than 100 feet to another junction. Burl Tree Way then turns right, off of the old road, and continues eastward. The old road continues northward and is signed as the Rudolph Trail (EQ) until it ends at Moccasin Creek Road - FR 576.

After the junction with Rudolph Trail, the Burl Tree Way Trail descends slightly to cross a small creek. The route then rolls gently over several small ridges before passing a noticeable unmarked trail on the right. About 150 feet further along the trail, but out of sight, is the junction with the Tanager Trail (EQ), to the left.

From the Tanager Trail junction, Burl Tree Way descends steadily, crossing Cotton Place Road - FR 555 and then ending at the River Trail (EQ) next to the Uwharrie River.

MTB Tips: Most of the Burl Tree Way is rideable in either direction.

Buttermilk Trail

Map	page 94	**Difficulty**	Moderate
Length	0.92 mile	**Configuration**	One Way
Trailhead	NA	**Elev Gain/Loss**	201' / 460'

Start Coordinates N35.40707, W80.03605;   17 S 587526 3918613

Buttermilk Trail (USFS Trail #720) is a moderate-rated equestrian trail on the east side of the equestrian trail system. The Buttermilk Trail is part of the Salmon blazed group of trails.

Maps from the 1960's show two dirt bike trails close to the area that Buttermilk Trail traverses. The Rattlesnake Trail passed through the saddle where Buttermilk starts, but it's not clear if it climbed towards the top of the mountain or if it stayed lower on the mountain. The Coon Trail started on Cotton Place Road where Buttermilk ends, but appears to have only run part of the way up the mountain.

Buttermilk Trail starts at its junction with the Hang Glider Trail (EQ) in a high saddle between Daniel and Shingle Trap Mountains. The route begins by climbing directly up a steep slope on Daniel Mountain. This section is covered with loose rocks. The route stops just short of going to the very top of the mountain, and instead turns sharply right and begins a long direct descent along a spur ridge.

The route eventually becomes less steep and rocky as it nears the bottom of the mountain. There is a fairly open field area with nice views across the Uwharrie River valley. Not far beyond this open area, the route ends at Cotton Place Road - FR 555, across from the end of River Trail (EQ).

EQ Tips: Although this trail is rated moderate, the rocky, steep upper section is definitely on the more challenging side of "moderate".

MTB Tips: The upper section of Buttermilk that runs towards the top of the mountain is steep and covered with loose rocks, making an ascent from either direction almost a guaranteed hike-a-bike. Approaching from the end of the trail at Cotton Place Road - FR 555 and riding up to the open field vista, and then backtracking out, is the only section I would recommend biking, unless the route is your last resort for crossing the mountains to/from the interior of the Badin Lake Recreation Area.

Fraley Trail

Map	page 96	**Difficulty**	Difficult
Length	2.16 miles	**Configuration**	One Way
Trailhead	NA	**Elev Gain/Loss**	389' / 655'

Start Coordinates N35.42416, W80.06900;   17 S 584516 3920480

Fraley Trail (USFS Trail #722) is a difficult rated trail in the southwestern section of the equestrian trail system. It is part of the Yellow blazed group of trails.

Fraley Trail starts at a junction with Todd Trail (EQ) just west of Moccasin Creek Road (FR 576), near the Flintlock Shooting Range. The route quickly crosses FR 576, and follows the gated and gravel road FR 6688.

As the route crosses FR 576, there are a couple of options. Going straight across FR 576 leads you up a small bank and around the left side of the gate, then down onto FR 6688. Crossing FR 576 at a slight angle to the right leads you past a small culvert and to a trail entrance that is signed for Fraley Trail. From the sign, there is a well-used trail that leads left back towards the gate and FR 6688. There is also a blazed trail leading more to the right from the sign. This trail section was nearly overgrown in 2012 and obviously doesn't get much use. It connects to the Fraley route at the top of the knoll to the east, but the popular traffic pattern is to simply follow FR 6688. The popular route is detailed in this guide.

About 0.2 mile up the graveled road, there is a junction with an old road bed to the right. The Fraley route turns right here. FR 6688 continues straight and ends where the route of the Sawmill Trail (OHV) takes it over. Guardrail has been erected to block OHV traffic from leaving Sawmill Trail and turning onto FR 6688.

After the turn, the Fraley route heads south over a small knoll and descends slightly to an intersection with Slab Pile Trail (OHV) and Sawmill Trail (OHV). The intersection is a broad open area and finding the continuation of the Fraley Trail can be little tricky. The old road bed that Fraley followed into the intersection continues across the clearing, but there is a small "Road Closed" sign where it enters into the tree line. Look on the left side for a short bypass route through a few trees to get to the old road bed.

From the clearing, the Fraley route descends gently for a few tenths of a mile, but then climbs up a mountain. The route then crosses over the three small peaks of this mountain before dropping down the southern end. The trail up and over this mountain is very rocky.

Near the bottom of the mountain, the route crosses the Dutch John Trail (OHV). Watch for some split rail fence along the OHV trail before reaching the intersection. After the intersection, the Fraley route continues a loose rocky descent until it reaches a crossing of Dutch John Creek.

Across the creek, the route turns right and then parallels the creek, offering a much gentler section of trail to travel. At one point the trail drops down to the edge of the creek before turning back away to continue paralleling it again.

The route crosses Dutch John Creek one final time, and then crosses a tributary creek less than 100 feet away. Just after the second creek crossing, the Fraley Trail ends at a junction with the Bates Trail (EQ). Dutch John Road (FR 553) is within sight to the left.

EQ Tips: Much of the Fraley Trail is relatively close to OHV trails, so expect to hear loud noises from ATV's and dirt bikes that could spook sensitive horses.

MTB Tips: The northern section of the Fraley Trail, north of its intersection with Slab Pile Trail (OHV), consists of unremarkable gravel road or old road bed. The southern section, south of the intersection with Dutch John Trail (OHV) is mostly rideable singletrack trail. The middle section over the mountain is primarily unpleasantly steep trail covered with large loose rocks. I would recommend simply avoiding this middle section of the trail and ride the connecting OHV trails instead.

Greg's Loop Trail

Map	page 98	**Difficulty**	Easy
Length	1.29 miles	**Configuration**	Loop, almost
Trailhead	NA	**Elev Gain/Loss**	246' / 249'

Start Coordinates N35.45446, W80.06105;   17 S 585205 3923848

Greg's Loop Trail (USFS Trail #700) is an easy rated trail in the northwestern section of the equestrian trail system. It is part of the Green blazed group of trails.

Greg's Loop Trail starts at a junction with the Blackburn Trail (EQ) and circles counterclockwise around the upper end of a valley before it ends at another junction with Blackburn, not far from the first junction. The route follows several sections of old road bed that run through the area, as well as some singletrack trail sections.

Old maps from the 1960's show several trails in the area of the current Greg's Loop Trail. The route follows some sections of these old trails, and crosses others. The old trails had names such as Black Snake Trail, Cross Road Trail, Crump Mine Trail, and Reeves Branch Trail.

Three sections of the trail on the western side of the loop are being relocated as this guide goes to press. The new alignment is shown on the maps and profile chart.

Along the route, there are several unsigned junctions with old roads or trails that connect to FR 597. The abundance of old road beds and junctions makes this route a little more difficult to follow. It's helpful to watch for the green blazes and keep up with where you are on the map provided in this guide.

EQ Tips: Keep an eye out for the green blazes to help stay on the correct route.

MTB Tips: This trail doesn't have any significant hills or rocky sections and is pleasant to ride in either direction.

Hang Glider Trail

Map	page 100	**Difficulty**	Difficult
Length	1.30 miles	**Configuration**	One Way
Trailhead	NA	**Elev Gain/Loss**	524' / 120'

Start Coordinates N35.41053, W80.04723;   17 S 586506 3918988

Hang Glider Trail (USFS Trail #719) is a difficult rated trail in the southeastern section of the equestrian trail system. It is part of the Salmon blazed group of trails.

Hang Glider Trail starts at a junction with the Morgan Trail (EQ) and Berner Trail (EQ), not far from Dutch John Road (FR 553). There is a fairly popular unofficial car-camping area between the road and the trail junction. The Morgan Trail passes through the camp area and crosses a small creek just before ending at this trail junction.

The route heads upstream, crossing the creek five times before reaching an open, well-worn area beside the Dickey Bell Trail (OHV). The Hang Glider route crosses the Dickey Bell Trail here, but the route on the far side of the intersection is difficult to spot. Look for a metal guardrail on the far side the Dickey Bell Trail. The Hang Glider route goes around the left end of the guardrail and then turns sharply back to the right behind the guardrail. It then climbs up a steep rocky hill.

After the intersection, the route generally parallels the Dickey Bell Trail for a while, and at one point comes within a few feet of it. Eventually the route climbs away from the OHV trail and follows a rocky path to a saddle between Daniel Mountain and Shingle Trap Mountain. The Buttermilk Trail (EQ) junctions with Hang Glider in this saddle, leading left up Daniel Mountain.

From the saddle, the route turns right and climbs over the top of the eastern peak of Shingle Trap Mountain. The route ends at an overlook that was cleared out for use as a hang gliding launch site in the 1990's. No one hang glides from here anymore, but the vista is still enjoyed by those who reach this spot.

As of the end of 2013, the upper section of the Hang Glider trail, from the saddle to the overlook, was closed due to resource damage. The USFS plans to rehab the trail and reopen it at a later date.

EQ Tips: This trail is close to OHV trails, so you may hear lots of noise from that traffic.

MTB Tips: The lower sections of the this trail are less difficult to ride, but the nearby roads and OHV trails offer better alternatives to get thru the area. The upper sections of trail are covered with lots of loose rocks. Visiting the overlook at the top would be the only reason to push your bike all the way to the top.

Helen's Loop Trail

Map	page 102	**Difficulty**	Easy
Length	2.11 miles	**Configuration**	Loop
Trailhead	NA	**Elev Gain/Loss**	286' / 286'

Start Coordinates N35.43733, W80.03246;   17 S 587818 3921973

Helen's Loop Trail (USFS Trail #712) is an easy rated trail in the northeastern section of the equestrian trail system. It is part of the Magenta blazed group of trails.

Helen's Loop Trail starts at a junction with the River Trail (EQ), beside the West Branch of McLean's Creek and a short distance north of McLean's Creek Road (FR 544).

The route heads upstream along West Branch. This section is often called Lower Helen's Loop. The route crosses the creek and soon junctions on the left with a side trail signed as Connector that leads to the Old Horse Camp and the Blue Hole (a large pool in the creek).

The route then climbs to a crossing of paved Mullinix Road (SR 1154). Across the road, the route passes through a small section of woods that borders the 4B Horse Farm.

The route then crosses Mullinix Road again, heading back south along the ridge top. This section is often called Upper Helen's Loop.

EQ Tips: Upper Helen's Loop follows an old road bed along the ridge and offers easy side by side riding.

Home Trail

Map	page 104	**Difficulty**	Easy
Length	2.35 miles	**Configuration**	One Way
Trailhead	NA	**Elev Gain/Loss**	460' / 431'

Start Coordinates N35.44539, W80.03852;   17 S 587260 3922861

Home Trail (USFS Trail #710) is an easy rated trail in the northern section of the equestrian trail system. It is part of the Magenta blazed group of trails.

Home Trail starts beside the West Branch of McLean's Creek, at the Mullinix Road (SR 1144) bridge over this creek. There is a large pool in the creek at this spot known as the Blue Hole.

The route climbs up from the creek and passes by the Old Horse Camp on Mullinix Road. The route then crosses a creek and passes by a junction with the Josh Trail (EQ) and Indian Trail (EQ) on the right. It then passes by the Canebrake Horse Camp and crosses McLean's Creek Road (FR 544).

After the road crossing, the route descends to cross an unnamed creek and then climbs over a ridge. Near the top of the ridge, the route intersects the Larry Trail (EQ). Running along the ridge top, the route passes by a junction with the Megan Trail (EQ) on the left. After dropping off the ridge, the route ends at Moccasin Creek Road (SR 576) where it crosses Moccasin Creek. On the far side of the road, a little to the left, is the start of the Burl Tree Way Trail (EQ).

EQ Tips: Upper Helen's Loop follows old road bed along the ridge and offers easy side by side riding.

Indian Trail

Map	page 106	**Difficulty**	Easy
Length	1.14 miles	**Configuration**	One Way
Trailhead	NA	**Elev Gain/Loss**	293' / 1445'
Start Coordinates	N35.44268, W80.04596;	17 S 586587 3922555	

Indian Trail (USFS Trail #708) is an easy rated trail in the northern section of the equestrian trail system. It is part of the Magenta blazed group of trails.

Indian Trail starts at a junction with the Home Trail (EQ) and Josh Trail (EQ), not far north of the Canebrake Horse Campground. The route runs westward over high ground and crosses McLean's Creek Road (FR 544).

From the road, the route climbs a short distance and then descends to cross a creek. Near the creek is an unmarked connector trail that leads to the Overflow Horse Camping field along FR 544. From the creek the route begins a long climb. The route eventually crosses a hill top with a broad open area known locally as the "Hitchin' Hill" or "Walmart" (parking lot).

The route ends at a junction with the Todd Trail (EQ) and Megan Trail (EQ). From here, riders can connect to the trails on the west side of the Badin Lake Recreational Area.

EQ Tips: Indian Trail is heavily used and therefore easy to follow.

Josh Trail

Map	page 108	**Difficulty**	Easy
Length	1.81 miles	**Configuration**	One Way
Trailhead	NA	**Elev Gain/Loss**	389' / 300'

Start Coordinates N35.44270, W80.04594;   17 S 586590 3922556

Josh Trail (USFS Trail #702) is an easy rated trail in the northern section of the equestrian trail system. It is part of the Green blazed group of trails.

Josh Trail starts at a junction with the Home Trail (EQ) and Indian Trail (EQ), not far north of the Canebrake Horse Campground. The route runs westward and crosses McLean's Creek Road (FR 544) twice.

At the second crossing of FR 544, you will see the start of the Blackburn Trail (EQ) directly across the road. The Josh Trail route continues on the far side of the road, about 50 feet to the left. The route climbs from the road crossing and then turns left at a junction with the end of the Blackburn Trail.

After crossing over a small knoll, the trail descends towards Badin Lake Road (FR 597). Less than 100 yards from the road crossing, there is an unmarked trail to the left. The trail straight ahead connects to FR 597 just north of the road intersection of FR 597 and 597A (which leads to the Badin Lake campgrounds). The unmarked trail to the left connects to a graveled pull-off area just south of the 597 and 597A intersection. The Josh route continues directly across FR 597 from this graveled pull-off area.

From the FR 597 crossing, the route climbs over another small knoll and is soon joined from the right by the white-blazed Badin Lake Hiking Trail. The two trails run together for about 100 feet before the hiking trail splits off to the left. A short distance further, the end of the Lake Trail (EQ) junctions on the right side. This intersection is unsigned. Both trails are blazed with Green paint.

The Josh Trail route continues along an old road bed. It runs along the edge of a small open field before ending at an intersection with the Lake Trail (EQ) and the Badin Lake Hiking Trail. This intersection is signed.

Lake Trail

Map	page 110	**Difficulty**	Easy
Length	1.48 miles	**Configuration**	One Way
Trailhead	NA	**Elev Gain/Loss**	217' / 213'

Start Coordinates N35.44076, W80.06083;   17 S 585240 3922329

Lake Trail (USFS Trail #703) is an easy rated trail in the northwestern section of the equestrian trail system. It is part of the Green blazed group of trails.

Lake Trail starts at a junction with the Todd Trail (EQ), not far west of the end of the Indian Trail (EQ). The route runs westward and crosses Badin Lake Road (FR 597). On maps from the 1960's, this first section of trail was known as the Red Oak Trail.

To continue on the route on the far side of FR 597, turn right on the road and follow it over a small creek, then look for a trail entrance on the left side of the road. The route then follows an old road bed to an intersection with the Badin Lake Hiking Trail and the end of the Josh Trail (EQ).

The Lake Trail route continues westward along the old road bed towards the lake shore. This section of trail is shared with the "Short Loop" option of the Badin Lake Hiking Trail. You will see both Green and White paint blazes along this section. About half way through this section, there is an unmarked trail to the right. It simply connects to the Lake Trail after it turns back from the lake.

The route doesn't actually run all the way to the lake shore, but it does come within sight of the lake in a well-worn area. The white-blazed Badin Lake Hiking Trail runs along the shoreline. The Green-blazed Lake Trail turns right and parallels the shoreline for a short distance in the clearing, but it lies a little further from the water.

The Green-blazed route then turns away from the lake and heads eastward. A few hundred feet from the lake is a junction with an unmarked road/trail. The Lake Trail route turns left. The unmarked road/trail simply connects to the Lake Trail further along, offering a small shortcut.

The route continues eastward, passing junctions with both of the unmarked connectors before it ends at a junction with the Josh Trail.

EQ Tips: The presence of several unmarked connectors running between the U-shaped portion of the trail near the lake make this trail a little confusing to navigate. Consulting the map of the trail should help make sense of how it is laid out.

Larry Trail

Map	page 112	**Difficulty**	Easy
Length	1.42 miles	**Configuration**	One Way
Trailhead	NA	**Elev Gain/Loss**	310' / 185'

Start Coordinates N35.44008, W80.03301;   17 S 587766 3922278

Larry Trail (USFS Trail #711) is an easy rated trail in the northwestern section of the equestrian trail system. It is part of the Magenta blazed group of trails.

Larry Trail starts at a junction with Helen' Loop Trail (EQ), on the west side of the West Branch of Moccasin Creek. The route climbs up from the creek, passes near a field on private land, and then intersects McLeans Creek Road (FR 544).

The route then drops down into the valley of another tributary of Moccasin Creek. It follows the creek upstream for a while, then crosses the creek and continues upstream on the other side.

Eventually the route climbs out of the valley and intersects the Home Trail (EQ). From that intersection, the route crosses fairly level ground until it ends at a junction with the Megan Trail (EQ).

EQ Tips: There are some unmarked trails connecting to this trail, which could make this trail a little confusing to navigate. Watch for the Magenta trail blazes and you should be fine.

Leslie Trail

Map	page 114	**Difficulty**	Moderate
Length	1.26 miles	**Configuration**	One Way
Trailhead	NA	**Elev Gain/Loss**	257' / 231'
Start Coordinates	N35.43932, W80.06165;	17 S 585167 3922169	

Leslie Trail (USFS Trail #704) is a moderate rated trail in the western section of the equestrian trail system. It is part of the Dark Green blazed group of trails. See map on page 114.

Leslie Trail starts at a junction with the Todd Trail (EQ) and heads westward. The route climbs over a small knoll and then drops to intersect Badin Lake Road (FR 597) near its intersection with the Cove Boat Ramp Road (FR 597B). The trail splits as you approach FR 597, with both leading to the road. The left fork of the split is the better route, as it avoids a large mud hole and lines up better with the trail continuation on the west side of FR 597.

From FR 597, the route climbs over a small mountain and passes by a storage field and retention ponds for the Arrowhead Campground. The route crosses a service road that leads to the Cover Boat Ramp Road (FR 597B).

The route then descends to a small creek at the head of a cove on Badin Lake. The route turns and heads up stream a short distance before crossing the creek and climbing the hill on the far side. Near the top of the hill, the route ends at a junction with the Tony Trail (EQ) and Big Rock Loop Trail (EQ).

EQ Tips: There is water for horses at the creek crossing near the lake.

Megan Trail

Map	page 116	**Difficulty**	Easy
Length	1.65 miles	**Configuration**	One Way
Trailhead	NA	**Elev Gain/Loss**	244' / 468'

Start Coordinates N35.41577, W80.06925;   17 S 584502 3919549

Megan Trail (USFS Trail #709) is an easy rated trail in the center section of the equestrian trail system. It is part of the Magenta blazed group of trails.

Megan Trail starts at a junction with the Todd Trail (EQ) and Indian Trail (EQ) and runs southeastward. The route starts high and follows a ridge line over a small mountain, then it makes a long descent to cross a creek.

Across the creek, the route climbs steeply up another ridge. This steep rocky climb is more like a "moderate" difficulty rated section. Once on top of this ridge, the route rolls more gently up and down over some smaller features but generally drops in elevation as it goes along.

The route passes a junction on the left with an old road bed that connects to Moccasin Creek Road (FR 576). This junction is within sight of the gravel road. The route then parallels FR 576 as it continues.

After passing through a field, a junction with the end of the Larry Trail (EQ) is passed on the left. The route ends at a junction with the Home Trail (EQ), not far from where the Home Trail ends at FR 576.

EQ Tips: There is water for horses at the creek crossing.

Morgan Trail

Map	page 118	**Difficulty**	Easy
Length	1.59 miles	**Configuration**	One Way
Trailhead	NA	**Elev Gain/Loss**	333' / 312'

Start Coordinates N35.42868, W80.04085;   17 S 587066 3921006

Morgan Trail (USFS Trail #718) is one of four equestrian trails that connect the northern half of the equestrian trail system to the more remote southern half of the system. It is an easy rated trail that is part of the Magenta blazed group of trails.

In 2010, the Morgan Trail was rehabbed by a trail maintenance contractor. The tread was graded with power equipment, the wooden bridges were removed, and drainage was improved. The "trail corridor" was cleared back to the USFS standard for equestrian trails. As a result of this work, the trail "flows" quite well for both horseback riders and mountain bikers.

Morgan Trail starts at a junction with Burl Tree Way Trail (EQ) just south of Moccasin Creek Road (FR 576). The route heads southward and climbs gently for the first 0.9 miles. Along the way it crosses the Rocky Mountain Trail (OHV), Dutch John Road (FR 553), and the Rocky Mountain Trail again.

From there the route climbs over a small mountain and crosses the Dickey Bell Trail (OHV). It then climbs over another small mountain before descending to cross Dutch John Road again. The trail ends at a junction with the Berner and Hanglider Trails (EQ), just across a tributary of Dutch John Creek.

EQ Tips: Much of the Morgan Trail is relatively close to OHV trails, so expect to hear loud noises from ATV's and dirt bikes that could spook sensitive horses.

MTB Tips: The first two-thirds of the Morgan Trail are pleasant to ride in either direction. The southernmost section that descends a mountain to Dutch John Road is fairly steep and would be a challenge for most riders to pedal back up, despite being clear of any major obstacles. Fortunately, Dutch John Road offers an easy alternate return route.

River Trail

Map	page 120	**Difficulty**	Moderate
Length	3.59 miles	**Configuration**	One Way
Trailhead	NA	**Elev Gain/Loss**	533' / 501'
Start Coordinates	N35.43741, W80.03246;	17 S 587819 3921982	

River Trail (USFS Trail #713) is a moderate rated trail in the eastern section of the equestrian trail system. It is part of the Salmon blazed group of trails.

River Trail starts at a junction with Helen's Loop Trail (EQ), at the southernmost point of its "loop". The route follows the West Branch of Moccasin Creek downstream to its confluence with Moccasin Creek. After crossing Moccasin Creek, the route crosses McLeans Creek Road (FR 544) and begins a gentle climb up a low ridge, paralleling the gravel road.

Near the intersection of FR 544 and Moccasin Creek Road (FR 576), the route crosses FR 544 again and parallels FR 576 for several hundred feet. A junction with the Wren Trail (EQ) is passed on the right. River Trail then crosses FR 576 and heads southward.

The route descends gently and crosses a small creek. From there it contours along the base of Daniel Mountain until it reaches a crossing of Cotton Place Road (FR 555).

After crossing FR 555, the route generally follows the Uwharrie River downstream. A junction with the end of Burl Tree Way Trail (EQ) is passed on the right. As the route heads south, the space between the river and FR 555 gets smaller and in places the trail is on a steep narrow slope.

Several large open fields will be found near the Cotton Place Trailhead that serves the OHV trails. An unmarked trail connects to that parking area. There are a few places to easily access the Uwharrie River in this area.

The route continues along the river, winding back and forth to work around some steep creek gullies. Eventually the trail leaves the river and climbs a hill to end at Cotton Place Road. There is a gate across the road at this point, and directly across the road is the end of the Buttermilk Trail (EQ).

Robbins Trail

Map	page 122	**Difficulty**	Easy
Length	1.65 miles	**Configuration**	One Way
Trailhead	NA	**Elev Gain/Loss**	213' / 455'

Start Coordinates N35.42037, W80.07223;   17 S 584227 3920057

Robbins Trail (USFS Trail #724) is an easy rated trail in the southwestern section of the equestrian trail system. It is part of the Yellow blazed group of trails.

Robbins Trail starts at a junction with Todd Trail (EQ), Tony Trail (EQ), and Bates Trail (EQ) just north of Moccasin Creek Road (FR 576), near its intersection with FR 516. The route for Robbins and Bates run together as they head southward and cross FR 576, following the graveled road FR 516. About 150 feet down FR 516, Robbins Trail turns off to the right into the trees. The Bates Trail route continues following FR 516.

The route climbs high up on the side of a mountain before beginning a relatively long descent. The descent is only broken by a short passage through a saddle.

Shortly after the route crosses a creek, there is a junction with a short side trail to the left that leads to a camping area at the end of Moccasin Creek Road (FR 576). The Robbins Trail route continues over a small knoll before ending at Moccasin Creek Road, across from the Deep Water Trail Road (FR 6560).

EQ Tips: This trail is an out and back route, as there are no other equestrian trails accessible from the end. A short distance down the Deep Water Trail Road is a large grassy field known as the Deep Water Trail Camp.

Rudolph Trail

Map	page 124	**Difficulty**	Easy
Length	0.26 miles	**Configuration**	One Way
Trailhead	NA	**Elev Gain/Loss**	58' / 17'

Start Coordinates N35.42931, W80.03640;   17 S 587470 3921080

Rudolph Trail (USFS Trail #716) is an easy rated trail in the eastern section of the equestrian trail system. It is part of the Salmon blazed group of trails. The route is an old gated Forest Service road (FR 6607).

On maps from the 1960's, Rudolph Trail was shown as a jeep trail that followed the currently described section, but it then turned westward and did not climb up Daniel Mountain. Several dirt bike trails (Wildcat Trail and White Oak Trail) branched off this jeep trail and did climb a little further up the mountain. Later, the road was extended up the mountain to end at a junction with the Daniel Trail (OHV). In 1993, the upper half of the trail was closed due to erosion problems.

The route begins at a small pull off along Moccasin Creek Road (FR 576). It goes around a gate and follows an old road bed. Not far from the start is a junction with the Tanager Trail (EQ) on the left.

The route then gently climbs towards Daniel Mountain. The Rudolph Trail officially ends at a junction with the Burl Tree Way Trail (EQ). Burl Tree Way is a singletrack trail leading the left of the old road bed. The next 100 feet of the old road is part of the Burl Tree Way route, until that route turns off to the right at a signed junction. The old road bed continues southward from here, but is no longer part of a named trail.

Tanager Trail

Map	page 126	**Difficulty**	Easy
Length	0.70 miles	**Configuration**	One Way
Trailhead	NA	**Elev Gain/Loss**	135' / 117'

Start Coordinates N35.42892, W80.03635;   17 S 587475 3921037

Tanager Trail (USFS Trail #715) is an easy rated trail in the eastern section of the equestrian trail system. It is part of the Salmon blazed group of trails.

Tanager Trail starts at a junction with the Rudolph Trail (EQ). The route heads eastward along fairly level ground for about 0.3 miles before it turns sharply right and descends to cross a creek.

At the creek crossing, a junction with the Wren Trail (EQ) will be seen on the left, leading across the creek. An old gold mine can be seen on the far side of the creek.

The route climbs from the creek until it junctions with the Burl Tree Way Trail (EQ) on the lower slopes of Daniel Mountain.

EQ Tips: There is a steep eroded section between the creek and Burl Tree Way that can get pretty slick when it is wet.

Todd Trail

Map	page 128	**Difficulty**	Moderate
Length	2.04 miles	**Configuration**	One Way
Trailhead	NA	**Elev Gain/Loss**	372' / 319'

Start Coordinates N35.44078, W80.05958;   17 S 585353 3922332

Todd Trail (USFS Trail #707) is a moderate rated trail in the western section of the equestrian trail system. It is part of the Dark Green blazed group of trails.

Todd Trail starts at a junction with Indian Trail (EQ) and Megan Trail (EQ). The route heads westward initially, and soon passes a junction with the Lake Trail (EQ) on the right. The route then begins heading southward, which it does for most of it's length.

A junction with Leslie Trail (EQ) is passed on the right in a saddle. From there, the route winds its way around some low ridges until it comes close to Moccasin Creek Road (FR 576). The route then begins paralleling FR 576.

The route crosses Badin Lake Road (FR 597), within sight of where it ends at Moccasin Creek Road (FR 576). Just before the road intersection, you will pass a small field and see a concrete foundation slab from a building long gone. There is a creek crossing not far after FR 597.

The next junction is where the Fraley Trail (EQ) leads off to the left. This is just beyond the Flintlock Valley Shooting Range on FR 576.

The route then works its way upwards along a rocky ridge until it ends at a junction with the Tony Trail (EQ), Bates Trail (EQ), and Robbins Trail (EQ).

EQ Tips: The Todd Trail is fairly heavily used as it provides a good connector between the northern and southern sections of the equestrian trail system.

Tony Trail

Map	page 130	**Difficulty**	Moderate
Length	1.75 miles	**Configuration**	One Way
Trailhead	NA	**Elev Gain/Loss**	396' / 314'

Start Coordinates N35.43378, W80.07619;   17 S 583853 3921541

Tony Trail (USFS Trail #706) is a moderate rated trail in the western section of the equestrian trail system. It is part of the Dark Green blazed group of trails.

Todd Trail starts at a junction with the Leslie Trail (EQ) and Big Rock Loop Trail (EQ). The route leads westward and passes by a side tail that leads to the large rock formation known as Nifty Rocks or Big Rocks.

From the rocks, the route turns more southward and crosses Moccasin Creek Road (FR 576). The route then climbs over a rocky mountain and then descends to a creek crossing.

From the creek, the route climbs to cross FR 576 again. It then parallels the road until ending at a junction with Todd Trail (EQ), Bates Trail (EQ), and Robbins Trail (EQ).

EQ Tips: This trail is seldom used and offers a more wilderness-like experience. Watch for the Dark Green blazes to stay on track, as there are several unmarked trails in this area.

MTB Tips: The rocky mountain between the two crossings of FR 576 is very difficult to ride. FR 576 offers an easier alternative to connect the upper section of this trail with other trails.

Wren Trail

Map	page 132	**Difficulty**	Easy
Length	0.70 miles	**Configuration**	One Way
Trailhead	NA	**Elev Gain/Loss**	135' / 117'

Start Coordinates N35.42892, W80.03635;   17 S 587475 3921037

Wren Trail (USFS Trail #714) is an easy rated trail in the eastern section of the equestrian trail system. It is part of the Salmon blazed group of trails.

Wren Trail starts at a junction with the River Trail (EQ). The route heads southward and almost immediately crosses Moccasin Creek Road (FR 576). South of the road, the route passes by a gate and heads across a small field planted as a wildlife food plot. From the field, the route descends to cross a creek. After the creek crossing, the route turns right and follows the creek upstream until it ends at a junction with the Tanager Trail (EQ). On the south side of the creek near the junction can be seen an old gold mine.

EQ Tips: There is a short but steep section of trail across bare rock near the creek, but there is a bypass around it.

Bates Trail

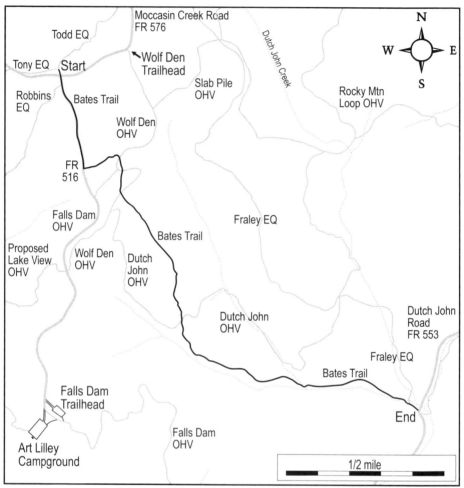

Elevation Profile: Bates Trail

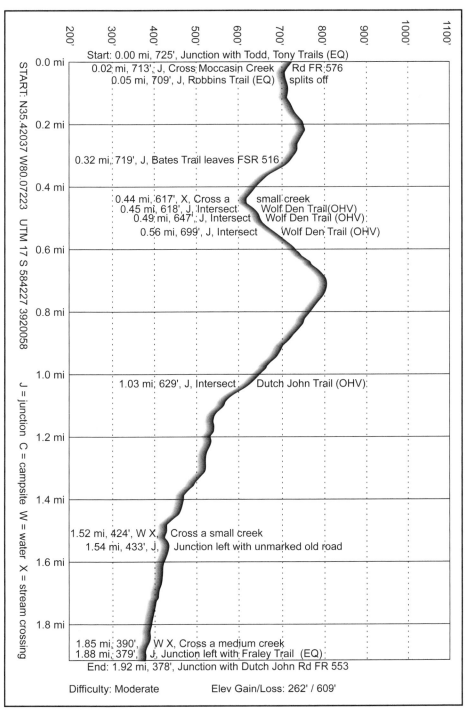

START: N35.42037 W80.07223 UTM 17 S 584227 3920058

J = junction C = campsite W = water X = stream crossing

200' 300' 400' 500' 600' 700' 800' 900' 1000' 1100'

0.0 mi — Start: 0.00 mi, 725', Junction with Todd, Tony Trails (EQ)
0.02 mi, 713', J, Cross Moccasin Creek Rd FR 576
0.05 mi, 709', J, Robbins Trail (EQ) splits off

0.2 mi

0.32 mi, 719', J, Bates Trail leaves FSR 516

0.4 mi
0.44 mi, 617', X, Cross a small creek
0.45 mi, 618', J, Intersect Wolf Den Trail(OHV)
0.49 mi, 647', J, Intersect Wolf Den Trail (OHV)
0.56 mi, 699', J, Intersect Wolf Den Trail (OHV)

0.6 mi

0.8 mi

1.0 mi
1.03 mi, 629', J, Intersect Dutch John Trail (OHV)

1.2 mi

1.4 mi

1.52 mi, 424', W X, Cross a small creek
1.54 mi, 433', J, Junction left with unmarked old road

1.6 mi

1.8 mi

1.85 mi, 390', W X, Cross a medium creek
1.88 mi, 379', J, Junction left with Fraley Trail (EQ)
End: 1.92 mi, 378', Junction with Dutch John Rd FR 553

Difficulty: Moderate   Elev Gain/Loss: 262' / 609'

Berner Trail

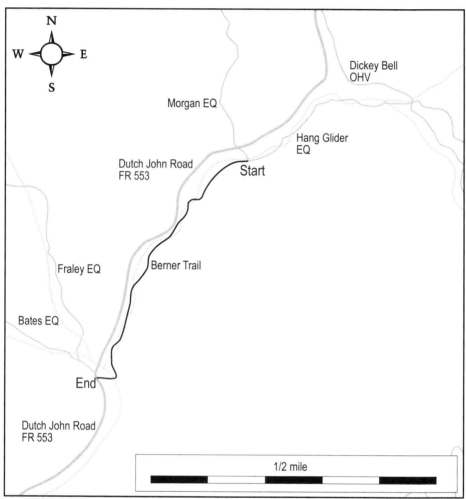

Elevation Profile: Berner Trail

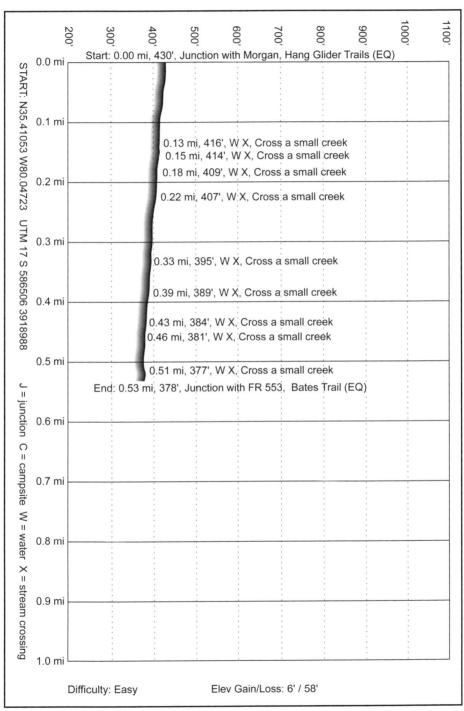

START: N35.41053 W80.04723 UTM 17 S 586506 3918988

J = junction C = campsite W = water X = stream crossing

Start: 0.00 mi, 430', Junction with Morgan, Hang Glider Trails (EQ)

0.13 mi, 416', W X, Cross a small creek
0.15 mi, 414', W X, Cross a small creek
0.18 mi, 409', W X, Cross a small creek

0.22 mi, 407', W X, Cross a small creek

0.33 mi, 395', W X, Cross a small creek

0.39 mi, 389', W X, Cross a small creek

0.43 mi, 384', W X, Cross a small creek
0.46 mi, 381', W X, Cross a small creek

0.51 mi, 377', W X, Cross a small creek
End: 0.53 mi, 378', Junction with FR 553, Bates Trail (EQ)

Difficulty: Easy   Elev Gain/Loss: 6' / 58'

Big Rock Loop Trail

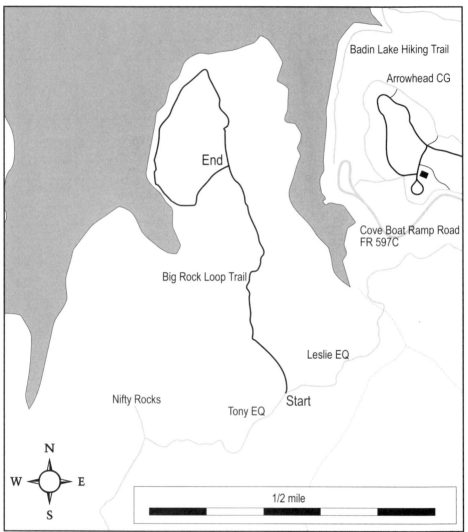

Badin Lake Hiking Trail

Arrowhead CG

End

Cove Boat Ramp Road
FR 597C

Big Rock Loop Trail

Leslie EQ

Nifty Rocks

Tony EQ   Start

N
W — E
S

1/2 mile

Elevation Profile: Big Rock Loop Trail

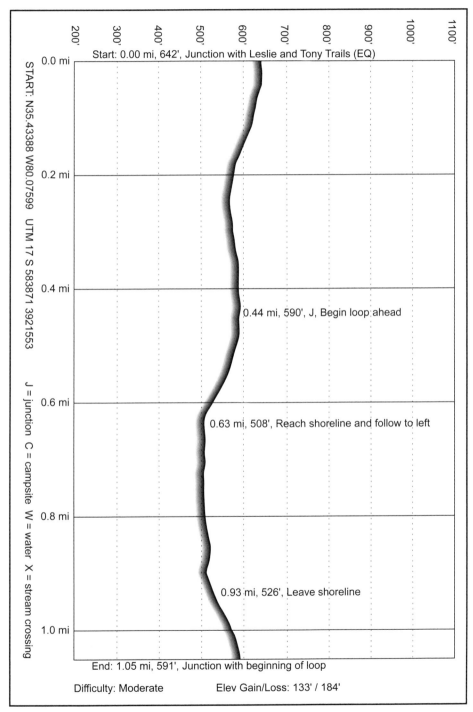

START: N35.43388 W80.07599 UTM 17 S 583871 3921553   J = junction C = campsite W = water X = stream crossing

Start: 0.00 mi, 642', Junction with Leslie and Tony Trails (EQ)

0.44 mi, 590', J, Begin loop ahead

0.63 mi, 508', Reach shoreline and follow to left

0.93 mi, 526', Leave shoreline

End: 1.05 mi, 591', Junction with beginning of loop

Difficulty: Moderate   Elev Gain/Loss: 133' / 184'

Blackburn Trail

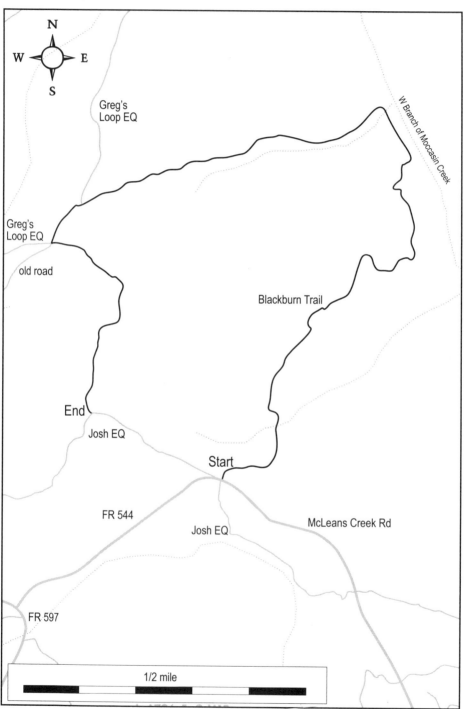

Elevation Profile: Blackburn Trail

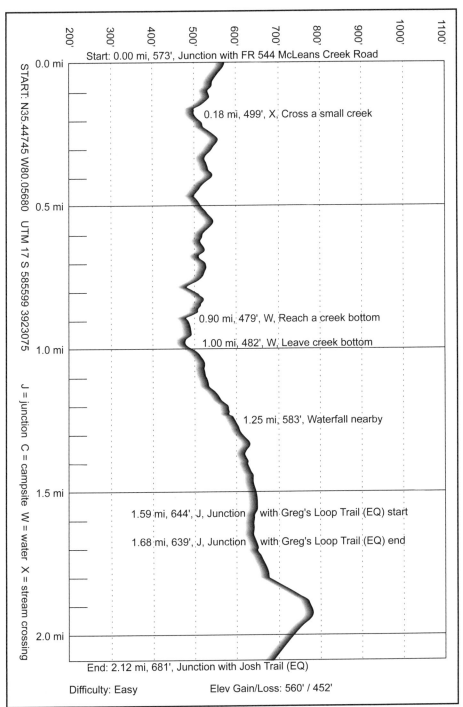

START: N35.44745 W80.05680   UTM 17 S 585599 3923075

J = junction C = campsite W = water X = stream crossing

Start: 0.00 mi, 573', Junction with FR 544 McLeans Creek Road

0.18 mi, 499', X, Cross a small creek

0.90 mi, 479', W, Reach a creek bottom

1.00 mi, 482', W, Leave creek bottom

1.25 mi, 583', Waterfall nearby

1.59 mi, 644', J, Junction with Greg's Loop Trail (EQ) start

1.68 mi, 639', J, Junction with Greg's Loop Trail (EQ) end

End: 2.12 mi, 681', Junction with Josh Trail (EQ)

Difficulty: Easy   Elev Gain/Loss: 560' / 452'

Burl Tree Way Trail

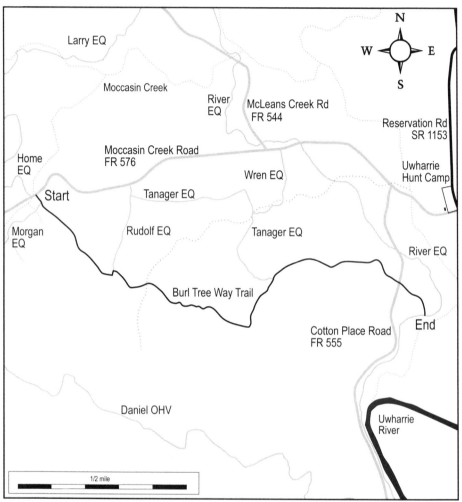

Elevation Profile: Burl Tree Way

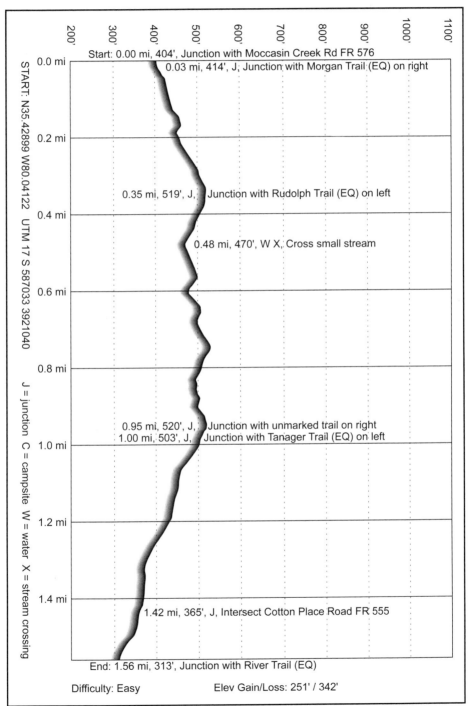

START: N35.42899 W80.04122 UTM 17 S 587033 3921040

J = junction C = campsite W = water X = stream crossing

Start: 0.00 mi, 404', Junction with Moccasin Creek Rd FR 576

0.03 mi, 414', J, Junction with Morgan Trail (EQ) on right

0.35 mi, 519', J, Junction with Rudolph Trail (EQ) on left

0.48 mi, 470', W X, Cross small stream

0.95 mi, 520', J, Junction with unmarked trail on right
1.00 mi, 503', J, Junction with Tanager Trail (EQ) on left

1.42 mi, 365', J, Intersect Cotton Place Road FR 555

End: 1.56 mi, 313', Junction with River Trail (EQ)

Difficulty: Easy   Elev Gain/Loss: 251' / 342'

Buttermilk Trail

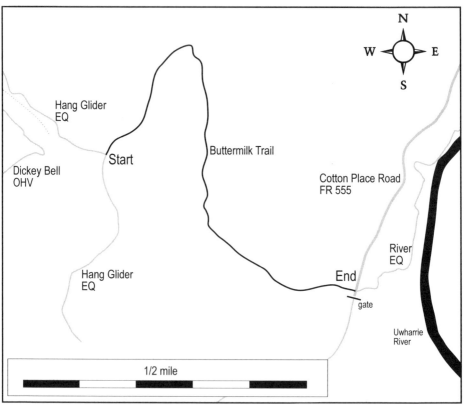

Elevation Profile: Buttermilk Trail

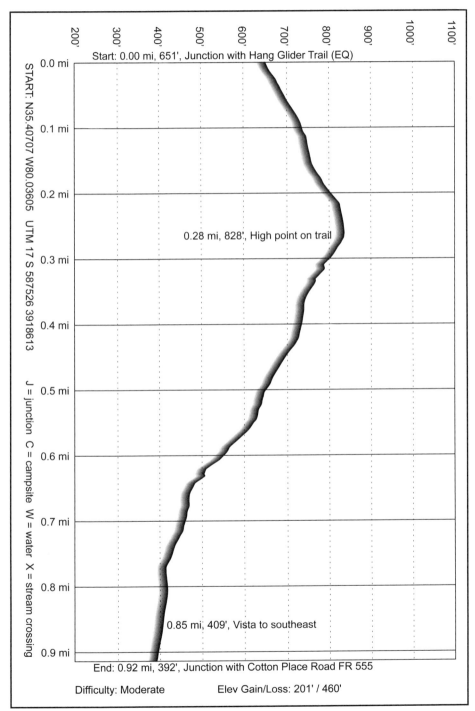

START: N35.40707 W80.03605   UTM 17 S 587526 3918613   J = junction C = campsite W = water X = stream crossing

Start: 0.00 mi, 651', Junction with Hang Glider Trail (EQ)

0.28 mi, 828', High point on trail

0.85 mi, 409', Vista to southeast

End: 0.92 mi, 392', Junction with Cotton Place Road FR 555

Difficulty: Moderate   Elev Gain/Loss: 201' / 460'

Fraley Trail

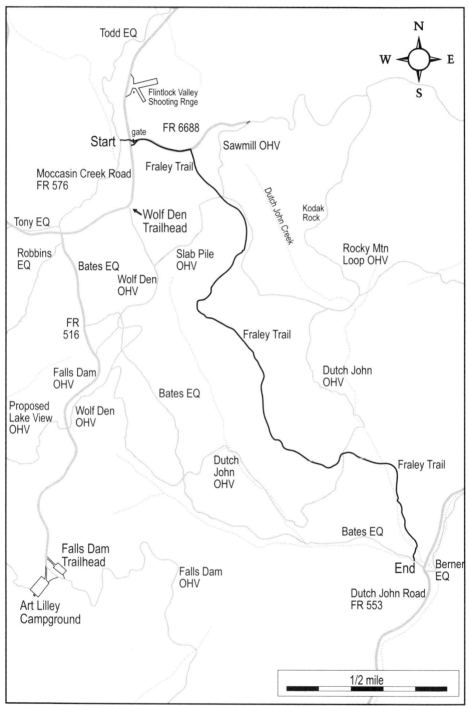

Elevation Profile: Fraley Trail

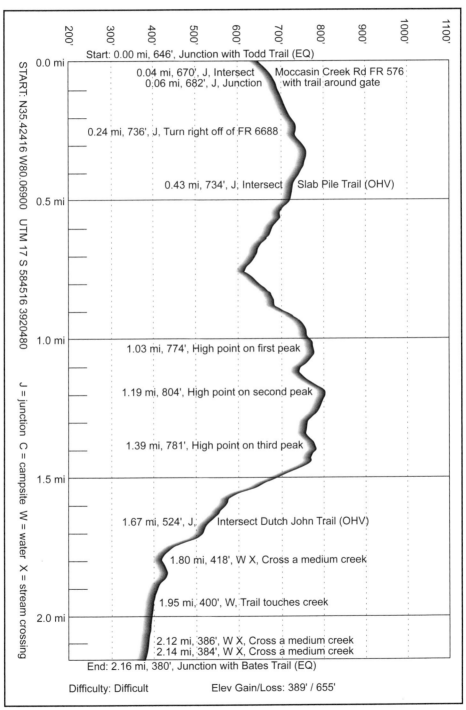

Start: 0.00 mi, 646', Junction with Todd Trail (EQ)

0.04 mi, 670', J, Intersect Moccasin Creek Rd FR 576
0.06 mi, 682', J, Junction with trail around gate

0.24 mi, 736', J, Turn right off of FR 6688

0.43 mi, 734', J, Intersect Slab Pile Trail (OHV)

START: N35.42416 W80.06900 UTM 17 S 584516 3920480

J = junction C = campsite W = water X = stream crossing

1.03 mi, 774', High point on first peak

1.19 mi, 804', High point on second peak

1.39 mi, 781', High point on third peak

1.67 mi, 524', J, Intersect Dutch John Trail (OHV)

1.80 mi, 418', W X, Cross a medium creek

1.95 mi, 400', W, Trail touches creek

2.12 mi, 386', W X, Cross a medium creek
2.14 mi, 384', W X, Cross a medium creek

End: 2.16 mi, 380', Junction with Bates Trail (EQ)

Difficulty: Difficult   Elev Gain/Loss: 389' / 655'

Greg's Loop Trail

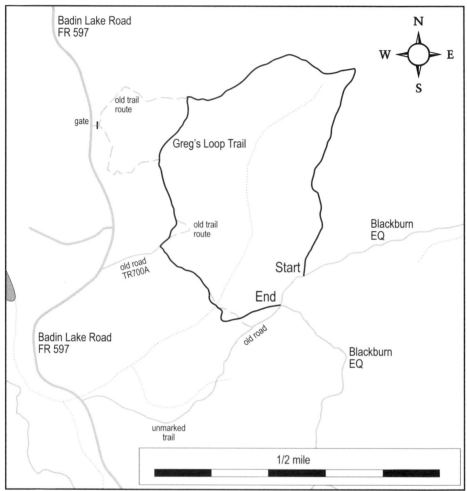

Badin Lake Road
FR 597

N
W — E
S

old trail
route

gate

Greg's Loop Trail

old trail
route

Blackburn
EQ

old road
TR700A

Start

End

Badin Lake Road
FR 597

old road

Blackburn
EQ

unmarked
trail

1/2 mile

Elevation Profile: Greg's Loop Trail

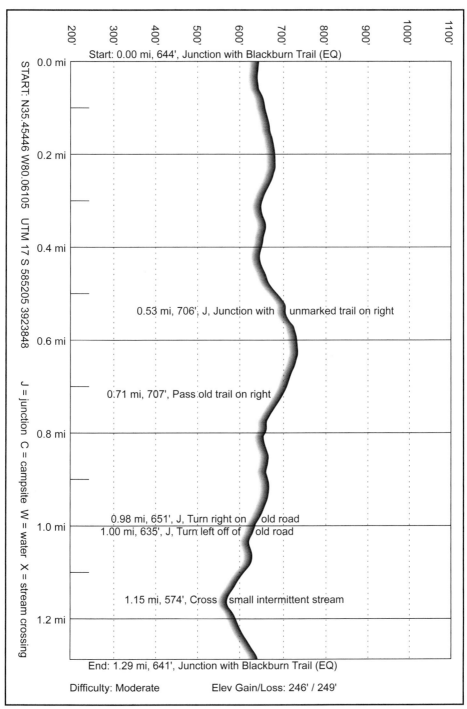

START: N35.45446 W80.06105 UTM 17 S 585205 3923848

J = junction C = campsite W = water X = stream crossing

Start: 0.00 mi, 644', Junction with Blackburn Trail (EQ)

0.53 mi, 706', J, Junction with unmarked trail on right

0.71 mi, 707', Pass old trail on right

0.98 mi, 651', J, Turn right on old road
1.00 mi, 635', J, Turn left off of old road

1.15 mi, 574', Cross small intermittent stream

End: 1.29 mi, 641', Junction with Blackburn Trail (EQ)

Difficulty: Moderate   Elev Gain/Loss: 246' / 249'

Hang Glider Trail

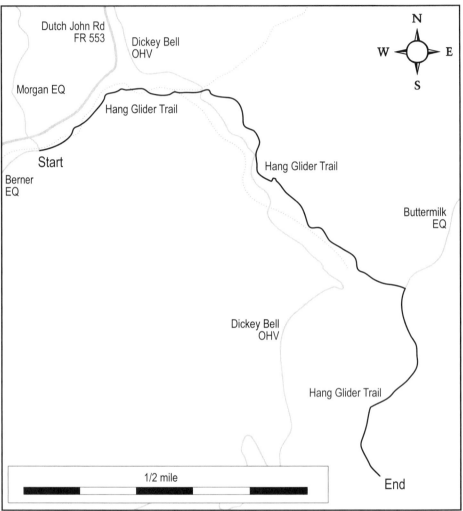

Elevation Profile: Hang Glider Trail

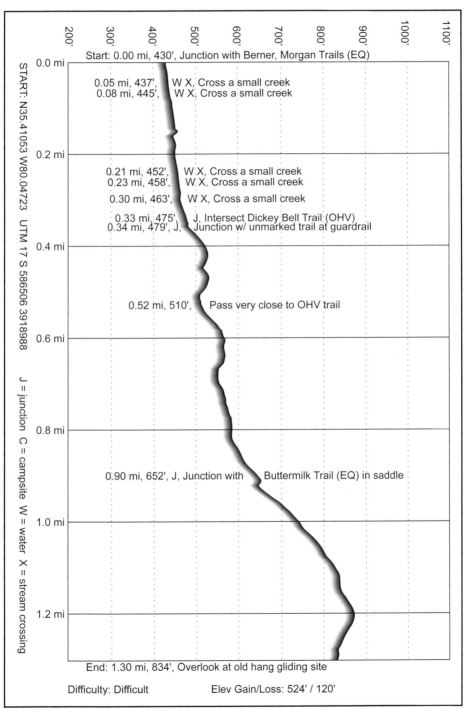

START: N35.41053 W80.04723 UTM 17 S 586506 3918988   J = junction   C = campsite   W = water   X = stream crossing

200' 300' 400' 500' 600' 700' 800' 900' 1000' 1100'

0.0 mi — Start: 0.00 mi, 430', Junction with Berner, Morgan Trails (EQ)

0.05 mi, 437', W X, Cross a small creek
0.08 mi, 445', W X, Cross a small creek

0.2 mi

0.21 mi, 452', W X, Cross a small creek
0.23 mi, 458', W X, Cross a small creek
0.30 mi, 463', W X, Cross a small creek
0.33 mi, 475', J, Intersect Dickey Bell Trail (OHV)
0.34 mi, 479', J, Junction w/ unmarked trail at guardrail

0.4 mi

0.52 mi, 510', Pass very close to OHV trail

0.6 mi

0.8 mi

0.90 mi, 652', J, Junction with Buttermilk Trail (EQ) in saddle

1.0 mi

1.2 mi

End: 1.30 mi, 834', Overlook at old hang gliding site

Difficulty: Difficult   Elev Gain/Loss: 524' / 120'

Helen's Loop Trail

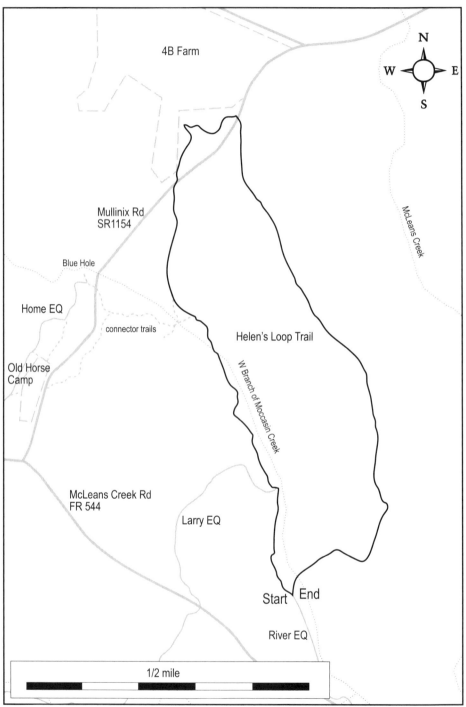

4B Farm

N
W — E
S

Mullinix Rd
SR1154

Blue Hole

McLeans Creek

Home EQ

connector trails

Helen's Loop Trail

Old Horse
Camp

W Branch of Moccasin Creek

McLeans Creek Rd
FR 544

Larry EQ

Start End

River EQ

1/2 mile

Elevation Profile: Helen's Loop Trail

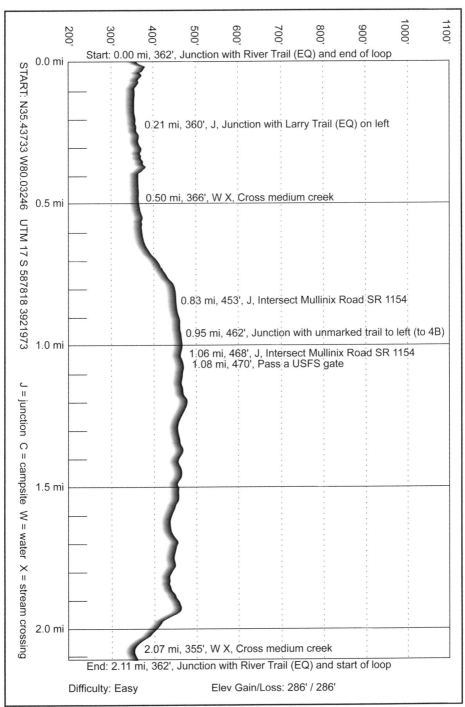

START: N35.43733 W80.03246   UTM 17 S 587818 3921973

J = junction   C = campsite   W = water   X = stream crossing

Start: 0.00 mi, 362', Junction with River Trail (EQ) and end of loop

0.0 mi

0.21 mi, 360', J, Junction with Larry Trail (EQ) on left

0.5 mi

0.50 mi, 366', W X, Cross medium creek

0.83 mi, 453', J, Intersect Mullinix Road SR 1154

0.95 mi, 462', Junction with unmarked trail to left (to 4B)

1.0 mi

1.06 mi, 468', J, Intersect Mullinix Road SR 1154
1.08 mi, 470', Pass a USFS gate

1.5 mi

2.0 mi

2.07 mi, 355', W X, Cross medium creek

End: 2.11 mi, 362', Junction with River Trail (EQ) and start of loop

Difficulty: Easy   Elev Gain/Loss: 286' / 286'

Home Trail

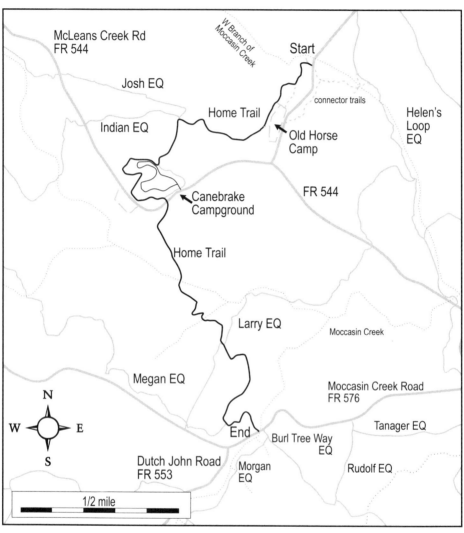

McLeans Creek Rd
FR 544

W Branch of Moccasin Creek

Start

Josh EQ

connector trails

Home Trail

Helen's
Loop
EQ

Indian EQ

Old Horse
Camp

Canebrake
Campground

FR 544

Home Trail

Larry EQ

Moccasin Creek

Megan EQ

Moccasin Creek Road
FR 576

N

W — E

S

End

Burl Tree Way
EQ

Tanager EQ

Dutch John Road
FR 553

Morgan
EQ

Rudolf EQ

1/2 mile

Elevation Profile: Home Trail

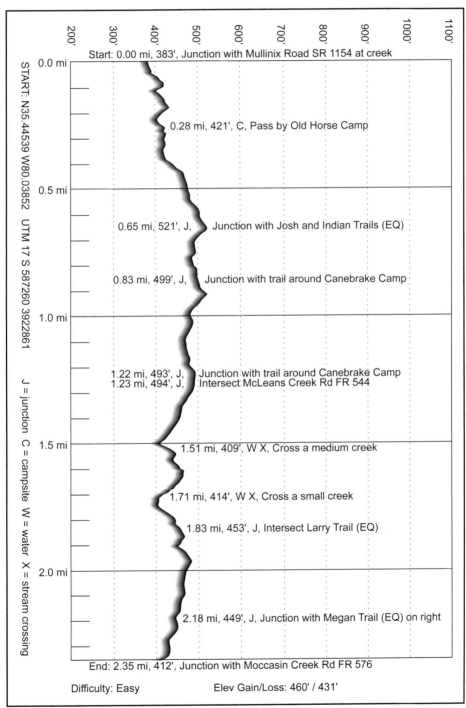

Start: 0.00 mi, 383', Junction with Mullinix Road SR 1154 at creek

START: N35.44539 W80.03852   UTM 17 S 587260 3922861

J = junction   C = campsite   W = water   X = stream crossing

0.28 mi, 421', C, Pass by Old Horse Camp

0.65 mi, 521', J,   Junction with Josh and Indian Trails (EQ)

0.83 mi, 499', J,   Junction with trail around Canebrake Camp

1.22 mi, 493', J,   Junction with trail around Canebrake Camp
1.23 mi, 494', J,   Intersect McLeans Creek Rd FR 544

1.51 mi, 409', W X, Cross a medium creek

1.71 mi, 414', W X, Cross a small creek

1.83 mi, 453', J, Intersect Larry Trail (EQ)

2.18 mi, 449', J, Junction with Megan Trail (EQ) on right

End: 2.35 mi, 412', Junction with Moccasin Creek Rd FR 576

Difficulty: Easy   Elev Gain/Loss: 460' / 431'

Indian Trail

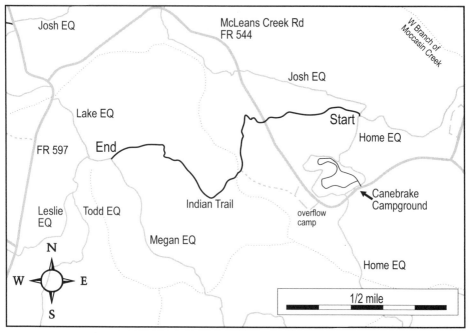

Elevation Profile: Indian Trail

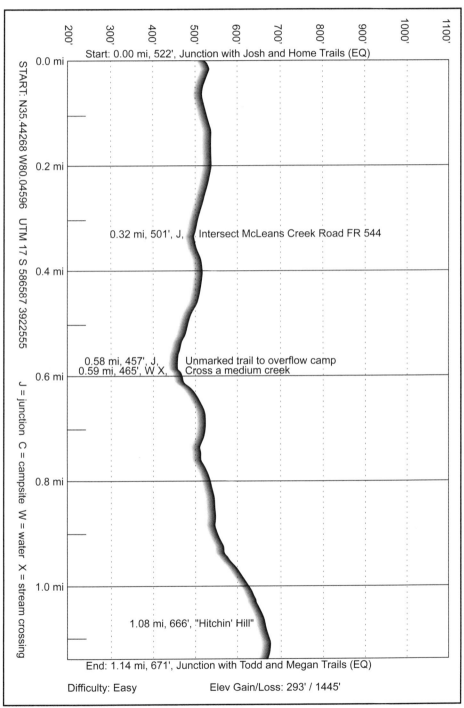

START: N35.44268 W80.04596 UTM 17 S 586587 3922555

J = junction C = campsite W = water X = stream crossing

Start: 0.00 mi, 522', Junction with Josh and Home Trails (EQ)

0.32 mi, 501', J,   Intersect McLeans Creek Road FR 544

0.58 mi, 457', J,   Unmarked trail to overflow camp
0.59 mi, 465', W X, Cross a medium creek

1.08 mi, 666', "Hitchin' Hill"

End: 1.14 mi, 671', Junction with Todd and Megan Trails (EQ)

Difficulty: Easy   Elev Gain/Loss: 293' / 1445'

Josh Trail

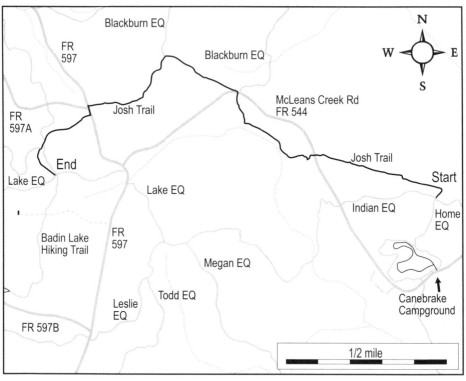

Elevation Profile: Josh Trail

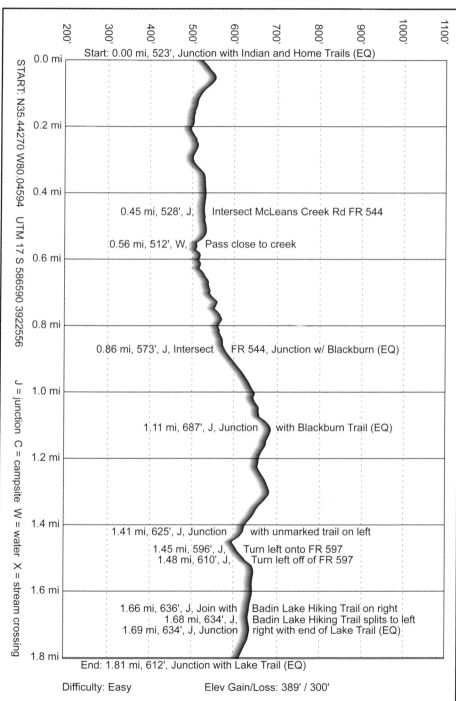

START: N35.44270 W80.04594   UTM 17 S 586590 3922556

J = junction C = campsite W = water X = stream crossing

200' 300' 400' 500' 600' 700' 800' 900' 1000' 1100'

Start: 0.00 mi, 523', Junction with Indian and Home Trails (EQ)

0.0 mi

0.2 mi

0.4 mi

0.45 mi, 528', J,   Intersect McLeans Creek Rd FR 544

0.56 mi, 512', W,   Pass close to creek

0.6 mi

0.8 mi

0.86 mi, 573', J, Intersect   FR 544, Junction w/ Blackburn (EQ)

1.0 mi

1.11 mi, 687', J, Junction   with Blackburn Trail (EQ)

1.2 mi

1.4 mi

1.41 mi, 625', J, Junction   with unmarked trail on left
1.45 mi, 596', J,   Turn left onto FR 597
1.48 mi, 610', J,   Turn left off of FR 597

1.6 mi

1.66 mi, 636', J, Join with   Badin Lake Hiking Trail on right
1.68 mi, 634', J,   Badin Lake Hiking Trail splits to left
1.69 mi, 634', J, Junction   right with end of Lake Trail (EQ)

1.8 mi

End: 1.81 mi, 612', Junction with Lake Trail (EQ)

Difficulty: Easy   Elev Gain/Loss: 389' / 300'

Lake Trail

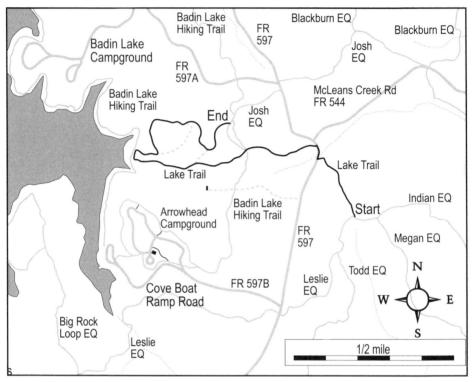

Elevation Profile: Lake Trail

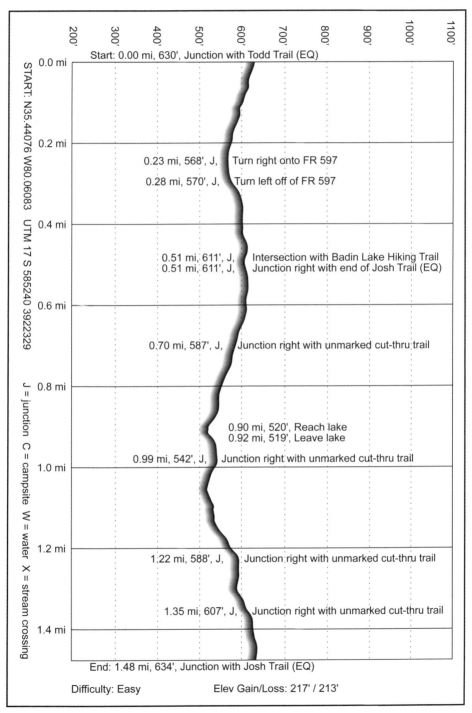

START: N35.44076 W80.06083   UTM 17 S 585240 3922329   J = junction C = campsite W = water X = stream crossing

Start: 0.00 mi, 630', Junction with Todd Trail (EQ)

0.23 mi, 568', J, Turn right onto FR 597

0.28 mi, 570', J, Turn left off of FR 597

0.51 mi, 611', J, Intersection with Badin Lake Hiking Trail
0.51 mi, 611', J, Junction right with end of Josh Trail (EQ)

0.70 mi, 587', J, Junction right with unmarked cut-thru trail

0.90 mi, 520', Reach lake
0.92 mi, 519', Leave lake
0.99 mi, 542', J, Junction right with unmarked cut-thru trail

1.22 mi, 588', J, Junction right with unmarked cut-thru trail

1.35 mi, 607', J, Junction right with unmarked cut-thru trail

End: 1.48 mi, 634', Junction with Josh Trail (EQ)

Difficulty: Easy   Elev Gain/Loss: 217' / 213'

Larry Trail

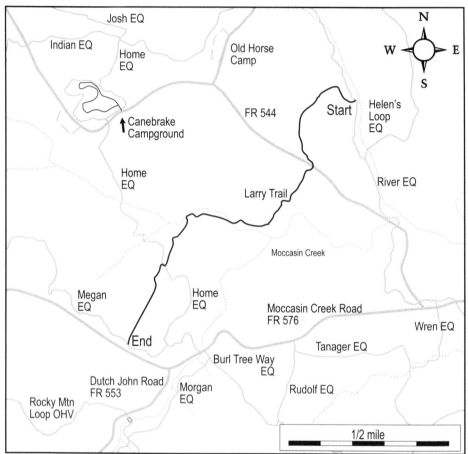

Elevation Profile: Larry Trail

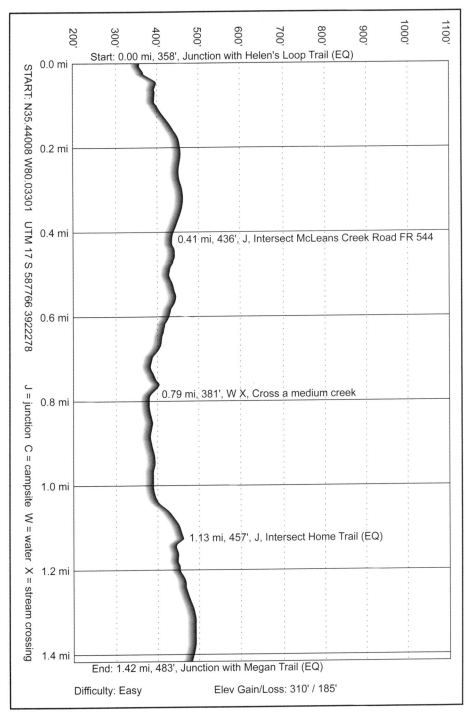

Start: 0.00 mi, 358', Junction with Helen's Loop Trail (EQ)

0.41 mi, 436', J, Intersect McLeans Creek Road FR 544

0.79 mi, 381', W X, Cross a medium creek

1.13 mi, 457', J, Intersect Home Trail (EQ)

End: 1.42 mi, 483', Junction with Megan Trail (EQ)

START: N35.44008 W80.03301 UTM 17 S 587766 3922278

J = junction C = campsite W = water X = stream crossing

Difficulty: Easy   Elev Gain/Loss: 310' / 185'

Leslie Trail

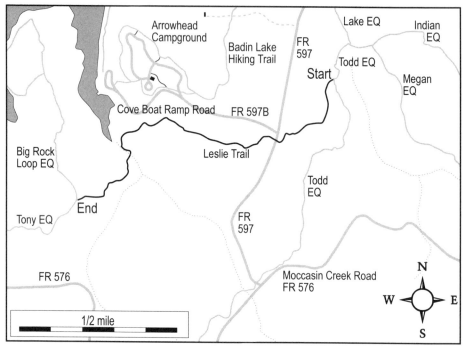

Elevation Profile: Leslie Trail

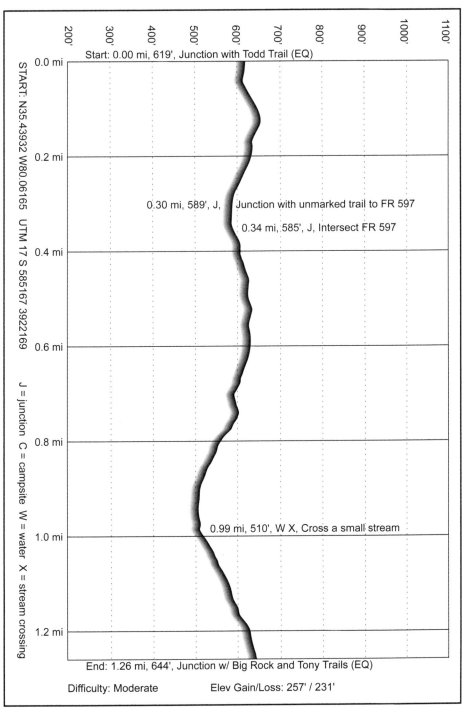

START: N35.43932 W80.06165 UTM 17 S 585167 3922169

J = junction C = campsite W = water X = stream crossing

Start: 0.00 mi, 619', Junction with Todd Trail (EQ)

0.30 mi, 589', J, Junction with unmarked trail to FR 597

0.34 mi, 585', J, Intersect FR 597

0.99 mi, 510', W X, Cross a small stream

End: 1.26 mi, 644', Junction w/ Big Rock and Tony Trails (EQ)

Difficulty: Moderate   Elev Gain/Loss: 257' / 231'

Megan Trail

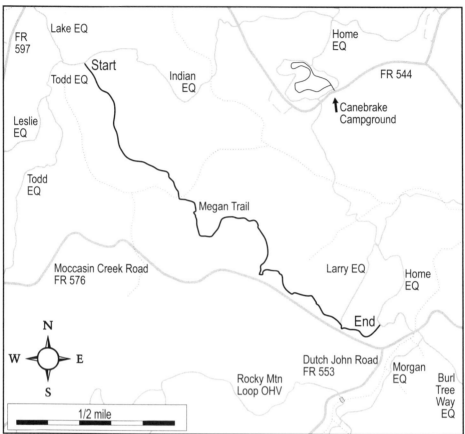

Elevation Profile: Megan Trail

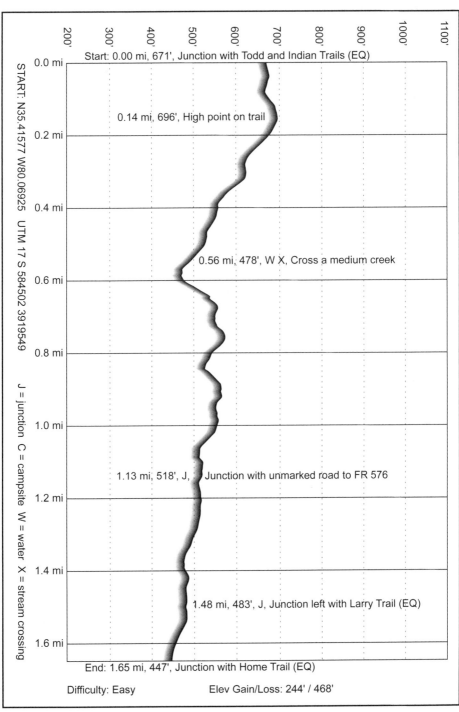

START: N35.41577 W80.06925   UTM 17 S 584502 3919549

J = junction C = campsite W = water X = stream crossing

Start: 0.00 mi, 671', Junction with Todd and Indian Trails (EQ)

0.14 mi, 696', High point on trail

0.56 mi, 478', W X, Cross a medium creek

1.13 mi, 518', J, Junction with unmarked road to FR 576

1.48 mi, 483', J, Junction left with Larry Trail (EQ)

End: 1.65 mi, 447', Junction with Home Trail (EQ)

Difficulty: Easy   Elev Gain/Loss: 244' / 468'

Morgan Trail

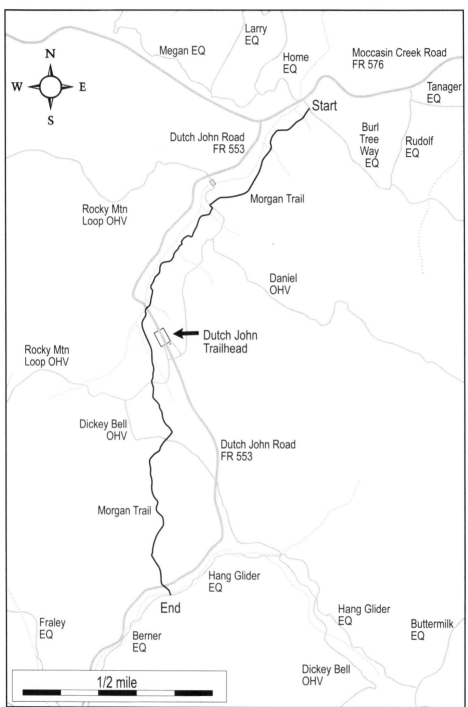

Elevation Profile: Morgan Trail

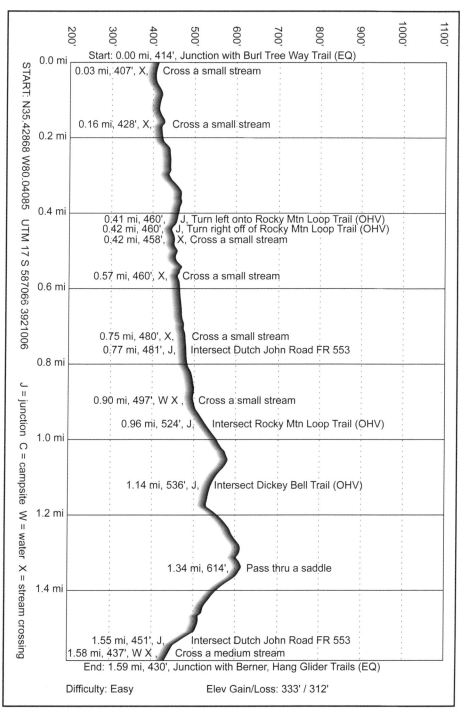

START: N35.42868 W80.04085 UTM 17 S 587066 3921006

J = junction C = campsite W = water X = stream crossing

0.0 mi
0.2 mi
0.4 mi
0.6 mi
0.8 mi
1.0 mi
1.2 mi
1.4 mi

200' 300' 400' 500' 600' 700' 800' 900' 1000' 1100'

Start: 0.00 mi, 414', Junction with Burl Tree Way Trail (EQ)
0.03 mi, 407', X,   Cross a small stream
0.16 mi, 428', X,   Cross a small stream
0.41 mi, 460',   J, Turn left onto Rocky Mtn Loop Trail (OHV)
0.42 mi, 460',   J, Turn right off of Rocky Mtn Loop Trail (OHV)
0.42 mi, 458',   X, Cross a small stream
0.57 mi, 460', X,   Cross a small stream
0.75 mi, 480', X,   Cross a small stream
0.77 mi, 481', J,   Intersect Dutch John Road FR 553
0.90 mi, 497', W X , Cross a small stream
0.96 mi, 524', J,   Intersect Rocky Mtn Loop Trail (OHV)
1.14 mi, 536', J,   Intersect Dickey Bell Trail (OHV)
1.34 mi, 614',   Pass thru a saddle
1.55 mi, 451', J,   Intersect Dutch John Road FR 553
1.58 mi, 437', W X , Cross a medium stream
End: 1.59 mi, 430', Junction with Berner, Hang Glider Trails (EQ)

Difficulty: Easy   Elev Gain/Loss: 333' / 312'

River Trail

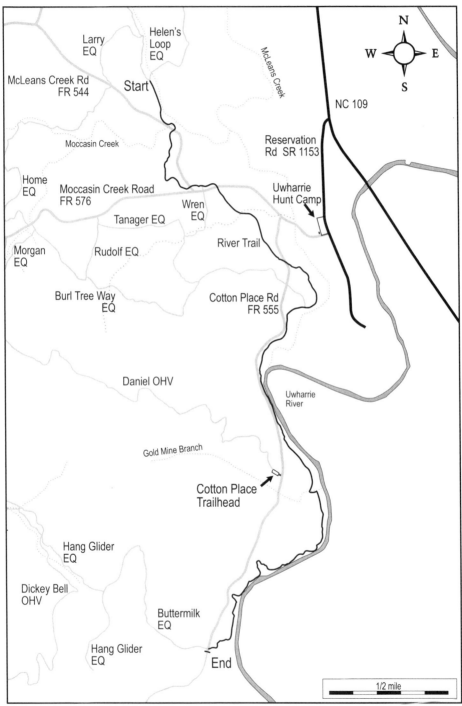

Elevation Profile: River Trail

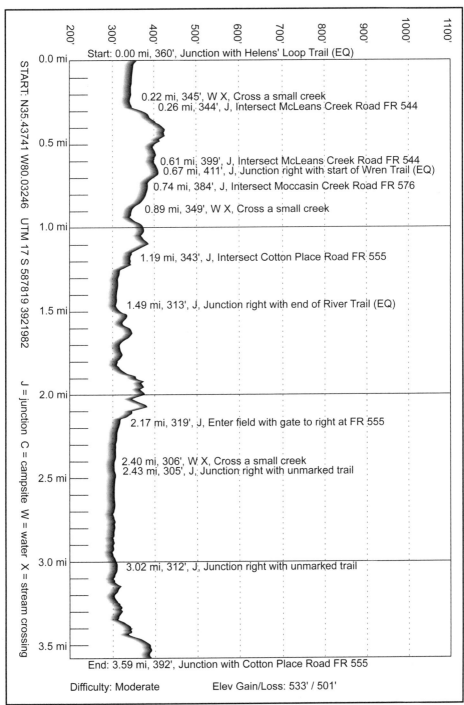

Start: 0.00 mi, 360', Junction with Helens' Loop Trail (EQ)

0.22 mi, 345', W X, Cross a small creek
0.26 mi, 344', J, Intersect McLeans Creek Road FR 544

0.61 mi, 399', J, Intersect McLeans Creek Road FR 544
0.67 mi, 411', J, Junction right with start of Wren Trail (EQ)
0.74 mi, 384', J, Intersect Moccasin Creek Road FR 576

0.89 mi, 349', W X, Cross a small creek

1.19 mi, 343', J, Intersect Cotton Place Road FR 555

1.49 mi, 313', J, Junction right with end of River Trail (EQ)

2.17 mi, 319', J, Enter field with gate to right at FR 555

2.40 mi, 306', W X, Cross a small creek
2.43 mi, 305', J, Junction right with unmarked trail

3.02 mi, 312', J, Junction right with unmarked trail

End: 3.59 mi, 392', Junction with Cotton Place Road FR 555

Difficulty: Moderate   Elev Gain/Loss: 533' / 501'

START: N35.43741 W80.03246   UTM 17 S 587819 3921982   J = junction C = campsite W = water X = stream crossing

Robbins Trail

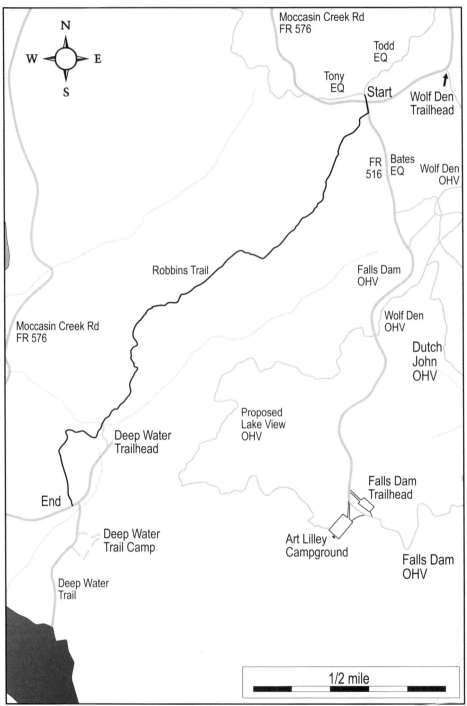

N
W   E
S

Moccasin Creek Rd
FR 576

Todd
EQ

Tony
EQ

Start

Wolf Den
Trailhead

FR 516

Bates
EQ

Wolf Den
OHV

Falls Dam
OHV

Robbins Trail

Moccasin Creek Rd
FR 576

Wolf Den
OHV

Dutch
John
OHV

Proposed
Lake View
OHV

Deep Water
Trailhead

Falls Dam
Trailhead

End

Deep Water
Trail Camp

Art Lilley
Campground

Falls Dam
OHV

Deep Water
Trail

1/2 mile

Elevation Profile: Robbins Trail

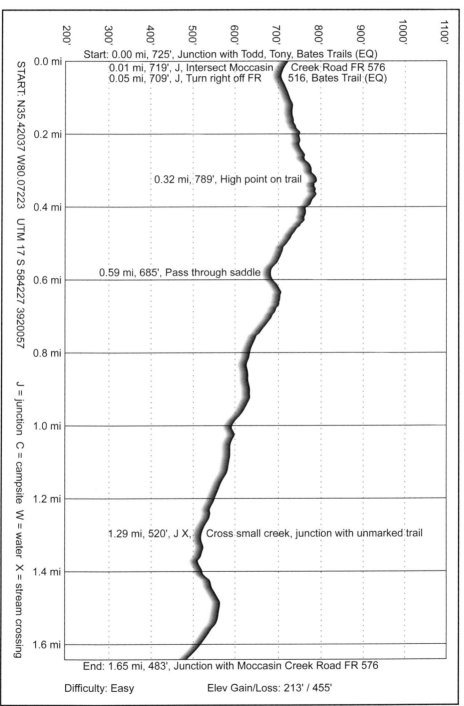

Start: 0.00 mi, 725', Junction with Todd, Tony, Bates Trails (EQ)

0.01 mi, 719', J, Intersect Moccasin Creek Road FR 576
0.05 mi, 709', J, Turn right off FR 516, Bates Trail (EQ)

0.32 mi, 789', High point on trail

0.59 mi, 685', Pass through saddle

1.29 mi, 520', J X, Cross small creek, junction with unmarked trail

START: N35.42037 W80.07223   UTM 17 S 584227 3920057

J = junction C = campsite W = water X = stream crossing

End: 1.65 mi, 483', Junction with Moccasin Creek Road FR 576

Difficulty: Easy   Elev Gain/Loss: 213' / 455'

Rudolph Trail

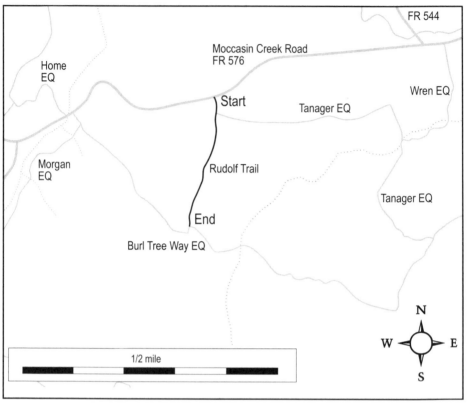

Elevation Profile: Rudolph Trail

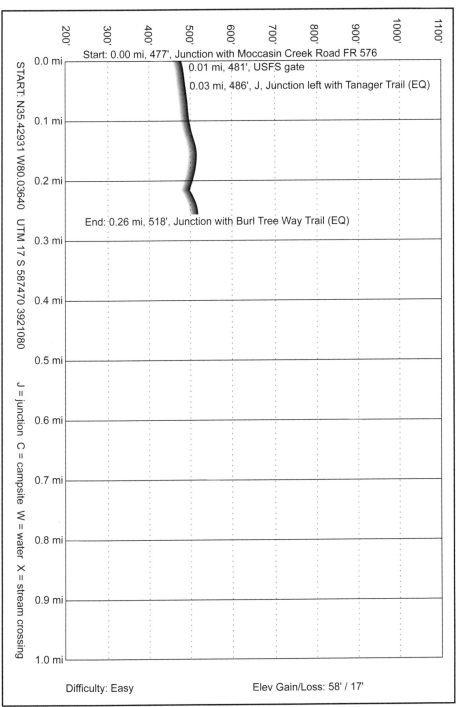

START: N35.42931 W80.03640 UTM 17 S 587470 3921080

J = junction C = campsite W = water X = stream crossing

Start: 0.00 mi, 477', Junction with Moccasin Creek Road FR 576

0.01 mi, 481', USFS gate

0.03 mi, 486', J, Junction left with Tanager Trail (EQ)

End: 0.26 mi, 518', Junction with Burl Tree Way Trail (EQ)

Difficulty: Easy

Elev Gain/Loss: 58' / 17'

Tanager Trail

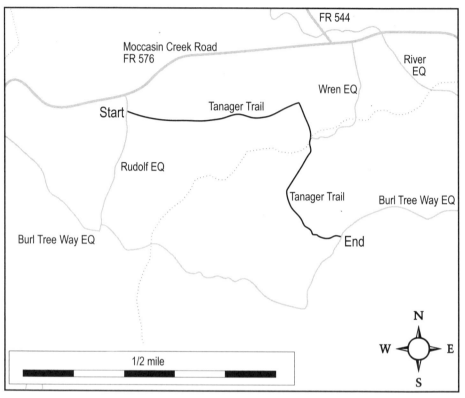

Elevation Profile: Tanager Trail

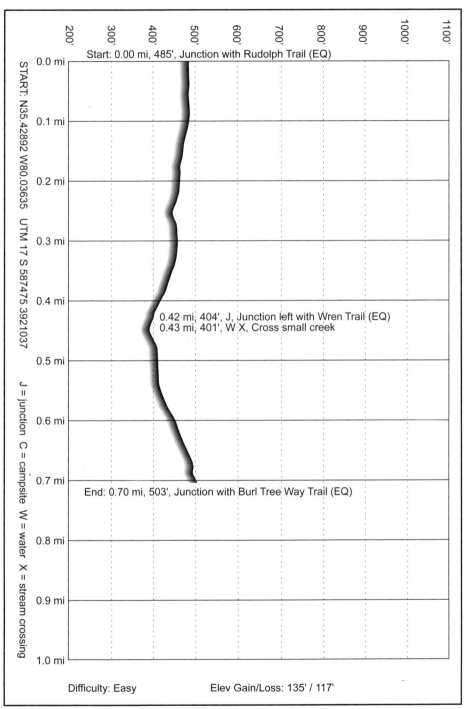

START: N35.42892 W80.03635   UTM 17 S 587475 3921037

J = junction C = campsite W = water X = stream crossing

Start: 0.00 mi, 485', Junction with Rudolph Trail (EQ)

0.42 mi, 404', J, Junction left with Wren Trail (EQ)
0.43 mi, 401', W X, Cross small creek

End: 0.70 mi, 503', Junction with Burl Tree Way Trail (EQ)

Difficulty: Easy   Elev Gain/Loss: 135' / 117'

Todd Trail

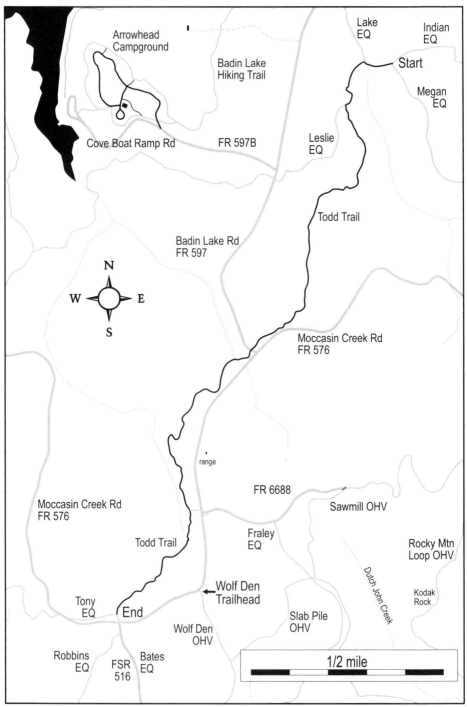

Elevation Profile: Todd Trail

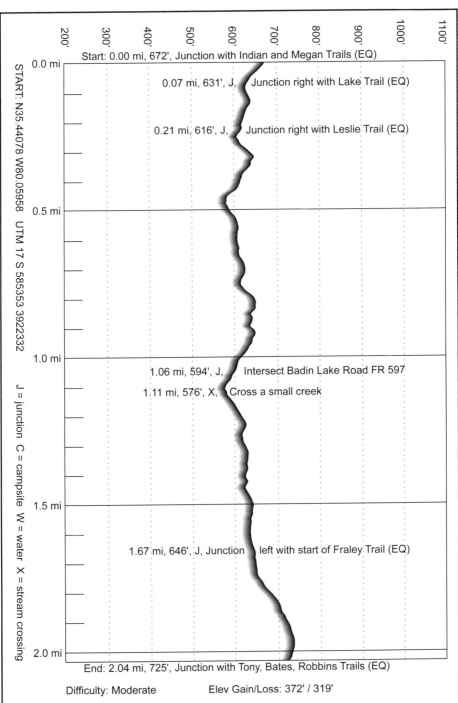

START: N35.44078 W80.05958 UTM 17 S 585353 3922332

J = junction C = campsite W = water X = stream crossing

Start: 0.00 mi, 672', Junction with Indian and Megan Trails (EQ)

0.07 mi, 631', J, Junction right with Lake Trail (EQ)

0.21 mi, 616', J, Junction right with Leslie Trail (EQ)

1.06 mi, 594', J, Intersect Badin Lake Road FR 597

1.11 mi, 576', X, Cross a small creek

1.67 mi, 646', J, Junction left with start of Fraley Trail (EQ)

End: 2.04 mi, 725', Junction with Tony, Bates, Robbins Trails (EQ)

Difficulty: Moderate   Elev Gain/Loss: 372' / 319'

Tony Trail

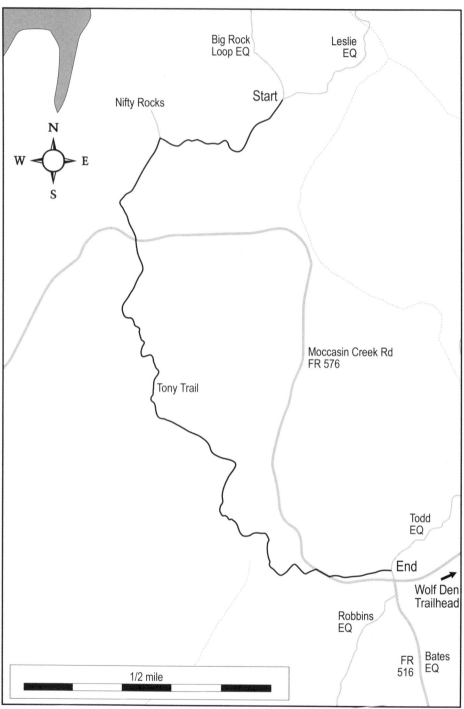

Big Rock
Loop EQ

Leslie
EQ

Nifty Rocks

Start

N
W E
S

Moccasin Creek Rd
FR 576

Tony Trail

Todd
EQ

End

Wolf Den
Trailhead

Robbins
EQ

1/2 mile

FR
516

Bates
EQ

Elevation Profile: Tony Trail

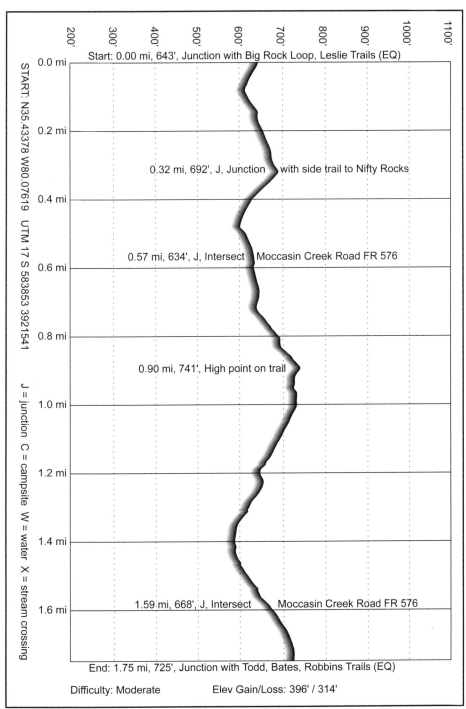

START: N35.43378 W80.07619 UTM 17 S 583853 3921541

J = junction C = campsite W = water X = stream crossing

Start: 0.00 mi, 643', Junction with Big Rock Loop, Leslie Trails (EQ)

0.32 mi, 692', J, Junction with side trail to Nifty Rocks

0.57 mi, 634', J, Intersect Moccasin Creek Road FR 576

0.90 mi, 741', High point on trail

1.59 mi, 668', J, Intersect Moccasin Creek Road FR 576

End: 1.75 mi, 725', Junction with Todd, Bates, Robbins Trails (EQ)

Difficulty: Moderate   Elev Gain/Loss: 396' / 314'

Wren Trail

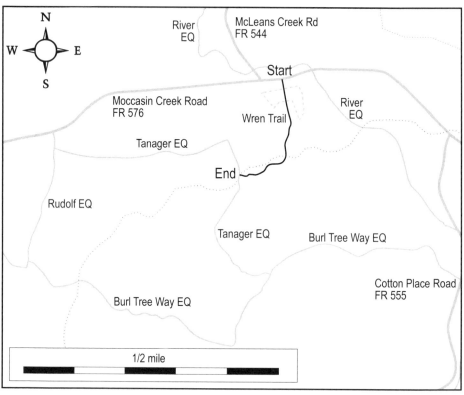

Elevation Profile: Wren Trail

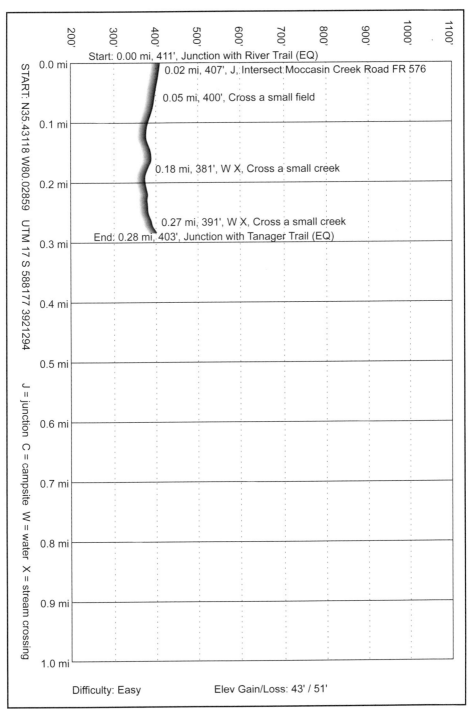

START: N35.43118 W80.02859 UTM 17 S 588177 3921294

J = junction C = campsite W = water X = stream crossing

Start: 0.00 mi, 411', Junction with River Trail (EQ)

0.02 mi, 407', J, Intersect Moccasin Creek Road FR 576

0.05 mi, 400', Cross a small field

0.18 mi, 381', W X, Cross a small creek

0.27 mi, 391', W X, Cross a small creek

End: 0.28 mi, 403', Junction with Tanager Trail (EQ)

Difficulty: Easy   Elev Gain/Loss: 43' / 51'

Badin Lake Equestrian Trips

Trip	Use	Length (miles)	Elevation Gain/Loss	Difficulty Rating	Page
BLRA Trip C	EBH	5.30	948' / 942'	Easy	136
BLRA Trip D	EBH	4.72	844' / 844'	Easy	138
BLRA Trip E	EBH	6.10	1,038' / 1,044'	Easy	140
BLRA Trip F	EBH	9.43	1,698' / 1,698'	Moderate	142
BLRA Trip G	EBH	10.58	1,890' / 1,890'	Moderate	144
BLRA Trip H	EBH	10.87	2,189' / 2,183'	Difficult	146

This set of trips for equestrians was suggested by Elizabeth Earnhardt of the Uwharrie Trail Riders Association. They were described in her booklet *Badin Lake Recreation Area Uwharrie National Forest Trail Guide*, published in 2007.

With the high number of horse-legal trails in the Badin Lake Recreation Area and numerous trailheads, there are many other trip route options possible. This is just a set to get you started. Piece together your own unique routes based on the trail sections you enoy riding the most!

BLRA Trip C - The Bat Cave

Map	page 136	**Difficulty**	Easy
Length	5.30 miles	**Configuration**	Loop
Trailhead	Canebrake Campground	**Elev Gain/Loss**	948' / 942'

Start Coordinates N35.43920, W80.04675;   17 S 586519 3922168

BLRA Trip D - The Lake Ride

Map	page 138	**Difficulty**	Easy
Length	4.72 miles	**Configuration**	Lollipop
Trailhead	Canebrake Campground	**Elev Gain/Loss**	844' / 844'

Start Coordinates N35.44068, W80.04709;   17 S 586487 3922332

BLRA Trip E - The River Ride

Map	page 140	**Difficulty**	Easy
Length	6.10 miles	**Configuration**	Loop
Trailhead	Canebrake Campground	**Elev Gain/Loss**	1,038' / 1,044'

Start Coordinates N35.44068, W80.04709;   17 S 586487 3922332

BLRA Trip F - Big Rocks

Map	page 142	**Difficulty**	Moderate
Length	9.43 miles	**Configuration**	Lollipops
Trailhead	Canebrake Campground	**Elev Gain/Loss**	1,698' / 1,698'

Start Coordinates N35.44068, W80.04709;   17 S 586487 3922332

BLRA Trip G - Deep Water Camp

Map	page 144	**Difficulty**	Moderate
Length	10.58 miles	**Configuration**	Lollipop
Trailhead	Canebrake Campground	**Elev Gain/Loss**	1,890' / 1,890'

Start Coordinates N35.44068, W80.04709;   17 S 586487 3922332

BLRA Trip H - Hang Glider

Map	page 146	**Difficulty**	Difficult
Length	10.87 miles	**Configuration**	Loop
Trailhead	Canebrake Campground	**Elev Gain/Loss**	2,189' / 2,183'

Start Coordinates N35.43920, W80.04675;   17 S 586519 3922168

Badin Lake Trip C

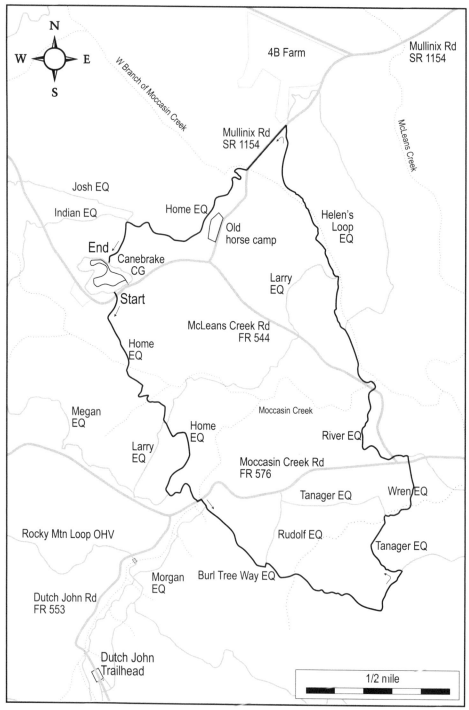

N W E S

W Branch of Moccasin Creek

4B Farm

Mullinix Rd
SR 1154

Mullinix Rd
SR 1154

McLeans Creek

Josh EQ

Indian EQ

Home EQ

Helen's
Loop
EQ

Old
horse camp

End

Canebrake
CG

Larry
EQ

Start

McLeans Creek Rd
FR 544

Home
EQ

Megan
EQ

Moccasin Creek

Home
EQ

River EQ

Larry
EQ

Moccasin Creek Rd
FR 576

Wren EQ

Tanager EQ

Rocky Mtn Loop OHV

Rudolf EQ

Tanager EQ

Morgan
EQ

Burl Tree Way EQ

Dutch John Rd
FR 553

Dutch John
Trailhead

1/2 mile

Elevation Profile: BLRA Trip C - The Bat Cave

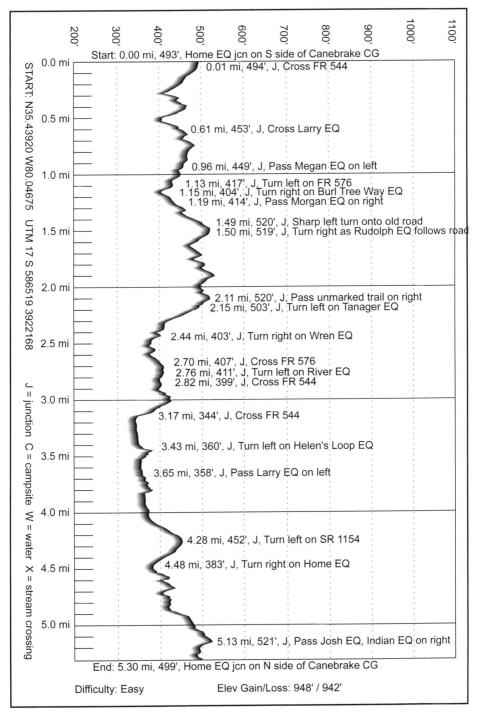

START: N35.43920 W80.04675 UTM 17 S 586519 3922168

J = junction C = campsite W = water X = stream crossing

200' 300' 400' 500' 600' 700' 800' 900' 1000' 1100'

Start: 0.00 mi, 493', Home EQ jcn on S side of Canebrake CG

0.0 mi   0.01 mi, 494', J, Cross FR 544

0.5 mi   0.61 mi, 453', J, Cross Larry EQ

0.96 mi, 449', J, Pass Megan EQ on left

1.0 mi   1.13 mi, 417', J, Turn left on FR 576
1.15 mi, 404', J, Turn right on Burl Tree Way EQ
1.19 mi, 414', J, Pass Morgan EQ on right

1.49 mi, 520', J, Sharp left turn onto old road
1.5 mi   1.50 mi, 519', J, Turn right as Rudolph EQ follows road

2.0 mi   2.11 mi, 520', J, Pass unmarked trail on right
2.15 mi, 503', J, Turn left on Tanager EQ

2.44 mi, 403', J, Turn right on Wren EQ
2.5 mi

2.70 mi, 407', J, Cross FR 576
2.76 mi, 411', J, Turn left on River EQ
2.82 mi, 399', J, Cross FR 544

3.0 mi

3.17 mi, 344', J, Cross FR 544

3.43 mi, 360', J, Turn left on Helen's Loop EQ
3.5 mi

3.65 mi, 358', J, Pass Larry EQ on left

4.0 mi

4.28 mi, 452', J, Turn left on SR 1154

4.48 mi, 383', J, Turn right on Home EQ
4.5 mi

5.0 mi

5.13 mi, 521', J, Pass Josh EQ, Indian EQ on right

End: 5.30 mi, 499', Home EQ jcn on N side of Canebrake CG

Difficulty: Easy   Elev Gain/Loss: 948' / 942'

Badin Lake Trip D

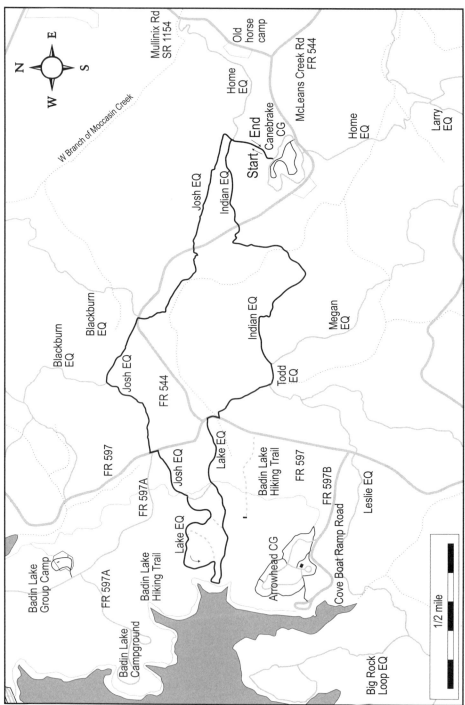

Elevation Profile: BLRA Trip D - The Lake Ride

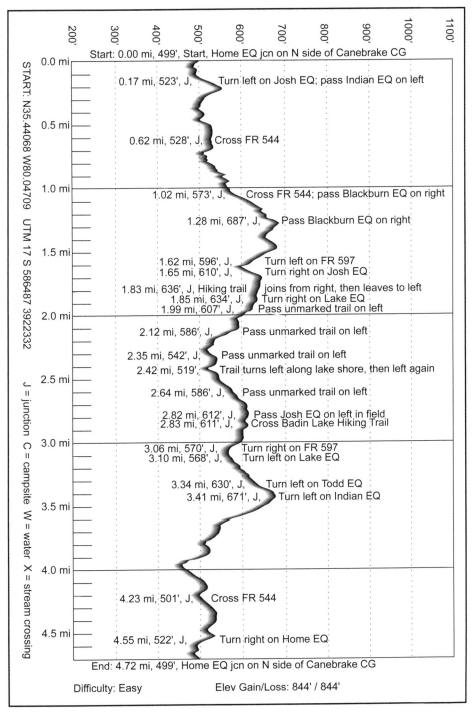

START: N35.44068 W80.04709 UTM 17 S 586487 3922332

J = junction C = campsite W = water X = stream crossing

200' 300' 400' 500' 600' 700' 800' 900' 1000' 1100'

Start: 0.00 mi, 499', Start, Home EQ jcn on N side of Canebrake CG

0.0 mi

0.17 mi, 523', J, Turn left on Josh EQ; pass Indian EQ on left

0.5 mi

0.62 mi, 528', J, Cross FR 544

1.0 mi

1.02 mi, 573', J, Cross FR 544; pass Blackburn EQ on right

1.28 mi, 687', J, Pass Blackburn EQ on right

1.5 mi

1.62 mi, 596', J, Turn left on FR 597
1.65 mi, 610', J, Turn right on Josh EQ
1.83 mi, 636', J, Hiking trail joins from right, then leaves to left
1.85 mi, 634', J, Turn right on Lake EQ
1.99 mi, 607', J, Pass unmarked trail on left

2.0 mi

2.12 mi, 586', J, Pass unmarked trail on left

2.35 mi, 542', J, Pass unmarked trail on left
2.42 mi, 519', Trail turns left along lake shore, then left again

2.5 mi

2.64 mi, 586', J, Pass unmarked trail on left

2.82 mi, 612', J, Pass Josh EQ on left in field
2.83 mi, 611', J, Cross Badin Lake Hiking Trail

3.0 mi

3.06 mi, 570', J, Turn right on FR 597
3.10 mi, 568', J, Turn left on Lake EQ

3.34 mi, 630', J, Turn left on Todd EQ
3.41 mi, 671', J, Turn left on Indian EQ

3.5 mi

4.0 mi

4.23 mi, 501', J, Cross FR 544

4.5 mi

4.55 mi, 522', J, Turn right on Home EQ

End: 4.72 mi, 499', Home EQ jcn on N side of Canebrake CG

Difficulty: Easy   Elev Gain/Loss: 844' / 844'

Badin Lake Trip E

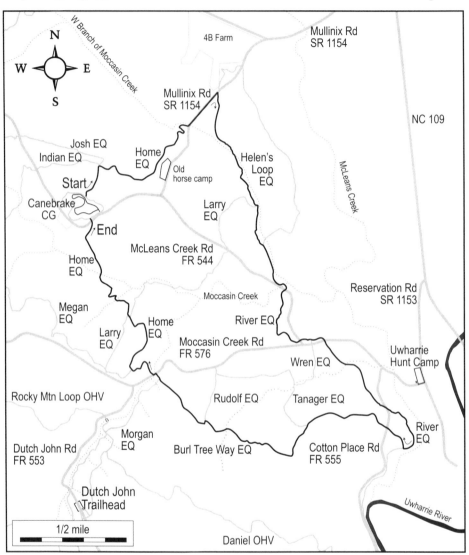

Elevation Profile: BLRA Trip E - The River Ride

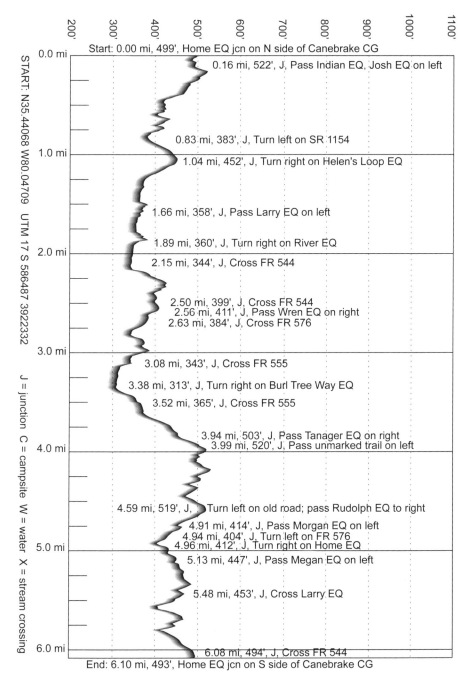

START: N35.44068 W80.04709 UTM 17 S 586487 3922332

J = junction C = campsite W = water X = stream crossing

Start: 0.00 mi, 499', Home EQ jcn on N side of Canebrake CG

0.16 mi, 522', J, Pass Indian EQ, Josh EQ on left

0.83 mi, 383', J, Turn left on SR 1154

1.04 mi, 452', J, Turn right on Helen's Loop EQ

1.66 mi, 358', J, Pass Larry EQ on left

1.89 mi, 360', J, Turn right on River EQ

2.15 mi, 344', J, Cross FR 544

2.50 mi, 399', J, Cross FR 544
2.56 mi, 411', J, Pass Wren EQ on right
2.63 mi, 384', J, Cross FR 576

3.08 mi, 343', J, Cross FR 555

3.38 mi, 313', J, Turn right on Burl Tree Way EQ

3.52 mi, 365', J, Cross FR 555

3.94 mi, 503', J, Pass Tanager EQ on right
3.99 mi, 520', J, Pass unmarked trail on left

4.59 mi, 519', J, Turn left on old road; pass Rudolph EQ to right

4.91 mi, 414', J, Pass Morgan EQ on left
4.94 mi, 404', J, Turn left on FR 576
4.96 mi, 412', J, Turn right on Home EQ

5.13 mi, 447', J, Pass Megan EQ on left

5.48 mi, 453', J, Cross Larry EQ

6.08 mi, 494', J, Cross FR 544

End: 6.10 mi, 493', Home EQ jcn on S side of Canebrake CG

Difficulty: Easy   Elev Gain/Loss: 1,038' / 1,044'

Badin Lake Trip F

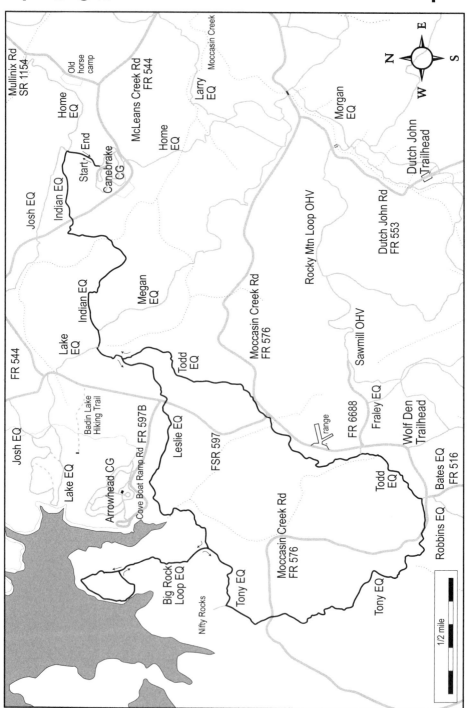

Elevation Profile: BLRA Trip F - Big Rocks

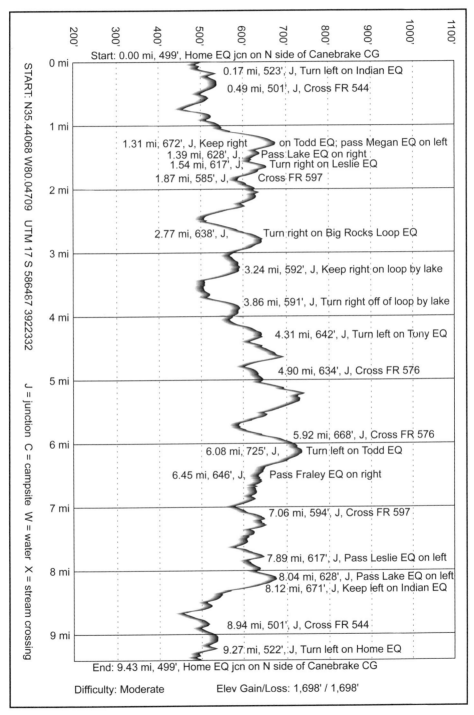

START: N35.44068 W80.04709 UTM 17 S 586467 3922332   J = junction C = campsite W = water X = stream crossing

Start: 0.00 mi, 499', Home EQ jcn on N side of Canebrake CG

0 mi
0.17 mi, 523', J, Turn left on Indian EQ
0.49 mi, 501', J, Cross FR 544

1 mi
1.31 mi, 672', J, Keep right on Todd EQ; pass Megan EQ on left
1.39 mi, 628', J, Pass Lake EQ on right
1.54 mi, 617', J, Turn right on Leslie EQ
1.87 mi, 585', J, Cross FR 597

2 mi
2.77 mi, 638', J, Turn right on Big Rocks Loop EQ

3 mi
3.24 mi, 592', J, Keep right on loop by lake
3.86 mi, 591', J, Turn right off of loop by lake

4 mi
4.31 mi, 642', J, Turn left on Tony EQ
4.90 mi, 634', J, Cross FR 576

5 mi

5.92 mi, 668', J, Cross FR 576
6 mi
6.08 mi, 725', J, Turn left on Todd EQ
6.45 mi, 646', J, Pass Fraley EQ on right

7 mi
7.06 mi, 594', J, Cross FR 597

7.89 mi, 617', J, Pass Leslie EQ on left
8 mi
8.04 mi, 628', J, Pass Lake EQ on left
8.12 mi, 671', J, Keep left on Indian EQ

8.94 mi, 501', J, Cross FR 544
9 mi
9.27 mi, 522', J, Turn left on Home EQ
End: 9.43 mi, 499', Home EQ jcn on N side of Canebrake CG

Difficulty: Moderate   Elev Gain/Loss: 1,698' / 1,698'

Badin Lake Trip G

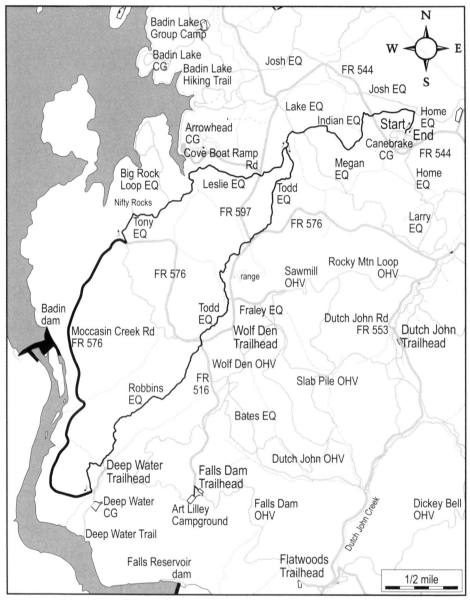

Elevation Profile: BLRA Trip G - Deep Water Camp

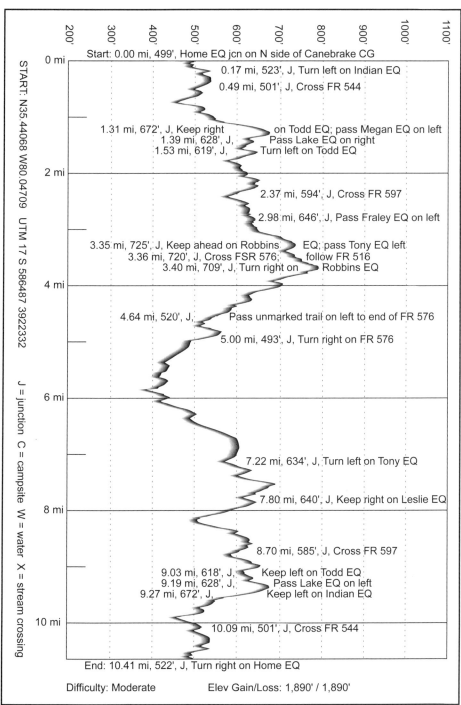

START: N35.44068 W80.04709   UTM 17 S 586487 3922332

J = junction   C = campsite   W = water   X = stream crossing

200'   300'   400'   500'   600'   700'   800'   900'   1000'   1100'

0 mi   Start: 0.00 mi, 499', Home EQ jcn on N side of Canebrake CG
0.17 mi, 523', J, Turn left on Indian EQ
0.49 mi, 501', J, Cross FR 544

1.31 mi, 672', J, Keep right   on Todd EQ; pass Megan EQ on left
1.39 mi, 628', J,   Pass Lake EQ on right
1.53 mi, 619', J,   Turn left on Todd EQ

2 mi

2.37 mi, 594', J, Cross FR 597

2.98 mi, 646', J, Pass Fraley EQ on left

3.35 mi, 725', J, Keep ahead on Robbins   EQ; pass Tony EQ left
3.36 mi, 720', J, Cross FSR 576;   follow FR 516
3.40 mi, 709', J, Turn right on   Robbins EQ

4 mi

4.64 mi, 520', J,   Pass unmarked trail on left to end of FR 576

5.00 mi, 493', J, Turn right on FR 576

6 mi

7.22 mi, 634', J, Turn left on Tony EQ

7.80 mi, 640', J, Keep right on Leslie EQ

8 mi

8.70 mi, 585', J, Cross FR 597

9.03 mi, 618', J,   Keep left on Todd EQ
9.19 mi, 628', J,   Pass Lake EQ on left
9.27 mi, 672', J,   Keep left on Indian EQ

10 mi

10.09 mi, 501', J, Cross FR 544

End: 10.41 mi, 522', J, Turn right on Home EQ

Difficulty: Moderate   Elev Gain/Loss: 1,890' / 1,890'

Badin Lake Trip H

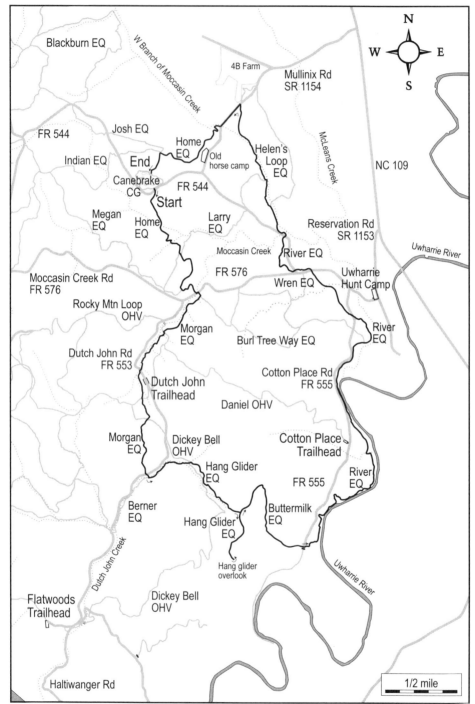

Elevation Profile: BLRA Trip H - Hang Glider

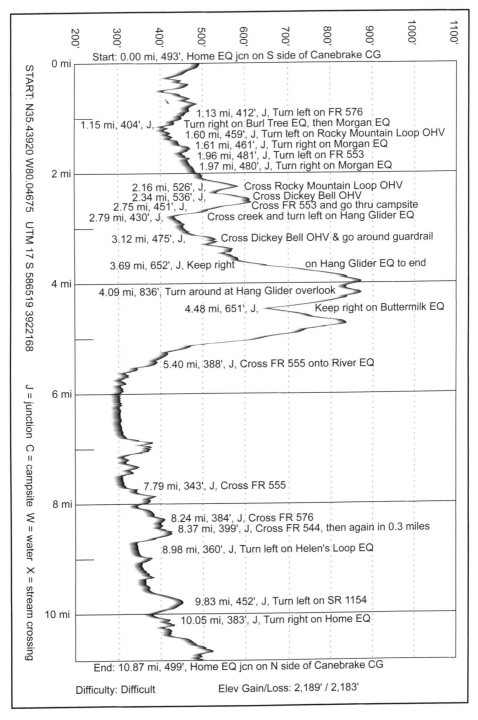

START: N35.43920 W80.04675   UTM 17 S 586519 3922168

J = junction C = campsite W = water X = stream crossing

200' 300' 400' 500' 600' 700' 800' 900' 1000' 1100'

0 mi   Start: 0.00 mi, 493', Home EQ jcn on S side of Canebrake CG

1.13 mi, 412', J, Turn left on FR 576
1.15 mi, 404', J,   Turn right on Burl Tree EQ, then Morgan EQ
1.60 mi, 459', J, Turn left on Rocky Mountain Loop OHV
1.61 mi, 461', J, Turn right on Morgan EQ
1.96 mi, 481', J, Turn left on FR 553
1.97 mi, 480', J, Turn right on Morgan EQ

2 mi
2.16 mi, 526', J,   Cross Rocky Mountain Loop OHV
2.34 mi, 536', J,   Cross Dickey Bell OHV
2.75 mi, 451', J,   Cross FR 553 and go thru campsite
2.79 mi, 430', J,   Cross creek and turn left on Hang Glider EQ

3.12 mi, 475', J,   Cross Dickey Bell OHV & go around guardrail

3.69 mi, 652', J, Keep right   on Hang Glider EQ to end

4 mi
4.09 mi, 836', Turn around at Hang Glider overlook
4.48 mi, 651', J,   Keep right on Buttermilk EQ

5.40 mi, 388', J, Cross FR 555 onto River EQ

6 mi

7.79 mi, 343', J, Cross FR 555

8 mi
8.24 mi, 384', J, Cross FR 576
8.37 mi, 399', J, Cross FR 544, then again in 0.3 miles

8.98 mi, 360', J, Turn left on Helen's Loop EQ

9.83 mi, 452', J, Turn left on SR 1154

10 mi
10.05 mi, 383', J, Turn right on Home EQ

End: 10.87 mi, 499', Home EQ jcn on N side of Canebrake CG

Difficulty: Difficult   Elev Gain/Loss: 2,189' / 2,183'

Badin Lake OHV Trails

Trail Name	Length (miles)	Elevation Gain/Loss	Difficulty Rating	Map (page)
Daniel	1.86	567' / 681'	Difficult	162
Dickey Bell	3.39	726' / 871'	Difficult	164
Dutch John	2.04	548' / 754'	Moderate	166
Falls Dam	2.69	390' / 645'	Moderate	168
Lake View	1.50	396' / 459'	Easy	170
Rocky Mountain	2.74	614' / 592'	Difficult	172
Sawmill	0.92	233' / 178'	Moderate	174
Slab Pile	1.07	210' / 294'	Moderate	176
Wolf Den	0.93	221' / 94'	Easy	178

Off Highway Vehicle (OHV) Trail System
In 1972, a Presidential Order directed the National Forests to establish policies for off-road vehicles, including dirtbikes. At that time there were numerous roads and trails in USFS-owned areas open to public travel. Cross-country travel was also permitted. Increasing use resulted in noticeable environmental impacts and damage, and safety issues arising with vehicles not licensed for public road use.

A network of connecting routes was identified and signed for off road vehicle use. The Uwharrie National Forest's Off-Road Vehicle plan officially went into effect March 25, 1977. These trails were referred to as ORV trails at the time. This network of trails used many of the existing roadbeds that ran through the area. Cross-country travel was prohibited, and motorized use was restricted to only trails designated for such use.

Up through the late-1980's the OHV trails were designated in two use categories - trailbike use only, and all-type use. Jeeps were limited to four trails on the west side of the area - Wolf Den, Big Branch, CCC, and Falls Dam Trails. All other trails were "trailbike use only", which meant they were open to four-wheelers, motorcycles, mountain bikes, horses, and hikers. By 2012, upgrades to the trail treads have allowed all types of Off Highway Vehicles to be allowed on all of the trails.

On September 23, 1994, several of the OHV trails on the west side of the area, near the Yadkin River, were permanently closed to improve the chance that visiting bald eagles might nest in the area. Eagles are frequently spotted along the river, often feeding on injured fish below the dams. Protection of archeological and soil and water resources were also cited as reasons for the closures. The closed trails were: Elk Horn, Big Branch, CCC, and part of Falls Dam Trail. The Gold Mine Trail on the eastern side of the Badin Lake Area was also closed, due to excessive erosion problems. Several illegal trails were also closed off at that time.

A trial fee project was started in 1996 on the OHV trail system. User fees were channeled back into trail needs at the location where the fees are collected. Users were asked to pay $3 per day visit or $30 for a season pass. Roughly 90% of the fees collected remained in the Local USFS District. A few years later the "trail pass" system became more or less permanent. It is reviewed periodically and so far has been renewed each time. As of 2013, the "trail passes" are $5 per day. Season passes are still $30. Trail passes are required for all wheeled vehicles, including mountain bikes. Passes can be purchased at most local stores, like the Eldorado Outpost.

During January and February of 1997, the Forest Service temporarily closed all OHV trails due to excessively wet conditions that resulted in increased trail erosion. This practice has been continued each year. OHV trails are now closed from December 15th to March 31st.

The OHV trails are very popular with four-wheelers and off roaders, attracting over 500 users a day on most weekends. This heavy use leads to various problems, such as erosion and user conflicts. The USFS is always looking for ways to address these problems, so changes to how these trail are managed and where they go are likely to occur.

During deer hunting season, which usually begins in September or October and ends around January 1, the Badin Lake Recreation Area attracts scores of avid hunters who often camp along the roads at the pull-offs. It's not unusual to find all of these sites filled on weekends during hunting season. If you ride at this time of year, it's wise to wear plenty of blaze orange clothing and don't ride alone.

Volunteers from local and statewide groups have assisted in maintaining this system over the years.

Before the Wood Run Mountain Bike Trails were built in the 1990's, most mountain bikers who visited the Uwharries came to the Badin Lake Area and rode the OHV trails. Their descriptions would often include words like "wicked", "heinous", "not for beginners", etc. Rightly so in some cases. These trails were laid out for motorized users, not bicyclists. As a result, some of the hills are a bit too steep for the average mortal to pedal up. Several of these sections are challenging just to push a bike up.

On the positive side, most sections of the OHV trails are not that difficult. These trails resemble wide singletrack, 6 to 10 feet across on average. There usually aren't any defined tracks, single or double. These trails get a lot of motorized use so much of the tread is somewhat eroded and rocky. I once saw a steep rocky section of the Dickey Bell Trail that was covered in 4" to 6" of loose, powdered clay. It looked like gray flour. I'm not sure what to call that trail "condition"!

OHV trails shouldn't be ridden carelessly, no matter how much experience or suspension you have. If you ride clean, pick the best line and stay in control, you'll have a good time, get a great workout, and will certainly have a better chance of going home with fewer injuries and fewer broken parts on your bike.

Fortunately, it's hard for OHV's to sneak up on a mountain biker. My experience encountering OHV riders and drivers has always been positive. They are usually amazed that someone is crazy enough to be out there on a bicycle to start with and will often stop and chat.

All of the OHV trails are blazed with plastic orange diamonds. Many of the orange diamonds have the specific USFS trail number written on them.

USFS OHV Trail Rules

- No double riding on ATVs or dirtbikes

- NC DOT helmets required / ATVs & bikes

- Stay on OHV trails with orange diamonds

- Trail pass required

- Pick up trash

Daniel Trail

Map	page 162	**Difficulty**	Difficult
Length	1.86 miles	**Configuration**	One Way
Trailhead	Cotton Place	**Elev Gain/Loss**	567' / 681'

Start Coordinates N35.42376, W80.04540;   17 S 586659 3920456

Daniel Trail (USFS Trail #390) is the most difficult of the OHV trails. It is the only Uwharrie OHV trail rated as "Extremely Difficult". All OHV trails are marked with orange, diamond-shaped markers.

On a map from the 1960's, a "Daniel Trail" is shown starting at Dutch John Road (FR 553) and following the same route as today's Rocky Mountain Trail to just south of where Daniel Trail starts today. It was shown as a dirtbike trail at that time, and was shown as ending not far beyond the current intersection.

USGS maps place the "Daniel Mountain" name on the slightly lower and less massive mountain just south of the mountain that today's Daniel Trail climbs over. It's not clear if the USGS name is misplaced, or if both mountains are considered part of "Daniel Mountain". Either way, it's likely that the "Daniel Trail" was named after the mountain, which is one of three major mountains that lie along the Uwharrie River on the eastern side of the Badin Lake area.

Daniel Trail was one of the trails included in the initial ORV Trail System designated in 1977. It was signed for "Trailbike Use Only" at that time, but was upgraded to allow full-size vehicles not long after the nearby Gold Mine Trail was closed in 1994.

Daniel Trail starts at its junction with the Rocky Mountain Trail, east of Dutch John Road (FR 553). At the start there used to be a sign saying "This trail extremely dangerous when wet." The first obstacle is a long steep climb up a red clay trail with a series of drainage dips. After that the trail presents an even longer and steeper rocky climb. One notable obstacle in this section is a set of exposed bedrock slabs. The route climbs up these relatively low-angle slabs.

Once on top of the mountain, Daniel Trail works its way around two of the mountain's three peaks. Along the way, the trail features a few tricky descents and ledges. Alternate routes exist around most of these obstacles.

After the second saddle, the route presents visitors with a fairly open vista to the southeast. From there it turns and abruptly descends down the mountain through a series of rocky sections, ledges, and steep turns. The OHV community has given these features names such as 3 Path Climb, Little Ledge, Z Turn, "The" Ledge, and Gatekeeper.

Part of the way down, the route makes a sharp switchback turn. From this switchback there is a old roadbed that leads out on a small spur ridge where you'll find something of a vista looking to the northwest.

A short distance beyond the switchback is a challenging section consisting of two steep and severely eroded switchbacks, back to back. The bypass route is also difficult, which is likely why this trail earns the "most difficult" rating.

Below these obstacles, the trail crosses much easier terrain before ending at the Cotton Place Trailhead parking lot.

MTB Tips: For mountain bikers, it's a toss-up as the to the best direction to ride this trail. Riding it west to east gives you three probable pushes (not rides) going up and a controlled fall down the east end. Starting from Cotton Place Trailhead and riding it east to west will give most riders a couple of long pushes to get to the top of the ridge to begin with. The ridge top is nearly 400 feet higher than the trailhead. There's a decent vista from the top. Once on top, the route coming off the west end of the ridge should be rideable for anyone who made it to the top of the mountain.

Like the other OHV trails, Daniel Trail is closed in the winter from December 15th to April 1st. During the rest of the year, it is open 7 days a week, 24 hours a day, rain or shine.

Dickey Bell Trail

Map	page 164	**Difficulty**	Difficult
Length	3.39 miles	**Configuration**	One Way
Trailhead	Flatwoods Trailhead	**Elev Gain/Loss**	726' / 871'
Start Coordinates N35.41777, W80.04942; 17 S 586300 3919789			

Dickey Bell Trail (USFS Trail #91) is rated "Difficult" by the USFS. Prior to 2012, Dickey Bell Trail was trail #96A in the USFS system.

On maps from the 1960's, a jeep trail, labeled "Gold Mine Road", was shown starting at Dutch John Road (FR 553) where the Dickey Bell Trail crosses it today. It ran eastward across the mountain to Cotton Place Road (FR 555). Another jeep trail, labeled "Big Dickey Bell Road", started at a junction with Gold Mine Road and ran southward along the same route as today's Dickey Bell Trail to end at the saddle just south of the main ridge of Shingle Trap Mountain.

When the original ORV Trail System was designated in 1977, the Gold Mine Road became the Gold Mine Trail and was extended west of Dutch John Road to connect to the Rocky Mountain Trail. The Dickey Bell Trail was established as a dirtbike trail that ran from the Gold Mine Trail southward over Shingle Trap Mountain to connect to the end of Dutch John Road and the Falls Dam Trail.

In 1994, the Gold Mine Trail was closed due to erosion and resource impact problems on its eastern end. The Dickey Bell Trail route was extended along the remaining western portion of Gold Mine to where it junctioned with the Rocky Mountain Trail.

Dickey Bell Trail rolls gently from its start at Rocky Mountain Trail and drops slightly to cross Dutch John Road (FR 553) and several small tributaries of Dutch John Creek. Once past the second logged stream crossing, the route begins a long, moderate climb to the top of Shingle Trap Mountain, the highest in the area at just over 900' in elevation.

There is a relatively flat area on top of Shingle Trap Mountain. From there, Dickey Bell begins descending the south side of the mountain. There are three short but notably difficult downhill sections to negotiate before intersecting with the graveled Green Gap Road (FR 6584). The largest of these difficult sections is about 100 yards of steep, rocky, loose, and eroded trail. Some OHV users refer to this as the "Little Daniel hill climb". The other two sections are rocky but much shorter.

After Green Gap Road, the route crosses Dutch John Creek. This crossing used to be the widest of all the creek fords in the OHV trail system, at about 20 feet wide. A one-lane steel beam bridge was constructed over the creek in 2010 to stop stream damage and avoid possible trail closure. This bridge is dedicated to a fallen Marine, Sgt Josh D. Desforges, an OHV enthusiast and trail volunteer who was killed in Afghanistan in 2010.

A short distance beyond the bridge, the route turns left and follows the public gravel Haltiwanger Road (SR1214) for a short distance before turning right and climbing a short hill and circling back to join the very end of Dutch John Road (FR 553). The final 100 yards or so leading to the Flatwoods Trailhead parking area is also shared with public road traffic.

MTB Tips: Following this trail in the direction described should allow the best chance for mountain bikers to ride nearly all of the route. The climb up the north end of the mountain is gradual enough for most riders to spin up. All but one of the rocky downhills on the south end should be rideable. I suspect only highly skilled riders will be able to negotiate their way through that one steep, rocky, loose section. For the rest of us, it's less than 100 yards of hike-a-bike. Riding the trail south to north presents a smooth but much steeper ascent up the south side of the mountain and a guaranteed hike-a-bike up that steepest rocky section. I found myself pushing up a lot more of the route when going in this direction.

OHV Tips: The steepest rocky section presents a notable hill climb when traveling Dickey from South to North.

All OHV trails are marked with orange, diamond-shaped markers. Like the other OHV trails, Dickey Bell Trail is now closed in the winter from December 15th to April 1st. During the rest of the year, it is open 7 days a week, 24 hours a day, rain or shine.

Dutch John Trail

Map	page 166	**Difficulty**	Moderate
Length	2.04 miles	**Configuration**	One Way
Trailhead	NA	**Elev Gain/Loss**	548' / 754'
Start Coordinates N35.41403, W80.06931;   17 S 584498 3919356

Dutch John Trail (USFS Trail #90) is one of the OHV trails rated "Difficult" by the USFS. All OHV trails are marked with orange, diamond-shaped markers.

Dutch John Trail was signed when the original ORV Trail System was created in 1977. Part of the route follows old roadbeds near Dutch John Creek and along one of its tributaries. The trail is most likely named after Dutch John Creek. In fact, prior to 1996, the trail actually ran down the middle of the rocky creekbed for about 50 yards.

The first half mile of trail on the western end of Dutch John follows an old roadbed once called the Crome Mine Road. This road may have also been part of the route of the long-abandoned Dutch John Hiking Trail. The Crome Mine Road ran from the Wolf Den Trail eastward to Dutch John Road.

In 2012, the western ends of Dutch John and Wolf Den Trails were both relocated from the top of the ridgeline, moving their intersection several hundred feet further east from the Falls Dam Trail (OHV)/FR 516.

The Dutch John Trail route goes over two significant mountains, one at each end of the trail. Between these mountains the trail goes over two smaller hills and through a rather rocky section along a creek.

The Dutch John Trail begins at its junction with Wolf Den Trail (OHV). From here it climbs gently for a short distance before beginning a long descent. The descent is broken up when the route crosses over a low spur ridge. Dutch John Trail crosses the Bates Trail (EQ) on this spur ridge.

The route then continues dropping on the far side of the spur, passing through an entrenched section before reaching a rocky creek. After crossing this creek, the route turns right and then parallels it. The fairly long section beside the creek is covered in loose rocks.

Eventually the route climbs away from the creek and circles up and across the side of the adjacent mountain. Once around the corner of the ridge, the route starts to descend again. Not far from the crest the route crosses the Fraley Trail (EQ). Dutch John then drops to cross over Dutch John Creek itself. It soon crosses back and begins climbing through a steep, severely entrenched section of trail. This section was entrenched 8-10 feet deep in the fall of 2012.

This section of the route that now climbs away from the creek used to follow Dutch John Creek. About 50 yards of the trail actually ran in the middle of the creekbed. A relocation in 1996 changed the route to climb up the side of the mountain instead.

Once through the entrenched section, the trail soon begins a long descent before ending at a junction with Slab Pile Trail.

MTB Tips: Perhaps the most enjoyable way to approach mountain biking the Dutch John Trail is to plan on not riding all the way through it. Turning downhill onto either of the two equestrian trails that cross it allows one to continue riding towards Dutch John Road (FR 553) and avoid the long steep climbs on either end of the trail. Starting from the end at Wolf Den Trail (OHV) offers less of a climb at the beginning and the rocky section along the creek is more negotiable going downstream.

Like the other OHV trails, Dutch John Trail is closed in the winter from December 15th to April 1st. During the rest of the year, it is open 7 days a week, 24 hours a day, rain or shine.

Falls Dam Trail

Map	page 168	**Difficulty**	Moderate
Length	2.69 miles	**Configuration**	One Way
Trailhead	Flatwoods	**Elev Gain/Loss**	390' / 645'
Start Coordinates N35.41594, W80.06891; 17 S 584532 3919569			

Falls Dam Trail (USFS Trail #96) forms the southwestern perimeter of the OHV trail system. All OHV trails are marked with orange, diamond-shaped markers.

Falls Dam Trail was part of the ORV trail system designated in 1977. At that time, its western end extended to the end of Moccasin Creek Road (FR 576) along what was previously part of the Wolf Den Trail.

On maps from the 1960's, there was no Falls Dam Trail shown. A short dead end dirtbike trail was shown heading east from the then Wolf Den Trail at what is now the Falls Dam Trailhead. This dirtbike trail was labeled the Narrows Trail. It ran east along the ridge top but did not drop down off the mountain.

In 1994, several trails on the western side of the ORV Trail System were closed. The closures were made in order to improve chances that Bald Eagles might nest on the slopes above the lake. The section of Falls Dam Trail dropping off the mountain to the end of Moccasin Creek Road was closed. The end of the trail was rerouted to run northward along FR 516 to end at Moccasin Creek Road, where a gate was established, blocking that end of FR 516. Along the way, the new route went past a junction with a connector to the Wolf Den Trail. The CCC Trail, another one of the ORV trails closed at that time, ran from that junction westward down Falls Dam Mountain to connect to the end of Moccasin Creek Road (FR 576).

In 2009, the northernmost section of trail, along FR 516, was further improved and re-opened to public vehicular traffic. The improvements extended all the way to the top of Falls Dam Mountain, providing public access to the new Falls Dam Trailhead and Art Lilley Memorial Campground. The road to the trailhead and campground is FR 516 and Falls Dam Trail.

Falls Dam Trail now starts at its junction with the Wolf Den Trail (OHV), and climbs to the ridge top where it turns left on FR 516. In the first edition of this guide, this first uphill section was called the Wolf Den Connector and Falls Dam Trail extended along FR 516 to Moccasin Creek Road.

From the turn onto FR 516, the route follows the road to the Falls Dam Trailhead and Art Lilley Campground. From the Falls Dam Trailhead, it meanders along the broad top of the mountain before dropping down the east slope.

After leaving the mountaintop, Falls Dam Trail assumes the normal OHV trail look with a narrower width and more erosion, rocks, and roots. The moderate descent eventually leads to flatter terrain. There are several spots along the way that provide views of the lakes and surrounding mountains, especially when the leaves are down in the winter. The last section of the trail is relatively gentle as it contours around Falls Mountain and heads towards the Dutch John Creek valley.

Falls Dam Trail ends at the Flatwoods Trailhead, near the end of Dutch John Road (FR 553).

Like the other OHV trails, Falls Dam Trail is closed in the winter from December 15th to April 1st. During the rest of the year, it is open 7 days a week, 24 hours a day, rain or shine.

Lake View Trail

Map	page 170	**Difficulty**	Easy
Length	~1.50 miles	**Configuration**	One Way
Trailhead	Falls Dam	**Elev Gain/Loss**	TBD

Start Coordinates N35.40434, W80.07384;   17 S 584097 3918278

As of the beginning of 2014, the proposed Lake View Trail was still working its way through the paperwork process and trying to pass sensitive resource inspections along the proposed route.

While the general route has been flagged on the ground, it has been changed several times already. The map shown here is based on the route as flagged in November 2012, but it was known then that certain sections would have to be rerouted. However, this should provide a fairly close representation of what the trail will look like when it is finally approved, constructed, and opened for use.

Rocky Mountain Loop Trail

Map	page 172	**Difficulty**	Difficult
Length	2.74 miles	**Configuration**	One Way
Trailhead	Dutch John Trailhead	**Elev Gain/Loss**	614' / 592'

Start Coordinates N35.41983, W80.04769;   17 S 586455 3920019

Rocky Mountain Loop Trail (USFS Trail #92) is the only OHV trail that actually forms a loop by connecting back to itself. It was part of the original ORV trail system designated in 1977. All OHV trails are marked with orange, diamond-shaped markers.

In the first edition of this guidebook, this trail was called "Rocky Mount Trail", according to the USFS name at that time. After years of confusion, the name was officially changed to "Rocky Mountain Loop Trail" in 2009. Some signs along the trail still say "Rocky Mount".

The trail begins low, near Moccasin Creek, at the Dutch John Trailhead on Dutch John Road (FR 553). The first trail intersection encountered is with the Morgan Trail (EQ). The route then passes a junction with Dickey Bell Trail (OHV) on the left on top of a low ridge.

At the junction with Slab Pile Trail (OHV), the Rocky Mountain Trail route turns right and climbs an unnamed mountain. Along the way up, trail users will encounter the well-known Kodak Rock obstacle. This section of exposed rock ledges presents a perfect opportunity for OHV drivers to put themselves and their equipment to the test, and for others to take pictures of the attempts. Not sure how long the Kodak Rock name will remain, since the iconic photo film company has now gone out of business. There is an easier bypass route around Kodak Rock.

As of the beginning of 2014, the section of Rocky Mountain Trail between Slab Pile and Samwill Trails is temporarily closed until a solution for resource protection can be put in place. This may take several years to complete.

The route tops out at about 800' in elevation. The trail then passes a junction on the left with Sawmill Trail (OHV) before beginning a rocky descent to Dutch John Road (FR 553).

Shortly after crossing the gravel road, there is a narrow bridge over Moccasin Creek. This one-lane steel beam bridge was constructed over the creek in 2010 to avoid stream damage and possible trail closure. The route then intersects with the Morgan Trail (EQ) again and then passes a junction on the left with Daniel Trail (OHV). The route passes by the Dutch John Trailhead parking lot , crosses Dutch John Road (FR 553), and ends a few feet further at a junction with itself.

MTB Tips: Following the trail as described gives you a shorter push uphill, allowing you to enjoy more downhill miles on the rest of the trail. Although Rocky Mountain Loop certainly deserves its name, I couldn't tell that it was any rockier than the other OHV trails.

Like the other OHV trails, Rocky Mountain Loop is closed in the winter from December 15th to April 1st. During the rest of the year, it is open 7 days a week, 24 hours a day, rain or shine.

Sawmill Trail

Map	page 174	**Difficulty**	Moderate
Length	0.92 miles	**Configuration**	One Way
Trailhead	NA	**Elev Gain/Loss**	233' / 178'
Start Coordinates N35.42626, W80.05522; 17 S 585765 3920725			

Sawmill Trail (USFS Trail #93) lies in the northwest corner of the OHV trail system. All OHV trails are marked with orange, diamond-shaped markers.

Sawmill was part of the first set of ORV trails designated in 1977. Sawmill Trail has previously been known as trail #92A in the USFS system, but was renumbered in 2012. Sawmill Trail runs from the Slab Pile Trail (OHV) to Rocky Mountain Trail (OHV).

The initial 1977 trail route was 1.6 miles long. The trail climbed up onto the mountain just north of the current trail location and ran along its U-shaped ridge line. On older maps from the 1960's, this ridge top section of trail was part of two dirtbike trails, one labeled Powder Keg Trail and the other Low Gap Trail. The "Sawmill Trail" labeled on those old maps was a short dead end section that is now part of the Rocky Mountain Trail, running from its junction with Slab Pile Trail towards Kodak Rock.

Part of the route was relocated in 2006 in order to move it further away from the Flintlock Valley Shooting Range on Moccasin Creek Road (FR 576). Bullets whizzing through the trees over the trail were deemed to be a little too adventurous. The ridge top portion of the trail was removed with this relocation.

In 2011, another relocation was completed, moving most of the trail onto an old roadbed upgraded to trail standards. This change moved the trail even further from the firing range and protected heritage resources that were being impacted by the previous relocation. The overall length of Sawmill Trail was reduced to the current length of 1.0 mile by this change.

The west end of Sawmill Trail starts at a junction with Slab Pile Trail (OHV). The route drops gently to begin with, climbs up to 830' in the middle, and has a minor climb at the end where it junctions with Rocky Mountain Trail (OHV). The trail snakes in and out of two valleys that are the headwaters of the Dutch John Creek drainage.

Like the other OHV trails, Sawmill Trail is now closed in the winter from December 15th to April 1st. During the rest of the year, it is open 7 days a week, 24 hours a day, rain or shine.

Slab Pile Trail

Map	page 176	**Difficulty**	Moderate
Length	1.07 miles	**Configuration**	One Way
Trailhead	NA	**Elev Gain/Loss**	210' / 294'

Start Coordinates N35.41866, W80.06695;   17 S 584708 3919872

Overall, Slab Pile Trail (USFS Trail #79) is one of the easier trails in the OHV trail system. The route cuts across the OHV trail area, providing a link from the west side to the east side of the trail system. All OHV trails are marked with orange, diamond-shaped markers.

Slab Pile was signed when the ORV trails were designated in 1977. Slab Pile Trail was previously known as trail #89A in the USFS system, but was renumbered in 2012.

Older maps from the 1960's show Slab Pile Trail as a dead end dirtbike trail starting from its current east end at Rocky Mountain Trail (OHV) and heading northwest and staying on the north side of Dutch John Creek. The name most likely refers to a pile of "slabs" at a nearby sawmill operation.

Slab Pile Trail starts at Wolf Den Trail (OHV) and offers a moderate climb to a ridge top. An intersection with the Fraley Trail (EQ) and a junction to the left with Sawmill Trail (OHV) is found at the top. The route then descends to cross a few rolling ravines before passing a junction on the right with Dutch John Trail (OHV).

A final descent leads to a crossing of Dutch John Creek on a bottomless arch structure, built in 2012-13. This structure replaces a log corduroy crossing. A short and gentle climb leads to the route's end at Rocky Mountain Trail (OHV).

Like the other OHV trails, Slab Pile Trail is now closed in the winter from December 15th to April 1st. During the rest of the year, it is open 7 days a week, 24 hours a day, rain or shine.

Wolf Den Trail

Map	page 178	**Difficulty**	Easy
Length	0.93 miles	**Configuration**	One Way
Trailhead	Wolf Den Trailhead	**Elev Gain/Loss**	221' / 94'
Start Coordinates	N35.42133, W80.06846;	17 S 584568 3920167	

Wolf Den Trail (USFS Trail #89) is fairly gentle compared to most of the other OHV trails, although there is a noticeable climb near its end. It is the only trail rated "Easy" by the USFS. All OHV trails are marked with orange, diamond-shaped markers.

In the 1960's, Wolf Den Trail was a jeep trail that ran from its current start location all the way over Falls Dam Mountain (through the present Falls Dam Trailhead) and connected to the end of Moccasin Creek Road (FR 576). Wolf Den Trail was shortened to its present length in the late 1970's when FR 516 was built on part of the route and the ORV trail system was designated. The section of Wolf Den from Falls Dam Mountain westward to the end of FR 576 became part of Falls Dam Trail (OHV) at that time. This western section of trail was closed in 1994.

In late 2012, the ends of the Wolf Den and Dutch John Trails were relocated from the top of the ridge to just below it. This only moved their intersection a few hundred feet further east. The end of Wolf Den Trail at FR 516/Falls Dam Trail is now also a few hundred feet further north.

From the start at Wolf Den Trailhead, this trail drops gently downhill, passing a junction with Slab Pile Trail (OHV) on the left. There is a small creek crossing at the bottom of the hill.

After crossing the creek, the route intersects the Bates Trail (equestrian). A short distance from there, the route passes a junction with the end of Falls Dam Trail (OHV) on the right. After that junction, the route intersects the Bates Trail two more times as it climbs a ridge. A junction with the end of Dutch John Trail (OHV) is passed on the left, just below the top of the ridge. The route ends at its junction with the Falls Dam Trail.

Like the other OHV trails, Wolf Den Trail is now closed in the winter from December 15th to April 1st. During the rest of the year, it is open 7 days a week, 24 hours a day, rain or shine.

Daniel Trail

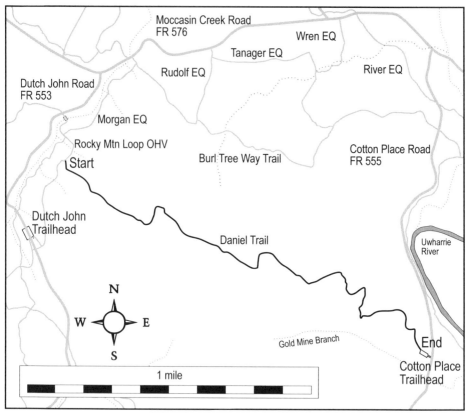

Elevation Profile: Daniel Trail

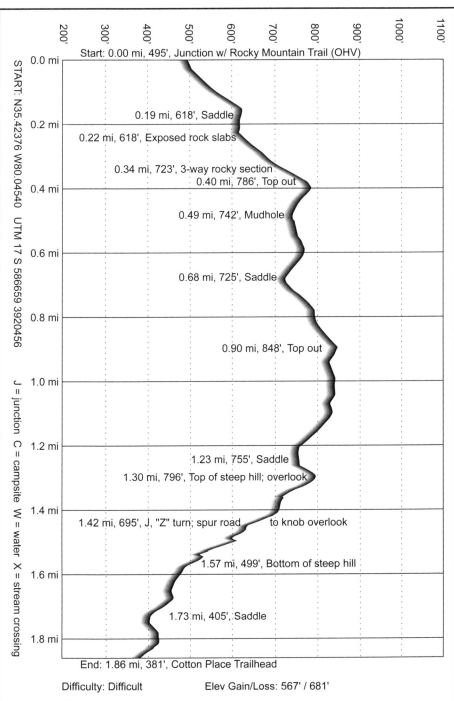

START: N35.42376 W80.04540 UTM 17 S 586659 3920456

J = junction C = campsite W = water X = stream crossing

Start: 0.00 mi, 495', Junction w/ Rocky Mountain Trail (OHV)

0.19 mi, 618', Saddle

0.22 mi, 618', Exposed rock slabs

0.34 mi, 723', 3-way rocky section

0.40 mi, 786', Top out

0.49 mi, 742', Mudhole

0.68 mi, 725', Saddle

0.90 mi, 848', Top out

1.23 mi, 755', Saddle

1.30 mi, 796', Top of steep hill; overlook

1.42 mi, 695', J, "Z" turn; spur road   to knob overlook

1.57 mi, 499', Bottom of steep hill

1.73 mi, 405', Saddle

End: 1.86 mi, 381', Cotton Place Trailhead

Difficulty: Difficult   Elev Gain/Loss: 567' / 681'

Dickey Bell Trail

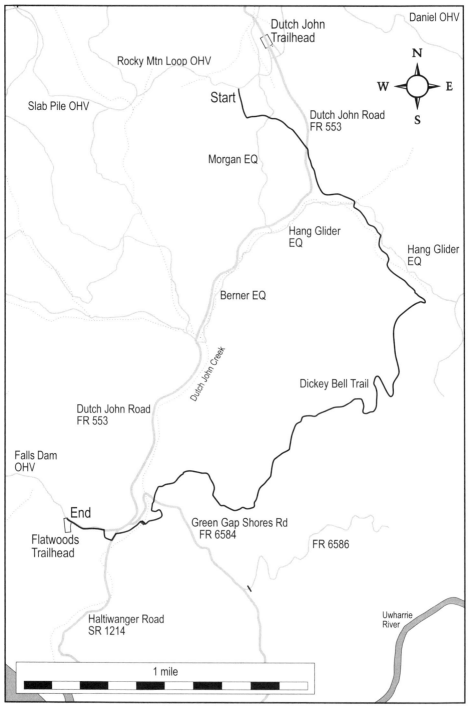

Daniel OHV

Dutch John Trailhead

Rocky Mtn Loop OHV

N
W   E
S

Slab Pile OHV

Start

Dutch John Road
FR 553

Morgan EQ

Hang Glider EQ

Hang Glider EQ

Berner EQ

Dutch John Creek

Dickey Bell Trail

Dutch John Road
FR 553

Falls Dam
OHV

End

Flatwoods
Trailhead

Green Gap Shores Rd
FR 6584

FR 6586

Haltiwanger Road
SR 1214

Uwharrie
River

1 mile

Elevation Profile: Dickey Bell Trail

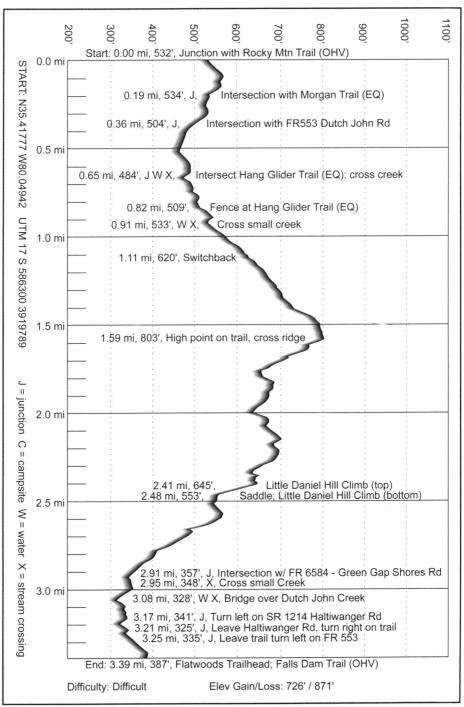

Start: 0.00 mi, 532', Junction with Rocky Mtn Trail (OHV)

0.19 mi, 534', J,   Intersection with Morgan Trail (EQ)

0.36 mi, 504', J,   Intersection with FR553 Dutch John Rd

0.65 mi, 484', J W X,   Intersect Hang Glider Trail (EQ); cross creek

0.82 mi, 509',   Fence at Hang Glider Trail (EQ)
0.91 mi, 533', W X,   Cross small creek

1.11 mi, 620', Switchback

1.59 mi, 803', High point on trail, cross ridge

2.41 mi, 645',   Little Daniel Hill Climb (top)
2.48 mi, 553',   Saddle; Little Daniel Hill Climb (bottom)

2.91 mi, 357', J, Intersection w/ FR 6584 - Green Gap Shores Rd
2.95 mi, 348', X, Cross small Creek
3.08 mi, 328', W X, Bridge over Dutch John Creek
3.17 mi, 341', J, Turn left on SR 1214 Haltiwanger Rd
3.21 mi, 325', J, Leave Haltiwanger Rd, turn right on trail
3.25 mi, 335', J, Leave trail turn left on FR 553

End: 3.39 mi, 387', Flatwoods Trailhead; Falls Dam Trail (OHV)

Difficulty: Difficult   Elev Gain/Loss: 726' / 871'

START: N35.41777 W80.04942 UTM 17 S 586300 3919789

J = junction C = campsite W = water X = stream crossing

Dutch John Trail

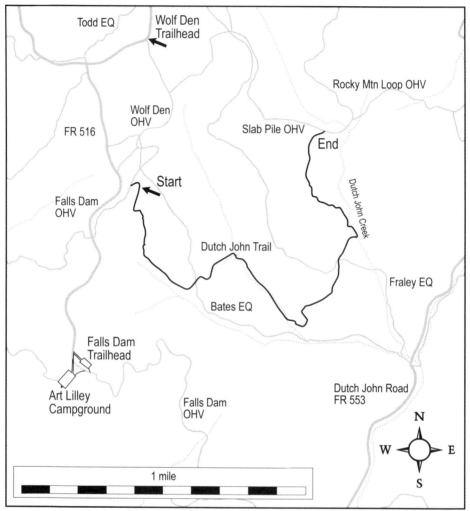

Elevation Profile: Dutch John Trail

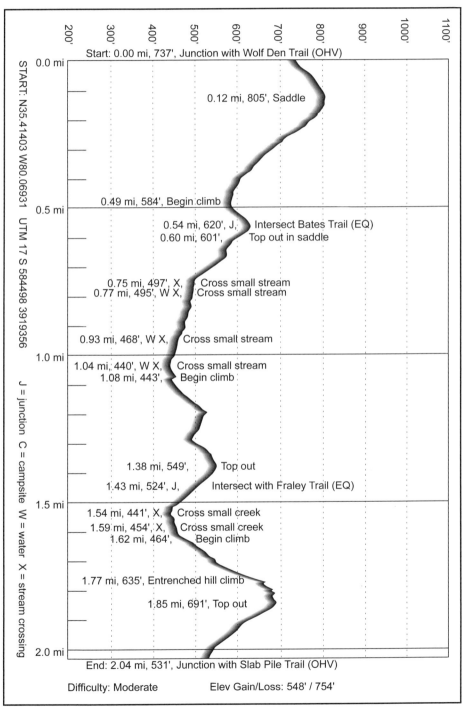

START: N35.41403 W80.06931 UTM 17 S 584498 3919356

J = junction C = campsite W = water X = stream crossing

Start: 0.00 mi, 737', Junction with Wolf Den Trail (OHV)

0.12 mi, 805', Saddle

0.49 mi, 584', Begin climb

0.54 mi, 620', J, Intersect Bates Trail (EQ)
0.60 mi, 601',   Top out in saddle

0.75 mi, 497', X, Cross small stream
0.77 mi, 495', W X, Cross small stream

0.93 mi, 468', W X, Cross small stream

1.04 mi, 440', W X, Cross small stream
1.08 mi, 443', Begin climb

1.38 mi, 549', Top out

1.43 mi, 524', J, Intersect with Fraley Trail (EQ)

1.54 mi, 441', X, Cross small creek
1.59 mi, 454', X, Cross small creek
1.62 mi, 464', Begin climb

1.77 mi, 635', Entrenched hill climb

1.85 mi, 691', Top out

End: 2.04 mi, 531', Junction with Slab Pile Trail (OHV)

Difficulty: Moderate   Elev Gain/Loss: 548' / 754'

Falls Dam Trail

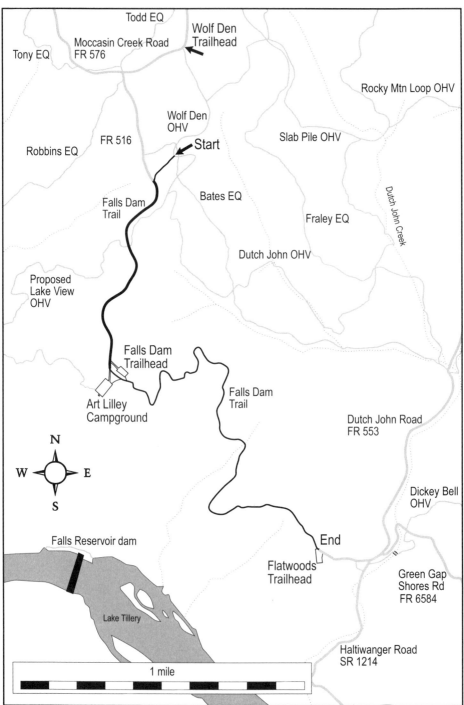

Elevation Profile: Falls Dam Trail

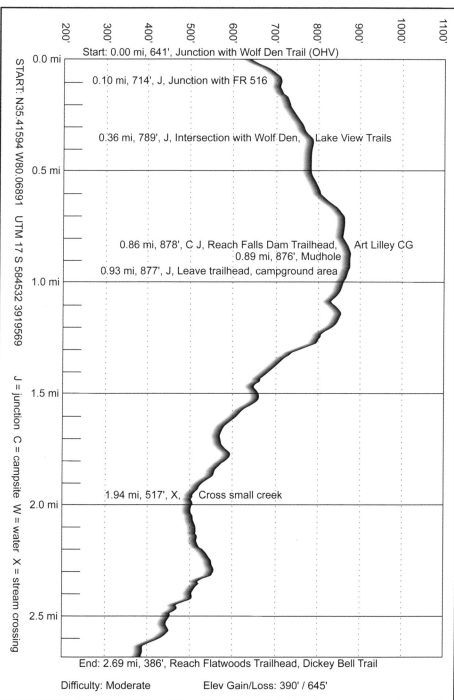

START: N35.41594 W80.06891 UTM 17 S 584532 3919569

J = junction C = campsite W = water X = stream crossing

200' 300' 400' 500' 600' 700' 800' 900' 1000' 1100'

0.0 mi — Start: 0.00 mi, 641', Junction with Wolf Den Trail (OHV)

0.10 mi, 714', J, Junction with FR 516

0.36 mi, 789', J, Intersection with Wolf Den, Lake View Trails

0.5 mi

0.86 mi, 878', C J, Reach Falls Dam Trailhead, Art Lilley CG
0.89 mi, 876', Mudhole
0.93 mi, 877', J, Leave trailhead, campground area

1.0 mi

1.5 mi

1.94 mi, 517', X, Cross small creek

2.0 mi

2.5 mi

End: 2.69 mi, 386', Reach Flatwoods Trailhead, Dickey Bell Trail

Difficulty: Moderate   Elev Gain/Loss: 390' / 645'

Lake View Trail

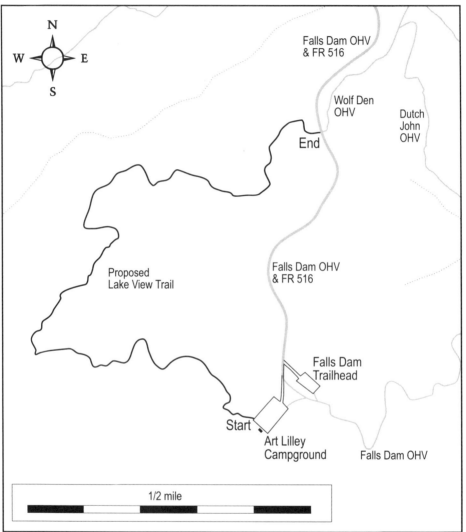

Elevation Profile: Lake View Trail (proposed)

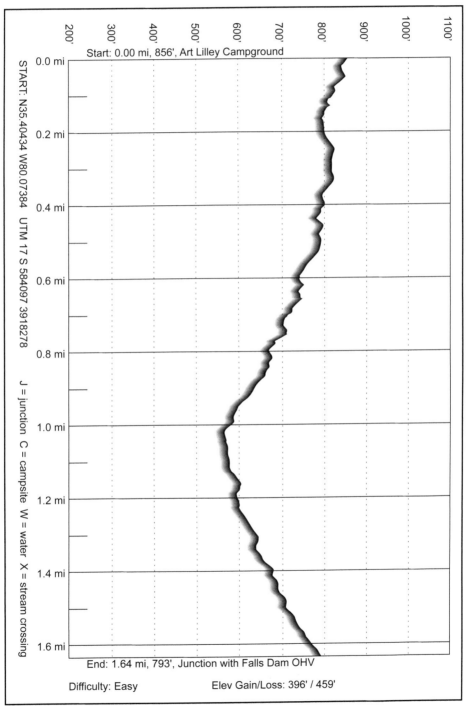

Start: 0.00 mi, 856', Art Lilley Campground

START: N35.40434 W80.07384 UTM 17 S 584097 3918278 J = junction C = campsite W = water X = stream crossing

End: 1.64 mi, 793', Junction with Falls Dam OHV

Difficulty: Easy   Elev Gain/Loss: 396' / 459'

Rocky Mountain Trail

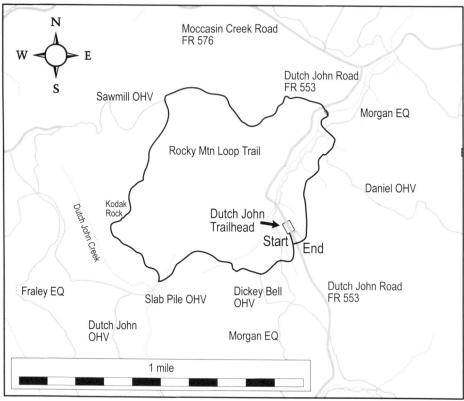

As of the beginning of 2014, the section of Rocky Mountain Trail between Slab Pile and Samwill Trails (containing Kodak Rock) was temporarily closed until a solution for resource protection can be put in place. This may take several years to be completed.

Elevation Profile: Rocky Mountain Trail

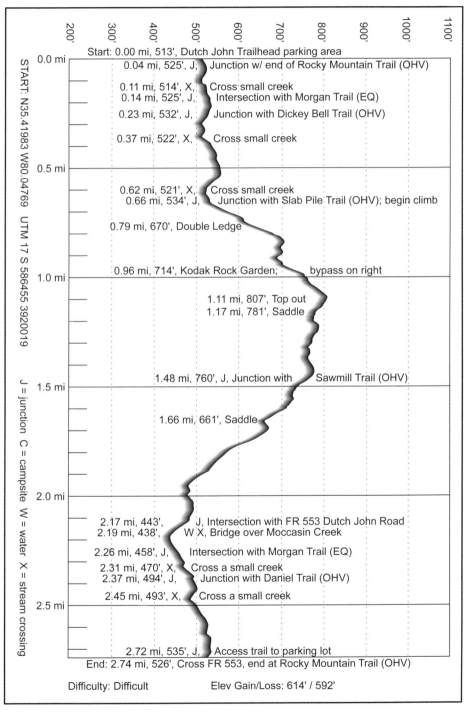

START: N35.41983 W80.04769 UTM 17 S 586455 3920019

J = junction C = campsite W = water X = stream crossing

200' 300' 400' 500' 600' 700' 800' 900' 1000' 1100'	

Start: 0.00 mi, 513', Dutch John Trailhead parking area

0.0 mi

0.04 mi, 525', J, Junction w/ end of Rocky Mountain Trail (OHV)

0.11 mi, 514', X, Cross small creek
0.14 mi, 525', J, Intersection with Morgan Trail (EQ)

0.23 mi, 532', J, Junction with Dickey Bell Trail (OHV)

0.37 mi, 522', X, Cross small creek

0.5 mi

0.62 mi, 521', X, Cross small creek
0.66 mi, 534', J, Junction with Slab Pile Trail (OHV); begin climb

0.79 mi, 670', Double Ledge

0.96 mi, 714', Kodak Rock Garden; bypass on right

1.0 mi

1.11 mi, 807', Top out
1.17 mi, 781', Saddle

1.48 mi, 760', J, Junction with Sawmill Trail (OHV)

1.5 mi

1.66 mi, 661', Saddle

2.0 mi

2.17 mi, 443', J, Intersection with FR 553 Dutch John Road
2.19 mi, 438', W X, Bridge over Moccasin Creek

2.26 mi, 458', J, Intersection with Morgan Trail (EQ)

2.31 mi, 470', X, Cross a small creek
2.37 mi, 494', J, Junction with Daniel Trail (OHV)

2.45 mi, 493', X, Cross a small creek

2.5 mi

2.72 mi, 535', J, Access trail to parking lot

End: 2.74 mi, 526', Cross FR 553, end at Rocky Mountain Trail (OHV)

Difficulty: Difficult   Elev Gain/Loss: 614' / 592'

Sawmill Trail

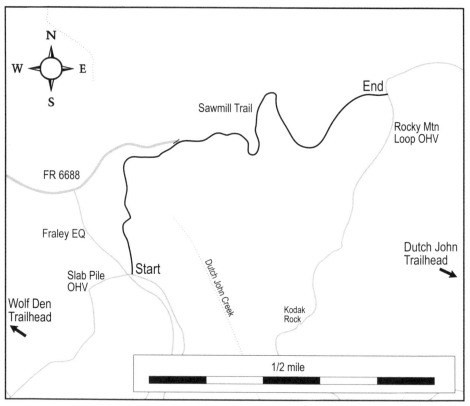

Elevation Profile: Sawmill Trail

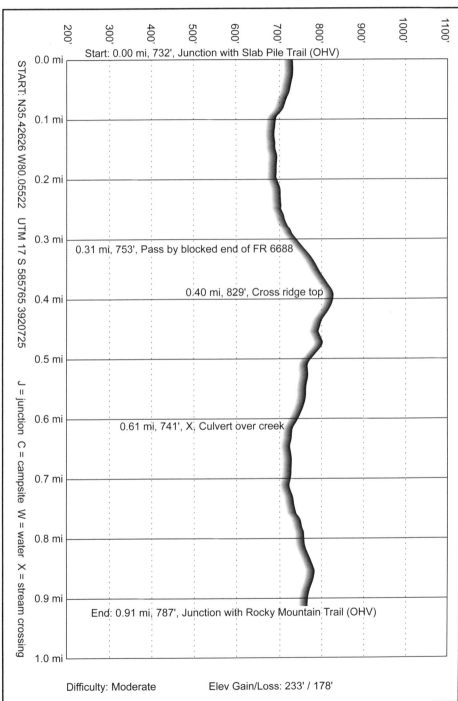

START: N35.42626 W80.05522   UTM 17 S 585765 3920725

J = junction C = campsite W = water X = stream crossing

200' 300' 400' 500' 600' 700' 800' 900' 1000' 1100'

0.0 mi   Start: 0.00 mi, 732', Junction with Slab Pile Trail (OHV)

0.1 mi

0.2 mi

0.3 mi   0.31 mi, 753', Pass by blocked end of FR 6688

0.40 mi, 829', Cross ridge top

0.4 mi

0.5 mi

0.6 mi   0.61 mi, 741', X, Culvert over creek

0.7 mi

0.8 mi

0.9 mi   End: 0.91 mi, 787', Junction with Rocky Mountain Trail (OHV)

1.0 mi

Difficulty: Moderate   Elev Gain/Loss: 233' / 178'

Slab Pile Trail

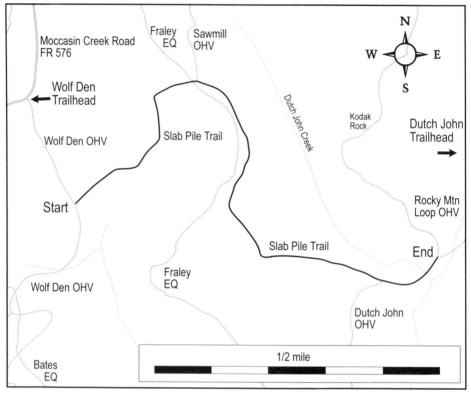

Elevation Profile: Slab Pile Trail

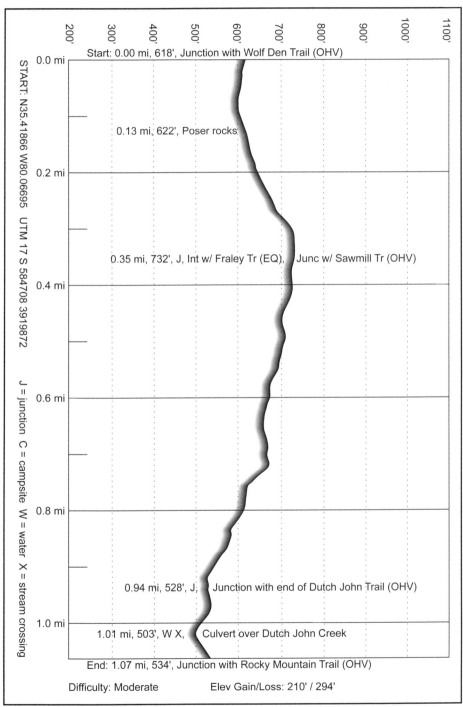

Start: 0.00 mi, 618', Junction with Wolf Den Trail (OHV)

0.13 mi, 622', Poser rocks

0.35 mi, 732', J, Int w/ Fraley Tr (EQ),   Junc w/ Sawmill Tr (OHV)

0.94 mi, 528', J,   Junction with end of Dutch John Trail (OHV)

1.01 mi, 503', W X,   Culvert over Dutch John Creek

End: 1.07 mi, 534', Junction with Rocky Mountain Trail (OHV)

START: N35.41866 W80.06695   UTM 17 S 584708 3919872   J = junction C = campsite W = water X = stream crossing

Difficulty: Moderate   Elev Gain/Loss: 210' / 294'

Wolf Den Trail

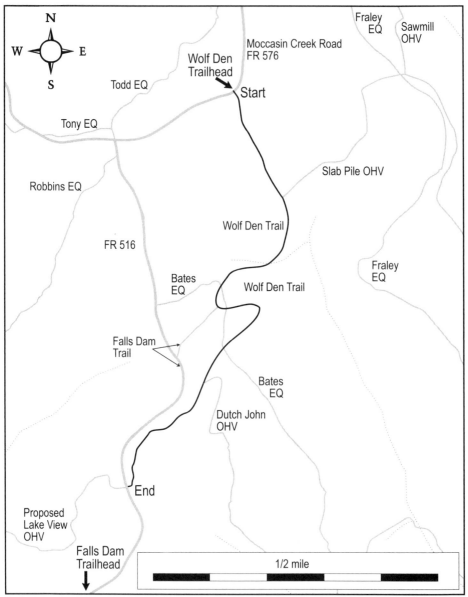

Elevation Profile: Wolf Den Trail

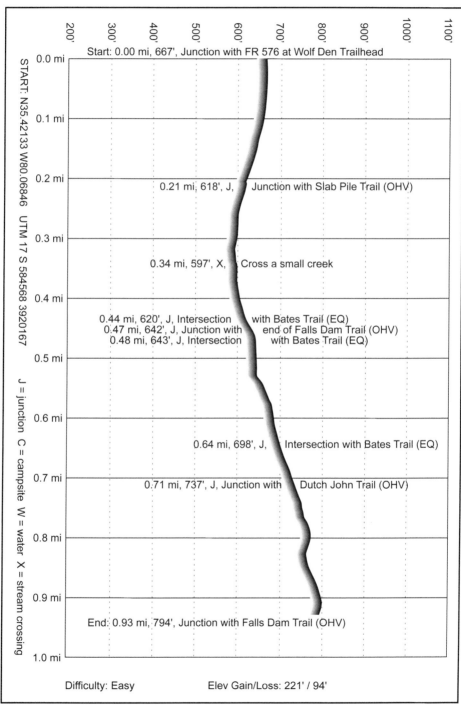

START: N35.42133 W80.06846 UTM 17 S 584568 3920167

J = junction C = campsite W = water X = stream crossing

Start: 0.00 mi, 667', Junction with FR 576 at Wolf Den Trailhead

0.21 mi, 618', J, Junction with Slab Pile Trail (OHV)

0.34 mi, 597', X, Cross a small creek

0.44 mi, 620', J, Intersection with Bates Trail (EQ)
0.47 mi, 642', J, Junction with end of Falls Dam Trail (OHV)
0.48 mi, 643', J, Intersection with Bates Trail (EQ)

0.64 mi, 698', J, Intersection with Bates Trail (EQ)

0.71 mi, 737', J, Junction with Dutch John Trail (OHV)

End: 0.93 mi, 794', Junction with Falls Dam Trail (OHV)

Difficulty: Easy   Elev Gain/Loss: 221' / 94'

Badin Lake OHV Trips

Trip	Use	Length (miles)	Elevation Gain/ Loss	Difficulty Rating	Page
BLRA Trip I	OEBH	6.75	1,288' / 1,288'	Moderate	182
BLRA Trip J	OEBH	6.75	1,170' / 1,170'	Moderate	184
BLRA Trip K	OEBH	9.24	1,972' / 1,972'	Difficult	186
BLRA Trip L	OEBH	11.02	2,600' / 2,600'	Difficult	188
BLRA Trip M	OEBH	5.39	371' / 645'	Difficult +	190

BLRA Trip I

Map	page 182	**Difficulty**	Moderate
Length	6.75 miles	**Configuration**	Lollipop
Trailhead	Falls Dam	**Elev Gain/Loss**	1,288' / 1,288'

Start Coordinates N35.40499, W80.07279;   17 S 584192 3918351

OHV Trip A is a Moderate route that starts at the Falls Dam Trailhead / Art Lilley Campground. This trip follows a lollipop route and features a visit to Kodak Rock on the Rocky Mountain Loop Trail (there is a moderate-rated bypass). This Trip stays on OHV trails and is suitable for vehicles that are not street-legal.

BLRA Trip J

Map	page 184	**Difficulty**	Moderate
Length	6.75 miles	**Configuration**	Loop
Trailhead	Flatwoods	**Elev Gain/Loss**	1,170' / 1,170'

Start Coordinates N35.41577, W80.06925;   17 S 584502 3919549

OHV Trip B is a Moderate route that starts at the Flatwoods Trailhead. This trip follows a Loop route and features a climb up the Falls Dam Trail. This Trip uses a section of Dutch John Road FR 553, so is only suitable for vehicles that are street-legal.

BLRA Trip K

Map	page 186	**Difficulty**	Difficult
Length	9.24 miles	**Configuration**	Loop
Trailhead	Dutch John	**Elev Gain/Loss**	1,972' / 1,972'

Start Coordinates N35.41983, W80.04769;   17 S 586455 3920019

OHV Trip C is a Difficult route that starts at the Dutch John Trailhead. This trip follows a Loop route around most of the OHV trail system. This Trip stays on OHV trails and is suitable for vehicles that are not street-legal.

BLRA Trip L

Map	page 188	**Difficulty**	Difficult
Length	11.02 miles	**Configuration**	Loop
Trailhead	Dutch John	**Elev Gain/Loss**	2,600' / 2,600'

Start Coordinates N35.41983, W80.04769;   17 S 586455 3920019

OHV Trip D is a Difficult route that starts at the Dutch John Trailhead. This trip follows a Loop route that includes a run through the Dutch John Trail. This Trip stays on OHV trails and is suitable for vehicles that are not street-legal.

BLRA Trip M

Map	page 190	**Difficulty**	Very Difficult
Length	5.39 miles	**Configuration**	Loop
Trailhead	Dutch John	**Elev Gain/Loss**	371' / 645'

Start Coordinates N35.41998, W80.04735;   17 S 586486 3920035

OHV Trip E is an Extremely difficult route that starts at the Dutch John Trailhead. This trip follows a Loop route and features a climb Daniel Mountain. The Extremely Difficult section of this route is the descent down the east end of the mountain.

This Trip uses sections of three Forest Service roads to complete the loop, so is only suitable for vehicles that are street-legal. If you prefer to climb through the toughest section, this Trip can be done in the opposite direction.

An alternative for non-street-legal vehicles is to turn around at Cotton Place Trailhead and backtrack the 2.26 mles to the Start.

BLRA Trip I

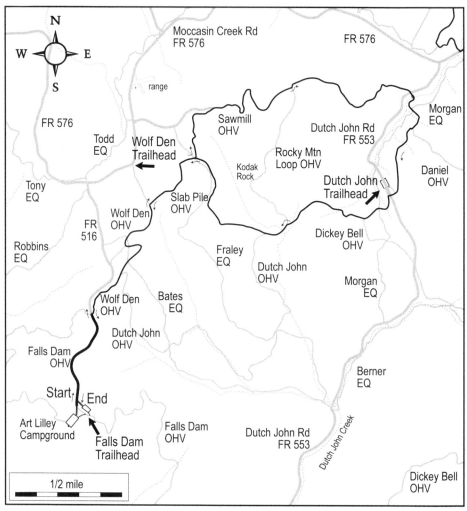

Elevation Profile: BLRA Trip I

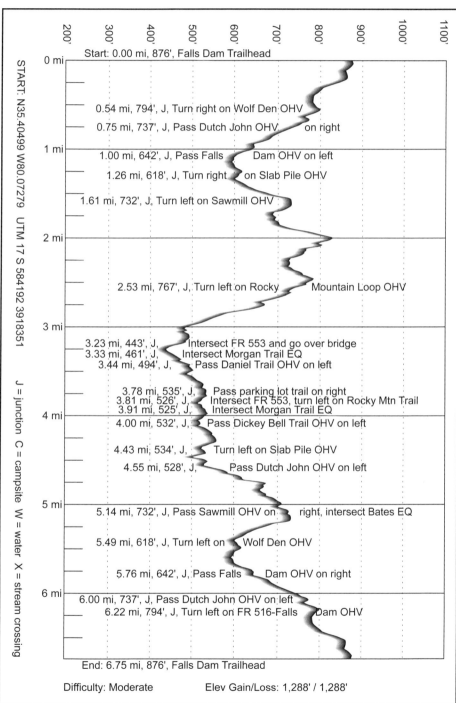

START: N35.40499 W80.07279 UTM 17 S 584192 3918351   J = junction C = campsite W = water X = stream crossing

Start: 0.00 mi, 876', Falls Dam Trailhead

0.54 mi, 794', J, Turn right on Wolf Den OHV
0.75 mi, 737', J, Pass Dutch John OHV on right

1.00 mi, 642', J, Pass Falls Dam OHV on left
1.26 mi, 618', J, Turn right on Slab Pile OHV

1.61 mi, 732', J, Turn left on Sawmill OHV

2.53 mi, 767', J, Turn left on Rocky Mountain Loop OHV

3.23 mi, 443', J, Intersect FR 553 and go over bridge
3.33 mi, 461', J, Intersect Morgan Trail EQ
3.44 mi, 494', J, Pass Daniel Trail OHV on left

3.78 mi, 535', J, Pass parking lot trail on right
3.81 mi, 526', J, Intersect FR 553, turn left on Rocky Mtn Trail
3.91 mi, 525', J, Intersect Morgan Trail EQ
4.00 mi, 532', J, Pass Dickey Bell Trail OHV on left

4.43 mi, 534', J, Turn left on Slab Pile OHV

4.55 mi, 528', J, Pass Dutch John OHV on left

5.14 mi, 732', J, Pass Sawmill OHV on right, intersect Bates EQ

5.49 mi, 618', J, Turn left on Wolf Den OHV

5.76 mi, 642', J, Pass Falls Dam OHV on right

6.00 mi, 737', J, Pass Dutch John OHV on left
6.22 mi, 794', J, Turn left on FR 516-Falls Dam OHV

End: 6.75 mi, 876', Falls Dam Trailhead

Difficulty: Moderate   Elev Gain/Loss: 1,288' / 1,288'

BLRA Trip J

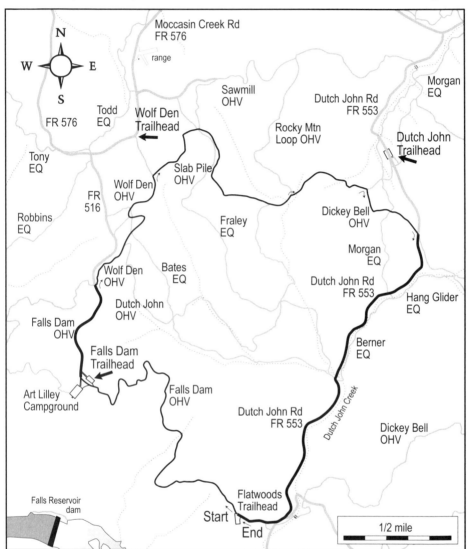

Elevation Profile: BLRA Trip J

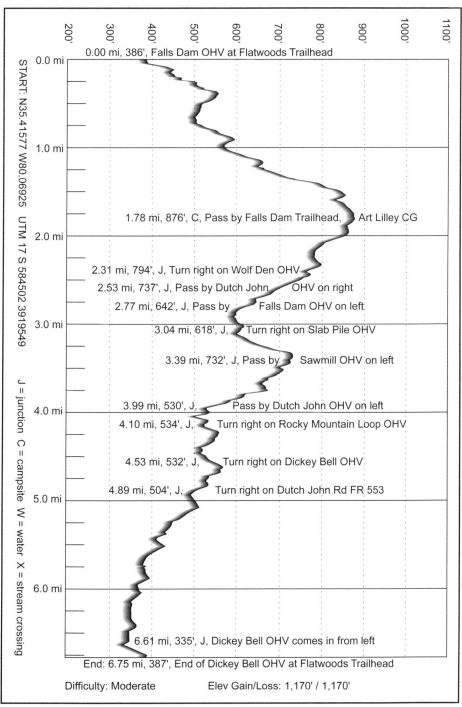

START: N35.41577 W80.06925 UTM 17 S 584502 3919549

J = junction C = campsite W = water X = stream crossing

0.00 mi, 386', Falls Dam OHV at Flatwoods Trailhead

1.78 mi, 876', C, Pass by Falls Dam Trailhead,   Art Lilley CG

2.31 mi, 794', J, Turn right on Wolf Den OHV

2.53 mi, 737', J, Pass by Dutch John   OHV on right

2.77 mi, 642', J, Pass by   Falls Dam OHV on left

3.04 mi, 618', J,   Turn right on Slab Pile OHV

3.39 mi, 732', J, Pass by   Sawmill OHV on left

3.99 mi, 530', J,   Pass by Dutch John OHV on left

4.10 mi, 534', J,   Turn right on Rocky Mountain Loop OHV

4.53 mi, 532', J,   Turn right on Dickey Bell OHV

4.89 mi, 504', J,   Turn right on Dutch John Rd FR 553

6.61 mi, 335', J, Dickey Bell OHV comes in from left

End: 6.75 mi, 387', End of Dickey Bell OHV at Flatwoods Trailhead

Difficulty: Moderate   Elev Gain/Loss: 1,170' / 1,170'

BLRA Trip K

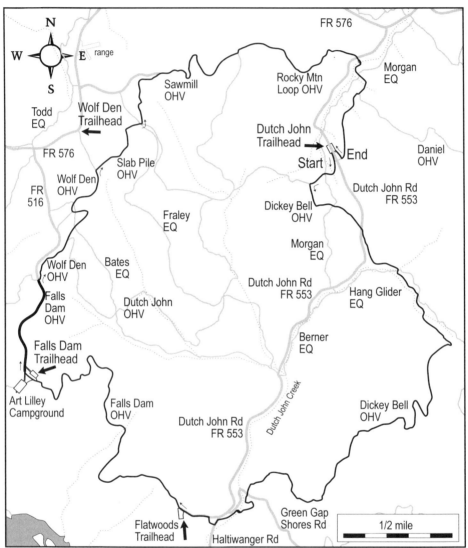

Elevation Profile: BLRA Trip K

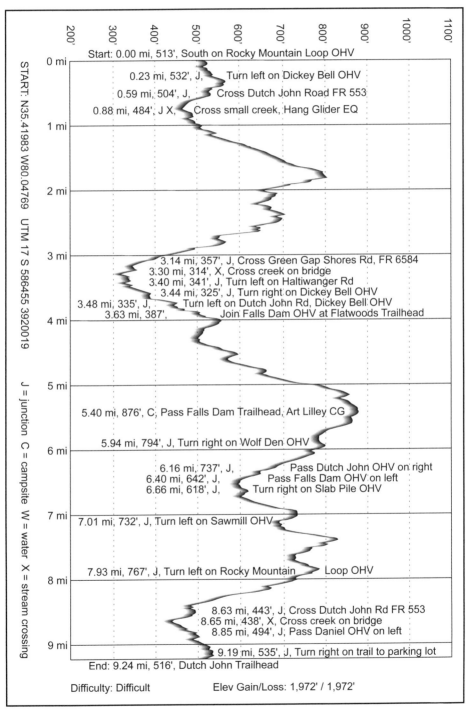

START: N35.41983 W80.04769   UTM 17 S 586455 3920019

J = junction C = campsite W = water X = stream crossing

Start: 0.00 mi, 513', South on Rocky Mountain Loop OHV

0.23 mi, 532', J, Turn left on Dickey Bell OHV

0.59 mi, 504', J, Cross Dutch John Road FR 553

0.88 mi, 484', J X, Cross small creek, Hang Glider EQ

3.14 mi, 357', J, Cross Green Gap Shores Rd, FR 6584

3.30 mi, 314', X, Cross creek on bridge

3.40 mi, 341', J, Turn left on Haltiwanger Rd

3.44 mi, 325', J, Turn right on Dickey Bell OHV

3.48 mi, 335', J, Turn left on Dutch John Rd, Dickey Bell OHV

3.63 mi, 387', Join Falls Dam OHV at Flatwoods Trailhead

5.40 mi, 876', C, Pass Falls Dam Trailhead, Art Lilley CG

5.94 mi, 794', J, Turn right on Wolf Den OHV

6.16 mi, 737', J, Pass Dutch John OHV on right

6.40 mi, 642', J, Pass Falls Dam OHV on left

6.66 mi, 618', J, Turn right on Slab Pile OHV

7.01 mi, 732', J, Turn left on Sawmill OHV

7.93 mi, 767', J, Turn left on Rocky Mountain Loop OHV

8.63 mi, 443', J, Cross Dutch John Rd FR 553

8.65 mi, 438', X, Cross creek on bridge

8.85 mi, 494', J, Pass Daniel OHV on left

9.19 mi, 535', J, Turn right on trail to parking lot

End: 9.24 mi, 516', Dutch John Trailhead

Difficulty: Difficult   Elev Gain/Loss: 1,972' / 1,972'

BLRA Trip L

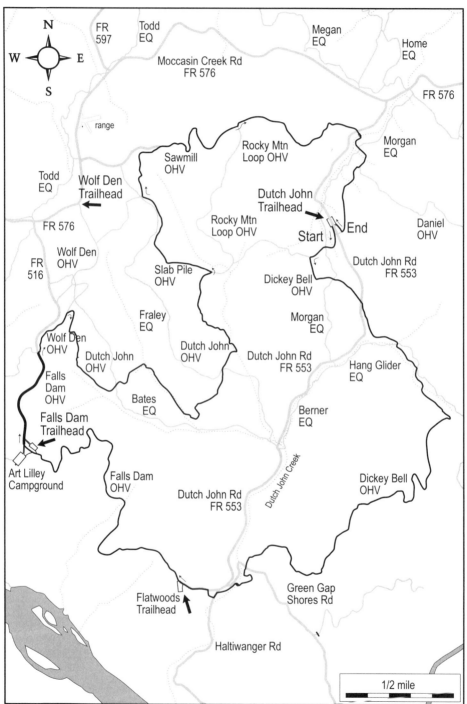

Elevation Profile: BLRA Trip L

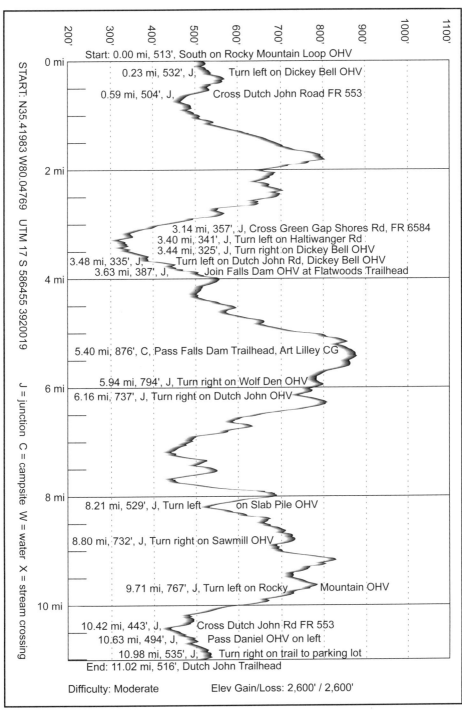

START: N35.41983 W80.04769 UTM 17 S 586455 3920019

J = junction C = campsite W = water X = stream crossing

Start: 0.00 mi, 513', South on Rocky Mountain Loop OHV

0.23 mi, 532', J, Turn left on Dickey Bell OHV

0.59 mi, 504', J, Cross Dutch John Road FR 553

3.14 mi, 357', J, Cross Green Gap Shores Rd, FR 6584
3.40 mi, 341', J, Turn left on Haltiwanger Rd
3.44 mi, 325', J, Turn right on Dickey Bell OHV
3.48 mi, 335', J, Turn left on Dutch John Rd, Dickey Bell OHV
3.63 mi, 387', J, Join Falls Dam OHV at Flatwoods Trailhead

5.40 mi, 876', C, Pass Falls Dam Trailhead, Art Lilley CG

5.94 mi, 794', J, Turn right on Wolf Den OHV
6.16 mi, 737', J, Turn right on Dutch John OHV

8.21 mi, 529', J, Turn left on Slab Pile OHV

8.80 mi, 732', J, Turn right on Sawmill OHV

9.71 mi, 767', J, Turn left on Rocky Mountain OHV

10.42 mi, 443', J, Cross Dutch John Rd FR 553
10.63 mi, 494', J, Pass Daniel OHV on left
10.98 mi, 535', J, Turn right on trail to parking lot

End: 11.02 mi, 516', Dutch John Trailhead

Difficulty: Moderate   Elev Gain/Loss: 2,600' / 2,600'

BLRA Trip M

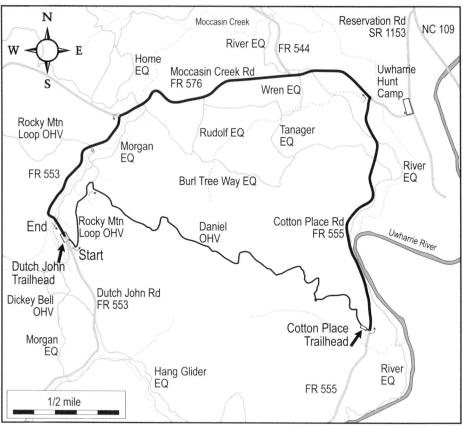

Elevation Profile: BLRA Trip M

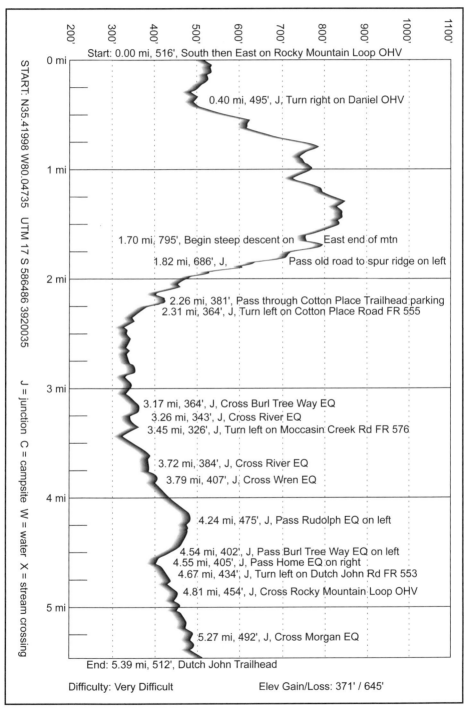

START: N35.41998 W80.04735 UTM 17 S 586486 3920035

J = junction C = campsite W = water X = stream crossing

Start: 0.00 mi, 516', South then East on Rocky Mountain Loop OHV

0.40 mi, 495', J, Turn right on Daniel OHV

1.70 mi, 795', Begin steep descent on   East end of mtn

1.82 mi, 686', J,   Pass old road to spur ridge on left

2.26 mi, 381', Pass through Cotton Place Trailhead parking
2.31 mi, 364', J, Turn left on Cotton Place Road FR 555

3.17 mi, 364', J, Cross Burl Tree Way EQ
3.26 mi, 343', J, Cross River EQ
3.45 mi, 326', J, Turn left on Moccasin Creek Rd FR 576

3.72 mi, 384', J, Cross River EQ
3.79 mi, 407', J, Cross Wren EQ

4.24 mi, 475', J, Pass Rudolph EQ on left

4.54 mi, 402', J, Pass Burl Tree Way EQ on left
4.55 mi, 405', J, Pass Home EQ on right
4.67 mi, 434', J, Turn left on Dutch John Rd FR 553

4.81 mi, 454', J, Cross Rocky Mountain Loop OHV

5.27 mi, 492', J, Cross Morgan EQ

End: 5.39 mi, 512', Dutch John Trailhead

Difficulty: Very Difficult   Elev Gain/Loss: 371' / 645'

Badin Lake Bike Trips

Trip	Use	Length (miles)	Elevation Gain/ Loss	Difficulty Rating	Page
BLRA Trip N	EBH	6.56	1,220' / 1,220'	Moderate	194
BLRA Trip O	OEBH	6.86	1,169' / 1,169'	Moderate	196
BLRA Trip P	EBH	8.79	1,646' / 1,646'	Difficult	198
BLRA Trip Q	EBH	16.16	2,907' / 2,907'	Difficult +	200

This selection of trips was chosen to offer a range of mountain bike riding experiences, mostly differentiated by length. The length of the trips vary - 6+miles, 9+ miles, and 16+ miles. These Trips are rated from Moderate to Extremely Difficult.

Although this section is labeled "Bike Trips", any of these routes can be legally used by horseback riders or hikers. Trip O can even be used by street-legal OHVs. Refer to the use icons at the top of each page for appropriate use types.

For visitors staying overnight, the three main USFS campgrounds in the Badin Lake Recreation Area are relatively close to each other. Three of the Trips start at an intersection that is centrally located to these campgrounds, allowing you to ride out and return without having to drive.

Most of the Trips pass through trailheads and can be started there as an alternative. There is a small pull-off parking area near the intersection where the other Trips start, similar to other pull-offs found throughout the Forest. This spot can accomodate 2-3 vehicles, but it is not maintained as an official parking place.

Trips O and Q include OHV trail sections. Trail passes are required on the OHV trails for all wheeled vehicles, including mountain bikes. As of 2014, "trail passes" are $5 per day. Season passes are $30. Passes can be purchased at most local stores, like the Eldorado Outpost. All OHV trails are closed each year from around December 15th to March 31st.

BLRA Trip N

Map	page 194	**Difficulty**	Moderate
Length	6.55 miles	**Configuration**	Loop
Trailhead	Near BL CGs	**Elev Gain/Loss**	1,209' / 1,209'

Start Coordinates N35.44642, W80.06492;   17 S 584863 3922952

BLRA Trip N starts at the intersection of FR 597 and FR 597A. This Trip follows equestrian trails and a section of FR 597, making it suitable for bikes, horses, and hikers.

BLRA Trip O

Map	page 196	**Difficulty**	Moderate
Length	6.86 miles	**Configuration**	Loop
Trailhead	Falls Dam	**Elev Gain/Loss**	1,169' / 1,169'

Start Coordinates N35.40499, W80.07279;   17 S 584192 3918351

BLRA Trip O starts at the Falls Dam Trailhead, which is adjacent to the Art Lilley Campground. This Trip follows OHV trails and a long section of FR 553. It is suitable for bikes, horses, hikers, and street-legal OHVs.

BLRA Trip P

Map	page 198	**Difficulty**	Difficult
Length	8.79 miles	**Configuration**	Loop
Trailhead	Near BL CGs	**Elev Gain/Loss**	1,646' / 1,646'

Start Coordinates N35.44642, W80.06492;   17 S 584863 3922952

BLRA Trip P starts at the intersection of FR 597 and FR 597A. This Trip follows equestrian trails and a section of FR 597. It is suitable for bikes, horses, and hikers.

BLRA Trip Q

Map	page 200	**Difficulty**	Difficult +
Length	16.16 miles	**Configuration**	Loop
Trailhead	Near BL CGs	**Elev Gain/Loss**	2,907' / 2,907'

Start Coordinates N35.44642, W80.06492;   17 S 584863 3922952

BLRA Trip Q is a longer route on the harder side of Difficult. The trip starts at the intersection of FR 597 and FR 597A. This trip generally follows a Loop route, although you could call it a double lollipop with the small loop out to the lakeshore near the end. This Trip follows equestrian trails, OHV trails, and a few sections of graveled Forest Service roads. It is suitable for bikes, horses, and hikers.

Badin Lake Trip N

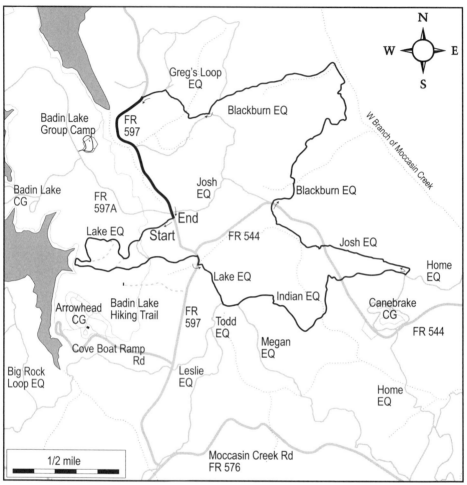

Elevation Profile: BLRA Trip N

START: N35.44642 W80.06492 UTM 17 S 584863 3922952   J = junction C = campsite W = water X = stream crossing

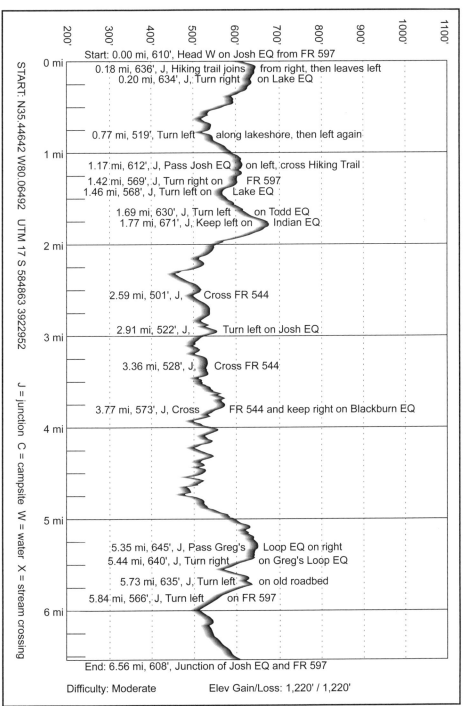

Start: 0.00 mi, 610', Head W on Josh EQ from FR 597

0.18 mi, 636', J, Hiking trail joins from right, then leaves left
0.20 mi, 634', J, Turn right on Lake EQ

0.77 mi, 519', Turn left along lakeshore, then left again

1.17 mi, 612', J, Pass Josh EQ on left, cross Hiking Trail
1.42 mi, 569', J, Turn right on FR 597
1.46 mi, 568', J, Turn left on Lake EQ

1.69 mi, 630', J, Turn left on Todd EQ
1.77 mi, 671', J, Keep left on Indian EQ

2.59 mi, 501', J, Cross FR 544

2.91 mi, 522', J, Turn left on Josh EQ

3.36 mi, 528', J, Cross FR 544

3.77 mi, 573', J, Cross FR 544 and keep right on Blackburn EQ

5.35 mi, 645', J, Pass Greg's Loop EQ on right
5.44 mi, 640', J, Turn right on Greg's Loop EQ

5.73 mi, 635', J, Turn left on old roadbed
5.84 mi, 566', J, Turn left on FR 597

End: 6.56 mi, 608', Junction of Josh EQ and FR 597

Difficulty: Moderate   Elev Gain/Loss: 1,220' / 1,220'

Badin Lake Trip O

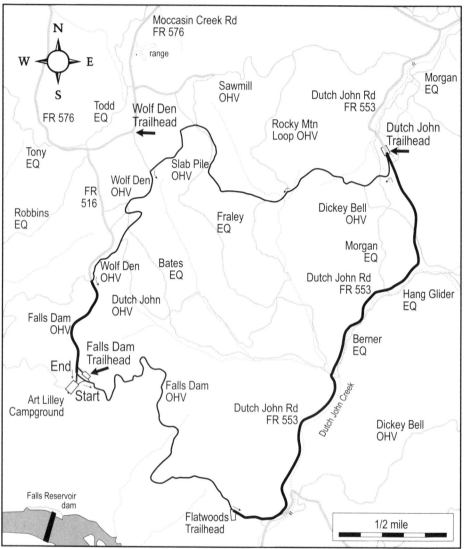

Elevation Profile: BLRA Trip O

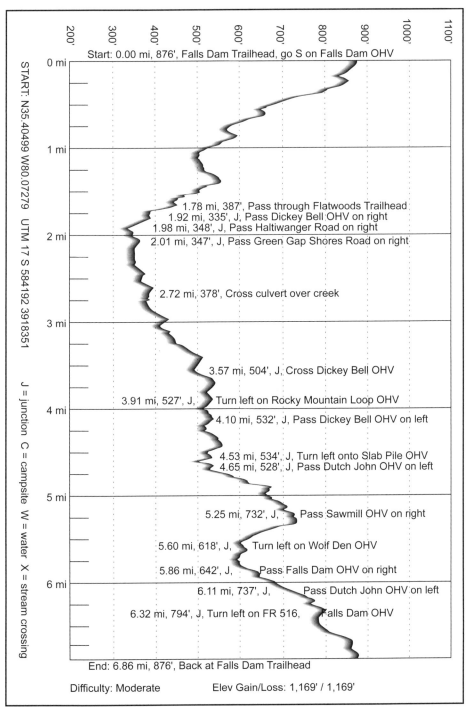

START: N35.40499 W80.07279   UTM 17 S 584192 3918351   J = junction C = campsite W = water X = stream crossing

Start: 0.00 mi, 876', Falls Dam Trailhead, go S on Falls Dam OHV

1.78 mi, 387', Pass through Flatwoods Trailhead
1.92 mi, 335', J, Pass Dickey Bell OHV on right
1.98 mi, 348', J, Pass Haltiwanger Road on right
2.01 mi, 347', J, Pass Green Gap Shores Road on right

2.72 mi, 378', Cross culvert over creek

3.57 mi, 504', J, Cross Dickey Bell OHV

3.91 mi, 527', J, Turn left on Rocky Mountain Loop OHV

4.10 mi, 532', J, Pass Dickey Bell OHV on left

4.53 mi, 534', J, Turn left onto Slab Pile OHV
4.65 mi, 528', J, Pass Dutch John OHV on left

5.25 mi, 732', J, Pass Sawmill OHV on right

5.60 mi, 618', J, Turn left on Wolf Den OHV

5.86 mi, 642', J, Pass Falls Dam OHV on right

6.11 mi, 737', J, Pass Dutch John OHV on left

6.32 mi, 794', J, Turn left on FR 516, Falls Dam OHV

End: 6.86 mi, 876', Back at Falls Dam Trailhead

Difficulty: Moderate   Elev Gain/Loss: 1,169' / 1,169'

Badin Lake Trip P

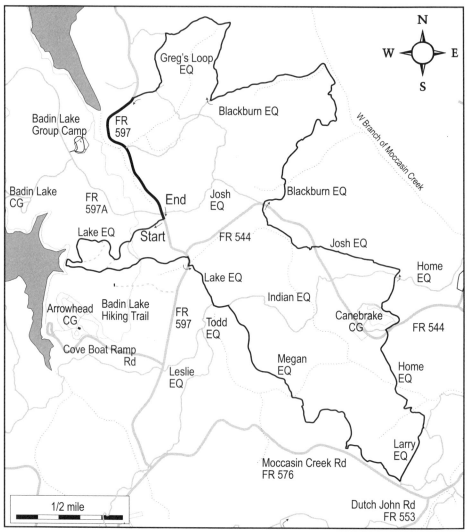

Elevation Profile: BLRA Trip P

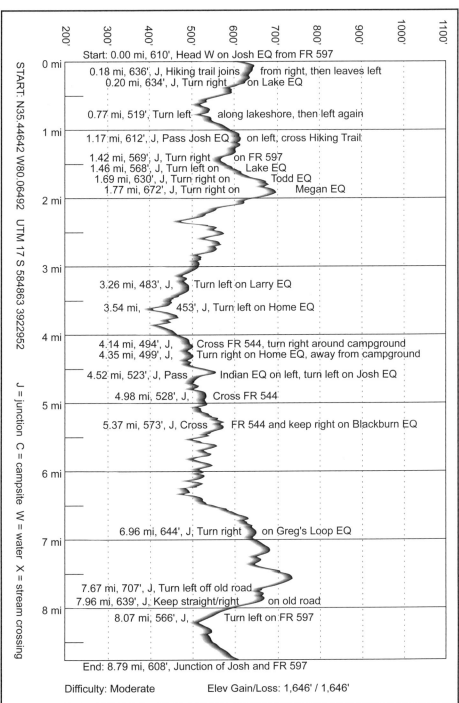

START: N35.44642 W80.06492 UTM 17 S 584863 3922952   J = junction C = campsite W = water X = stream crossing

Start: 0.00 mi, 610', Head W on Josh EQ from FR 597

0.18 mi, 636', J, Hiking trail joins from right, then leaves left
0.20 mi, 634', J, Turn right on Lake EQ

0.77 mi, 519', Turn left along lakeshore, then left again

1.17 mi, 612', J, Pass Josh EQ on left, cross Hiking Trail

1.42 mi, 569', J, Turn right on FR 597
1.46 mi, 568', J, Turn left on Lake EQ
1.69 mi, 630', J, Turn right on Todd EQ
1.77 mi, 672', J, Turn right on Megan EQ

3.26 mi, 483', J, Turn left on Larry EQ

3.54 mi, 453', J, Turn left on Home EQ

4.14 mi, 494', J, Cross FR 544, turn right around campground
4.35 mi, 499', J, Turn right on Home EQ, away from campground

4.52 mi, 523', J, Pass Indian EQ on left, turn left on Josh EQ

4.98 mi, 528', J, Cross FR 544

5.37 mi, 573', J, Cross FR 544 and keep right on Blackburn EQ

6.96 mi, 644', J, Turn right on Greg's Loop EQ

7.67 mi, 707', J, Turn left off old road
7.96 mi, 639', J, Keep straight/right on old road
8.07 mi, 566', J, Turn left on FR 597

End: 8.79 mi, 608', Junction of Josh and FR 597

Difficulty: Moderate   Elev Gain/Loss: 1,646' / 1,646'

Badin Lake Trip Q

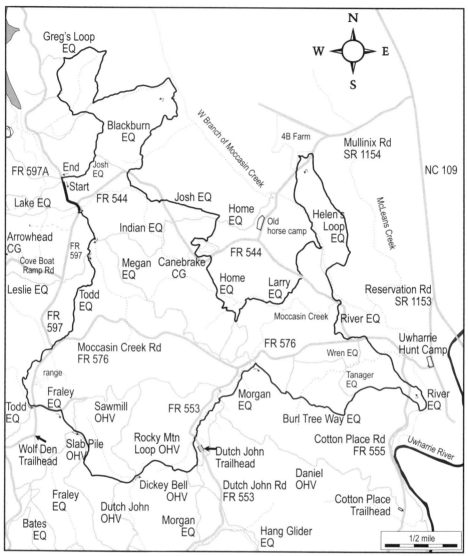

Elevation Profile: BLRA Trip Q

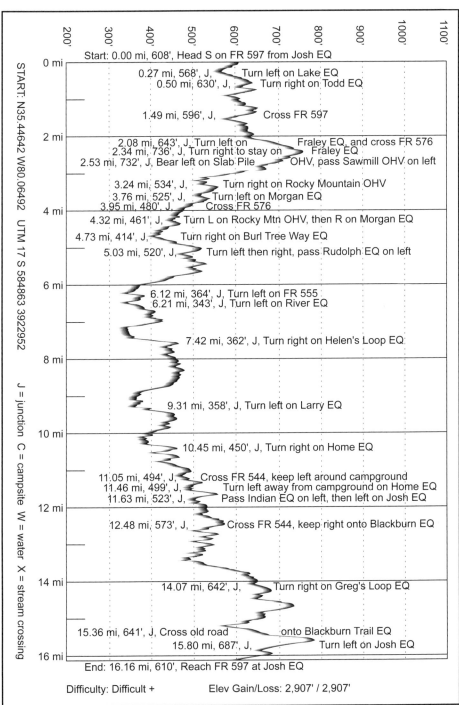

START: N35.44642 W80.06492 UTM 17 S 584863 3922952

J = junction C = campsite W = water X = stream crossing

Start: 0.00 mi, 608', Head S on FR 597 from Josh EQ

0.27 mi, 568', J,   Turn left on Lake EQ
0.50 mi, 630', J,   Turn right on Todd EQ

1.49 mi, 596', J,   Cross FR 597

2.08 mi, 643', J, Turn left on   Fraley EQ, and cross FR 576
2.34 mi, 736', J, Turn right to stay on   Fraley EQ
2.53 mi, 732', J, Bear left on Slab Pile   OHV, pass Sawmill OHV on left

3.24 mi, 534', J,   Turn right on Rocky Mountain OHV
3.76 mi, 525', J,   Turn left on Morgan EQ
3.95 mi, 480', J,   Cross FR 576
4.32 mi, 461', J,   Turn L on Rocky Mtn OHV, then R on Morgan EQ

4.73 mi, 414', J,   Turn right on Burl Tree Way EQ
5.03 mi, 520', J,   Turn left then right, pass Rudolph EQ on left

6.12 mi, 364', J, Turn left on FR 555
6.21 mi, 343', J, Turn left on River EQ

7.42 mi, 362', J, Turn right on Helen's Loop EQ

9.31 mi, 358', J, Turn left on Larry EQ

10.45 mi, 450', J, Turn right on Home EQ

11.05 mi, 494', J,   Cross FR 544, keep left around campground
11.46 mi, 499', J,   Turn left away from campground on Home EQ
11.63 mi, 523', J,   Pass Indian EQ on left, then left on Josh EQ

12.48 mi, 573', J,   Cross FR 544, keep right onto Blackburn EQ

14.07 mi, 642', J,   Turn right on Greg's Loop EQ

15.36 mi, 641', J, Cross old road   onto Blackburn Trail EQ
15.80 mi, 687', J,   Turn left on Josh EQ

End: 16.16 mi, 610', Reach FR 597 at Josh EQ

Difficulty: Difficult +   Elev Gain/Loss: 2,907' / 2,907'

Birkhead Mountains Wilderness Area

A long mountain ridge runs north-south through the center of the Birkhead Mountains Wilderness. The north end of this ridge is Coolers Knob Mountain. The south end is Birkhead Mountain. Coolers Knob tops out around 940' in elevation. The area surrounding this mountain ridge is commonly known as the Birkhead Mountains.

Two tributaries of Hannahs Creek parallel the ridge; Robbins Branch on the west side, and the North Prong of Hannahs Creek on the east side. The creeks join together at the south end of the mountain.

About 3,000 acres were once owned by Watt Birkhead, a local farmer and mill operator. Mr. Birkhead had a house built on his "plantation" in 1904 and lived there for over ten years. The plantation was made up of several different home places. Many of these home places and family graveyards can still be found along the trails. There are also several old gold mines adjacent to the trails. Joe Moffitt, who was raised nearby, collected a lot of the local history of these mountains and recorded it in two books, one of which is titled *An Afternoon Hike Into The Past*, written in the mid-1970's.

Mr. Moffitt and Mike Chisholm, another hiking enthusiast, started working towards establishing the Uwharrie Trail in the late 1960's. Joe wanted to create a system of trails that could help teach young people proper values by reconnecting them to the land and our cultural history. Joe and Mike worked with USFS District Ranger Robert "Bob" Carey in planning out and getting approval for the trail on USFS lands. They also met with private property owners and arranged permission to run trail across their land.

The first sections of trail were put on the ground in late 1960's. Boy Scouts from Moffitt's troop put in a significant amount of the volunteer labor required to create the trails. Scouts working on Eagle Projects built many of the stone fireplaces found at the various campsites in the Birkheads. A few of these fireplaces were removed in subsequent years.

Scouts continue to work on these trails today, including projects such as the bridge on the Thornburg Trail. Moffitt also founded the Uwharrie Trail Club, a group of outdoor enthusiasts who volunteer their time to help maintain the trails as well as organize outdoor fun trips.

In the beginning, part of the original Uwharrie Trail followed the route of what is now the Robbins Branch Trail. The original trail route was located so it would run by various places of interest in the area, such as old home places and gold mines. The Uwharrie Trail ran south from the Birkhead Mountains across private lands to other USFS lands in Montgomery County. From there the trail followed public land southward for over 20 miles to end at NC 24-27. The total length of the trail was about 35 miles.

Sections of the original trail that crossed private property were "unrecognized" by the USFS around 1980, partly due to the process of applying for National Recreation Trail designation for the southern end of the Uwharrie Trail, and partly because of real and perceived disputes with landowners. This closure effectively separated trails in the Birkhead Mountains area from the southern portions of the Uwharrie Trail.

In 1984, nearly 4,800 acres of public land southwest of Asheboro, NC were designated as the Birkhead Mountains Wilderness Area. The area is rich in historical sites, most of which are hidden in the forest that has reclaimed the numerous homesteads that once dotted this mountainous region. Five main hiking trails connect to form a trail network through the Birkheads. Several side trails extend from these main trails to provide access to campsites or other points of interest. Because of the Wilderness designation, trails in the Birkhead Mountains are only open to foot travel. These trails, unlike most in Wilderness areas, are marked and occasionally maintained. In 2013, the USFS expressed an interest in removing some of the newer signage placed in the Wilderness.

In 1997, a group of trail enthusiasts formed the Uwharrie Trail Partnership and began serious efforts to reconnect the Birkhead Mountains Wilderness Area with the southern section of the Uwharrie Trail. This organization later grew into the Greater Uwharrie Conservation Partnership. See the Volunteer Opportunities chapter for more information about these organizations. More details about efforts to protect and reopen the trail can be found in the chapter on the Uwharrie Trail.

CAMPING

In addition to establishing trails in the Birkhead Mountains, Joe Moffitt's Boy Scouts also established several permanent campsites. Most of these campsites have rock fireplace/grills. Most are located near a spring or other water source. The exception is Camp 5, which was intended to be a dry campsite. There are other informal camp sites throughout the area and camping is allowed anywhere, but it is especially important that campers follow Leave No Trace ethics when doing so.

MAPS

A black and white topographic map for the "Birkhead Mountains Wilderness Trail", updated 5/10/11, was available online from the USFS website at the time of this guide's publication. This map does not include the Camp Three Trail or side trails, shows the Thornburg and Robbins Branch trailheads too far from the road, and incorrectly shows the southern end of Birkhead Mountain Trail connecting to a public road.

USGS topographic quadrangle maps covering this area are: Eleazer, Farmer. The 1994 revisions show a rough approximation of the main trails, but are missing the Camp Three and Thornburg Trails.

ACCESS

Tot Hill Farm Trailhead

Tot Hill Farm Trailhead is located at the north end of the area, on Tot Hill Farm Road (SR 1163).
You should see brown and white Forest Service signs on NC 49

UTM	17S 599168 3944206
Lat/Lon	N35.63669 W79.90472

indicating the turn for the trailhead. There is a small parking lot for 10-15 cars and a map kiosk at this trailhead. Birkhead Mountain Trail begins at this trailhead. In the first edition of this guidebook, this trailhead was called Talbott's Branch Trailhead. The parking area was built around 2008.

Thornburg Trailhead

Thornburg Trailhead is located on the north west side of the area. Turn north onto Science Hill Road (SR 1163) from NC 49. This is the same intersection as the

UTM	17S 595471 3942421
Lat/Lon	N35.62097 W79.94575

western end of Tot Hill Farm Road. The road is named Science Hill Road to the north of NC 49 and Tot Hill Farm Road to the south. From the end of Science Hill Road, turn left onto Lassiter Mill Road (SR 1107). After driving 2.7 miles, turn left into the graveled drive for the trailhead. You should see brown and white Forest Service signs indicating the turn for the trailhead. There is a small parking lot for 6 to 10 cars at the farm. The Thornburg Trail begins at this trailhead.

Robbins Branch Trailhead

Robbins Branch Trailhead is located on the south west side of the area. From NC 49, turn north onto Science Hill Road (SR 1163), then left onto Lassiter Mill Road (SR

UTM	17S 594422 3938673
Lat/Lon	N35.58728 W79.95777

1107). At 2.7 miles you will pass by the Thornburg Trailhead. After driving 5.4

Birkhead Mountains Wilderness Area

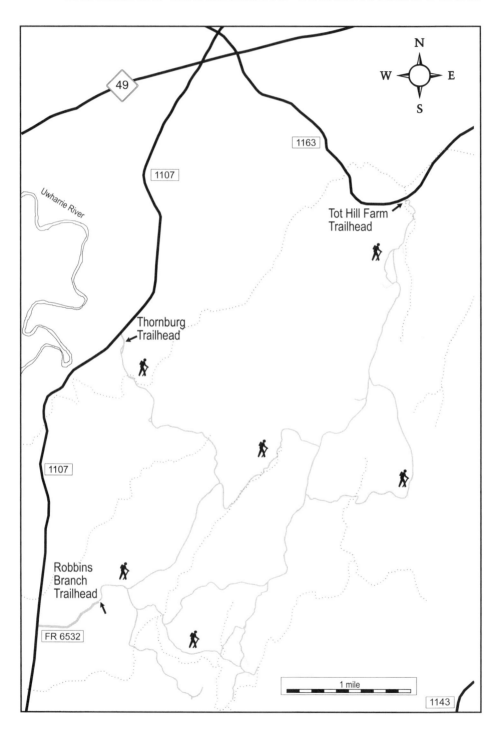

miles, turn left onto graveled Robbins Branch Road (FR 6532). You should see brown and white Forest Service signs indicating the turn for the trailhead. Robbins Branch Trailhead is a small grassy parking area at the end of Robbins Branch Road, with room for 15-20 vehicles. Robbins Branch Trail begins at this trailhead.

NOTES OF INTEREST
Although parts of this area were cleared for farming in the past, and all of the forest has been logged at least once before, most of the scenic vistas and open fields along the trails have disappeared as forest reclaimed the land.

WHAT IS WILDERNESS?
(Reprinted from the 1987 USFS Birkhead Mountains Wilderness map & brochure)

The goal of Wilderness designation is to protect and preserve the natural resources and wilderness character, provide for public use, and reduce conflicts between this use and the values of wilderness. Wilderness values include solitude and naturalness, as well as ecological features. Wilderness exists for its own intrinsic values. Economy, user comfort and convenience, or commercial value are not standards of wilderness management or use. Where a choice must be made between wilderness values and human use, preserving the wilderness resource is the overriding value. The guiding principle is to allow the natural processes to shape the environment.

What is allowed?
Primitive recreation activities such as backpacking and camping
Hunting and fishing according to State regulations
Trail construction and maintenance to primitive standards
Collection of nuts, berries, cones for personal use

What is prohibited?
Timber harvesting
Mechanical Transport (bicycles, wagons, carts)
Motorized vehicles and equipment
Removal of artifacts

As a visitor to the wilderness, you should be aware that you are entering a primitive environment. You will meet and live with nature on its own terms, and become familiar with the sometimes scary feeling of being completely on your own, away from the comforts and conveniences of civilization. Path finding is an integral part of the wilderness experience. To ensure this opportunity, wilderness trails are kept primitive, rugged, and often steep. You will experience a challenge of traveling through these mountains similar to that of the early pioneers and settlers. You should know how to read a topographic map and use a compass.

Birkhead Mountains Wilderness Trails

Trail Name	Length (miles)	Elevation Gain/Loss	Difficulty Rating	Map (page)
Birkhead Mountain	5.01	800' / 860'	Moderate	216
Camp Four	0.38	35' / 150'	Moderate	218
Camp Three	2.19	400' / 410'	Moderate	220
Cooper Mtn Cemetary	1.21	320' / 190'	Moderate	222
Hannah's Creek	1.35	250' / 230'	Easy	224
Old Road	1.08	260' / 90'	Moderate	224
Robbins Branch	3.06	630' / 340'	Moderate	226
Thornburg	1.74	350' / 155'	Moderate	228

Birkhead Mountain Trail

Map	page 216	**Difficulty**	Moderate
Length	5.01 miles	**Configuration**	One Way
Trailhead	Tot Hill Farm	**Elev Gain/Loss**	800' / 860'

Start Coordinates N35.63636, W79.90460;   17 S 584227 3920058

Birkhead Mountain Trail begins at Tot Hill Farm Trailhead, at the north end of the Wilderness Area. This trail was part of the original Uwharrie Trail in the early 1970's. The name was changed to Birkhead Mountain Trail in the 1980's when the sections of trail on private land just south of the Wilderness Area were closed. Birkhead Mountain Trail is marked with white paint blazes.

The Tot Hill Farm Trailhead and parking lot was built in the late 2000's. In the first edition of this guide, this end of the Birkhead Mountain Trail was called the Talbott's Branch Trailhead. There were no parking spaces there at that time.

After crossing Talbott's Branch, the route ascends towards the top of Coolers Knob. Most of the trail lies under forest cover now, so long distance views are mostly limited to winter time.

Forrester Road

On the way up the mountain, an optional route to the left offers a slightly different way up the mountain. This alternative is known as the Forrester Road. The Forrester family home place was located along this road. Their old sawmill site can be seen along the way. This 0.3 mile long section of old road takes a more direct route up the mountain. The Birkhead Mountain Trail wanders off to the west a short way before rejoining the old road further up the mountain. The Forrester Road is shown on the map on page 216.

Uphill of the Forrester Road option, the white-blazed trail follows the old roadbed southward on the ridge. There is a junction where the Birkhead Mountain Trail turns to the right off of the road. The Camp Three Trail continues on the old roadbed. There is an unofficial sign at the junction which incorrectly labels the road south as leading to "Camp 7", but this sign may get removed. If you're not paying attention, it's easy to miss the trail as it turns to the right (west).

A short distance beyond the Camp Three Trail intersection, Camp 1B is located in a saddle, right beside the trail. The faint side trail to Camp One and its spring can be found by dropping downhill to the west from the saddle. You'll have to search closely to spot the faint yellow blazes that mark the route.

Continuing southward along the ridge, the Birkhead Mountain Trail route reaches a junction with Robbins Branch Trail on the right. Further down the ridge you will come to a junction with the start of Camp Three Trail on the left. Camp Five is located on the right side of the trail at this junction. There is no water source at Camp Five. Camp Five was intended to be a dry campsite, in order to help campers learn to deal with limited water supplies.

From Camp Five, the route begins dropping down the south end of Birkhead Mountain. Watt Birkhead's plantation was located on the ridge between Camp Five and the side trail to Camp Four. The Scouts erected a sign at this spot giving some details about the Birkheads. Look for the side trail to Camp Four in a small saddle. This side trail hasn't been used or maintained in some time. It leads to the right and can be followed by searching for the remaining yellow blazes. A small creek serves as a water source at Camp Four.

According to Joe Moffitt, the old roadbed that the Birkhead Mountain Trail follows at the south end of the mountain ridge was once part of the Salisbury-Fayetteville Byway or Trail. He suspects that it was once traveled by the likes of Daniel Boone and Jesse and Frank James.

The route then passes a junction to the left with Hannahs Creek Trail. A short distance beyond is the junction to the left with the Camp Six side trail. Camp Six is located near the North Prong of Hannahs Creek.

Birkhead Mountain Trail eventually crosses the North Prong of Hannahs Creek. From the creek the route ascends and ends at the Forest Service property line. On the maps in this guide, the Birkhead Mountain Trail line is shown ending at the North Prong of Hannahs Creek.

Camp One Trail
Camp One Trail begins at the Birkhead Mountain Trail, south of the junction of the north end of the Camp Three Trail. The indistinct Camp One Trail starts in a saddle on the ridgeline and can be hard to find. There is a sign in the saddle indicating Camp One. I must admit that I missed this trail when exploring for the first edition of this book in the 1990's. I misinterpreted the sign as meaning that the "camp" was in the fairly flat saddle itself. The saddle area was labeled Camp 1B in the first edition of this guide book.

As I re-explored the area again in 2012, I lucked upon a faint yellow blaze on the west edge of the saddle. Although there were no signs of a trail on the ground, I descended the rocky slope a little further and discovered another faint yellow blaze. I kept this up until I was standing in the real Camp One!

The trail route descends westward from the saddle for about 0.1 mile and leads to a less-steeply sloped area. Camp One is tucked into a slightly sheltered valley high on the side of the mountain. There is a small rock fire pit in the middle of the camp site. The Camp One Trail is shown, but not labeled, on the map on page 216.

An aluminum sign mounted on a tree indicates that Camp One was built July 22, 1976. The upper portion of the sign is covered by the tree growing over it, but enough of the wording is visible to tell us that the camp was built as an Eagle Scout project planned by Mike Stout. More details about this and other "camps" can be found in the Uwharrie Trail chapter.

Camp Four Trail
Map	page 218	**Difficulty**	Moderate
Length	0.38 miles	**Configuration**	One Way
Trailhead	n/a	**Elev Gain/Loss**	35' / 150'
Start Coordinates	N35.58736, W79.92756; 17 S 597160 3938711		

Camp Four Trail is a footpath first marked by Boy Scouts in the late 1970's. Camp Four Trail begins at its junction with the Birkhead Mountain Trail. This junction is located about a third of a mile north of the junction of the Hannahs Creek Trail and the Birkhead Mountain Trail.

The indistinct Camp Four Trail starts in a small saddle on the ridgeline and can be hard to find. There is no sign in the saddle indicating the Camp Four Trail. As with the trail to Camp One, I missed this trail when exploring for the first edition of this book in the 1990's. I knew from other sources generally where it started and where it went, but that was all.

As I re-explored the area again in 2012, I was determined to find this trail and record its location with a GPS. Working my way north from the Hannah's Creek and the Birkhead Mountain Trail junction, I looked hard at every tree and likely route for a trail to head down the hill to the west. My hiking partner Marcey finally noticed a faint yellow blaze on the west side of the trail in a slight saddle. Although there were no signs of a trail on the ground, we guessed that the trail would have led to the southwest and contoured around the hillside on its way down to the creek. We carefully leapfrogged from one faint blaze to another along the route, expanding our search even wider when the next logical blaze couldn't be found, until we finally dropped into Camp Four!

The trail route leaves the Birkhead Mountain Trail in the saddle and climbs slightly before beginning a gradual descent along the west side of the main ridgeline. There is one section where several blazes are missing. This section crosses a large gully and leaves you to make a large leap of faith in choosing which direction to continue in. But a general southwest direction and gradual descent will keep you on track. Closer to the creek bottom, the laurel undergrowth thickens, but there is still a faint path to follow. Camp Four is tucked neatly into a sheltered valley next to a creek. There is a small stone fireplace hearth in the middle of the camp site.

An unmarked but well-used trail leads from the Camp #4 site southward along the creek and junctions with the Hannahs Creek Trail, about 50 feet east of the prominent chimney along that trail. The distance from the camp site to Hannahs Creek Trail is not much more than 100 feet.

An aluminum sign cemented into the back side of the stone hearth indicates that Camp Four was completed March 3, 1979. More details about this and other "camps" can be found in the Uwharrie Trail chapter.

Camp Three Trail

Map	page 220	Difficulty	Moderate
Length	2.19 miles	Configuration	One Way
Trailhead	n/a	Elev Gain/Loss	400' / 410'

Start Coordinates N35.60246, W79.91892;   17 S 597924 3940394

Camp Three Trail was marked by Boy Scouts in the early 1970's. Camp Three Trail begins at the Birkhead Mountain Trail at Camp Five. The first part of the trail follows a footpath created by the Scouts. Much of the trail tread is hard to follow, due in part to its light use by hikers. I found the trail easier to follow when starting at the Camp Five end (south end). Camp Three Trail is blazed sporadically with various colors of paint. Sometimes there are horizontal green slashes, sometimes there are yellow blazes.

The route descends from the ridge top at Camp Five and passes by several locations that have interesting stories behind them. These spots include Twin Rocks, Bootleg Hollow, Fern Valley, and the old Rush gold mine.

Bootleg Hollow got its name from the story of a gun battle between revenue agents and bootleggers at the site of their moonshine still along the creek in that hollow. Fern Valley is filled with its namesake, but there is also the story of Alfred Hanes. He supposedly grew weary of his wife and made plans to run away with another man's wife. They disappeared but she returned a month or so later. He was never heard from again. The stories told suggest he was caught by the woman's husband and was buried somewhere in Fern Valley, perhaps near where the trail crosses the North Prong of Hannah's Creek in Fern Valley. Perhaps his ghost still wanders there on lonely nights?

If you can find a copy of Joe Moffitt's book *An Afternoon Hike Into The Past*, it is filled with more of the legends and folklore about these and other interesting spots in the Birkhead Mountains.

The route then climbs over a low ridge and passes by several old mines and home sites before dropping into the valley that hosts Camp Three. A stone-walled spring provides water at this camp site. Hancock's guide referred to this as Rush's Mine Camp.

Near Camp #3 the trail passes by the old Rush Gold Mine. The route follows old roadbeds from this point on. Look for forks in the roadbed and always take the left fork. The route gradually ascends and curves back to the left before reaching the top of Coolers Knob Mountain. The route ends at Birkhead Mountain Trail, a short distance north of Camp 1B.

Camp Six Trail

Camp Six Trail was marked by Boy Scouts in the late 1970's. Camp Six Trail begins at its junction with the Birkhead Mountain Trail. This junction is located a few hundred feet south of the junction of the Hannahs Creek Trail and the Birkhead Mountain Trail. There are a couple of old roadbeds converging in this area, as well as the marked trails, which can make this area confusing. There is no sign indicating the start of the Camp Six Trail. The most prominent feature here is the Bingham Graveyard.

The Bingham Graveyard sits on a flat ridge top and is identified by a large aluminum sign and a number of small plain head stones. According to Joseph Moffitt in *An Afternoon Hike Into The Past*, this graveyard was started around

1770 and was last used about 1900. There may be as many as 40 graves here, including several generations of Christopher "Kit" Bingham's family and possibly some of the family's slaves.

The Camp Six Trail heads eastward from the graveyard and drops off the ridge top before turning northward and descending along the hillside to the creek below. The trail is well used and easy to follow. At the Camp #6 site, there is a rock fireplace hearth. More details about this and other "camps" can be found in the Uwharrie Trail chapter.

The Camp Six Trail is about 0.15 miles long and drops about 50 feet in elevation. The Camp Six Trail is shown on the map on page 218.

Cooper Mountain Cemetery Trail

Map	page 222	**Difficulty**	Moderate
Length	1.21 miles	**Configuration**	One Way
Trailhead	n/a	**Elev Gain/Loss**	320' / 190'
Start Coordinates	N35.58922, W79.94326;	17 S 595735 3938902	

Cooper Mountain Cemetery Trail begins at its intersection with the Hannah's Creek Trail, in the southwest corner of the Wilderness Area. This trail was not included in the first edition of this guide, and may not have been fully in existence at that time. There is no sign at the intersection.

The trail route starts out as a faint hiking trail that gently drops downhill. As it nears Hannah's Creek it makes a sharp turn to the left and begins following an old road bed. The route crosses the creek on stepping stones.

After crossing Hannah's Creek, the route begins climbing and soon passes by its namesake. On the left side of the trail is the Cooper Mountain Cemetery. This small cemetery is fenced in and has a new wooden cross bearing the cemetery name.

The route continues following the old road up the mountain. In a saddle near the top is a junction with another old road that leads to the right and south onto private property. The route follows the road as it curves northward and ends on the top of a mountain overlooking the valley through which Hannah's Creek flows.

Hannah's Creek Trail

Map	page 224	**Difficulty**	Easy
Length	1.35 miles	**Configuration**	One Way
Trailhead	n/a	**Elev Gain/Loss**	250' / 230"

Start Coordinates N35.59157, W79.94459;   17 S 595611 3939162

Hannah's Creek Trail starts at its junction with the Robbins Branch Trail. This fairly short trail parallels Hannah's Creek, although not within sight of it, until it leaves to climb a short distance to end at the Birkhead Mountain Trail. Hannah's Creek Trail is marked with white blazes.

The route follows an old roadbed most of the way. It was marked as a trail in the early 1970's, when the other trails were being built in the area by the Boy Scouts.

There are no views from this trail as it stays in the creek bottom for its entire length. An interesting rock chimney from the Bingham home place used to stand beside the trail near the third creek crossing, but it fell down in July of 2013.

Old Road Trail

The unimaginatively named Old Road Trail is my unofficial name for the route that follows an old road bed from the Hannahs Creek Trail to the Birkhead Mountain Trail. Although not officially signed, this 1.08 mile route apparently gets a fair amount of use by hikers. The northern end that joins the Birkhead Mountain Trail is somewhat overgrown and may sometimes be partially obscured by fallen limbs. I've included mention of this trail for the value it adds in creating your own alternate trip routings through this area. The elevation gain/loss is 260' / 90'. The Old Road Trail can be seen on the map on page 224.

Robbins Branch Trail

Map	page 226	**Difficulty**	Moderate
Length	3.06 miles	**Configuration**	One Way
Trailhead	n/a	**Elev Gain/Loss**	630' / 340'

Start Coordinates N35.59014, W79.94873;   17 S 595238 3939000

Robbins Branch Trail starts at the Robbins Branch Trailhead. The route follows an old roadbed most of the way. It was marked as a trail in the early 1970's, when the other trails were being marked and built in the area by the Boy Scouts. This road was originally part of the Uwharrie Trail route. Robbins Branch Trail is marked with white blazes.

A short distance from the trailhead, the route passes a junction with Hannahs Creek Trail, which leads to the right. The route then ascends along a low ridge paralleling Robbins Branch. The next junction reached is with the Thornburg Trail, which leads to the left.

After the Thornburg junction, the route descends to and crosses its namesake. The route crisscrosses the branch several times as it makes its way upstream. There is a small but pretty, informal campsite on the far side of Robbins Branch about 3/4 of a mile up the branch. The route then climbs away from the branch, circling around its headwaters, and ascends to end at the Birkhead Mountain Trail at the southern end of Coolers Knob Mountain.

Thornburg Trail

Map	page 228	**Difficulty**	Moderate
Length	1.74 miles	**Configuration**	One Way
Trailhead	n/a	**Elev Gain/Loss**	350' / 155'
Start Coordinates	N35.61997, W79.94499;	17 S 595541 3942312	

In 1993, the USFS purchased a tract of property along Lassiter Mill Road (SR 1163) known as the Thornburg Farm. The Thornburg Trail was built on this property in 1996 by volunteers from the Uwharrie Trail Club in cooperation with the USFS. This project created a new access route into the Wilderness Area.

In 1997, Cale Lohr, a Boy Scout from High Point, organized and carried out the building of the footbridge over Betty McGees Creek as his Eagle project. The route is marked with white paint blazes.

Thornburg Trail starts at Thornburg Trailhead. A major portion of the trail follows old roadbeds through the Thornburg Farm. The route goes right past the farmhouse and between several barns as it follows a dirt road through the farm and down to Betty McGees Creek. The route continues along the farm road as it passes by several fields. The fields on the farm are often used by dove hunters in September. I mention this because you don't normally encounter dove hunters on a hiking trail, but you might here.

Eventually the route leaves the farm fields and enters the woods to ascend a low ridge. The route then drops to cross a shallow valley before making a final climb to end at the Robbins Branch Trail.

Birkhead Mountain Trail

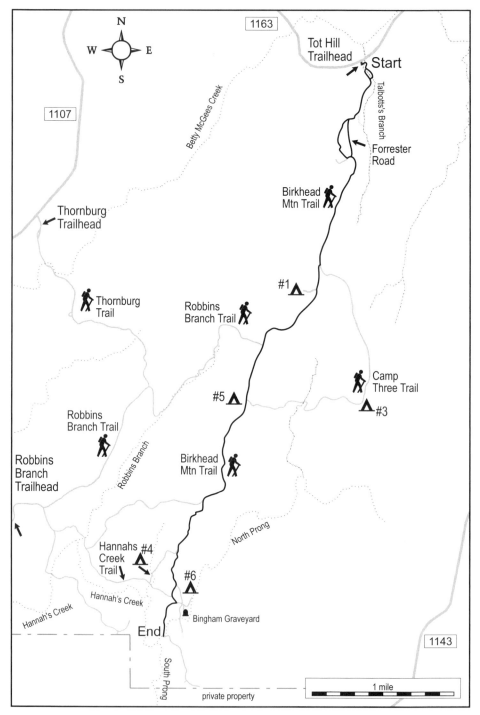

Elevation Profile: Birkhead Mountain Trail

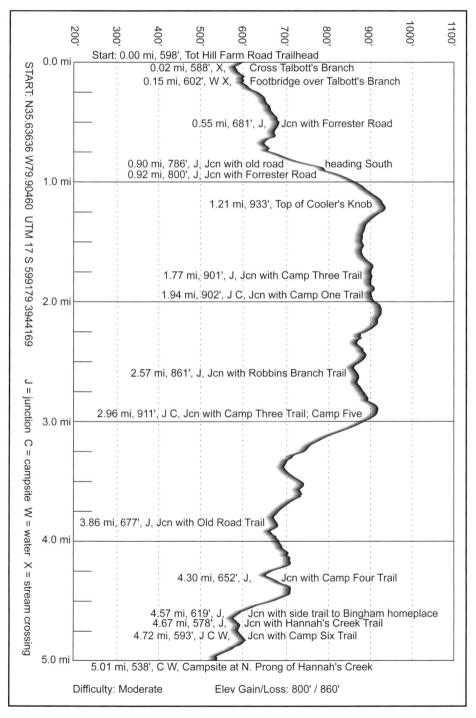

START: N35.63636 W79.90460 UTM 17 S 599179 3944169

J = junction C = campsite W = water X = stream crossing

200' 300' 400' 500' 600' 700' 800' 900' 1000' 1100'

Start: 0.00 mi, 598', Tot Hill Farm Road Trailhead

0.0 mi

0.02 mi, 588', X,   Cross Talbott's Branch
0.15 mi, 602', W X,   Footbridge over Talbott's Branch

0.55 mi, 681', J,   Jcn with Forrester Road

0.90 mi, 786', J, Jcn with old road   heading South
0.92 mi, 800', J, Jcn with Forrester Road

1.0 mi

1.21 mi, 933', Top of Cooler's Knob

1.77 mi, 901', J, Jcn with Camp Three Trail
1.94 mi, 902', J C, Jcn with Camp One Trail

2.0 mi

2.57 mi, 861', J, Jcn with Robbins Branch Trail

2.96 mi, 911', J C, Jcn with Camp Three Trail; Camp Five

3.0 mi

3.86 mi, 677', J, Jcn with Old Road Trail

4.0 mi

4.30 mi, 652', J,   Jcn with Camp Four Trail

4.57 mi, 619', J,   Jcn with side trail to Bingham homeplace
4.67 mi, 578', J,   Jcn with Hannah's Creek Trail
4.72 mi, 593', J C W,   Jcn with Camp Six Trail

5.0 mi

5.01 mi, 538', C W, Campsite at N. Prong of Hannah's Creek

Difficulty: Moderate   Elev Gain/Loss: 800' / 860'

Camp Four Trail

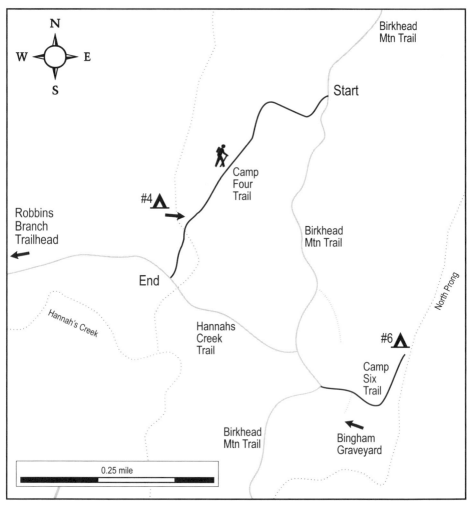

Elevation Profile: Camp Four Trail

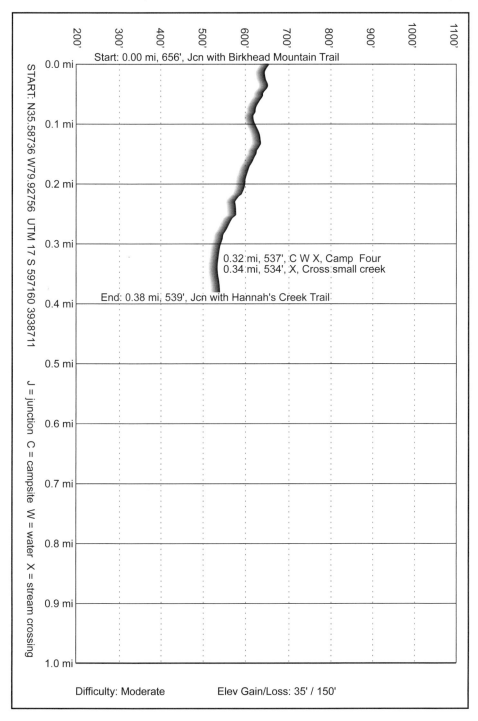

START: N35.58736 W79.92756 UTM 17 S 597160 3938711

J = junction C = campsite W = water X = stream crossing

Start: 0.00 mi, 656', Jcn with Birkhead Mountain Trail

0.32 mi, 537', C W X, Camp Four
0.34 mi, 534', X, Cross small creek

End: 0.38 mi, 539', Jcn with Hannah's Creek Trail

Difficulty: Moderate   Elev Gain/Loss: 35' / 150'

Camp Three Trail

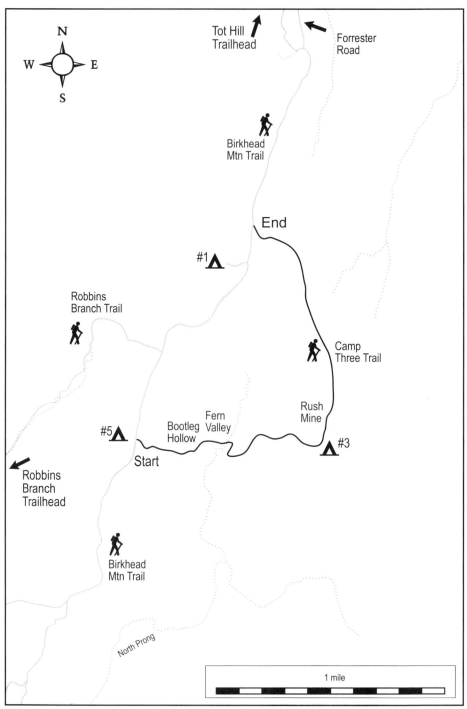

Elevation Profile: Camp Three Trail

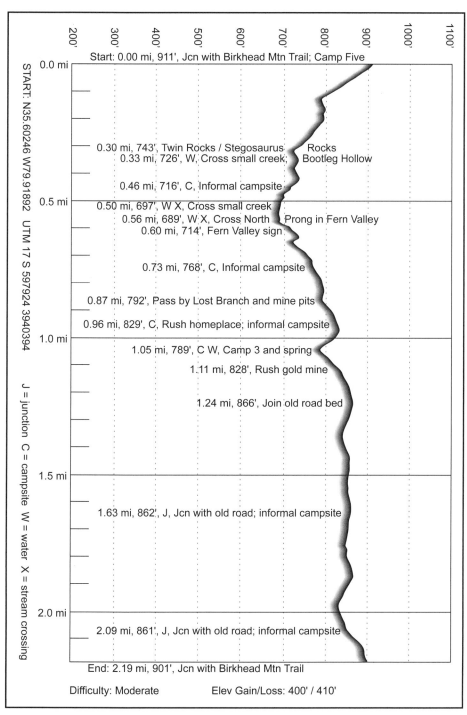

START: N35.60246 W79.91892 UTM 17 S 597924 3940394

J = junction C = campsite W = water X = stream crossing

200' 300' 400' 500' 600' 700' 800' 900' 1000' 1100'

Start: 0.00 mi, 911', Jcn with Birkhead Mtn Trail; Camp Five

0.0 mi

0.30 mi, 743', Twin Rocks / Stegosaurus   Rocks
0.33 mi, 726', W, Cross small creek;   Bootleg Hollow

0.46 mi, 716', C, Informal campsite

0.5 mi

0.50 mi, 697', W X, Cross small creek
0.56 mi, 689', W X, Cross North   Prong in Fern Valley
0.60 mi, 714', Fern Valley sign

0.73 mi, 768', C, Informal campsite

0.87 mi, 792', Pass by Lost Branch and mine pits

0.96 mi, 829', C, Rush homeplace; informal campsite

1.0 mi

1.05 mi, 789', C W, Camp 3 and spring

1.11 mi, 828', Rush gold mine

1.24 mi, 866', Join old road bed

1.5 mi

1.63 mi, 862', J, Jcn with old road; informal campsite

2.0 mi

2.09 mi, 861', J, Jcn with old road; informal campsite

End: 2.19 mi, 901', Jcn with Birkhead Mtn Trail

Difficulty: Moderate   Elev Gain/Loss: 400' / 410'

Cooper Mountain Cemetery Trail

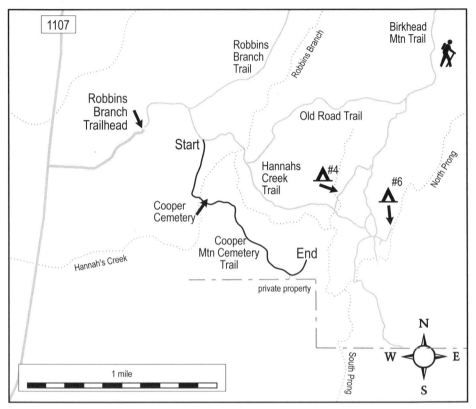

1107

Robbins Branch Trail

Robbins Branch

Birkhead Mtn Trail

Robbins Branch Trailhead

Old Road Trail

Start

Hannahs Creek Trail

#4

#6

North Prong

Cooper Cemetery

Cooper Mtn Cemetery Trail

End

Hannah's Creek

private property

1 mile

South Prong

N
W   E
S

Elevation Profile: Cooper Mtn Cemetery Trail

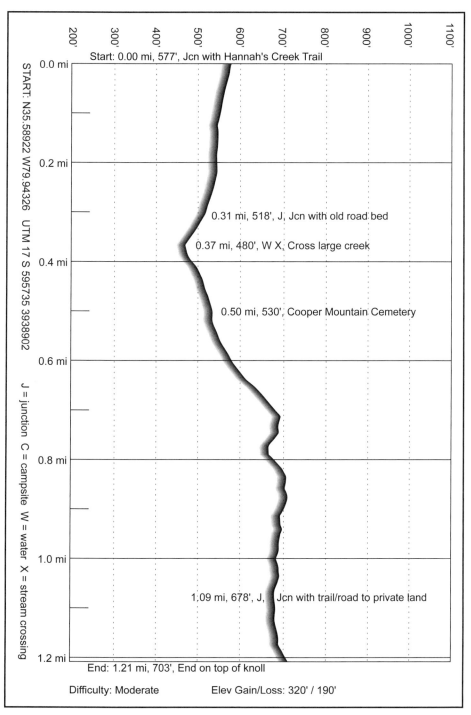

START: N35.58922 W79.94326 UTM 17 S 595735 3938902

J = junction C = campsite W = water X = stream crossing

Start: 0.00 mi, 577', Jcn with Hannah's Creek Trail

0.31 mi, 518', J, Jcn with old road bed

0.37 mi, 480', W X, Cross large creek

0.50 mi, 530', Cooper Mountain Cemetery

1.09 mi, 678', J, Jcn with trail/road to private land

End: 1.21 mi, 703', End on top of knoll

Difficulty: Moderate   Elev Gain/Loss: 320' / 190'

Hannah's Creek Trail

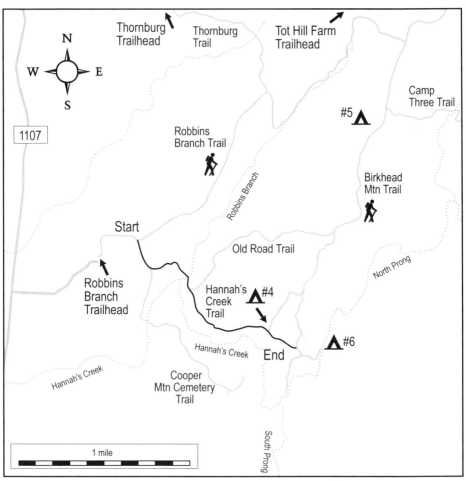

Thornburg Trailhead

Thornburg Trail

Tot Hill Farm Trailhead

Camp Three Trail

N
W · E
S

1107

#5 ⛺

Robbins Branch Trail

Robbins Branch

Birkhead Mtn Trail

Start

Old Road Trail

Robbins Branch Trailhead

Hannah's Creek Trail

#4 ⛺

North Prong

#6 ⛺

Hannah's Creek

End

Hannah's Creek

Cooper Mtn Cemetery Trail

South Prong

1 mile

Elevation Profile: Hannah's Creek Trail

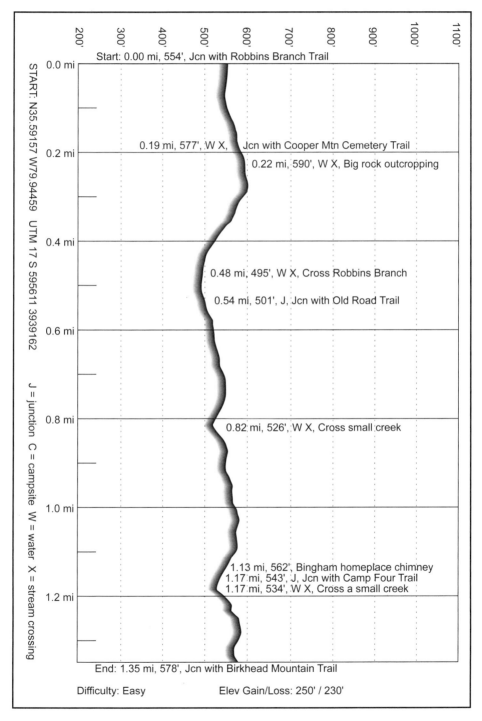

START: N35.59157 W79.94459 UTM 17 S 595611 3939162

J = junction C = campsite W = water X = stream crossing

Start: 0.00 mi, 554', Jcn with Robbins Branch Trail

0.19 mi, 577', W X, Jcn with Cooper Mtn Cemetery Trail

0.22 mi, 590', W X, Big rock outcropping

0.48 mi, 495', W X, Cross Robbins Branch

0.54 mi, 501', J, Jcn with Old Road Trail

0.82 mi, 526', W X, Cross small creek

1.13 mi, 562', Bingham homeplace chimney
1.17 mi, 543', J, Jcn with Camp Four Trail
1.17 mi, 534', W X, Cross a small creek

End: 1.35 mi, 578', Jcn with Birkhead Mountain Trail

Difficulty: Easy   Elev Gain/Loss: 250' / 230'

Robbins Branch Trail

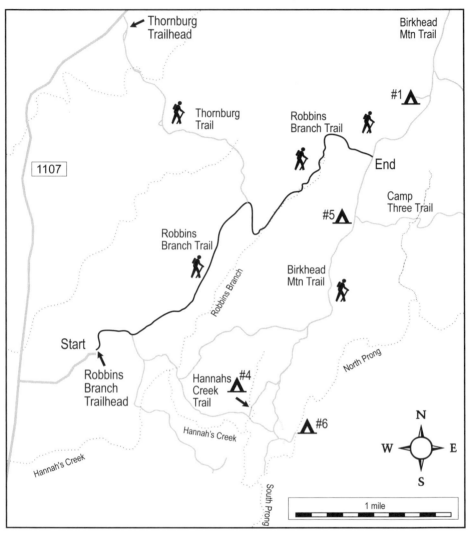

Thornburg
Trailhead

Birkhead
Mtn Trail

#1

Thornburg
Trail

Robbins
Branch Trail

1107

End

Camp
Three Trail

#5

Robbins
Branch Trail

Robbins Branch

Birkhead
Mtn Trail

Start

North Prong

Robbins
Branch
Trailhead

Hannahs
Creek
Trail

#4

Hannah's Creek

#6

Hannah's Creek

South Prong

N
W   E
S

1 mile

Elevation Profile: Robbins Branch Trail

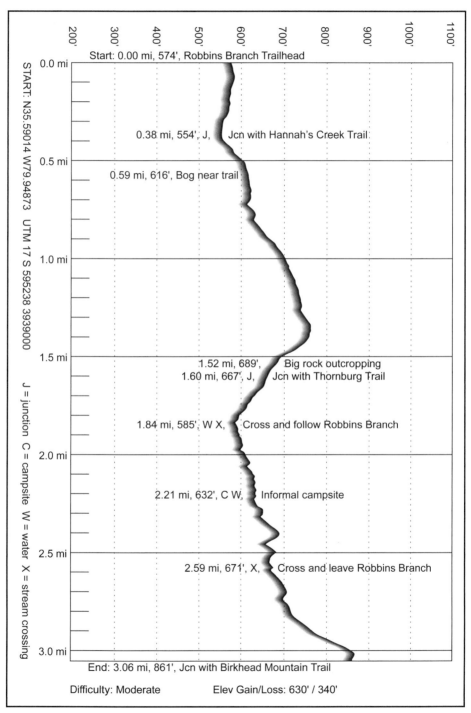

START: N35.59014 W79.94873 UTM 17 S 595238 3939000

J = junction C = campsite W = water X = stream crossing

Start: 0.00 mi, 574', Robbins Branch Trailhead

0.38 mi, 554', J, Jcn with Hannah's Creek Trail

0.59 mi, 616', Bog near trail

1.52 mi, 689', Big rock outcropping
1.60 mi, 667', J, Jcn with Thornburg Trail

1.84 mi, 585', W X, Cross and follow Robbins Branch

2.21 mi, 632', C W, Informal campsite

2.59 mi, 671', X, Cross and leave Robbins Branch

End: 3.06 mi, 861', Jcn with Birkhead Mountain Trail

Difficulty: Moderate   Elev Gain/Loss: 630' / 340'

Thornburg Trail

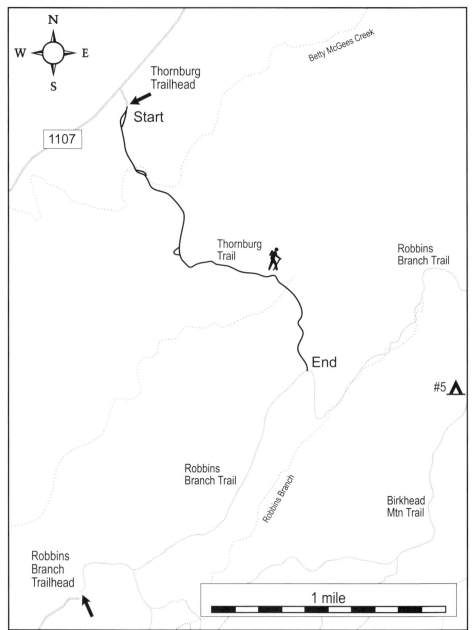

Elevation Profile: Thornburg Trail

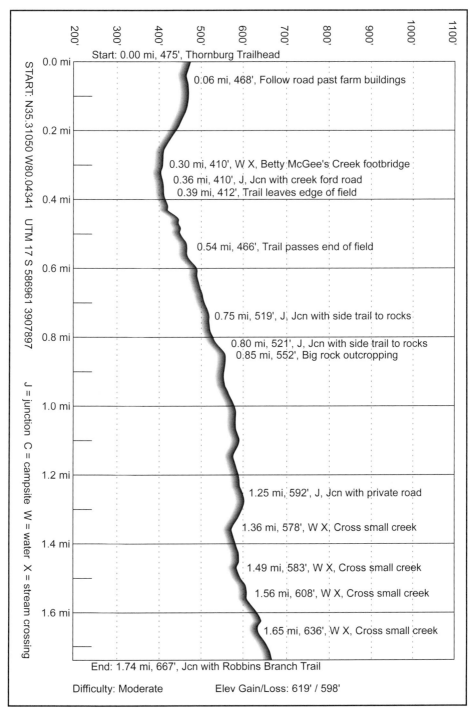

START: N35.31050 W80.04341 UTM 17 S 586961 3907897

J = junction C = campsite W = water X = stream crossing

200' 300' 400' 500' 600' 700' 800' 900' 1000' 1100'

Start: 0.00 mi, 475', Thornburg Trailhead

0.0 mi

0.06 mi, 468', Follow road past farm buildings

0.2 mi

0.30 mi, 410', W X, Betty McGee's Creek footbridge
0.36 mi, 410', J, Jcn with creek ford road
0.39 mi, 412', Trail leaves edge of field

0.4 mi

0.54 mi, 466', Trail passes end of field

0.6 mi

0.75 mi, 519', J, Jcn with side trail to rocks

0.8 mi

0.80 mi, 521', J, Jcn with side trail to rocks
0.85 mi, 552', Big rock outcropping

1.0 mi

1.2 mi

1.25 mi, 592', J, Jcn with private road

1.36 mi, 578', W X, Cross small creek

1.4 mi

1.49 mi, 583', W X, Cross small creek

1.56 mi, 608', W X, Cross small creek

1.6 mi

1.65 mi, 636', W X, Cross small creek

End: 1.74 mi, 667', Jcn with Robbins Branch Trail

Difficulty: Moderate   Elev Gain/Loss: 619' / 598'

Birkhead Mountains Wilderness Area Trips

Trip	Use	Length (miles)	Elevation Gain/ Loss	Difficulty Rating	Page
BMWA Trip A	H	9.83	1605' / 1605'	Difficult	232
BMWA Trip B	H	9.64	1595' / 1595'	Difficult	234
BMWA Trip C	H	12.22	2050' / 2050'	Difficult+	236
BMWA Trip D	H	6.86	1140' / 1140'	Difficult	238
BMWA Trip E	H	9.44	1595' / 1595'	Difficult	240
BMWA Trip F	H	12.27	2130' / 2130'	Difficult+	242
BMWA Trip G	H	6.91	1120' / 1120'	Difficult	244

Author's Choice

For dayhikers, I recommend Trip D. This trip gives you a chance to hike along a stream and a mountain ridgetop. The route is a little under 7 miles long, so make sure you can handle the distance and take along some food and drink.

For backpackers, I recommend Trip C. At more than 12 miles in length, this route gives you decent mileage but leaves times to enjoy the scenery. Options for established campsites can be found anywhere from 4 to 7 miles from the start. Along the way you can enjoy hiking beside babbling branches and ascending to the top of Birkhead Mountain.

Birkhead Trip A

Map	page 232	**Difficulty**	Difficult
Length	9.83 miles	**Configuration**	Lollipop
Trailhead	Thornburg	**Elev Gain/Loss**	1605' / 1605'

Start Coordinates N35.61997, W79.94499;   17 S 595541 3942312

Birkhead Trip B

Map	page 234	**Difficulty**	Difficult
Length	9.64 miles	**Configuration**	Lollipop
Trailhead	Thornburg	**Elev Gain/Loss**	1595' / 1595'

Start Coordinates N35.61997, W79.94499;   17 S 595541 3942312

Birkhead Trip C

Map	page 236	**Difficulty**	Difficult+
Length	12.22 miles	**Configuration**	Lollipop
Trailhead	Thornburg	**Elev Gain/Loss**	2050' / 2050'

Start Coordinates N35.61997, W79.94499;   17 S 595541 3942312

Birkhead Trip D

Map	page 238	**Difficulty**	Difficult
Length	6.86 miles	**Configuration**	Lollipop
Trailhead	Robbins Branch	**Elev Gain/Loss**	1140' / 1140'

Start Coordinates N35.59014, W79.94873;   17 S 595238 3939000

Birkhead Trip E

Map	page 240	**Difficulty**	Difficult
Length	9.44 miles	**Configuration**	Lollipop
Trailhead	Robbins Branch	**Elev Gain/Loss**	1595' / 1595'

Start Coordinates N35.59014, W79.94873;   17 S 595238 3939000

Birkhead Trip F

Map	page 242	**Difficulty**	Difficult+
Length	12.27 miles	**Configuration**	Lollipop
Trailhead	Tot Hill Farm	**Elev Gain/Loss**	2130' / 2130'

Start Coordinates N35.63636, W79.90460;   17 S 599179 3944169

Birkhead Trip G

Map	page 244	**Difficulty**	Difficult
Length	6.91 miles	**Configuration**	Lollipop
Trailhead	Tot Hill Farm	**Elev Gain/Loss**	1120' / 1120'

Start Coordinates N35.63636, W79.90460;   17 S 599179 3944169

BMWA Trip A

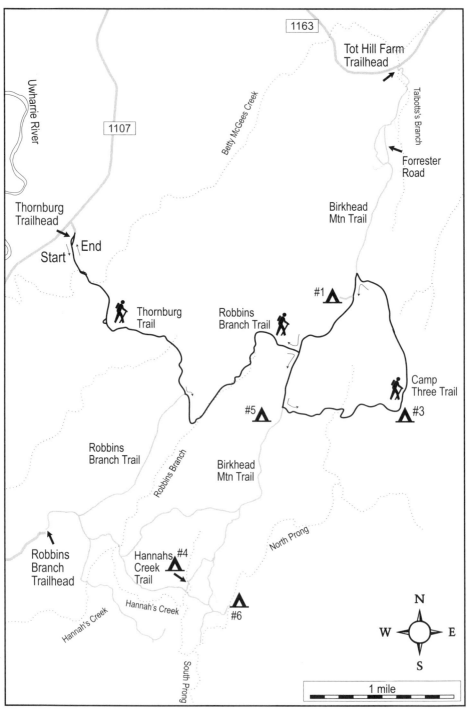

Elevation Profile: Birkhead Trip A

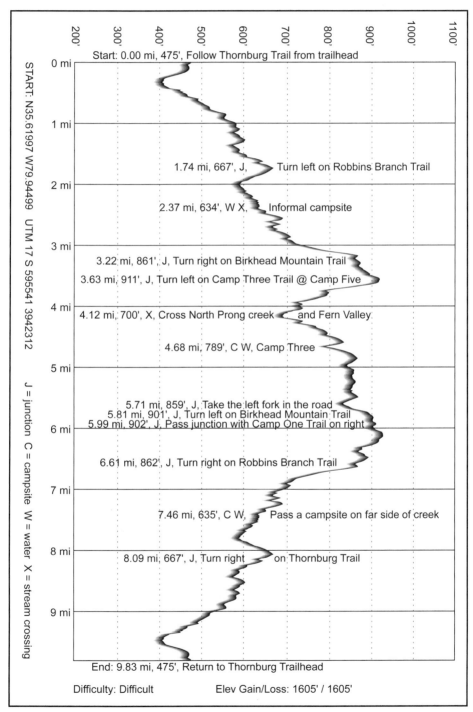

START: N35.61997 W79.94499 UTM 17 S 595541 3942312   J = junction C = campsite W = water X = stream crossing

Start: 0.00 mi, 475', Follow Thornburg Trail from trailhead

1.74 mi, 667', J,   Turn left on Robbins Branch Trail

2.37 mi, 634', W X,   Informal campsite

3.22 mi, 861', J, Turn right on Birkhead Mountain Trail

3.63 mi, 911', J, Turn left on Camp Three Trail @ Camp Five

4.12 mi, 700', X, Cross North Prong creek   and Fern Valley

4.68 mi, 789', C W, Camp Three

5.71 mi, 859', J, Take the left fork in the road
5.81 mi, 901', J, Turn left on Birkhead Mountain Trail
5.99 mi, 902', J, Pass junction with Camp One Trail on right

6.61 mi, 862', J, Turn right on Robbins Branch Trail

7.46 mi, 635', C W,   Pass a campsite on far side of creek

8.09 mi, 667', J, Turn right   on Thornburg Trail

End: 9.83 mi, 475', Return to Thornburg Trailhead

Difficulty: Difficult   Elev Gain/Loss: 1605' / 1605'

BMWA Trip B

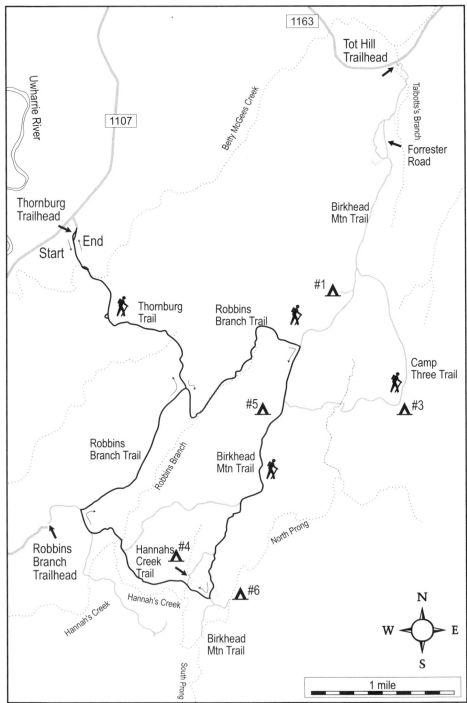

Elevation Profile: Birkhead Trip B

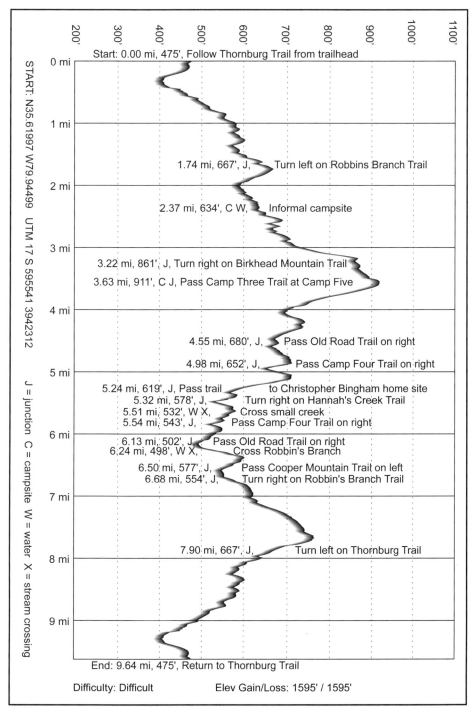

START: N35.61997 W79.94499   UTM 17 S 595541 3942312   J = junction C = campsite W = water X = stream crossing

200'   300'   400'   500'   600'   700'   800'   900'   1000'   1100'

Start: 0.00 mi, 475', Follow Thornburg Trail from trailhead

0 mi

1 mi

1.74 mi, 667', J,   Turn left on Robbins Branch Trail

2 mi

2.37 mi, 634', C W,   Informal campsite

3 mi

3.22 mi, 861', J, Turn right on Birkhead Mountain Trail

3.63 mi, 911', C J, Pass Camp Three Trail at Camp Five

4 mi

4.55 mi, 680', J,   Pass Old Road Trail on right

4.98 mi, 652', J,   Pass Camp Four Trail on right

5 mi

5.24 mi, 619', J, Pass trail   to Christopher Bingham home site

5.32 mi, 578', J,   Turn right on Hannah's Creek Trail

5.51 mi, 532', W X,   Cross small creek

5.54 mi, 543', J,   Pass Camp Four Trail on right

6 mi

6.13 mi, 502', J,   Pass Old Road Trail on right

6.24 mi, 498', W X,   Cross Robbin's Branch

6.50 mi, 577', J,   Pass Cooper Mountain Trail on left

6.68 mi, 554', J,   Turn right on Robbin's Branch Trail

7 mi

7.90 mi, 667', J,   Turn left on Thornburg Trail

8 mi

9 mi

End: 9.64 mi, 475', Return to Thornburg Trail

Difficulty: Difficult   Elev Gain/Loss: 1595' / 1595'

BMWA Trip C

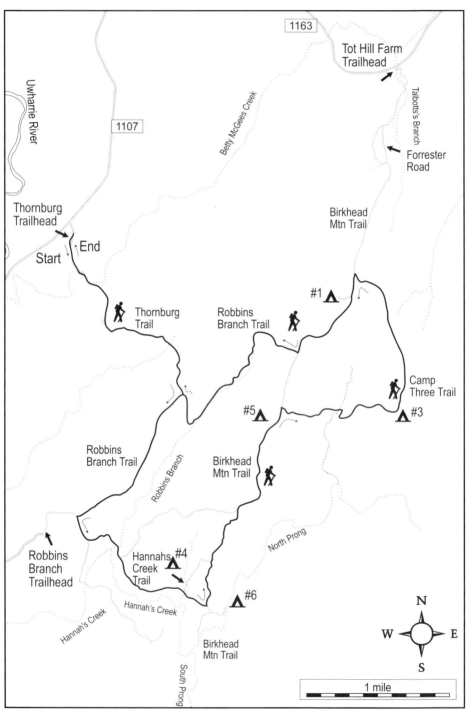

Elevation Profile: Birkhead Trip C

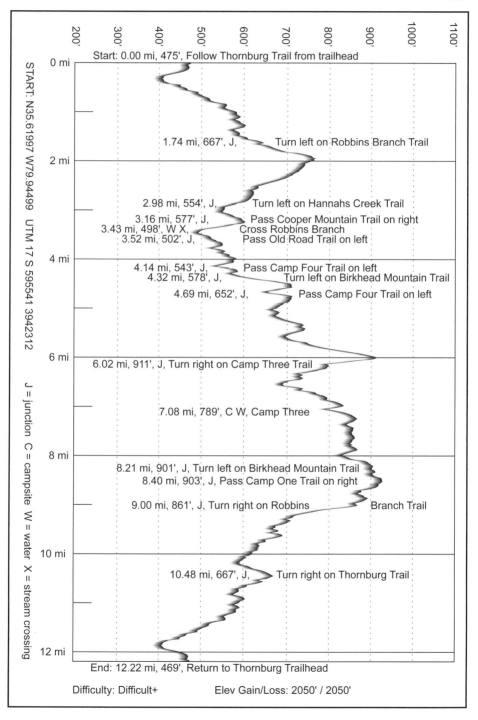

START: N35.61997 W79.94499 UTM 17 S 595541 3942312

J = junction C = campsite W = water X = stream crossing

200'   300'   400'   500'   600'   700'   800'   900'   1000'   1100'

Start: 0.00 mi, 475', Follow Thornburg Trail from trailhead

0 mi

1.74 mi, 667', J,   Turn left on Robbins Branch Trail

2 mi

2.98 mi, 554', J,   Turn left on Hannahs Creek Trail
3.16 mi, 577', J,   Pass Cooper Mountain Trail on right
3.43 mi, 498', W X,   Cross Robbins Branch
3.52 mi, 502', J,   Pass Old Road Trail on left

4 mi

4.14 mi, 543', J,   Pass Camp Four Trail on left
4.32 mi, 578', J,   Turn left on Birkhead Mountain Trail
4.69 mi, 652', J,   Pass Camp Four Trail on left

6 mi

6.02 mi, 911', J, Turn right on Camp Three Trail

7.08 mi, 789', C W, Camp Three

8 mi

8.21 mi, 901', J, Turn left on Birkhead Mountain Trail
8.40 mi, 903', J, Pass Camp One Trail on right

9.00 mi, 861', J, Turn right on Robbins   Branch Trail

10 mi

10.48 mi, 667', J,   Turn right on Thornburg Trail

12 mi

End: 12.22 mi, 469', Return to Thornburg Trailhead

Difficulty: Difficult+   Elev Gain/Loss: 2050' / 2050'

BMWA Trip D

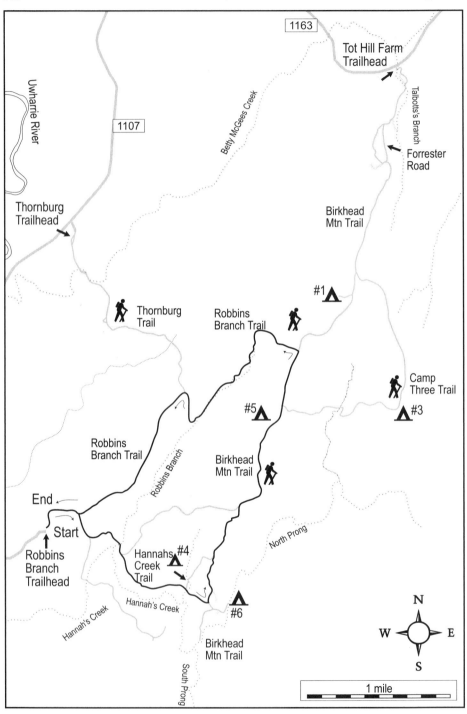

Elevation Profile: Birkhead Trip D

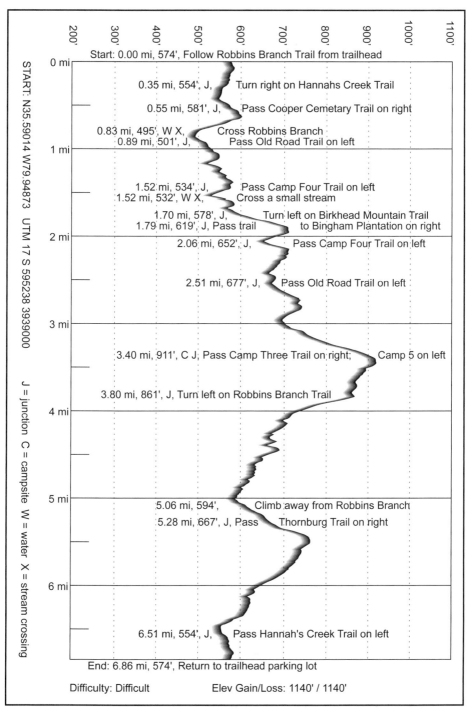

Start: 0.00 mi, 574', Follow Robbins Branch Trail from trailhead

0.35 mi, 554', J,   Turn right on Hannahs Creek Trail

0.55 mi, 581', J,   Pass Cooper Cemetary Trail on right

0.83 mi, 495', W X,   Cross Robbins Branch
0.89 mi, 501', J,   Pass Old Road Trail on left

1.52 mi, 534', J,   Pass Camp Four Trail on left
1.52 mi, 532', W X,   Cross a small stream

1.70 mi, 578', J,   Turn left on Birkhead Mountain Trail
1.79 mi, 619', J, Pass trail   to Bingham Plantation on right

2.06 mi, 652', J,   Pass Camp Four Trail on left

2.51 mi, 677', J,   Pass Old Road Trail on left

3.40 mi, 911', C J, Pass Camp Three Trail on right;   Camp 5 on left

3.80 mi, 861', J, Turn left on Robbins Branch Trail

5.06 mi, 594',   Climb away from Robbins Branch
5.28 mi, 667', J, Pass   Thornburg Trail on right

6.51 mi, 554', J,   Pass Hannah's Creek Trail on left

End: 6.86 mi, 574', Return to trailhead parking lot

Difficulty: Difficult   Elev Gain/Loss: 1140' / 1140'

START: N35.59014 W79.94873 UTM 17 S 595238 3939000

J = junction C = campsite W = water X = stream crossing

BMWA Trip E

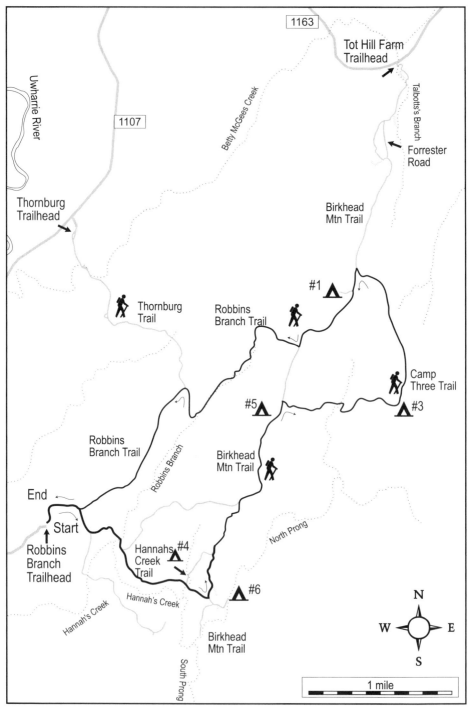

Elevation Profile: Birkhead Trip E

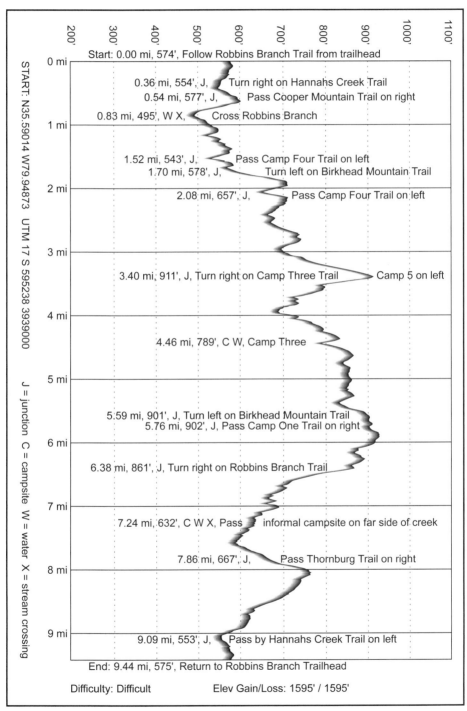

START: N35.59014 W79.94873 UTM 17 S 595238 3939000

J = junction C = campsite W = water X = stream crossing

200' 300' 400' 500' 600' 700' 800' 900' 1000' 1100'

0 mi   Start: 0.00 mi, 574', Follow Robbins Branch Trail from trailhead

0.36 mi, 554', J,   Turn right on Hannahs Creek Trail
0.54 mi, 577', J,   Pass Cooper Mountain Trail on right
0.83 mi, 495', W X,   Cross Robbins Branch

1 mi

1.52 mi, 543', J,   Pass Camp Four Trail on left
1.70 mi, 578', J,   Turn left on Birkhead Mountain Trail

2 mi   2.08 mi, 657', J,   Pass Camp Four Trail on left

3 mi

3.40 mi, 911', J, Turn right on Camp Three Trail   Camp 5 on left

4 mi

4.46 mi, 789', C W, Camp Three

5 mi

5.59 mi, 901', J, Turn left on Birkhead Mountain Trail
5.76 mi, 902', J, Pass Camp One Trail on right

6 mi

6.38 mi, 861', J, Turn right on Robbins Branch Trail

7 mi

7.24 mi, 632', C W X, Pass   informal campsite on far side of creek

7.86 mi, 667', J,   Pass Thornburg Trail on right

8 mi

9 mi

9.09 mi, 553', J,   Pass by Hannahs Creek Trail on left

End: 9.44 mi, 575', Return to Robbins Branch Trailhead

Difficulty: Difficult   Elev Gain/Loss: 1595' / 1595'

BMWA Trip F

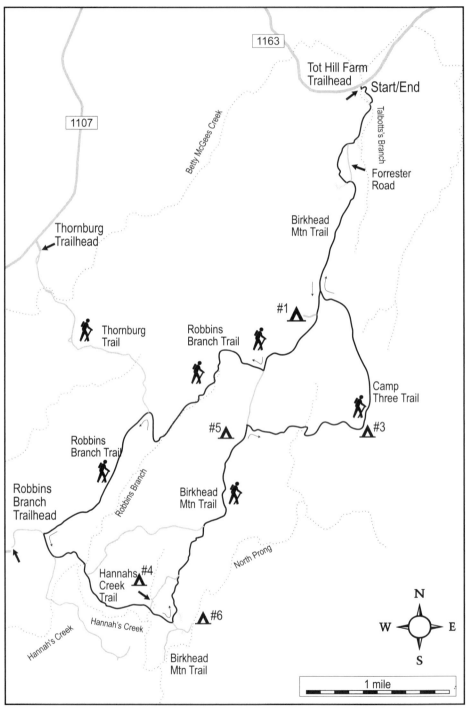

1163

Tot Hill Farm
Trailhead
Start/End

1107

Betty McGees Creek

Talbotts's Branch

Forrester
Road

Birkhead
Mtn Trail

Thornburg
Trailhead

#1

Thornburg
Trail

Robbins
Branch Trail

Camp
Three Trail

Robbins
Branch Trail

#5

#3

Robbins
Branch
Trailhead

Robbins Branch

Birkhead
Mtn Trail

North Prong

Hannahs
Creek
Trail

#4

#6

Hannah's Creek

Hannah's Creek

Birkhead
Mtn Trail

N
W   E
S

1 mile

Elevation Profile: Birkhead Trip F

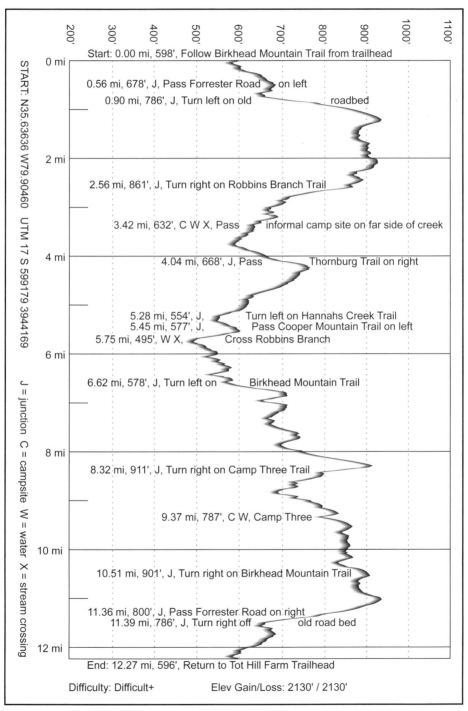

START: N35.63636 W79.90460   UTM 17 S 599179 3944169

J = junction   C = campsite   W = water   X = stream crossing

Start: 0.00 mi, 598', Follow Birkhead Mountain Trail from trailhead

0 mi

0.56 mi, 678', J, Pass Forrester Road on left

0.90 mi, 786', J, Turn left on old roadbed

2 mi

2.56 mi, 861', J, Turn right on Robbins Branch Trail

3.42 mi, 632', C W X, Pass informal camp site on far side of creek

4 mi

4.04 mi, 668', J, Pass Thornburg Trail on right

5.28 mi, 554', J, Turn left on Hannahs Creek Trail
5.45 mi, 577', J, Pass Cooper Mountain Trail on left
5.75 mi, 495', W X, Cross Robbins Branch

6 mi

6.62 mi, 578', J, Turn left on Birkhead Mountain Trail

8 mi

8.32 mi, 911', J, Turn right on Camp Three Trail

9.37 mi, 787', C W, Camp Three

10 mi

10.51 mi, 901', J, Turn right on Birkhead Mountain Trail

11.36 mi, 800', J, Pass Forrester Road on right
11.39 mi, 786', J, Turn right off old road bed

12 mi

End: 12.27 mi, 596', Return to Tot Hill Farm Trailhead

Difficulty: Difficult+   Elev Gain/Loss: 2130' / 2130'

BMWA Trip G

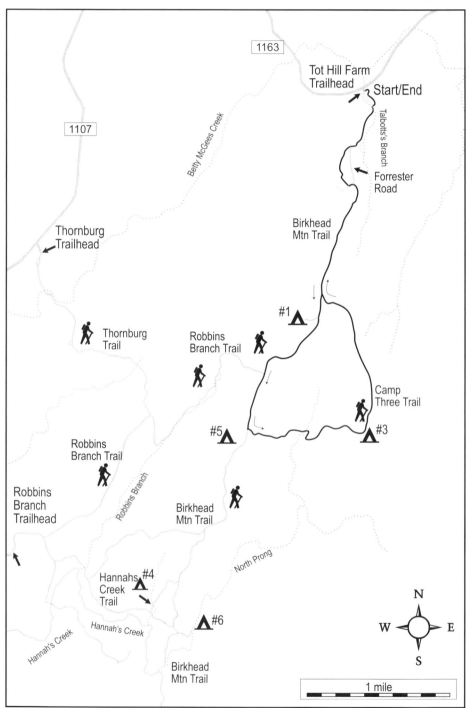

1163

Tot Hill Farm
Trailhead

Start/End

Talbotts's Branch

Betty McGees Creek

1107

Forrester
Road

Birkhead
Mtn Trail

Thornburg
Trailhead

#1

Thornburg
Trail

Robbins
Branch Trail

Camp
Three Trail

#3

#5

Robbins
Branch Trail

Robbins
Branch
Trailhead

Robbins Branch

Birkhead
Mtn Trail

North Prong

Hannahs
Creek
Trail

#4

N

W   E

S

#6

Hannah's Creek

Hannah's Creek

Birkhead
Mtn Trail

1 mile

Elevation Profile: Birkhead Trip G

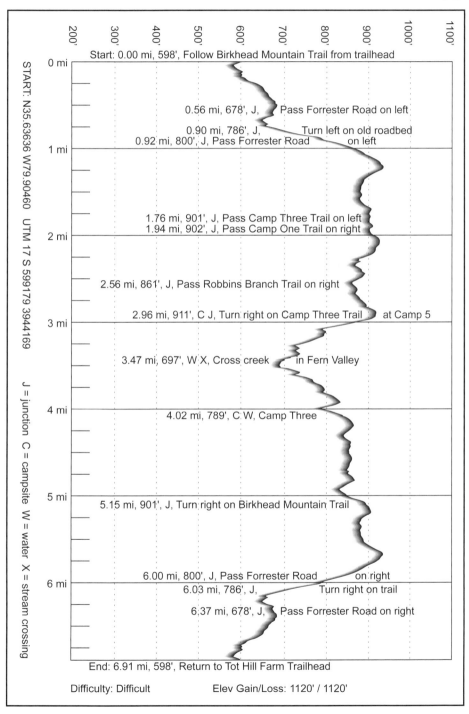

START: N35.63636 W79.90460 UTM 17 S 599179 3944169

J = junction C = campsite W = water X = stream crossing

200' 300' 400' 500' 600' 700' 800' 900' 1000' 1100'

0 mi — Start: 0.00 mi, 598', Follow Birkhead Mountain Trail from trailhead

0.56 mi, 678', J, Pass Forrester Road on left

0.90 mi, 786', J, Turn left on old roadbed
0.92 mi, 800', J, Pass Forrester Road on left

1 mi

1.76 mi, 901', J, Pass Camp Three Trail on left
1.94 mi, 902', J, Pass Camp One Trail on right

2 mi

2.56 mi, 861', J, Pass Robbins Branch Trail on right

2.96 mi, 911', C J, Turn right on Camp Three Trail at Camp 5

3 mi

3.47 mi, 697', W X, Cross creek in Fern Valley

4 mi

4.02 mi, 789', C W, Camp Three

5 mi

5.15 mi, 901', J, Turn right on Birkhead Mountain Trail

6.00 mi, 800', J, Pass Forrester Road on right
6.03 mi, 786', J, Turn right on trail

6 mi

6.37 mi, 678', J, Pass Forrester Road on right

End: 6.91 mi, 598', Return to Tot Hill Farm Trailhead

Difficulty: Difficult   Elev Gain/Loss: 1120' / 1120'

Boone's Cave Park

Boones's Cave Park is a small, roughly 100 acre county park on the bank of the Yadkin River. The park is managed by the Davidson County Parks and Recreation Department. The park address is 3552 Boone's Cave Park Road, Lexington, NC. The Park and Recreation Department office can be reached at 336-242-2285.

ACCESS

Picnic Shelter / Parking Trailhead
The main parking lot is located at the end of the park road, at the Picnic Shelter overlooking the Yadkin River. A short trail leads from here to Boone's Cave, just below the shelter. Several of the park trails can be accessed from this trailhead or not far from it.

UTM	17 S 548095 3961821
Lat/Lon	N35.79932 W80.46772

Entrance Trailhead
A small parking lot is located just inside the entrance gate of the park, at the park office. The Backcountry Trail and Wetlands and Woodlands Trail can be accessed from this trailhead.

UTM	17 S 548394 3961657
Lat/Lon	N35.79782 W80.46442

NOTES OF INTEREST
The namesake of the park is Boone's Cave. This small cave overlooking the river is rumored to have been used by Daniel Boone's family when they lived in the Yadkin River Valley in the 1750's. A short trail with wooden steps leads from the Picnic Shelter down to the cave and some of the other park trails.

A 1740's style log cabin was built in 2006 and is one of the interesting features of the park. It shows the type of early log cabin that the Boone family might have lived in when they were in this area. The log cabin project was organized by the Davidson County Historical Museum. Davidson County Community College created a special 8-week course to build the cabin.

A monument honoring Daniel Boone and the Boone Trail Highway is located within a paved circle drive off of the main park road. There are restrooms and vending machines at the monument circle. A trail to the main campsites starts at this circle.

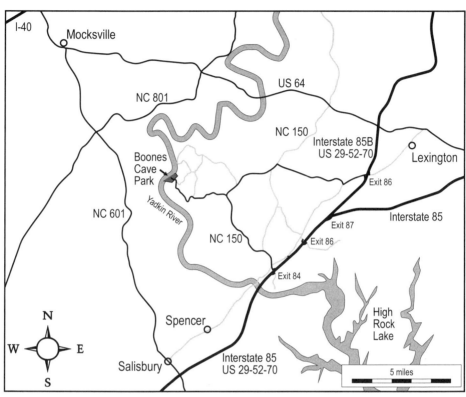

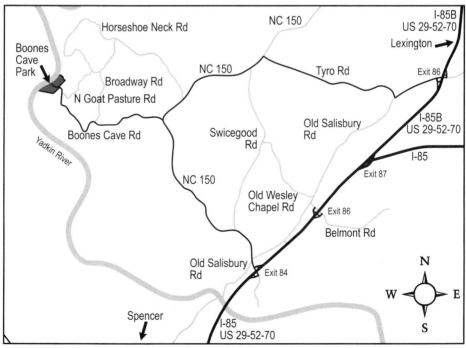

The park has about 3.5 miles of marked trails. Some of them follow graveled roads, but several are primitive footpaths much like what would have been found in the area in the 18th century.

The Cottonwood Trail leads to the state's tallest Cottonwood tree, at over 169 feet tall. The trunk is 16 feet around, and the canopy is 109 feet wide.

Park hours:

> May 1 – September 30
> 8 am – 8 pm, Monday – Saturday
> 1-8 pm, Sunday
>
> October 1 – April 30
> 8 am – 5:30 pm, Monday – Saturday
> 1-5:30 pm, Sunday

CAMPING
There are two sets of campsites within Boone's Cave Park. The main campground, accessed by a short trail leading from the monument circle loop, has eight tent pads. The primitive campsites accessed from the Runner's Loop Trail has four tentpads. Camping permits and reservations are required.

MAPS
A color brochure and photomap of the park was available online in 2013.

http://www.visitdavidsoncounty.com/images/PDF/boones%20cave%20 brochure%20%28new%29%2009.pdf

More park information is available at:

http://www.co.davidson.nc.us/ParksAndRecreation/ Boone%60sCaveParkInformation.aspx

Boone's Cave Park

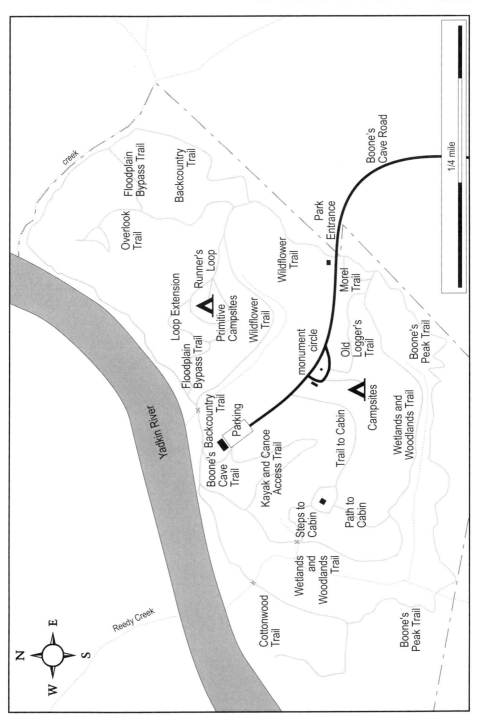

Boone's Cave Park Trails

Trail Name	Length (miles)	Elevation Gain/Loss	Difficulty Rating	Map (page)
Backcountry	0.61	208' / 725'	Moderate	256
Boone's Peak	0.54	164' / 66'	Moderate	258
Cottonwood	0.37	36' / 42'	Easy	260
Floodplain	0.40	170' / 154'	Moderate	262
Kayak and Canoe	0.25	18' / 107'	Easy	264
Overlook	0.25	89' / 114'	Easy	266
Runner's Loop	0.18	50' / 48'	Easy	268
Wetlands and Woodlands	0.52	181' / 51'	Easy	270
Wildflower	0.37	157' / 19'	Easy	272

Backcountry Trail

Map	page 256	**Difficulty**	Moderate
Length	0.61 miles	**Configuration**	One Way
Trailhead	n/a	**Elev Gain/Loss**	208' / 725'

Start Coordinates N35.79973, W80.46771;   17 S 548095 3961866

The Backcountry Trail is a narrow footpath that runs along the borders of the park on the northeast side of the main park road.

The Backcountry Trail starts on the banks of the Yadkin River at Boone's Cave, at a junction with the Boone's Cave and Cottonwood Trails. It follows the riverbank upstream, passing two other trails on the right near the beginning, the Wildflower Trail and the Floodplain Bypass Trail.

After about 0.3 miles, the trail turns away from the river and follows a small creek upstream. The other end of the Floodplain Bypass Trail is passed not long before the trail turns away from the creek and climbs steadily to end at the Wildflower Trail.

Boone's Peak Trail

Map	page 258	**Difficulty**	Moderate
Length	0.54 miles	**Configuration**	One Way
Trailhead	n/a	**Elev Gain/Loss**	164' / 66'

Start Coordinates N35.79771, W80.47068;   17 S 547828 3961641

The Boone's Peak Trail is a narrow footpath that generally runs along the southwest border of the park.

The trail begins at its junction with the Cottonwood Trail and soon crosses a small wet area on wooden puncheons, which are like a series of small bridges sitting just above the wet ground.

From the wet area, the trail works its way up and down until it eventually ends at a junction with the Wetlands and Woodlands Trail, near the park entrance.

A few short sections of the trail are relatively steep or run along a steep slope. These spots might be worthy of a "difficult" rating, but overall the trail is still a "moderate" difficulty trail.

Cottonwood Trail

Map	page 260	**Difficulty**	Easy
Length	0.37 miles	**Configuration**	One Way
Trailhead	n/a	**Elev Gain/Loss**	36' / 42'
Start Coordinates N35.79974, W80.46772; 17 S 548094 3961868			

The Cottonwood Trail is wide trail that runs through a flat floodplain along the Yadkin River. Much of the trail has been surfaced with mulch.

The trail starts at Boone's Cave, at a junction with the Boone's Cave and Backcountry Trails. The trail then heads downstream along the river. It soon passes the Kayak and Canoe Access Trail at Baptism Rock, a section of exposed bedrock on the edge of the river.

From Baptism Rock, the trail winds away from the river and through a low-lying area. The trail passes a junction with the Boone's Peak Trail. The route eventually ends at The Cottonwood Tree.

The Cottonwood Tree is North Carolina's prized Eastern Cottonwood Tree (Populus deltoids). It stands 160 feet tall and has a trunk circumference of 15'8" .

Floodplain Bypass Trail

Map	page 262	**Difficulty**	Moderate
Length	0.40 miles	**Configuration**	One Way
Trailhead	n/a	**Elev Gain/Loss**	170' / 154'
Start Coordinates N35.79995, W80.46680; 17 S 548177 3961892			

The Floodplain Bypass Trail is actually a combination of parts of several other trails, plus connecting trail sections at each end, that provide a drier route across the park when the low-lying sections of the Backcountry Trail are flooded by high river water.

The route starts at a junction with the Backcountry Trail near its start. The route climbs quickly to join with the Loop Extension, and then the Runner's Loop Trail. From there it follows the Wildflower Trail to the Overlook Trail. The route follows the Overlook Trail down to a saddle.

From the saddle, the route bears right and descends to end at the Backcountry Trail along a small creek. The final section of the Bypass Trail was not well-worn in 2012. The turn to the right off of the Overlook Trail took extra attention to spot.

Kayak and Canoe Access Trail

Map	page 264	Difficulty	Easy
Length	0.25 miles	Configuration	One Way
Trailhead	n/a	Elev Gain/Loss	18' / 107'

Start Coordinates N35.79932, W80.46772;   17 S 548095 3961821

The Kayak and Canoe Access Trail is a wide footpath designed to make it easier for paddlers to get their boats to and from the Yadkin River. Since the trail is a quarter mile long, paddlers might find portage wheels to be a helpful piece of gear.

The trail starts at the corner of the paved parking lot at the Picnic Shelter. It switchbacks along the slope to make losing 100' of elevation easier to negotiate. Near the bottom it passes a junction with the Wetlands and Woodlands Trail.

The trail ends where it crosses the Cottonwood Trail at the edge of the river. Baptism Rock is a large area of exposed bedrock that slopes into the river at this location.

Overlook Trail

Map	page 266	Difficulty	Easy
Length	0.25 miles	Configuration	Lollipop
Trailhead	n/a	Elev Gain/Loss	89' / 114'

Start Coordinates N35.79928, W80.46359;   17 S 548467 3961818

The Overlook Trail is a wide trail that ends with a small loop on a hilltop overlooking the Yadkin River.

The "overlook" views are limited by leafy vegetation, so they'll be better during the winter and early spring months. In 2012, the remains of a couple of benches were noted along the loop.

The only trail intersection along this trail is where the Floodplain Bypass Trail connects it to the Backcountry Trail.

Runner's Loop Trail

Map	page 268	**Difficulty**	Easy
Length	0.18 miles	**Configuration**	Lollipop
Trailhead	n/a	**Elev Gain/Loss**	50' / 48'

Start Coordinates N35.79943, W80.46404;   17 S 548427 3961836

The Runner's Loop Trail is a wide trail that basically just loops around the primitive campsites on a small hill.

A narrow footpath known as the Loop Extension has been built off of the trail. This extension drops a littel further down the hill towards the river. The Floodplain Bypass Trail connects to the Loop Extension.

There are four tent pads in the primitive camping area.

Wetlands and Woodlands Trail

Map	page 270	**Difficulty**	Easy
Length	0.52 miles	**Configuration**	One Way
Trailhead	n/a	**Elev Gain/Loss**	181' / 51

Start Coordinates N35.79913, W80.46873;   17 S 548003 3961800

The Wetlands and Woodlands Trail is a wide trail running as it is named - from the wetlands along the river to the woodlands on the higher side of the park.

This trail starts at a junction with the Kayak and Canoe Access Trail and climbs to the higher side of the park, ending at the main park road near the entrance.

Several side trails connect the Wetlands and Woodlands trail to key park features. Two side trails connect to the demonstration 1740's-style log cabin. Another side trail connects to the campground.

Wildflower Trail

Map	page 272	**Difficulty**	Easy
Length	0.37 miles	**Configuration**	One Way
Trailhead	n/a	**Elev Gain/Loss**	157' / 19'

Start Coordinates N35.79982, W80.46698;   17 S 548161 3961877

The Wildflower trail is a wide trail that climbs from near the river to the higher side of the park, ending near the entrance gate. Much of the route follows a graveled road.

Along this trail are informational signs noting many of the wildflowers found in the park. A number of the wildflowers are normally only found in the Appalachian Mountains, making this location a unique remnant of biodiversity.

Backcountry Trail

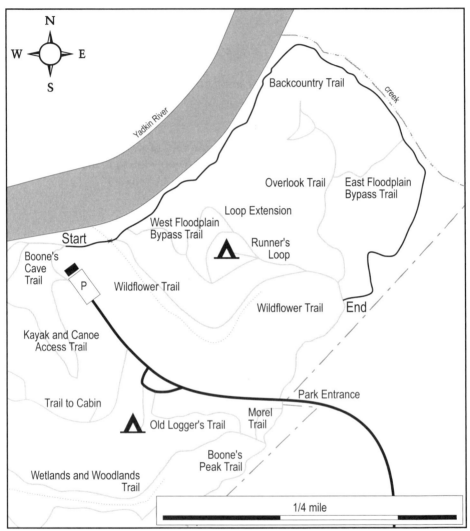

Elevation Profile: Backcountry Trail

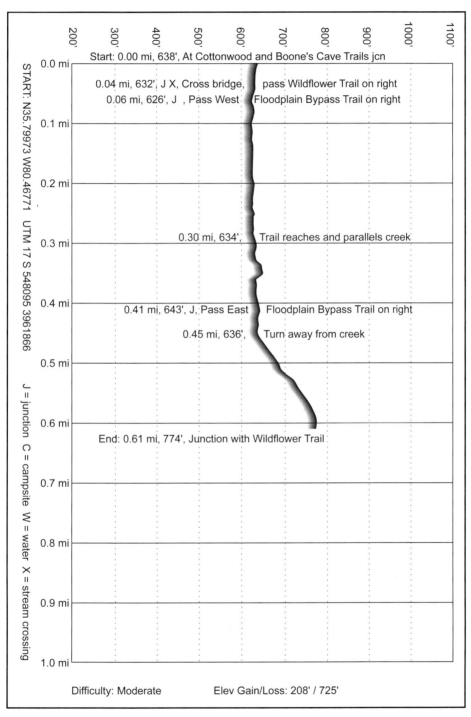

START: N35.79973 W80.46771 UTM 17 S 548095 3961866

J = junction C = campsite W = water X = stream crossing

200' 300' 400' 500' 600' 700' 800' 900' 1000' 1100'

0.0 mi — Start: 0.00 mi, 638', At Cottonwood and Boone's Cave Trails jcn

0.04 mi, 632', J X, Cross bridge,   pass Wildflower Trail on right
0.06 mi, 626', J , Pass West   Floodplain Bypass Trail on right

0.1 mi

0.2 mi

0.30 mi, 634',   Trail reaches and parallels creek

0.3 mi

0.4 mi — 0.41 mi, 643', J, Pass East   Floodplain Bypass Trail on right

0.45 mi, 636',   Turn away from creek

0.5 mi

0.6 mi — End: 0.61 mi, 774', Junction with Wildflower Trail

0.7 mi

0.8 mi

0.9 mi

1.0 mi

Difficulty: Moderate   Elev Gain/Loss: 208' / 725'

Boone's Peak Trail

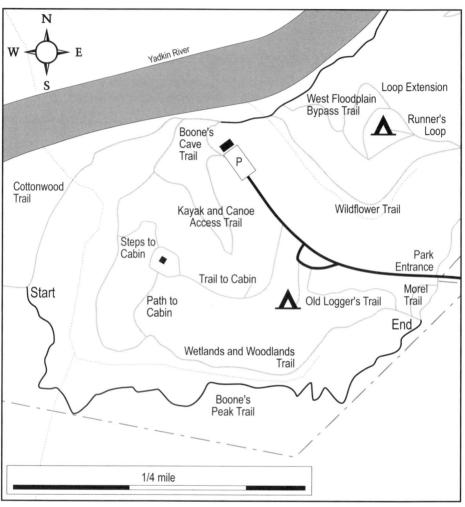

Elevation Profile: Boone's Peak Trail

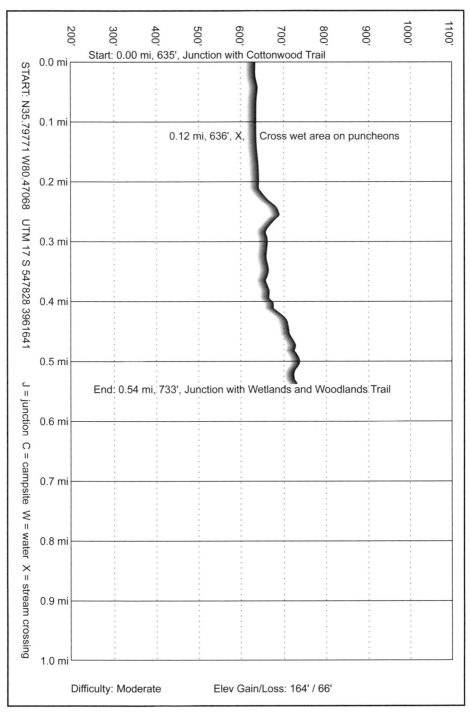

Difficulty: Moderate   Elev Gain/Loss: 164' / 66'

Cottonwood Trail

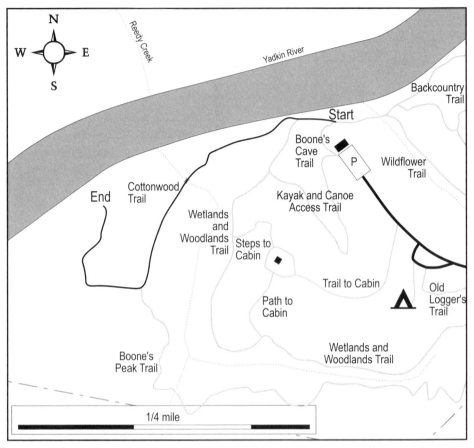

Elevation Profile: Cottonwood Trail

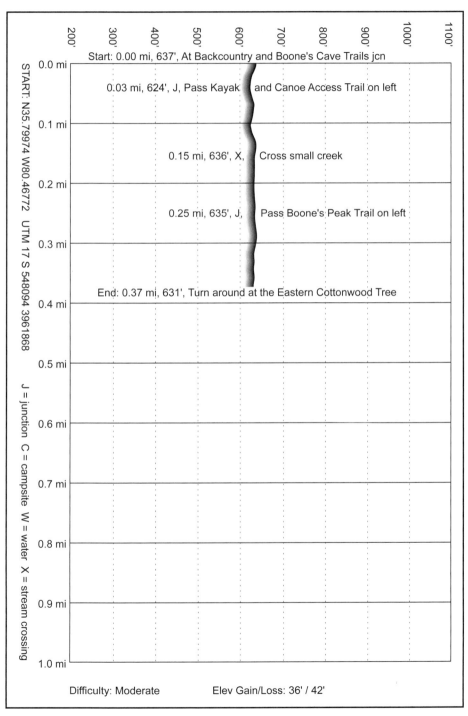

START: N35.79974 W80.46772 UTM 17 S 548094 3961868

J = junction C = campsite W = water X = stream crossing

200' 300' 400' 500' 600' 700' 800' 900' 1000' 1100'

Start: 0.00 mi, 637', At Backcountry and Boone's Cave Trails jcn

0.03 mi, 624', J, Pass Kayak and Canoe Access Trail on left

0.15 mi, 636', X, Cross small creek

0.25 mi, 635', J, Pass Boone's Peak Trail on left

End: 0.37 mi, 631', Turn around at the Eastern Cottonwood Tree

0.0 mi
0.1 mi
0.2 mi
0.3 mi
0.4 mi
0.5 mi
0.6 mi
0.7 mi
0.8 mi
0.9 mi
1.0 mi

Difficulty: Moderate   Elev Gain/Loss: 36' / 42'

Floodplain Bypass Trail

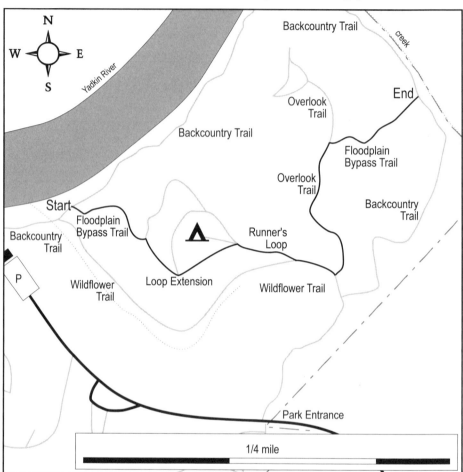

Elevation Profile: Floodplain Bypass Trail

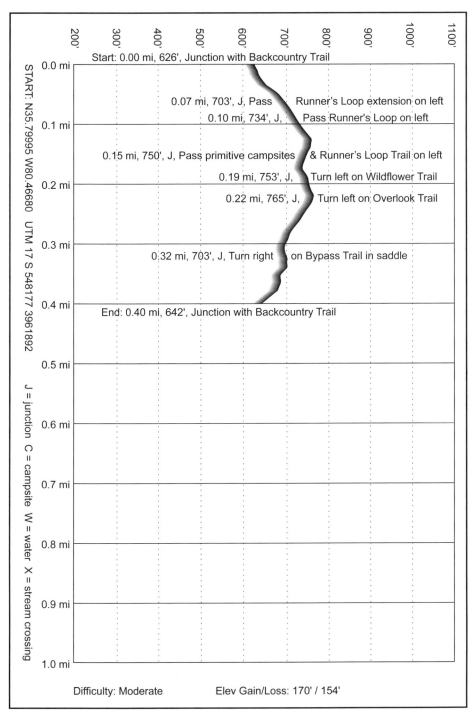

START: N35.79995 W80.46680 UTM 17 S 548177 3961892

J = junction C = campsite W = water X = stream crossing

Start: 0.00 mi, 626', Junction with Backcountry Trail

0.07 mi, 703', J, Pass Runner's Loop extension on left

0.10 mi, 734', J, Pass Runner's Loop on left

0.15 mi, 750', J, Pass primitive campsites & Runner's Loop Trail on left

0.19 mi, 753', J, Turn left on Wildflower Trail

0.22 mi, 765', J, Turn left on Overlook Trail

0.32 mi, 703', J, Turn right on Bypass Trail in saddle

End: 0.40 mi, 642', Junction with Backcountry Trail

Difficulty: Moderate   Elev Gain/Loss: 170' / 154'

Kayak and Canoe Access Trail

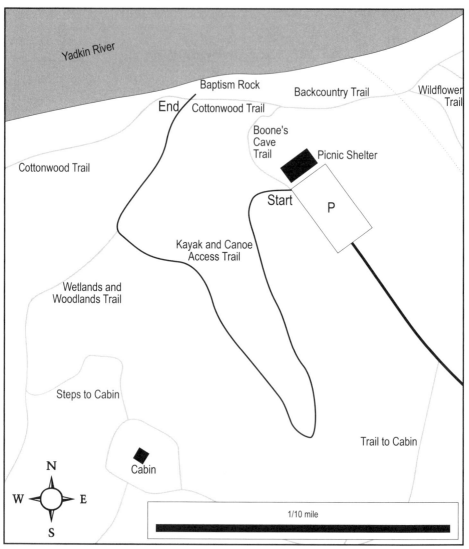

Elevation Profile: Kayak and Canoe Access Trail

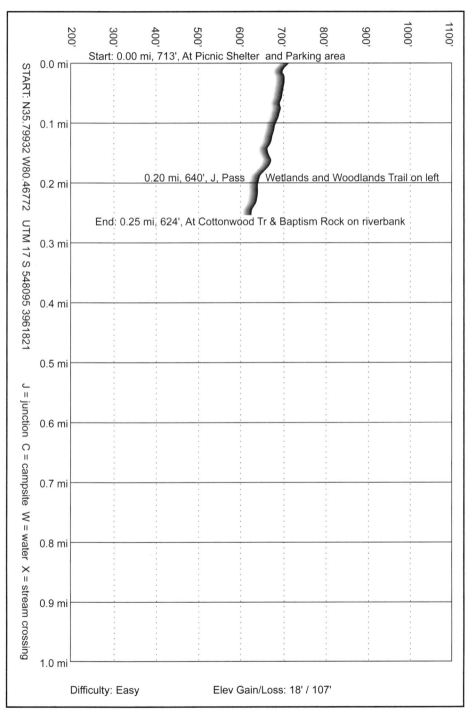

Difficulty: Easy   Elev Gain/Loss: 18' / 107'

Overlook Trail

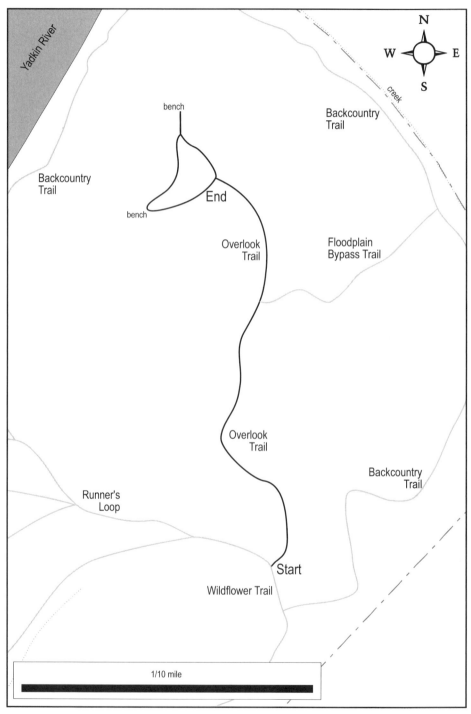

Yadkin River

N
W E
S

creek

bench

Backcountry
Trail

Backcountry
Trail

bench

End

Overlook
Trail

Floodplain
Bypass Trail

Overlook
Trail

Backcountry
Trail

Runner's
Loop

Start

Wildflower Trail

1/10 mile

Elevation Profile: Overlook Trail

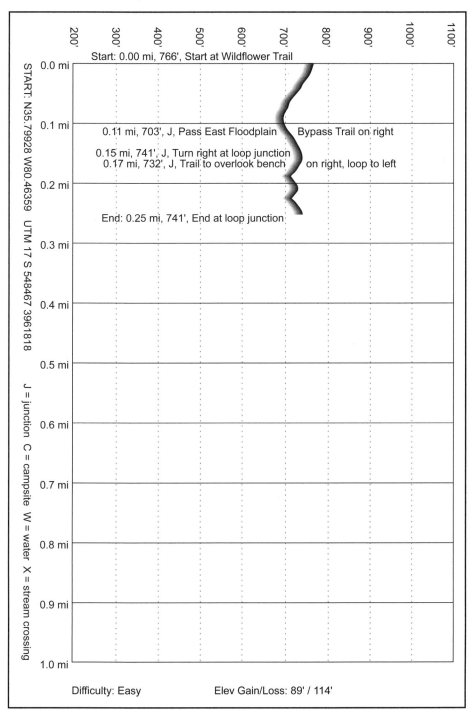

START: N35.79928 W80.46359 UTM 17 S 548467 3961818 J = junction C = campsite W = water X = stream crossing

Start: 0.00 mi, 766', Start at Wildflower Trail

0.11 mi, 703', J, Pass East Floodplain   Bypass Trail on right

0.15 mi, 741', J, Turn right at loop junction
0.17 mi, 732', J, Trail to overlook bench   on right, loop to left

End: 0.25 mi, 741', End at loop junction

Difficulty: Easy   Elev Gain/Loss: 89' / 114'

Runner's Loop Trail

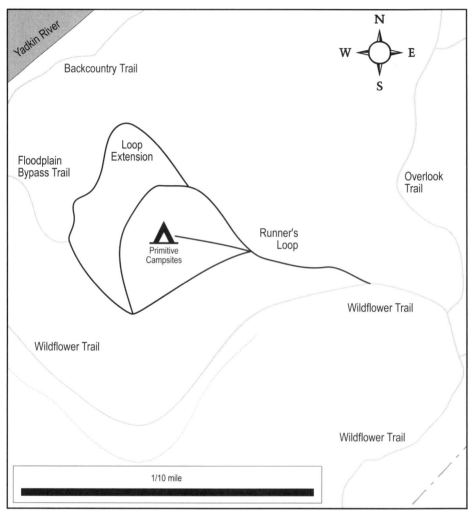

Elevation Profile: Runner's Loop Trail

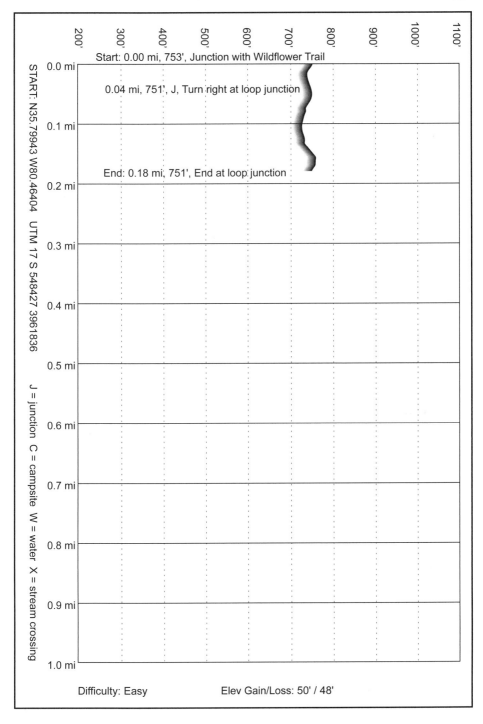

START: N35.79943 W80.46404 UTM 17 S 548427 3961836

J = junction C = campsite W = water X = stream crossing

Start: 0.00 mi, 753', Junction with Wildflower Trail

0.04 mi, 751', J, Turn right at loop junction

End: 0.18 mi, 751', End at loop junction

Difficulty: Easy   Elev Gain/Loss: 50' / 48'

Wetlands and Woodlands Trail

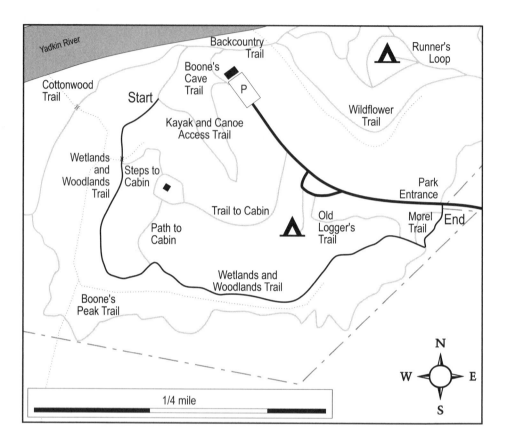

Elevation Profile: Wetlands and Woodlands Trail

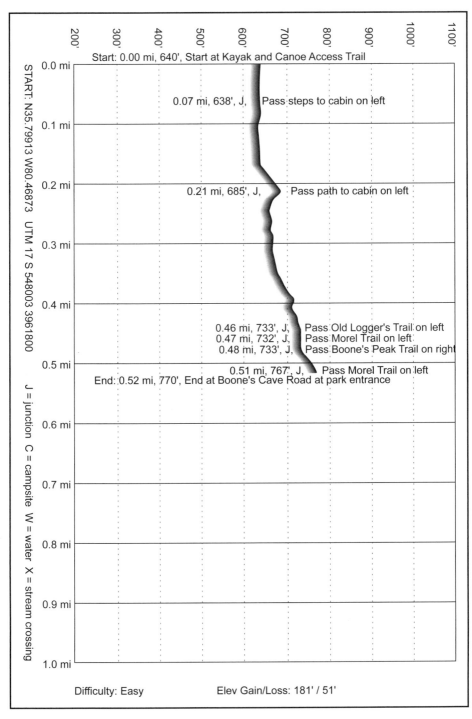

START: N35.79913 W80.46873 UTM 17 S 548003 3961800

J = junction C = campsite W = water X = stream crossing

200' 300' 400' 500' 600' 700' 800' 900' 1000' 1100'

Start: 0.00 mi, 640', Start at Kayak and Canoe Access Trail

0.0 mi

0.07 mi, 638', J, Pass steps to cabin on left

0.1 mi

0.2 mi 0.21 mi, 685', J, Pass path to cabin on left

0.3 mi

0.4 mi

0.46 mi, 733', J, Pass Old Logger's Trail on left
0.47 mi, 732', J, Pass Morel Trail on left
0.48 mi, 733', J, Pass Boone's Peak Trail on right

0.5 mi 0.51 mi, 767', J, Pass Morel Trail on left
End: 0.52 mi, 770', End at Boone's Cave Road at park entrance

0.6 mi

0.7 mi

0.8 mi

0.9 mi

1.0 mi

Difficulty: Easy   Elev Gain/Loss: 181' / 51'

Wildflower Trail

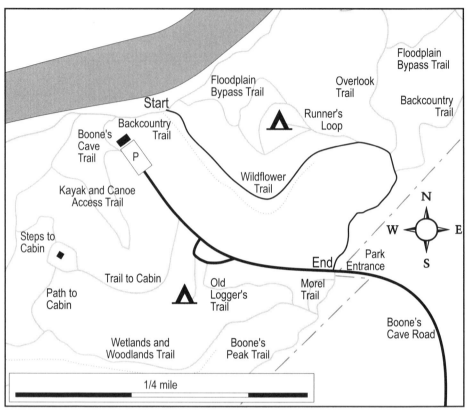

Elevation Profile: Wildflower Trail

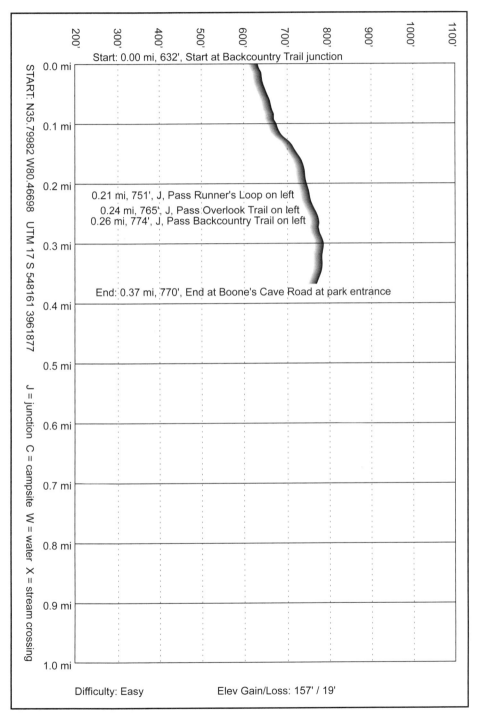

START: N35.79982 W80.46698   UTM 17 S 548161 3961877   J = junction   C = campsite   W = water   X = stream crossing

Start: 0.00 mi, 632', Start at Backcountry Trail junction

0.21 mi, 751', J, Pass Runner's Loop on left
0.24 mi, 765', J, Pass Overlook Trail on left
0.26 mi, 774', J, Pass Backcountry Trail on left

End: 0.37 mi, 770', End at Boone's Cave Road at park entrance

Difficulty: Easy   Elev Gain/Loss: 157' / 19'

Boone's Cave Park Trips

Trip	Use	Length (miles)	Elevation Gain/ Loss	Difficulty Rating	Page
BCP Trip A	H	1.00	298' / 298'	Moderate	276
BCP Trip B	H	1.22	249' / 203'	Moderate	278
BCP Trip C	H	2.68	573' / 571'	Moderate	280

BCP Trip A

Map	page 276	**Difficulty**	Easy
Length	1.00 miles	**Configuration**	Lollipop
Trailhead	Picnic Shelter	**Elev Gain/Loss**	298' / 298'

Start Coordinates N35.79930 W80.46767   UTM 17 S 548099 3961819

The Boone's Cave Park Trip A starts at the Picnic Shelter and makes a clockwise loop around the northeastern half of the park. This trip is the shortest trip route described for this park.

BCP Trip B

Map	page 278	**Difficulty**	Easy
Length	1.22 miles	**Configuration**	One Way
Trailhead	Picnic Shelter	**Elev Gain/Loss**	249' / 203'

Start Coordinates N35.79930 W80.46767   UTM 17 S 548099 3961819

The Boone's Cave Park Trip B starts at the Picnic Shelter and almost completes a clockwise loop around the southwestern half of the park. The route ends at the Boone monument, on the uphill side of the parking area.

BCP Trip C

Map	page 280	**Difficulty**	Moderate
Length	2.68 miles	**Configuration**	Combined
Trailhead	Picnic Shelter	**Elev Gain/Loss**	573' / 571'

Start Coordinates N35.79932 W80.46772   UTM 17 S 548095 3961821

The Boone's Cave Park Trip C includes most of the trails in the park without doubling back on any of them.

Other trips can be made by combining various segments of the other trails.

Boone's Cave Park Trip A

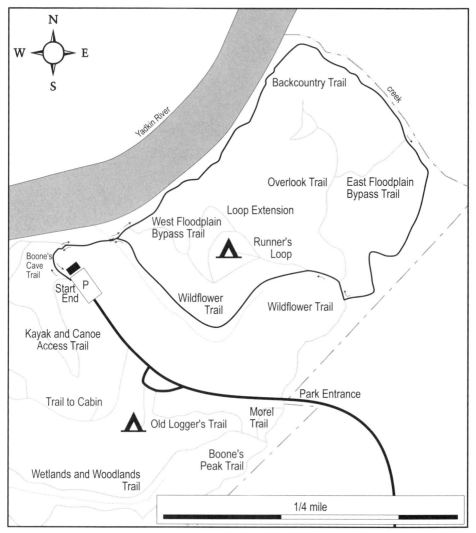

N
W — E
S

Yadkin River

creek

Backcountry Trail

Overlook Trail   East Floodplain
Bypass Trail

Loop Extension

West Floodplain
Bypass Trail

Runner's
Loop

Boone's
Cave
Trail

Start   P
End

Wildflower
Trail

Wildflower Trail

Kayak and Canoe
Access Trail

Trail to Cabin

Park Entrance

Morel
Trail

Old Logger's Trail

Boone's
Peak Trail

Wetlands and Woodlands
Trail

1/4 mile

Elevation Profile: Boone's Cave Park Trip A

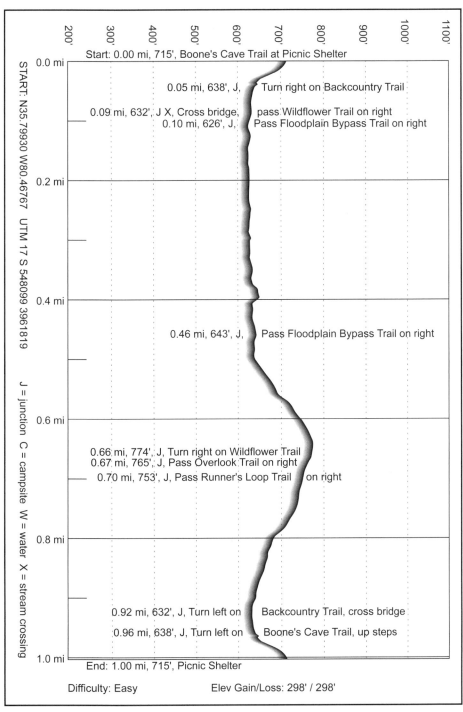

Boone's Cave Park Trip B

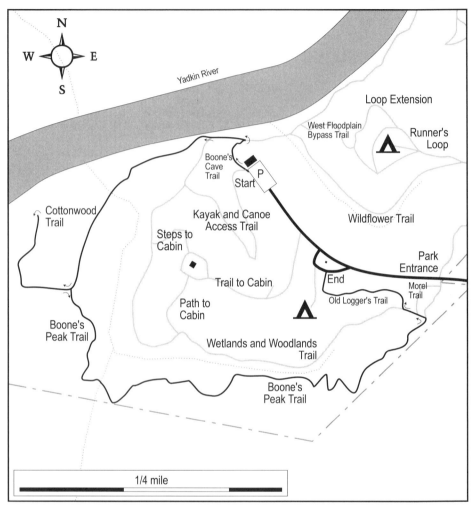

Elevation Profile: Boone's Cave Park Trip B

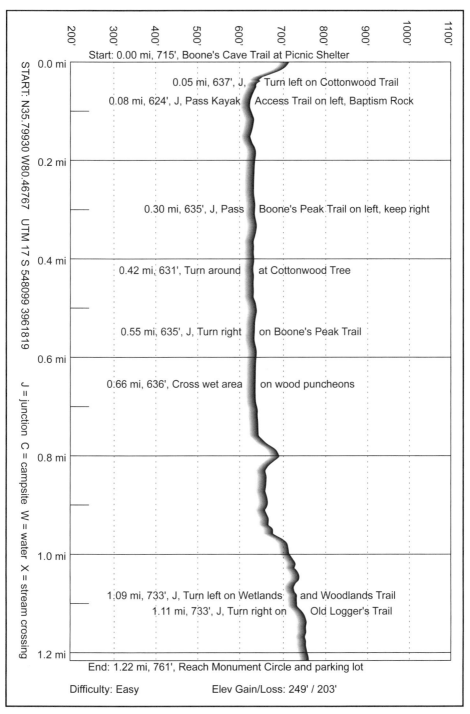

START: N35.79930 W80.46767 UTM 17 S 548099 3961819

J = junction C = campsite W = water X = stream crossing

Start: 0.00 mi, 715', Boone's Cave Trail at Picnic Shelter

0.05 mi, 637', J, Turn left on Cottonwood Trail

0.08 mi, 624', J, Pass Kayak Access Trail on left, Baptism Rock

0.30 mi, 635', J, Pass Boone's Peak Trail on left, keep right

0.42 mi, 631', Turn around at Cottonwood Tree

0.55 mi, 635', J, Turn right on Boone's Peak Trail

0.66 mi, 636', Cross wet area on wood puncheons

1.09 mi, 733', J, Turn left on Wetlands and Woodlands Trail

1.11 mi, 733', J, Turn right on Old Logger's Trail

End: 1.22 mi, 761', Reach Monument Circle and parking lot

Difficulty: Easy   Elev Gain/Loss: 249' / 203'

Boone's Cave Park Trip C

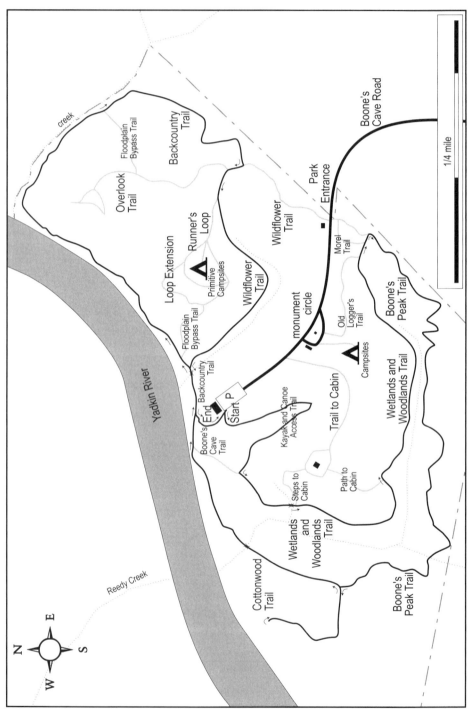

Elevation Profile: Boone's Cave Park Trip C

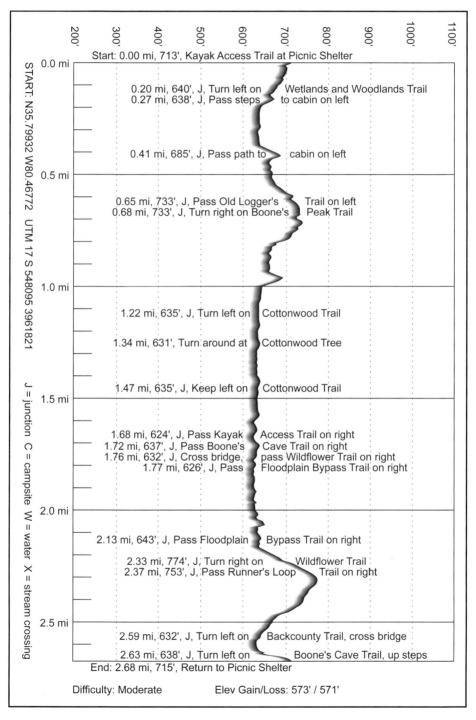

START: N35.79932 W80.46772 UTM 17 S 548095 3961821

J = junction C = campsite W = water X = stream crossing

Start: 0.00 mi, 713', Kayak Access Trail at Picnic Shelter

0.20 mi, 640', J, Turn left on Wetlands and Woodlands Trail
0.27 mi, 638', J, Pass steps to cabin on left

0.41 mi, 685', J, Pass path to cabin on left

0.65 mi, 733', J, Pass Old Logger's Trail on left
0.68 mi, 733', J, Turn right on Boone's Peak Trail

1.22 mi, 635', J, Turn left on Cottonwood Trail

1.34 mi, 631', Turn around at Cottonwood Tree

1.47 mi, 635', J, Keep left on Cottonwood Trail

1.68 mi, 624', J, Pass Kayak Access Trail on right
1.72 mi, 637', J, Pass Boone's Cave Trail on right
1.76 mi, 632', J, Cross bridge, pass Wildflower Trail on right
1.77 mi, 626', J, Pass Floodplain Bypass Trail on right

2.13 mi, 643', J, Pass Floodplain Bypass Trail on right

2.33 mi, 774', J, Turn right on Wildflower Trail
2.37 mi, 753', J, Pass Runner's Loop Trail on right

2.59 mi, 632', J, Turn left on Backcounty Trail, cross bridge

2.63 mi, 638', J, Turn left on Boone's Cave Trail, up steps

End: 2.68 mi, 715', Return to Picnic Shelter

Difficulty: Moderate   Elev Gain/Loss: 573' / 571'

Denson's Creek Area

Just east of Troy, NC is a relatively small but developing trail area that lies along Denson's Creek. There is a mix of USFS and Town of Troy properties in this area that contain several interconnected trails.

Behind the Uwharrie District Ranger Office in Troy, the USFS property extends all the way to Denson's Creek. Several trails have been built through this property, including an interpretive trail that educates visitors about features common to the area.

The Town dedicated the Roy J. Maness Nature Preserve in 2000. Within the Preserve is the Troy Reservoir, a 20-acre impoundment on Hughes Creek. The property is heavily wooded and provides beautiful vistas looking down on the reservoir. Hours for the Nature Preserve are posted at the park's entrance. The Preserve is generally open to the public from sunrise to 10:00 pm daily. For more information, contact the Town of Troy at 910-572-3661.

Bicycle and motorized use is prohibited on the trails in the Denson's Creek area.

ACCESS

Ranger Station Trailhead

The USFS District Ranger's Office is located on NC 24-27, 1.7 miles east of the courthouse in Troy. There is a small parking lot beside the office and another behind the office. The USFS Denson's Creek trails start at the back side of the

UTM	17 S 603281 3913745
Lat/Lon	N35.36167 W79.86316

office parking lot. The street address of the Ranger Station is 789 NC24/27, Troy, NC.

Fitness Loop Trailhead

A small parking area is located on Page Street (SR 1332), about 0.2 miles north of NC 24/27. This trailhead is 0.3 miles from the Ranger Station Trailhead. This parking area provides access to the

UTM	17 S 602817 3914037
Lat/Lon	N35.36435 W79.86824

Fitness Loop Trail.

Denson's Creek Area

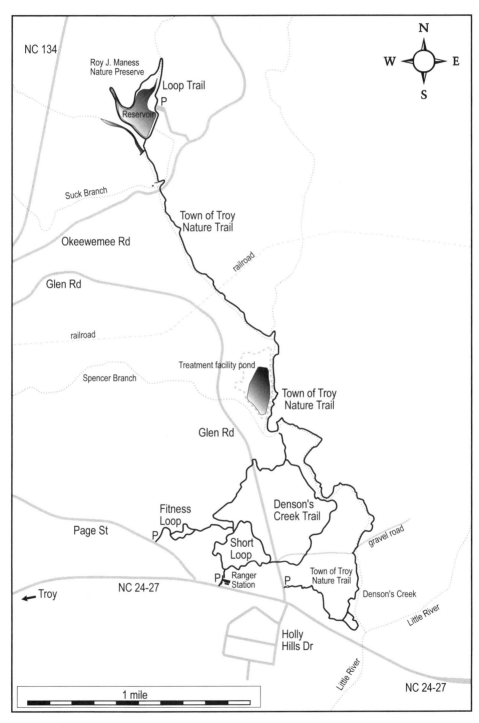

NC 134

Roy J. Maness
Nature Preserve

Loop Trail

P

Reservoir

N
W — E
S

Suck Branch

Town of Troy
Nature Trail

Okeewemee Rd

railroad

Glen Rd

railroad

Treatment facility pond

Spencer Branch

Town of Troy
Nature Trail

Glen Rd

Fitness
Loop

Denson's
Creek Trail

Page St

P

Short
Loop

gravel road

P   Ranger
    Station

P

Troy

NC 24-27

Town of Troy
Nature Trail

Denson's Creek

Little River

Holly
Hills Dr

Little River

NC 24-27

1 mile

Glen Road Trailhead

The 24/27 Parking Area is located on Glen Road (SR 1324), close to its intersection with NC 24/27. The Town Of Troy Nature Trail starts at this parking area.

UTM	17 S 603752 3913731
Lat/Lon	N35.36150 W79.85799

Nature Preserve Trailhead

The Roy J. Maness Nature Preserve is located on Okeewemee Road (SR 1323). From the parking area in the Preserve, you can access the Preserve Loop Trail and the northern end of the Town Of Troy Nature Trail.

UTM	17 S 602799 3917153
Lat/Lon	N35.39244 W79.86804

NOTES OF INTEREST

The trails in the Denson's Creek Area are not long.

CAMPING

There is no camping allowed along these trails. There is a small camping area in the Roy J. Maness Nature Preserve.

MAPS

The USFS produces a local brochure titled Denson's Creek Trail Map that shows the Denson's Creek Trail and the the Short Loop. It does not show the other trails in the area.

Denson's Creek Area Trails

Trail Name	Length (miles)	Elevation Gain/Loss	Difficulty Rating	Map (page)
Denson's Creek	2.20	320' / 320'	Moderate	288
Denson's Creek Short Loop	0.97	131' / 131'	Easy	290
Nature Preserve Loop	1.10	128' / 128'	Easy	292
Town of Troy Nature	3.98	505' / 589'	Moderate	294

Denson's Creek Trail

Map	page 288	**Difficulty**	Moderate
Length	2.22 miles	**Configuration**	Lollipop
Trailhead	Ranger Station	**Elev Gain/Loss**	320' / 320'

Start Coordinates N35.36210, W79.86276;   17 S 603318 3913793

The Denson's Creek Trail was built by Youth Conservation Corps crews in 1974. Hurricane Fran did significant damage to this area in 1996 and many of the trees were salvaged through a timber sale. The trail was renovated and remarked in 2004 by Boy Scout Troop 9 as part of an Eagle Scout project.

In addition to being a nice hiking trail, the Denson's Creek Trail is also an interpretive trail. Along the trail are twelve numbered markers that match up with a descriptive brochure. The numbered sites along the trail detail some of the plants you will see, the historical sites along the way, and some of the land management practices used in the area. Copies of the brochure are available at the kiosk outside the Ranger Station at the trailhead.

The Denson's Creek Trail starts and ends at the parking lot behind the ranger's office on NC 24/27. The route is marked with white blazes. About 50' from the parking lot is a trail junction. Turn right and follow the trail loop in a counterclockwise direction.

The route next passes a trail to the left. This trail is the Short Loop option. Continuing straight, the route soon crosses paved Glen Road (SR 1324). The route leaves the far side of the road and enters a graveled road, but the trail almost immediately splits off to the right into the woods. The route will cross back over the gravel road further down the hill.

The route passes over a small bluff overlooking Denson's Creek. At one time there was a small bench at this spot.

Farther along, the route passes a side trail that leads to Denson's Creek and the former site of a footbridge. Directly across the creek is the Town of Troy Nature Trail. The creek at this point is relatively deep and does not offer any decent rock hopping options. The route climbs back up to cross Glen Road again. Veer to the left as you cross the road to find the trail on the far side.

The next trail junction to the right leads to the USFS Fitness Trail loop. Not far from that junction is one with a trail to the left. This trail is the other end of the Short Loop option. There is small footbridge between these two junctions. The route then climbs back to the first junction not far from the parking lot.

Denson's Creek Short Loop Trail

Map	page 290	**Difficulty**	Easy
Length	0.97 miles	**Configuration**	Lollipop
Trailhead	Ranger Station	**Elev Gain/Loss**	131' / 131'

Start Coordinates N35.36210, W79.86276;   17 S 603318 3913793

The Short Loop does not feature any numbered markers. It provides a short hike from the ranger station that is just under a mile in length.

A short distance from the Short Loop along the west end of the Denson's Creek Trail, is a connector trail that leads to the Fitness Loop Trail. The Fitness Loop Trail features a series of exercise stations spaced out along it's length.

Nature Preserve Loop Trail

Map	page 292	**Difficulty**	Easy
Length	1.10 miles	**Configuration**	Loop
Trailhead	Nature Preserve	**Elev Gain/Loss**	128' / 128'

Start Coordinates N35.39232, W79.86810;   17 S 602794 3917140

The Roy J. Maness Nature Preserve was dedicated September 9, 2000. This nature preserve was created by the Town of Troy to protect and maintain the high quality of water in Denson's Creek and provide the benefit of conservation and recreation for all citizens.

The Nature Preserve is located on Okeewemee Road (SR 1323), about 1.1 miles east of NC 134, north of Troy, NC. There is a small camping area near the parking lot. Fishing is allowed in the preserve.

The Nature Preserve Loop Trail starts at the parking area and circles around the reservoir that serves the Town of Troy. Along the route are small wooden footbridges over two small creeks that feed into the reservoir. There are a couple of benches located along the trail.

Town of Troy Nature Trail

Map	page 294	**Difficulty**	Moderate
Length	3.98 miles	**Configuration**	One Way
Trailhead	24/27 Parking Area	**Elev Gain/Loss**	505' / 589'

Start Coordinates N35.36152, W79.85780;   17 S 603769 3913734

The Town of Troy Nature Trail was built in the late 2000's. The route starts at a small parking area on Glen Road, near NC 24/27, and follows Denson's Creek upstream about four miles to the Roy J. Maness Nature Preserve.

The route initially heads southeast paralleling the highway. As it nears Denson's Creek, there is an old road bed to the left that shortcuts a bend in the trail. Keeping right on the trail you will soon reach a junction with a spur trail. This spur trail drops down closer to the level of the creek and leads you under the NC 24-27 highway bridge. The spur trail ends at the bridge.

The Nature Trail route follows Denson's Creek upstream for most of its length. Trail maintenance crews have installed a number of features along the way that are not normally found on hiking trails. These include wood guardrails, steel cable handrails up steep climbs, wood stairs over short but steep sections, and fallen logs put into service as foot bridges.

Along the way the trail passes several small dams across the creek. Just north of Okeewemee Road there is a large wood footbridge over Denson's Creek. It connects the trail route with a small building and parking area on the far side of the creek. In 2012, a small dam at this location was removed to improve water flow in the creek. Remnants of the dam may still be visible.

As the route nears its end at the Roy J. Maness Nature Preserve, it climbs past a larger dam across Denson's Creek. The route ends where it junctions with the Nature Preserve Loop Trail on top of the reservoir dam.

Denson's Creek Trail

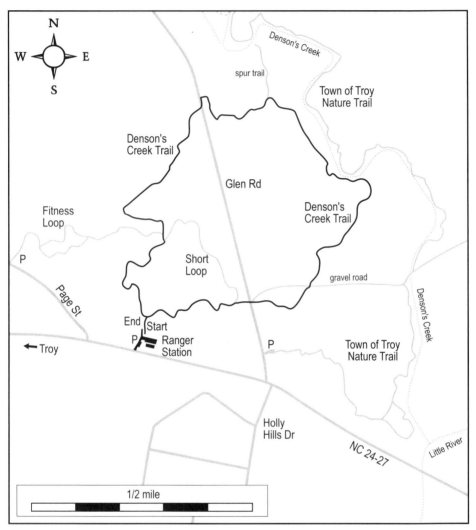

Elevation Profile: Denson's Creek Trail

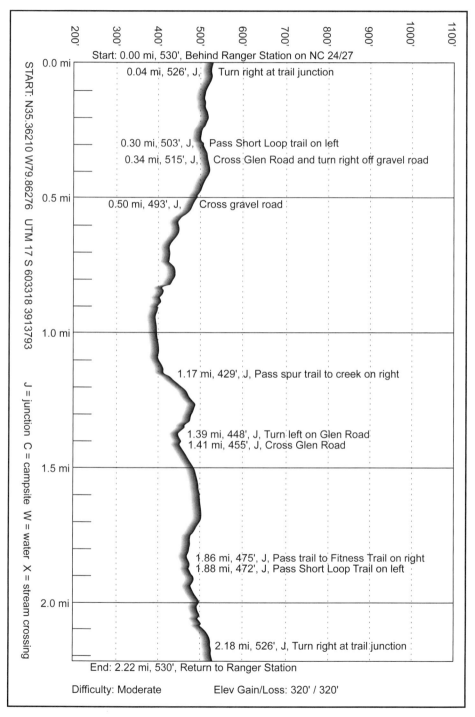

START: N35.36210 W79.86276 UTM 17 S 603318 3913793

J = junction C = campsite W = water X = stream crossing

Start: 0.00 mi, 530', Behind Ranger Station on NC 24/27

0.04 mi, 526', J, Turn right at trail junction

0.30 mi, 503', J, Pass Short Loop trail on left

0.34 mi, 515', J, Cross Glen Road and turn right off gravel road

0.50 mi, 493', J, Cross gravel road

1.17 mi, 429', J, Pass spur trail to creek on right

1.39 mi, 448', J, Turn left on Glen Road
1.41 mi, 455', J, Cross Glen Road

1.86 mi, 475', J, Pass trail to Fitness Trail on right
1.88 mi, 472', J, Pass Short Loop Trail on left

2.18 mi, 526', J, Turn right at trail junction

End: 2.22 mi, 530', Return to Ranger Station

Difficulty: Moderate   Elev Gain/Loss: 320' / 320'

Denson's Creek Short Loop Trail

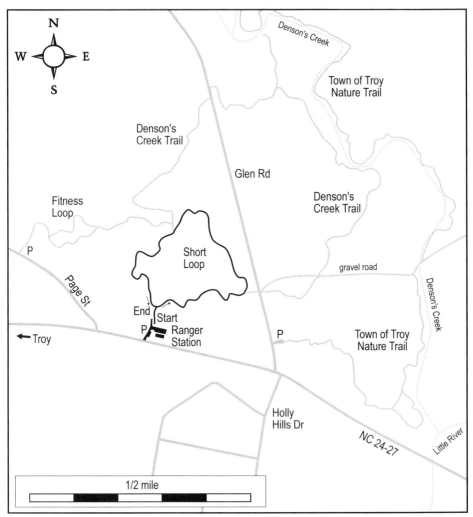

Elevation Profile: Denson's Creek Short Loop Trail

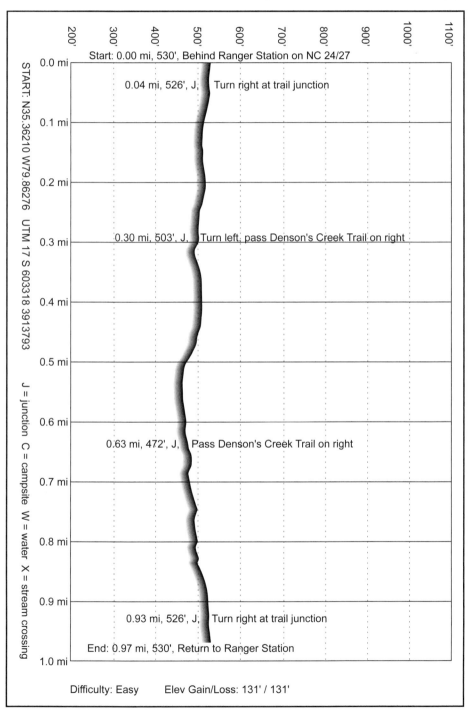

START: N35.36210 W79.86276   UTM 17 S 603318 3913793   J = junction C = campsite W = water X = stream crossing

200' 300' 400' 500' 600' 700' 800' 900' 1000' 1100'

START:

0.0 mi — Start: 0.00 mi, 530', Behind Ranger Station on NC 24/27

0.04 mi, 526', J, Turn right at trail junction

0.1 mi

0.2 mi

0.3 mi — 0.30 mi, 503', J, Turn left, pass Denson's Creek Trail on right

0.4 mi

0.5 mi

0.6 mi

0.63 mi, 472', J, Pass Denson's Creek Trail on right

0.7 mi

0.8 mi

0.9 mi

0.93 mi, 526', J, Turn right at trail junction

End: 0.97 mi, 530', Return to Ranger Station

1.0 mi

Difficulty: Easy   Elev Gain/Loss: 131' / 131'

Nature Preserve Loop Trail

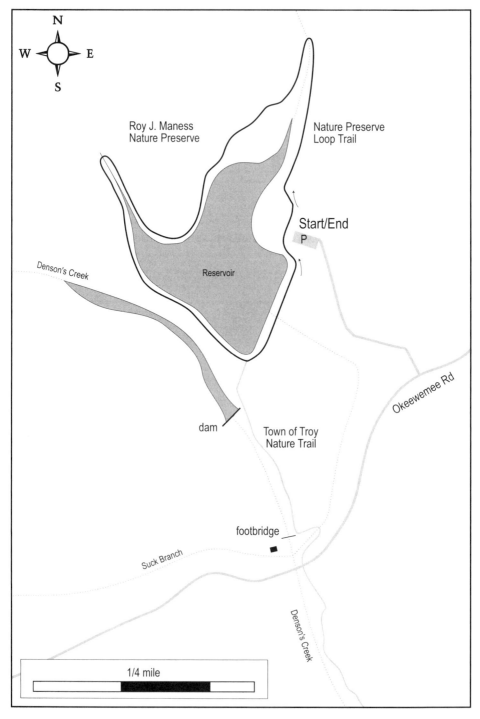

Elevation Profile: Nature Preserve Loop Trail

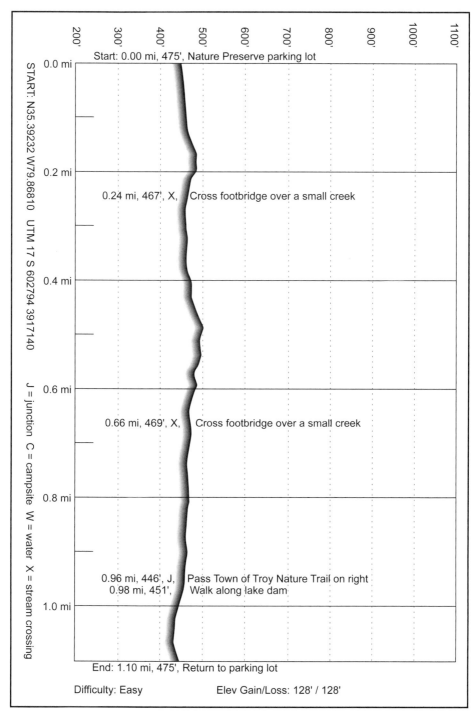

Start: 0.00 mi, 475', Nature Preserve parking lot

START: N35.39232 W79.86810 UTM 17 S 602794 3917140

J = junction C = campsite W = water X = stream crossing

0.24 mi, 467', X, Cross footbridge over a small creek

0.66 mi, 469', X, Cross footbridge over a small creek

0.96 mi, 446', J, Pass Town of Troy Nature Trail on right
0.98 mi, 451',   Walk along lake dam

End: 1.10 mi, 475', Return to parking lot

Difficulty: Easy   Elev Gain/Loss: 128' / 128'

Town of Troy Nature Trail

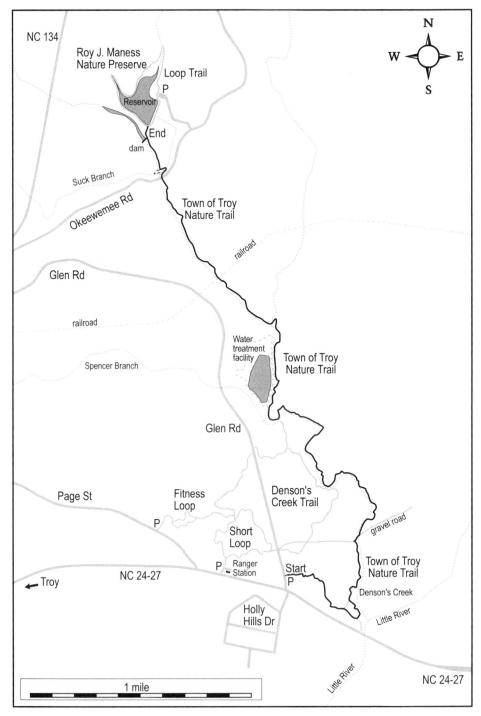

NC 134

Roy J. Maness
Nature Preserve

Loop Trail

P

Reservoir

End

dam

Suck Branch

Okeewemee Rd

Town of Troy
Nature Trail

railroad

Glen Rd

railroad

Spencer Branch

Water
treatment
facility

Town of Troy
Nature Trail

Glen Rd

Page St

Fitness
Loop

Denson's
Creek Trail

P

Short
Loop

gravel road

P · Ranger
Station

Start
P

Town of Troy
Nature Trail

Troy

NC 24-27

Denson's Creek

Holly
Hills Dr

Little River

Little River

NC 24-27

N
W   E
S

1 mile

Elevation Profile: Town of Troy Nature Trail

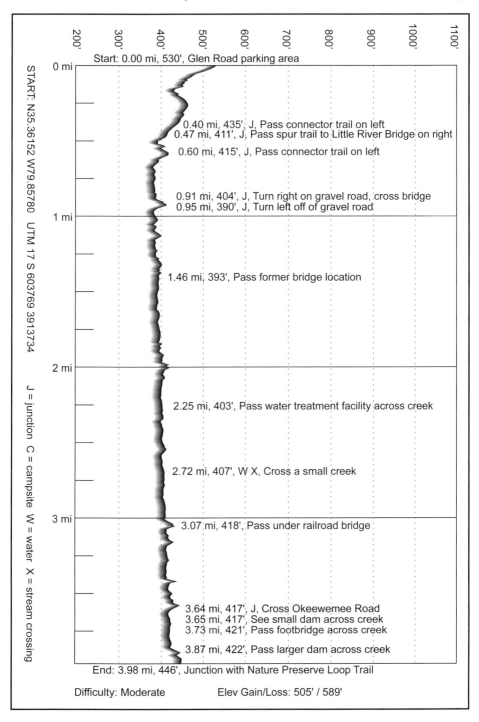

START: N35.36152 W79.85780   UTM 17 S 603769 3913734

J = junction C = campsite W = water X = stream crossing

200'   300'   400'   500'   600'   700'   800'   900'   1000'   1100'

Start: 0.00 mi, 530', Glen Road parking area

0 mi

0.40 mi, 435', J, Pass connector trail on left
0.47 mi, 411', J, Pass spur trail to Little River Bridge on right

0.60 mi, 415', J, Pass connector trail on left

0.91 mi, 404', J, Turn right on gravel road, cross bridge
0.95 mi, 390', J, Turn left off of gravel road

1 mi

1.46 mi, 393', Pass former bridge location

2 mi

2.25 mi, 403', Pass water treatment facility across creek

2.72 mi, 407', W X, Cross a small creek

3 mi

3.07 mi, 418', Pass under railroad bridge

3.64 mi, 417', J, Cross Okeewemee Road
3.65 mi, 417', See small dam across creek
3.73 mi, 421', Pass footbridge across creek

3.87 mi, 422', Pass larger dam across creek

End: 3.98 mi, 446', Junction with Nature Preserve Loop Trail

Difficulty: Moderate   Elev Gain/Loss: 505' / 589'

Denson's Creek Area Trips

Trip	Use	Length (miles)	Elevation Gain/ Loss	Difficulty Rating	Page
DCA Trip A	H	0.97	131' / 131'	Easy	298
DCA Trip B	H	3.31	549' / 549'	Moderate	300
DCA Trip C	H	11.37	1,387' / 1,387'	Difficult	302

Denson's Creek Trip A

Map	page 298	**Difficulty**	Easy
Length	0.97 miles	**Configuration**	Loop
Trailhead	Ranger Station	**Elev Gain/Loss**	131' / 131'

Start Coordinates N35.36210 W79.86276   UTM 17 S 603318 3913793

DCA Trip A follows the Denson's Creek Short Loop Trail route.

You can easily add 0.7 miles to this trip by adding in the Fitness Trail Loop. Turn right at the second Denson's Creek Trail intersection and then take the next left to the Fitness Loop. Go around the loop and return to the Short Loop Trail.

Denson's Creek Trip B

Map	page 320	**Difficulty**	Moderate
Length	3.31 miles	**Configuration**	Loop
Trailhead	Ranger Station	**Elev Gain/Loss**	549' / 549'

Start Coordinates N35.36210 W79.86276   UTM 17 S 603318 3913793

DCA Trip B starts with the Denson's Creek Trail and adds a portion of the Town of Troy Nature Trail for a slightly longer trip.

Denson's Creek Trip C

Map	page 302	**Difficulty**	Difficult
Length	11.37 miles	**Configuration**	Combined
Trailhead	Nature Preserve	**Elev Gain/Loss**	1,387' / 1,387'

Start Coordinates N35.39232 W79.86810   UTM 17 S 602794 3917140

DCA Trip C starts at the Nature Preserve and includes nearly all of the trails in the Denson's Creek Area except for the Fitness Trail and the Denson's Creek Short Loop Trail.

Denson's Creek Trip A

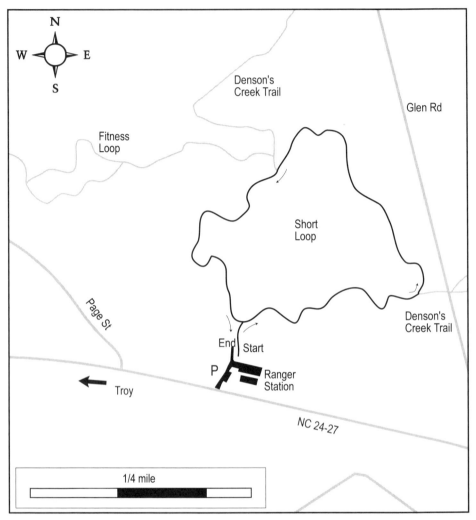

Elevation Profile: Denson's Creek Trip A

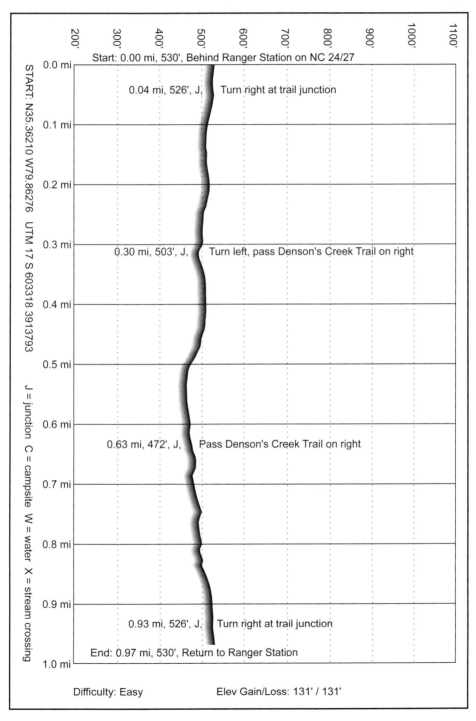

START: N35.36210 W79.86276 UTM 17 S 603318 3913793   J = junction C = campsite W = water X = stream crossing

200'   300'   400'   500'   600'   700'   800'   900'   1000'   1100'

0.0 mi Start: 0.00 mi, 530', Behind Ranger Station on NC 24/27

0.04 mi, 526', J,   Turn right at trail junction

0.1 mi

0.2 mi

0.3 mi 0.30 mi, 503', J,   Turn left, pass Denson's Creek Trail on right

0.4 mi

0.5 mi

0.6 mi

0.63 mi, 472', J,   Pass Denson's Creek Trail on right

0.7 mi

0.8 mi

0.9 mi

0.93 mi, 526', J,   Turn right at trail junction

End: 0.97 mi, 530', Return to Ranger Station

1.0 mi

Difficulty: Easy   Elev Gain/Loss: 131' / 131'

Denson's Creek Trip B

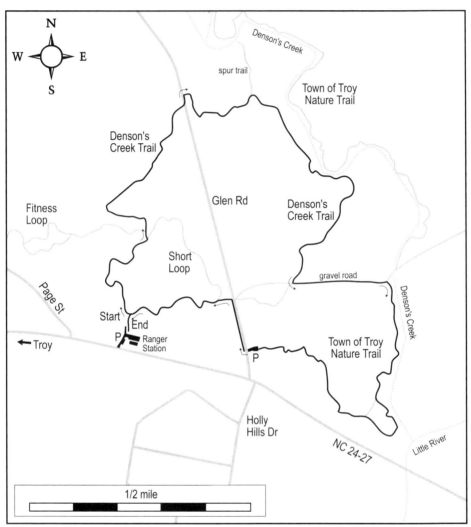

Elevation Profile: Denson's Creek Trip B

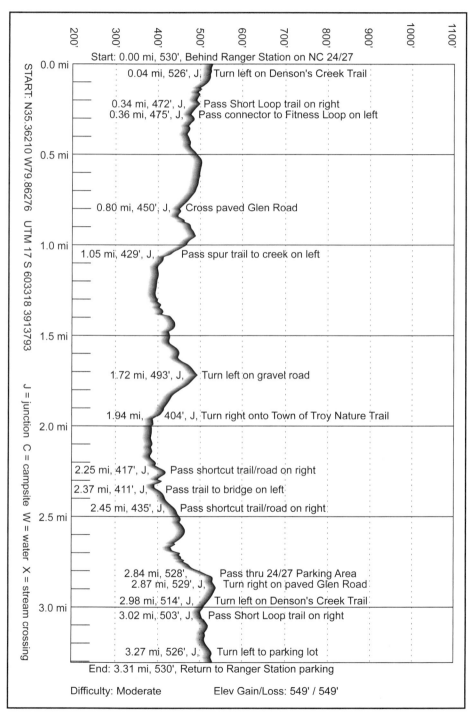

START: N35.36210 W79.86276   UTM 17 S 603318 3913793   J = junction C = campsite W = water X = stream crossing

Start: 0.00 mi, 530', Behind Ranger Station on NC 24/27

0.0 mi

0.04 mi, 526', J, Turn left on Denson's Creek Trail

0.34 mi, 472', J, Pass Short Loop trail on right
0.36 mi, 475', J, Pass connector to Fitness Loop on left

0.5 mi

0.80 mi, 450', J, Cross paved Glen Road

1.0 mi

1.05 mi, 429', J, Pass spur trail to creek on left

1.5 mi

1.72 mi, 493', J, Turn left on gravel road

1.94 mi, 404', J, Turn right onto Town of Troy Nature Trail

2.0 mi

2.25 mi, 417', J, Pass shortcut trail/road on right
2.37 mi, 411', J, Pass trail to bridge on left
2.45 mi, 435', J, Pass shortcut trail/road on right

2.5 mi

2.84 mi, 528', Pass thru 24/27 Parking Area
2.87 mi, 529', J, Turn right on paved Glen Road
2.98 mi, 514', J, Turn left on Denson's Creek Trail
3.02 mi, 503', J, Pass Short Loop trail on right

3.0 mi

3.27 mi, 526', J, Turn left to parking lot

End: 3.31 mi, 530', Return to Ranger Station parking

Difficulty: Moderate   Elev Gain/Loss: 549' / 549'

Denson's Creek Trip C

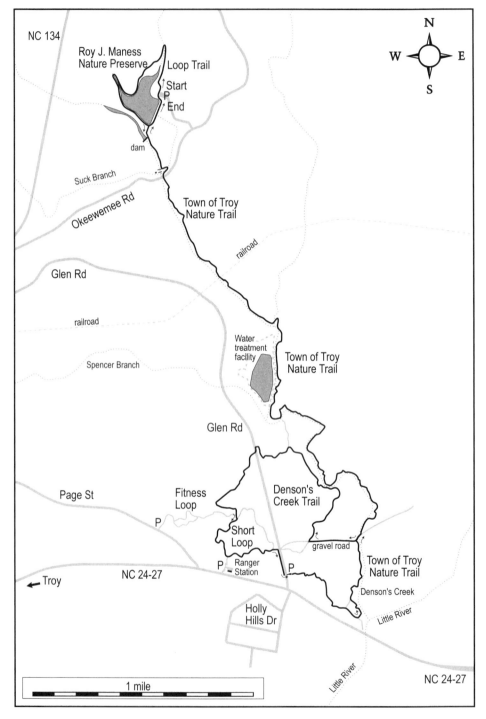

Elevation Profile: Denson's Creek Trip C

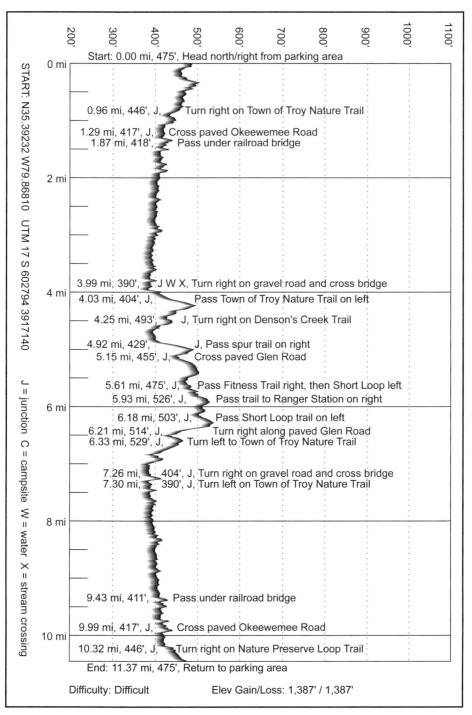

START: N35.39232 W79.86810 UTM 17 S 602794 3917140   J = junction C = campsite W = water X = stream crossing

200' 300' 400' 500' 600' 700' 800' 900' 1000' 1100'

0 mi — Start: 0.00 mi, 475', Head north/right from parking area

0.96 mi, 446', J,   Turn right on Town of Troy Nature Trail

1.29 mi, 417', J,   Cross paved Okeewemee Road
1.87 mi, 418',   Pass under railroad bridge

2 mi

3.99 mi, 390',   J W X, Turn right on gravel road and cross bridge
4 mi — 4.03 mi, 404', J,   Pass Town of Troy Nature Trail on left

4.25 mi, 493',   J, Turn right on Denson's Creek Trail

4.92 mi, 429',   J, Pass spur trail on right
5.15 mi, 455', J,   Cross paved Glen Road

5.61 mi, 475', J,   Pass Fitness Trail right, then Short Loop left
5.93 mi, 526', J,   Pass trail to Ranger Station on right
6 mi

6.18 mi, 503', J,   Pass Short Loop trail on left
6.21 mi, 514', J,   Turn right along paved Glen Road
6.33 mi, 529', J,   Turn left to Town of Troy Nature Trail

7.26 mi,   404', J, Turn right on gravel road and cross bridge
7.30 mi,   390', J, Turn left on Town of Troy Nature Trail

8 mi

9.43 mi, 411',   Pass under railroad bridge

9.99 mi, 417', J,   Cross paved Okeewemee Road
10 mi
10.32 mi, 446', J,   Turn right on Nature Preserve Loop Trail

End: 11.37 mi, 475', Return to parking area

Difficulty: Difficult   Elev Gain/Loss: 1,387' / 1,387'

Morris Mountain Area

The Morris Mountain Area is situated on the north side of NC 109, between Troy and the community of Uwharrie. Prior to the 1970's, a network of jeep trails criss-crossed Morris Mountain and its neighbors. This trail system even had signs posted at some of the intersections. A few of these signs were still standing when I first began exploring the area in the early 1990's. Most of these jeep trails were abandoned during the late 1970's when the ORV trail system was established in the Badin Lake Area. Eventually the roads were all gated and closed to jeep and ORV use.

Today the majority of trail users on Morris Mountain are hikers on the Uwharrie Trail. A few logging access roads in the area connect together and offer mountain bikers a place to do some riding. Unfortunately, loop routes for bikers in this area are scarce, but there are several out and back routes worth exploring. This chapter will cover the roads in this area, and the trips will include the Uwharrie Trail, but details about the Uwharrie Trail itself can be found in the chapter dedicated to that trail.

The bikeable routes are not signed or blazed and some of the older ones have not been maintained for a number of years. Morris Mountain's bike trips are best suited for those with an adventurous spirit. Although it is fairly easy to follow the roadbeds, you may have to go around fallen trees and other obstacles.

Morris Mountain and its subpeaks dominate the geography of this area, forming a ridge that runs generally north-south. The highest summits of Morris Mountain rise a little more than 820' above sea level. Spencer Creek and its tributaries parallel the east side of this ridge and separate Morris Mountain from a neighboring ridge of less defined mountains with similar elevations.

A few old homeplaces can still be recognized, as well as several sawmill sites and mining pits. Logging activity has taken place around Morris Mountain in recent years. New sections of logging roads were constructed. Panther Branch Road has been realigned since the first edition of this guide was written. Several timber cuts, or regeneration zones, can be seen along these trails and roads.

ACCESS

West Morris Mountain Trailhead

Located on the west side of the area, 1.1 miles north on Ophir Road (SR 1303) from Uwharrie, this trailhead can be found just beyond the West Morris Mountain Camp. Turn off of Ophir Road onto the graveled drive for the camp and

UTM	17 S 591378 3920970
Lat/Lon	N35.42797 W79.99336

continue past the old camping sites on the left side of the road. Just past the fork to the right (leading to the camping sites) is a small grassy clearing. A Forest Service gate marking the start of Camp Road is located on the far side of the clearing. Parking is available for 10 to so vehicles. There are no other facilities at this trailhead. Camp Road leads from this trailhead to the Uwharrie Trail (hiking only) and Morris Mountain Road. Bicycles are not permitted to use Camp Road.

109 Trailhead

On the south side of the area is the 109 Trailhead, serving the Uwharrie Trail. This trailhead is located on NC 109, 6.0 miles north of the courthouse in Troy (by way of NC 109 Business) and 1.9 miles south of the River Road (SR 1150)

UTM	17 S 592467 3917730
Lat/Lon	N35.39866 W79.98173

intersection at Uwharrie. There is a parking lot and bulletin board at this trailhead, with room to park 10 or so vehicles.

Cattail Creek Trailhead

Cattail Creek Trailhead is located on NC 109, 100 hundred yards south of the 109 Trailhead. Spencer Creek Road, a gated and graveled Forest System road, leads from this trailhead across Cattail Creek. The roadbed becomes

UTM	17 S 603752 3913731
Lat/Lon	N35.36150 W79.85799

progressively more overgrown the farther you go along it, but it does eventually connect to Morris Mountain Road. Parking space for 3 or 4 vehicles can be found here, but there are no other facilities.

Tower Road Trailhead

Tower Road Trailhead lies on the east side of the area, 2.1 miles past the end of pavement on Tower Road (SR 1134) 5.2 miles north of NC 109. The trailhead is 8.8 miles from Uwharrie by way of NC 109 and Tower Road, and 4.3 miles from

UTM	17 S 594476 3923484
Lat/Lon	N35.45034 W79.95895

the courthouse in Troy. Morris Mountain Road, a gated and graveled Forest System road, begins here. There is room to park 3 or 4 vehicles beside the gate. There are no other facilities.

Morris Mountain Area

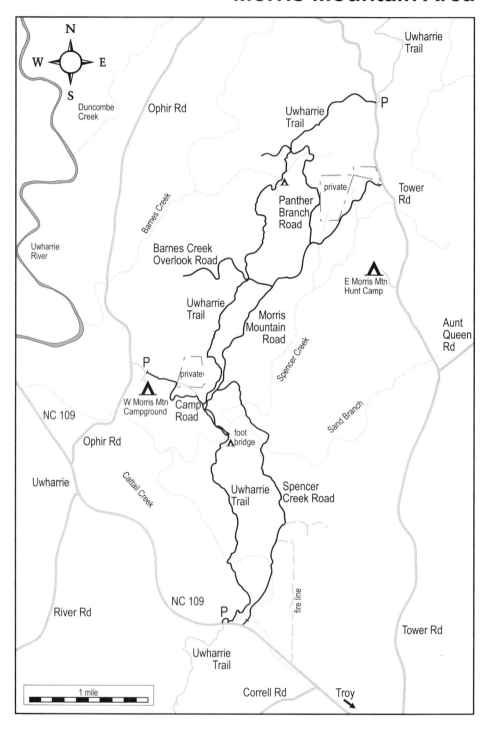

Horse Mountain Trailhead

Horse Mountain Trailhead is also located on the unpaved portion of Tower Road (SR 1134) 0.7 miles north of Tower Road Trailhead. This trailhead is located where the Uwharrie Trail crosses Tower Road. No provisions for parking have been

UTM	17 S 594375 3924546
Lat/Lon	N35.45993 W79.95994

made at this trailhead, although a few vehicles might squeeze in along a gated Forest road on the east side of Tower Road.

CAMPING

The Forest Service developed the Morris Mountain tract as an alternative to the heavily hunted Badin Lake Area. Two semi-developed camping areas, one on the east side of the area and one on the west, were built for hunters, although anyone can use them. There is no fee to use the East camp, but there is a $5 fee to use sites at the West camp.

East Morris Mountain Hunt Camp is located off of Tower Road (SR 1134). It's gate is opened during deer hunting season. There are no facilities at this site and no roads or trails that connect to the rest of the Morris Mountain Area.

West Morris Mountain Hunt Camp was renovated in 1993-94 by the Senior Community Service Work Program. It is located off a gravel road that connects to Ophir Road (SR 1303). This site now features 14 sites with picnic tables, fire rings, and pit toilets, but no water source. Camp Road, an older, gated logging road, connects West Morris Mountain Hunt Camp to the Uwharrie hiking trail and to Morris Mountain Road.

A well-used primitive camping area is located along the Uwharrie Trail at Spencer Creek. A nice wading hole is just downstream of the footbridge over Spencer Creek, located about 50 yards upstream of the camping area. Another popular campsite can be found where the Uwharrie Trail crosses Panther Branch.

MAPS

The local USFS District Ranger's office has produced simple maps covering the entire length of the Uwharrie Trail, which includes the Morris Mountain Area. The 2012 version of this map was titled "Uwharrie Hiking Trails". This map is printed on 8 1/2" by 14" paper and is generally accurate for this area but does not include topo lines or some of the oldest and newest sections of the logging roads.

Another map produced by the USFS office around 1985, titled the "Uwharrie Area Trail Map", was printed on 11" by 17" paper and included topo lines. This map indicated some of the old roadbeds in the area, including most of the ones in this guidebook. It also showed the abandoned West Morris Mountain Trail. The trail lines on this map were approximate locations, although they were generally accurate.

The USGS topographic map covering this area is the Lovejoy quadrangle. The 1983 revision does not show the trails. It does show a few pieces of the original jeep trail routes. The 1994 revision shows the Uwharrie Trail and some of the roadbeds described in this book.

Gemini Maps of NC, Inc. published a 1997 revision of its Uwharrie National Forest map. This large fold-out map includes the Morris Mountain Area. Although the map has topo lines, the trail lines are only a rough approximation of the trail locations. The Uwharrie Trail line is significantly off around Spencer Creek and is shown on the south side of Horse Mountain instead of the north side. None of the existing logging roads are shown on the map, although a few of the old jeep trail lines are included.

Morris Mountain Area Trails

Trail Name	Length (miles)	Elevation Gain/Loss	Difficulty Rating	Map (page)
Barnes Creek Overlook Road	1.07	98' / 278'	Easy	312
Camp Road	1.10	270' / 260'	Easy	314
Morris Mountain Road	2.69	389' / 434'	Easy	316
Panther Branch Road	1.51	170' / 338'	Easy	318
Spencer Creek Road	2.56	364' / 423'	Moderate	320

Barnes Creek Overlook Road

Map	page 312	**Difficulty**	Easy
Length	1.07 miles	**Configuration**	One way
Trailhead	N/A	**Elev Gain/Loss**	98' / 278'

Start Coordinates N35.43826, W79.97493;   17 S 593039 3922129

Barnes Creek Overlook Road, FR 6652A, is a gravel logging road that leads west over Morris Mountain to an early 1990's clear cut. Along the way are several brief vistas looking north over the valley of Barnes Creek and one of its tributaries, Panther Branch.

The route starts 1.4 miles in on Morris Mountain Road from the Tower Road Trailhead. After a short climb, the route crosses the Uwharrie hiking trail on a ridge top. From this point you will gradually descend, curving around the contours of the mountain before reaching a timber cut.

Barnes Creek Overlook Road ends at the landing in the middle of the timber cut. While you can't actually see Barnes Creek from the end, you can look out over the valley and see several surrounding mountains.

Camp Road

Map	page 314	**Difficulty**	Easy
Length	1.10 miles	**Configuration**	One way
Trailhead	West Morris Mtn	**Elev Gain/Loss**	270' / 260'

Start Coordinates N35.42797, W79.99336;   17 S 591378 3920970

Camp Road, FR 549, starts at the West Morris Mountain Trailhead and leads over a ridge to end at Spencer Creek. The first part of this road is also used to access a tract of private property. The road once passed through the property, but a newer road now bypasses the private land on the south side. The new road is the first turn to the right; a grassy road that is slightly overgrown. Bicycles are prohibited on Camp Road.

Camp Road climbs from the start. Just across the ridgetop, you may see the old footbridge from Spencer Creek laying to the left side of the road. It was left there in 1991 when the new bridge was built. Just past the old bridge you'll see Morris Mountain Road, leading left.

Camp Road then drops down the east side of the mountain. Where it joins with the Uwharrie hiking trail for a short distance, you'll notice several mining pits on either side of the trail. Just past these mine pits the road curves to the left, separating from the Uwharrie Trail. Camp Road ends at the wood footbridge over Spencer Creek. Spencer Creek campsites are a few yards to the right. A decent wading hole can be found just below the bridge, for those wanting to cool off a bit before climbing back over the ridge.

At one time, a hiking trail led from Camp Road, near the West Morris Mountain Camp, and circled southward and eastward to connect back to Camp Road near the intersection with Morris Mountain Road. Older USGS topo maps label this trail as USFS trail #96. I did not locate any signs of this trail during my explorations in the early 1990's.

Morris Mountain Road

Map	page 316	**Difficulty**	Easy
Length	2.69 miles	**Configuration**	One way
Trailhead	Tower Road	**Elev Gain/Loss**	389' / 434'

Start Coordinates N35.45034, W79.95895;   17 S 594476 3923484

Morris Mountain Road, FR 6652, is a gated and graveled Forest System road used primarily for logging access. Morris Mountain Road starts at the Tower Road Trailhead. It is fairly open for a mile and a half as it traverses the eastern slope of Morris Mountain. The last section of the route follows an old dirt road that ends at Camp Road.

Several out-and-back roads lead off of Morris Mountain Road. Some of these dead-ends offer curious travelers a chance to explore. Several of these roads connect to private property. Others lead to timber cut areas.

Panther Branch Road

Map	page 318	**Difficulty**	Moderate
Length	1.51 miles	**Configuration**	One way
Trailhead	N/A	**Elev Gain/Loss**	170' / 338'

Start Coordinates N35.44335, W79.96947;   17 S 593529 3922699

Panther Branch Road was an old overgrown road when I first explored it in the early 1990's. In 1997, the road was upgraded to provide logging access to an area of private land that was clear cut on the north side of Panther Branch. At that time the route began at Barnes Creek Overlook Road, about 50 yards from the intersection with Morris Mountain Road. The route climbed up and over Morris Mountain, crossing the Uwharrie hiking trail on top. A rather steep descent (for a logging road) took you down a spur ridge to Panther Branch. The road crossed the branch and ended in the timber cut.

When I explored the upgraded road in 1997, I was greeted with a severe summer thunderstorm upon reaching Panther Branch. Riding back up the wet clay road proved to be a slippery challenge. Booming thunder and the crackle of nearby lightning kept me moving pretty quickly.

Since then, a new road has been built to provide access to the same private land. The new road starts at Morris Mountain Road, north of Barnes Creel Overlook Road. This road doesn't share any of the previous alignment of the "Panther Branch Road" described in the first edition, but since that roadbed has been reclaimed and is no longer usable, I transferred the name to the new road.

Spencer Creek Road

Map	page 320	**Difficulty**	Moderate
Length	2.56 miles	**Configuration**	One way
Trailhead	Cattail Creek	**Elev Gain/Loss**	364' / 423'

Start Coordinates N35.39826, W79.97933;   17 S 592686 3917688

Spencer Creek Road is a gated Forest Service road, FR 6653. The first part of the road was relocated, graveled, and used for logging access in the mid 1990's. Sections of the road farther in are dirt and have been in existence for many years. They were most likely used to reach several home places and sawmill sites that can still be found in the area. The system of jeep trails that existed in the 1960's also used portions of Spencer Creek Road. You may still run across a few of the old signs that were put up along this trail system.

(continued on page 322)

Barnes Creek Overlook Road

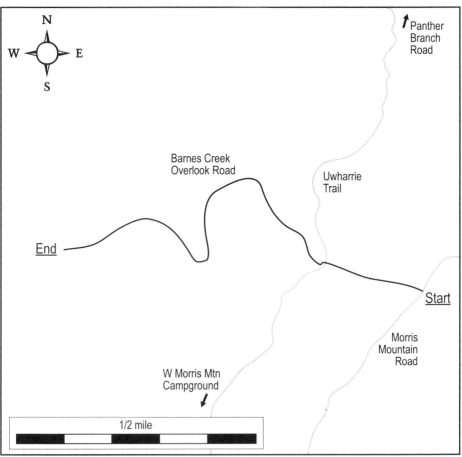

Elevation Profile: Barnes Creek Overlook Road

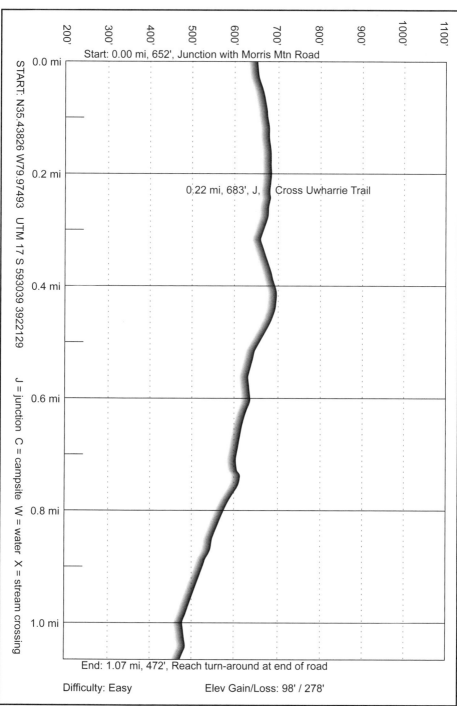

START: N35.43826 W79.97493 UTM 17 S 593039 3922129   J = junction C = campsite W = water X = stream crossing

Start: 0.00 mi, 652', Junction with Morris Mtn Road

0.22 mi, 683', J, Cross Uwharrie Trail

End: 1.07 mi, 472', Reach turn-around at end of road

Difficulty: Easy   Elev Gain/Loss: 98' / 278'

Camp Road

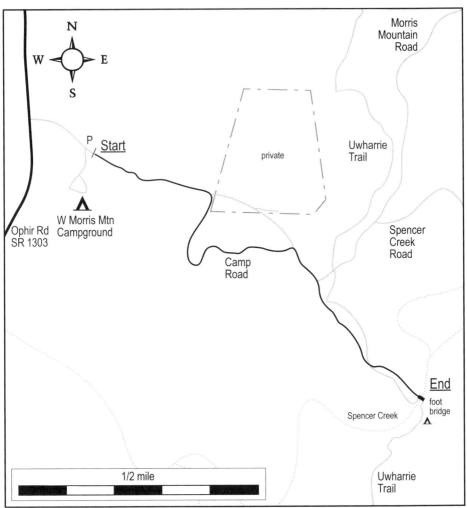

Elevation Profile: Camp Road

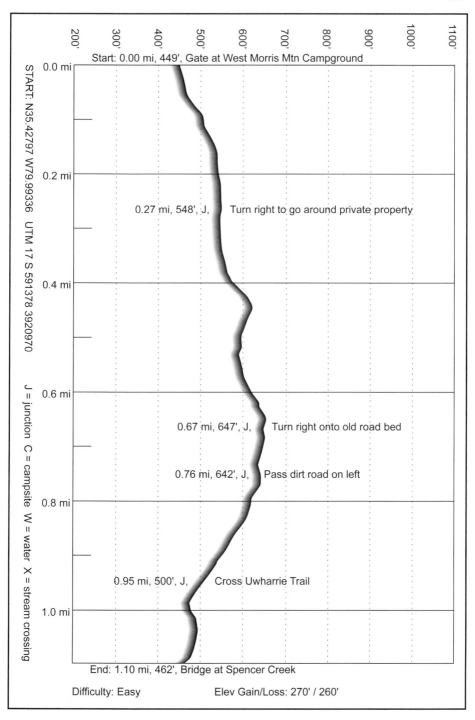

START: N35.42797 W79.99336 UTM 17 S 591378 3920970

J = junction C = campsite W = water X = stream crossing

Start: 0.00 mi, 449', Gate at West Morris Mtn Campground

0.27 mi, 548', J,   Turn right to go around private property

0.67 mi, 647', J,   Turn right onto old road bed

0.76 mi, 642', J,   Pass dirt road on left

0.95 mi, 500', J,   Cross Uwharrie Trail

End: 1.10 mi, 462', Bridge at Spencer Creek

Difficulty: Easy   Elev Gain/Loss: 270' / 260'

Morris Mountain Road

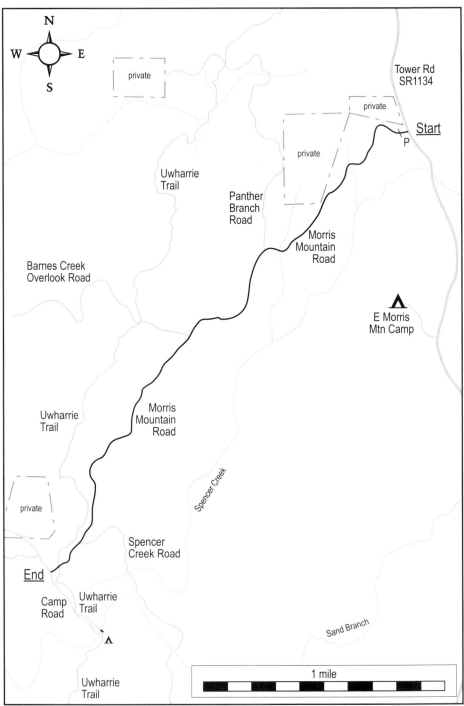

Elevation Profile: Morris Mountain Road

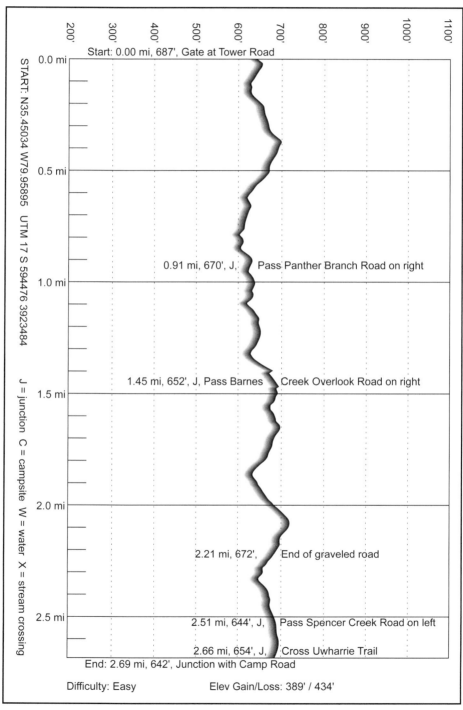

START: N35.45034 W79.95895 UTM 17 S 594476 3923484   J = junction C = campsite W = water X = stream crossing

Start: 0.00 mi, 687', Gate at Tower Road

0.91 mi, 670', J,   Pass Panther Branch Road on right

1.45 mi, 652', J, Pass Barnes   Creek Overlook Road on right

2.21 mi, 672',   End of graveled road

2.51 mi, 644', J,   Pass Spencer Creek Road on left

2.66 mi, 654', J,   Cross Uwharrie Trail

End: 2.69 mi, 642', Junction with Camp Road

Difficulty: Easy   Elev Gain/Loss: 389' / 434'

Panther Branch Road

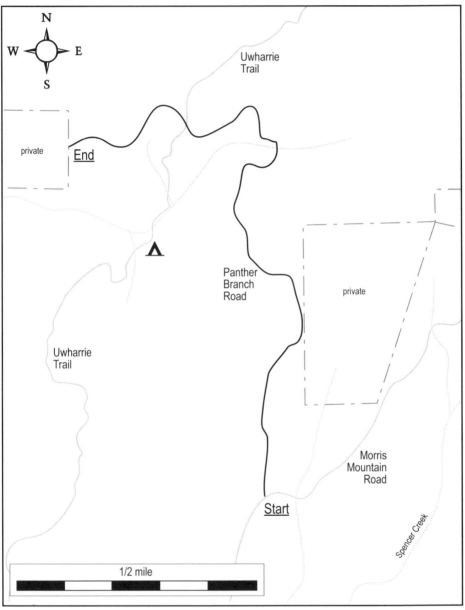

Elevation Profile: Panther Branch Road

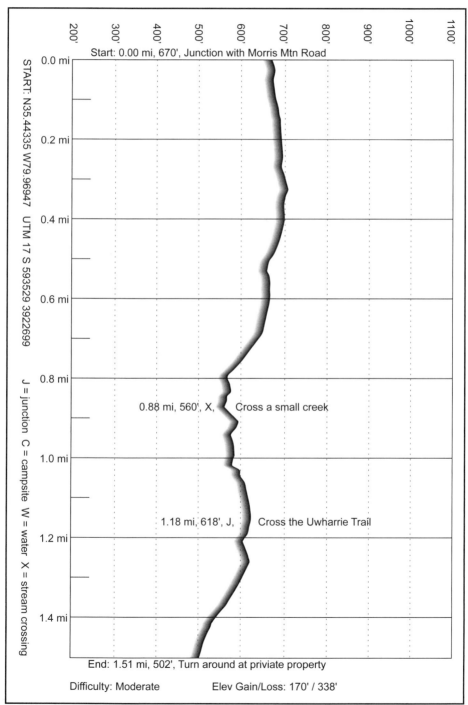

START: N35.44335 W79.96947   UTM 17 S 593529 3922699

J = junction C = campsite W = water X = stream crossing

Start: 0.00 mi, 670', Junction with Morris Mtn Road

0.88 mi, 560', X,   Cross a small creek

1.18 mi, 618', J,   Cross the Uwharrie Trail

End: 1.51 mi, 502', Turn around at priviate property

Difficulty: Moderate   Elev Gain/Loss: 170' / 338'

Spencer Creek Road

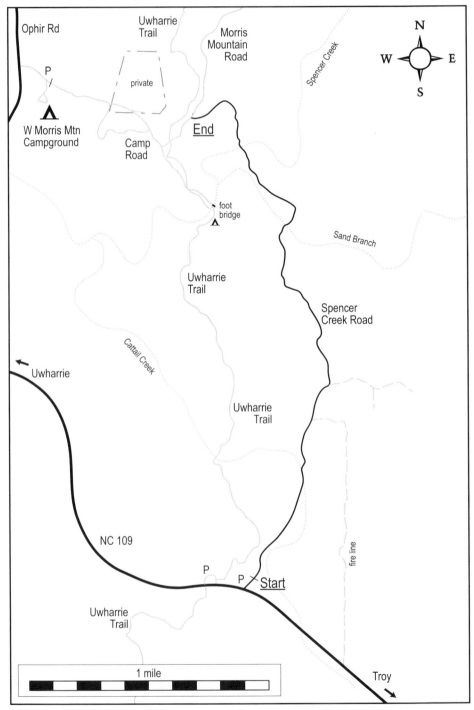

Ophir Rd

Uwharrie Trail

Morris Mountain Road

Spencer Creek

N
W   E
S

P

private

W Morris Mtn Campground

Camp Road

End

foot bridge

Sand Branch

Uwharrie Trail

Spencer Creek Road

Cattail Creek

← Uwharrie

Uwharrie Trail

fire line

NC 109

P

P Start

Uwharrie Trail

1 mile

Troy

Elevation Profile: Spencer Creek Road

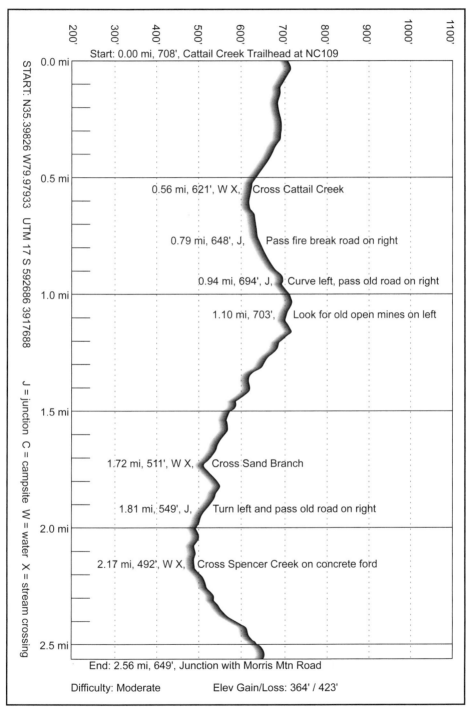

START: N35.39826 W79.97933   UTM 17 S 592686 3917688   J = junction C = campsite W = water X = stream crossing

Start: 0.00 mi, 708', Cattail Creek Trailhead at NC109

0.56 mi, 621', W X, Cross Cattail Creek

0.79 mi, 648', J, Pass fire break road on right

0.94 mi, 694', J, Curve left, pass old road on right

1.10 mi, 703', Look for old open mines on left

1.72 mi, 511', W X, Cross Sand Branch

1.81 mi, 549', J, Turn left and pass old road on right

2.17 mi, 492', W X, Cross Spencer Creek on concrete ford

End: 2.56 mi, 649', Junction with Morris Mtn Road

Difficulty: Moderate   Elev Gain/Loss: 364' / 423'

(continued)

Spencer Creek Road begins at the Forest Service gate at Cattail Creek Trailhead on NC 109. After passing over Cattail Creek, the route soon enters a timber cut and climbs over a small mountain. The road then drops down the far side of the mountain.

After reaching the end of the graveled portion of the road, the route follows a fire lane along the treeline down to cross Sand Branch. From there it picks up the old roadbed again. This last section can be tricky to follow.

After crossing Sand Branch, the road climbs a short distance to a junction with another woods road. To the right, the woods road leads to private property. To the left, Spencer Creek Road leads to a small concrete bridge structure over Spencer Creek itself. The section of Spencer Creek Road beyond Sand Branch hasn't been used by vehicles since the 1970's. You may encounter a number of trees down across the road, but the roadbed itself is fairly easy to identify and follow.

Once across Spencer Creek, the route follows an eroded section of roadbed as it climbs to meet the Morris Mountain Road on the southern ridge of Morris Mountain.

Spencer Creek Road is the only roadbed that crosses Spencer Creek, connecting the southern part of the Morris Mountain Area to the northern and western parts.

Morris Mountain Area Trips

Trip	Use	Length (miles)	Elevation Gain/ Loss	Difficulty Rating	Page
MMA Trip A	H	5.28	944' / 944'	Moderate	324
MMA Trip B	H	7.30	1,342' / 1,342'	Difficult	326
MMA Trip C	H	12.33	2,248' / 2,248'	Difficult	328

The Trips described here are hike-only trips that combine sections of the Uwharrie Trail and forest roads to form loops. Bike trip routes can be created by riding out and back on the forest roads described in the Morris Mountain Area Trails chapter.

Morris Mountain Trip A
Map	page 324	**Difficulty**	Moderate
Length	5.28 miles	**Configuration**	Loop
Trailhead	NC 109	**Elev Gain/Loss**	944' / 944'

Start Coordinates N35.39866, W79.98173;   17 S 592467 3917730

Morris Mountain Trip B
Map	page 326	**Difficulty**	Difficult
Length	7.3 miles	**Configuration**	Lollipop
Trailhead	W Morris Mtn Camp	**Elev Gain/Loss**	1,342' / 1,342'

Start Coordinates N35.42797, W79.99336;   17 S 591378 3920970

Morris Mountain Trip C
Map	page 328	**Difficulty**	Difficult
Length	12.33 miles	**Configuration**	Lollipop
Trailhead	W Morris Mtn Camp	**Elev Gain/Loss**	2,248' / 2,248'

Start Coordinates N35.42797, W79.99336;   17 S 591378 3920970

Morris Mountain Trip A

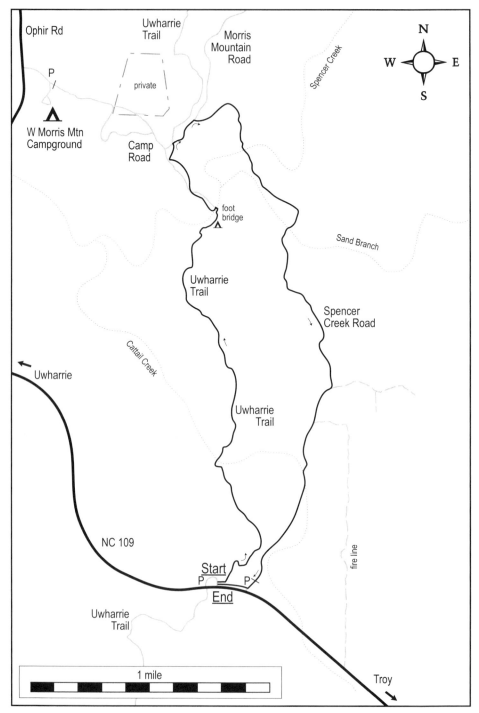

Ophir Rd

Uwharrie
Trail

Morris
Mountain
Road

Spencer Creek

N
W   E
S

P

private

W Morris Mtn
Campground

Camp
Road

foot
bridge

Sand Branch

Uwharrie
Trail

Spencer
Creek Road

Cattail Creek

Uwharrie

Uwharrie
Trail

NC 109

fire line

Start
P   P
End

Uwharrie
Trail

1 mile

Troy

Elevation Profile: Morris Mountain Trip A

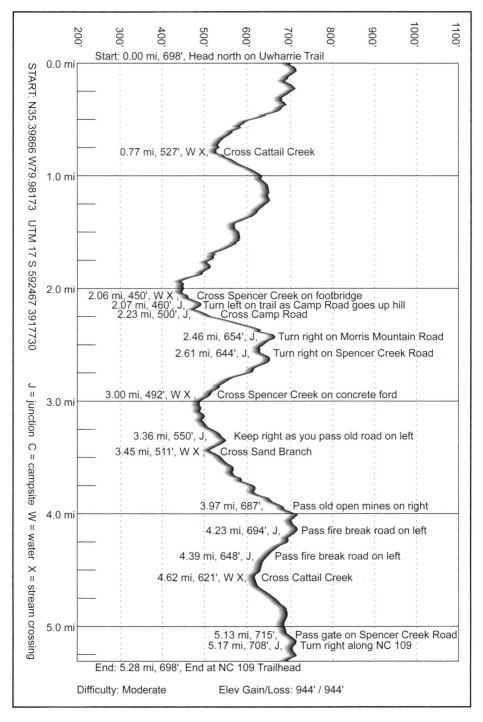

START: N35.39866 W79.98173   UTM 17 S 592467 3917730

J = junction C = campsite W = water X = stream crossing

Start: 0.00 mi, 698', Head north on Uwharrie Trail

0.0 mi

0.77 mi, 527', W X, Cross Cattail Creek

1.0 mi

2.0 mi

2.06 mi, 450', W X , Cross Spencer Creek on footbridge
2.07 mi, 460', J, Turn left on trail as Camp Road goes up hill
2.23 mi, 500', J, Cross Camp Road

2.46 mi, 654', J, Turn right on Morris Mountain Road
2.61 mi, 644', J, Turn right on Spencer Creek Road

3.00 mi, 492', W X , Cross Spencer Creek on concrete ford

3.0 mi

3.36 mi, 550', J, Keep right as you pass old road on left
3.45 mi, 511', W X , Cross Sand Branch

3.97 mi, 687', Pass old open mines on right

4.0 mi

4.23 mi, 694', J, Pass fire break road on left

4.39 mi, 648', J, Pass fire break road on left

4.62 mi, 621', W X, Cross Cattail Creek

5.0 mi

5.13 mi, 715', Pass gate on Spencer Creek Road
5.17 mi, 708', J, Turn right along NC 109

End: 5.28 mi, 698', End at NC 109 Trailhead

Difficulty: Moderate   Elev Gain/Loss: 944' / 944'

Morris Mountain Trip B

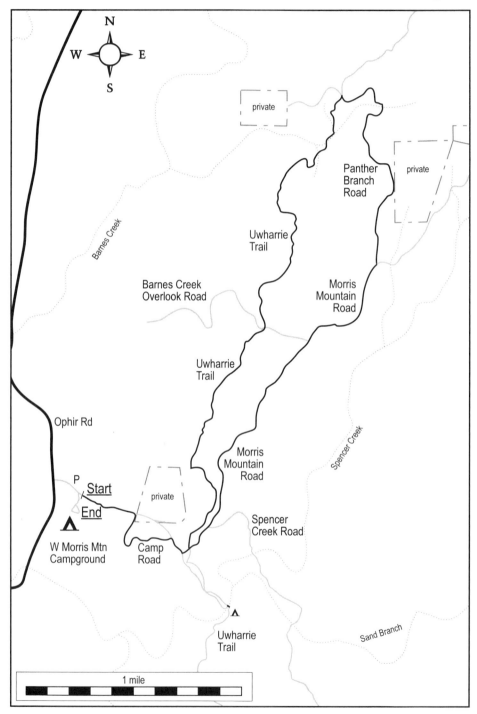

Elevation Profile: Morris Mountain Trip B

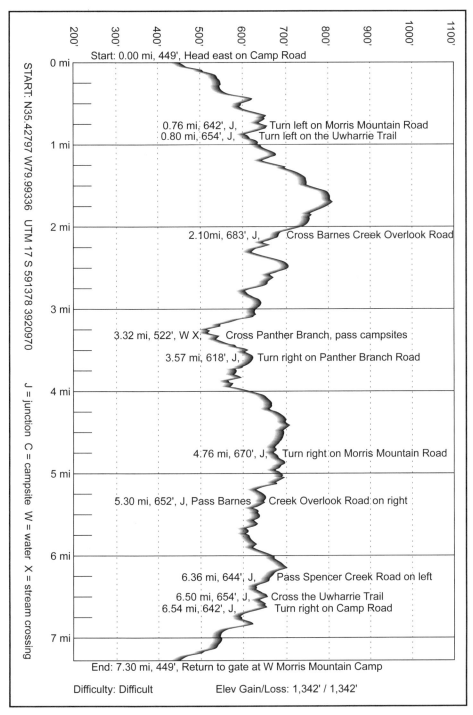

START: N35.42797 W79.99336   UTM 17 S 591378 3920970

J = junction C = campsite W = water X = stream crossing

Start: 0.00 mi, 449', Head east on Camp Road

0.76 mi, 642', J,   Turn left on Morris Mountain Road
0.80 mi, 654', J,   Turn left on the Uwharrie Trail

2.10mi, 683', J,   Cross Barnes Creek Overlook Road

3.32 mi, 522', W X,   Cross Panther Branch, pass campsites
3.57 mi, 618', J,   Turn right on Panther Branch Road

4.76 mi, 670', J,   Turn right on Morris Mountain Road

5.30 mi, 652', J, Pass Barnes   Creek Overlook Road on right

6.36 mi, 644', J,   Pass Spencer Creek Road on left
6.50 mi, 654', J,   Cross the Uwharrie Trail
6.54 mi, 642', J,   Turn right on Camp Road

End: 7.30 mi, 449', Return to gate at W Morris Mountain Camp

Difficulty: Difficult   Elev Gain/Loss: 1,342' / 1,342'

Morris Mountain Trip C

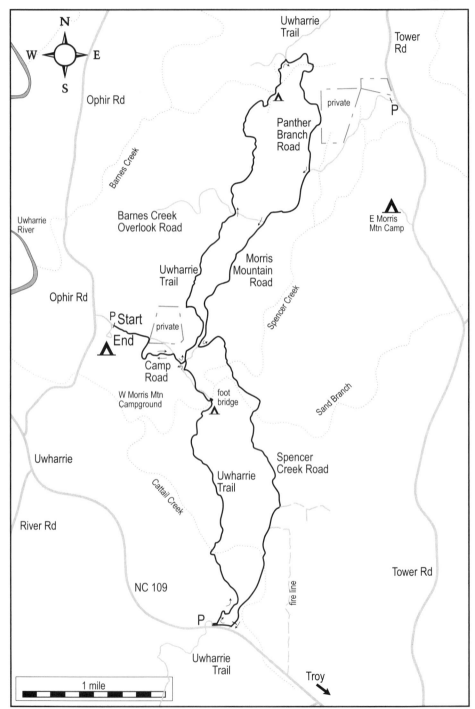

Elevation Profile: Morris Mountain Trip C

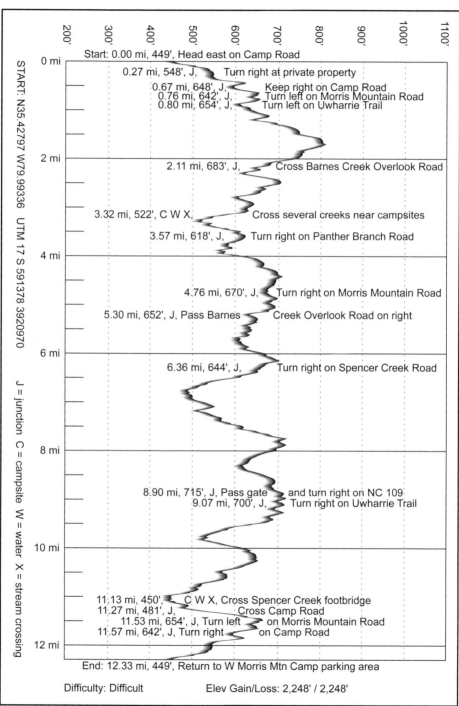

START: N35.42797 W79.99336 UTM 17 S 591378 3920970

J = junction C = campsite W = water X = stream crossing

200' 300' 400' 500' 600' 700' 800' 900' 1000' 1100'

0 mi Start: 0.00 mi, 449', Head east on Camp Road
0.27 mi, 548', J, Turn right at private property
0.67 mi, 648', J, Keep right on Camp Road
0.76 mi, 642', J, Turn left on Morris Mountain Road
0.80 mi, 654', J, Turn left on Uwharrie Trail

2 mi
2.11 mi, 683', J, Cross Barnes Creek Overlook Road

3.32 mi, 522', C W X, Cross several creeks near campsites

3.57 mi, 618', J, Turn right on Panther Branch Road

4 mi

4.76 mi, 670', J, Turn right on Morris Mountain Road
5.30 mi, 652', J, Pass Barnes Creek Overlook Road on right

6 mi
6.36 mi, 644', J, Turn right on Spencer Creek Road

8 mi

8.90 mi, 715', J, Pass gate and turn right on NC 109
9.07 mi, 700', J, Turn right on Uwharrie Trail

10 mi

11.13 mi, 450', C W X, Cross Spencer Creek footbridge
11.27 mi, 481', J, Cross Camp Road
11.53 mi, 654', J, Turn left on Morris Mountain Road
11.57 mi, 642', J, Turn right on Camp Road

12 mi

End: 12.33 mi, 449', Return to W Morris Mtn Camp parking area

Difficulty: Difficult   Elev Gain/Loss: 2,248' / 2,248'

Morrow Mountain State Park

Morrow Mountain State Park lies on the west side of Lake Tillery, across from the Badin Lake Area of the Uwharrie National Forest. Named after its dominant peak, the park contains several other mountains, reached by way of the park's various hiking and bridle trails. Like most other areas in the Uwharrie Lakes Region, Morrow Mountain State Park is rich in geologic and cultural history.

A museum building and several educational displays are available to help visitors understand the history of the region. The Kron House exhibit is a reconstruction of Dr. Francis Kron's home, doctor's office, and greenhouse as it appeared in the 1800's.

Thirteen named hiking trails run through the park, ranging from a short nature trail to four-mile-long Fall Mountain Trail. The hiking trails total about 17 miles. These trails are well marked with colored route markers. Most of the larger streams are crossed by footbridges. Three overlapping bridle trail routes offer an additional 20 miles of trail open to hikers and horseback riders.

Other recreational activities in the park include swimming, fishing, and boating. Mountain biking is not permitted in the park, except on the paved roads.

ACCESS
Morrow Mountain Road (SR 1798) is the only road entering the park. From the intersection of NC 24-27 and NC 740 in Albemarle, it is 4.0 miles to the intersection of Morrow Mountain Road and Valley Drive (SR 1720). Morrow Mountain Road leads straight into the park from this intersection. From the Tillery Bridges, it is 3.6 miles west on NC 24-27 to Valley Drive, a NC Scenic Byway, and then 2.8 miles north to Morrow Mountain Road.

There are five trailheads in the park, in addition to the campgrounds, which provide access to the trails. As in all NC State Parks, the entrance gate is locked at night. The gate opens at 8:00 AM year-round, but closes at 6:00 PM November-February, 7:00 PM in March and October, 8:00 PM in April, May and September, and 9:00 PM June-August.

Morrow Mountain State Park

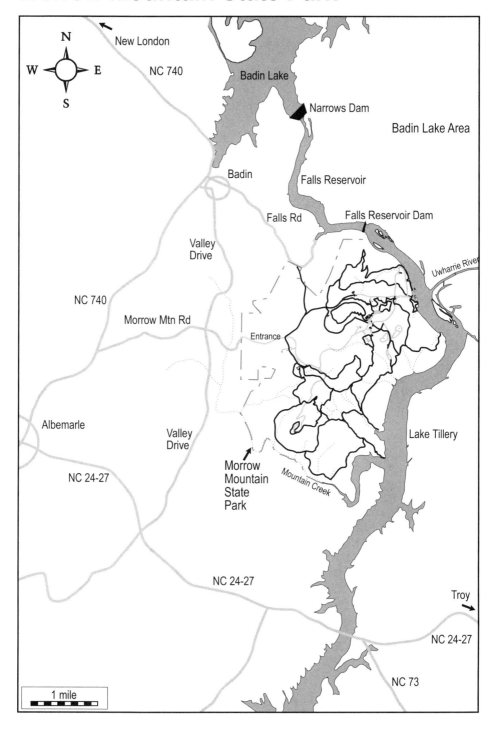

New London

NC 740

Badin Lake

Narrows Dam

Badin Lake Area

Badin

Falls Reservoir

Falls Rd

Falls Reservoir Dam

Valley Drive

Uwharrie River

NC 740

Morrow Mtn Rd

Entrance

Albemarle

Valley Drive

Lake Tillery

NC 24-27

Morrow Mountain State Park

Mountain Creek

NC 24-27

Troy

NC 24-27

NC 73

1 mile

Morrow Mountain State Park detail

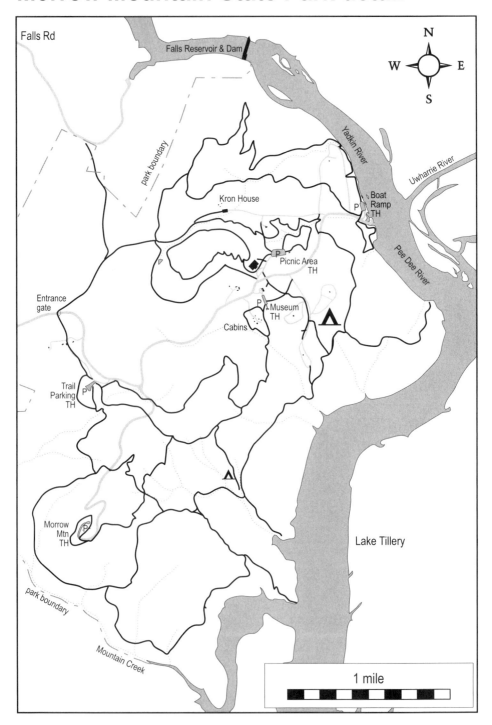

Trail Parking Trailhead

This is the first trailhead you reach upon entering the park. A short gravel road leads to the right, taking you to the large graveled parking lot, designed to easily accommodate horse trailers. There is a bulletin board for Morrow Mountain State

UTM	17 S 582472 3913921
Lat/Lon	N35.36520 W80.09217

Park and a water fountain at the entrance to the parking lot. The Sugarloaf Mountain hiking trail starts near the entrance on the left, in the east corner of the parking lot. The combined Short/Middle/Long Loop bridle trail route can be accessed from several trail entrances along the southeast side of the parking lot. There is a trail entrance in the west corner of the parking lot that ties to the Long Loop bridle trail, although the trail continues around to the east side and joins with the other bridle trails. There is a pit toilet and water spigot at this trailhead.

Morrow Mountain Trailhead

The paved parking lot on the summit of Morrow Mountain serves as a trailhead for the Mountain Loop Trail, which circles the upper slopes of the mountain. There is a picnic area on top with bathrooms and water sources. The Morrow Mountain

UTM	17 S 582440 3912399
Lat/Lon	N35.35147 W80.09268

Trail, which starts the Park Office and Museum, ends where it junctions with the Mountain Loop Trail just below the summit parking lot. Parking is available for 40-50 vehicles.

Museum Trailhead

The paved parking lot at the Park Office and Museum serves as a trailhead for the Morrow Mountain and Laurel trails, which share the same tread for a short distance. There are restrooms in the Office building. Maps and other

UTM	17 S 584186 3914734
Lat/Lon	N35.37238 W80.07323

information are available at the Office. Parking is available for 50-60 vehicles. Hikers can follow a shortcut trail and a service road eastward from the parking lot to connect to the Campground Trail.

Picnic Area Trailhead

The paved parking lot between the Picnic Area and the Pool serves as a trailhead for the short Quarry Trail and the Hattaway Mountain Trail. The Campground Trail ends in front of the pool bathhouse. There is room for 100+

UTM	17 S 584245 3915235
Lat/Lon	N35.37690 W80.07253

vehicles in the parking lot. Restrooms are available in the picnic area. There is one winterized water spigot in the picnic area. Water is available there year-round.

Boat Ramp Trailhead

The parking lot at the boat launch and canoe rental area on Lake Tillery serves as a trailhead for two hiking trails: Fall Mountain Trail and Three Rivers Trail. Parking space for 60-70 vehicles can be found at this trailhead. In the first edition of this guide, this trailhead was called the "Boathouse" Trailhead.

UTM	17 S 585147 3915656
Lat/Lon	N35.38061 W80.06255

NOTES OF INTEREST

Five mountains dominate the topography of Morrow Mountain State Park. Like the rest of the Uwharrie Mountain Range, these mountains are volcanic in origin. They are most likely the oldest mountains in North America, estimated to be 400 million years old. Time, wind, and water have worn these pinnacles down to their present height just under 1,000 feet above sea level.

A shallow sea once covered this region. Volcanic activity built up a layer of material called tuff. Later volcanic flows deposited rhyolite, a harder material, on top of the tuff. As the forces of erosion wore away the landscape, blocks of erosion-resistant rhyolite protected the tuff beneath them and became the mountains we have today. You'll find extensive deposits of rhyolite on top of the ridges and mountains. At lower elevations you can see the layers of volcanic tuff. Evidence of the volcanic slate formed from the ancient sea floor deposits can be seen at the lowest elevations, in particular on the Quarry Trail.

Several creeks drain the area, all of them running into Lake Tillery. The largest is Mountain Creek, which originates outside the park and flows along the southern boundary. A large cove is found where Mountain Creek empties into Lake Tillery. The first section of the bridle trail parallels the creek and cove. The Mountain Creek Spur Trail leads to the tip of the peninsula at the mouth of the cove.

As early as 10,000 years before Europeans arrived in the area, native Americans were enjoying the mountains of Morrow Mountain State Park. Rhyolite is an excellent material for making stone tools. The Indians mined rhyolite from the mountaintops to make stone tools and arrowheads, leaving behind piles of stone chips. They hunted and processed game in the area using the tools they made. They fished the river using stone walled fish traps, which can still be seen when the water level in Lake Tillery is lowered. They made clay pots, pieces of which can still be found in some places.

Europeans began settling in the area in the 1700's. John Kirk, a Scotch-Irish settler, established a ferry across the Yadkin River in 1780. The ferry site was located where the park's boat landing is today. A town called Tindalsville developed near the ferry site and served as the county seat until an epidemic wiped out the residents. The town was abandoned shortly thereafter and the courthouse moved across the river to several successive sites along the Uwharrie River.

Dr. Francis Kron emigrated to America in 1823 and eventually settled in the area between Fall and Hattaway Mountains. He was the first medical doctor to settle and practice medicine in the southern Piedmont of North Carolina. In the 1960's, his home, doctor's office, and greenhouse were reconstructed, as they might have appeared in the 1870's, and are maintained as an educational exhibit. Numerous other home sites and old roads can still be found throughout the park.

In the 1930's, a committee of local people began efforts to establish a state park. They acquired more than 3,000 acres by 1937, much of it donated by the citizens of Stanly County. Many of the facilities in the park were constructed by Civilian Conservation Corps and Work Projects Administration work crews between 1937 and 1942. The greenish volcanic slate used in the construction of numerous park structures came from the three slate quarries found in the park, one of which can be seen on the Quarry Trail. The park was opened to the public in 1939. The trails were built at a later date, some of them as late as the 1980's.

Projects on the trails are often performed by volunteers such as Boy Scout troops. Scouts placed the trail markers along all of the trails. They have also rebuilt many of the footbridges.

CAMPING
Camping opportunities in the park range from fully equipped vacation cabins to primitive backcountry campsites. For more information about current fees and reservations contact the park office at morrow.mountain@ncdenr.gov or 704-982-4402.

The family campground offers the most spaces, with 106 sites around three paved loop roads. Each loop has its own bathhouse, open from March 15 to November 30. One loop has been winterized and has water available all year.

There are six vacation cabins available by reservation. Summer months require a full week's rental, but weekend rentals are available in the spring and fall. Visit www.ncparks.gov or call 1-877-7-CAMP-NC to make reservations.

There are six group camp areas, each with its own pit toilet and winterized water source. A shared bathhouse is centrally located in the group camp area. A reservation and fee is required for use of the group camp areas.

The primitive backcountry sites have access to a pit toilet, but no water source. There are four sites, available by permit.

MAPS
North Carolina Parks and Recreation produces a map of each state park. Morrow Mountain State Park's version does not include topo lines in the background, but it does show major streams. It shows the trails with general accuracy. Older versions

of the maps did show faint topo lines. The local State Park office occasionally produces simple maps covering the park. These maps usually do not have topo lines.

USGS topographic quadrangle maps covering this area are: Morrow Mountain and Badin. The 1981 and 1994 printings do not show the trails, nor does the 2011 version.

Gemini Maps of NC, Inc. published a 1997 revision of its Uwharrie National Forest map. This large fold-out map includes Morrow Mountain State Park. Although the map has topo lines, the trail lines are only a rough approximation of the trail locations. The bridle trails are not shown. The Gemini map does not show the location of Park facilities such as the picnic area, office, or boathouse.

Morrow Mountain State Park Trails

Trail Name	Length (miles)	Elevation Gain/Loss	Difficulty Rating	Map (page)
Backpack	0.46	21' / 124'	Easy	345
Campground	0.60	37' / 82'	Easy	346
Duck Blind Spur	0.36	11' / 45'	Easy	347
Fall Mountain	4.02	760' / 760'	Moderate	348
Hattaway Mountain	2.07	555' / 555'	Moderate	350
Laurel	0.64	106' / 106'	Easy	352
Long Loop	10.15	1436' / 1436'	Difficult	354
Middle Loop	5.97	875' / 875'	Moderate	356
Morrow Mountain	2.42	863' / 419'	Moderate	358
Mountain Creek	0.50	17' / 92'	Easy	347
Mountain Loop	0.60	181' / 181'	Easy	360
Quarry	0.61	109' / 106'	Easy	361
Rocks	1.28	169' / 281'	Moderate	362
Short Loop	4.38	663' / 663'	Moderate	364
Sugarloaf	2.79	713' / 713'	Moderate	366
Three Rivers	0.73	92' / 92'	Easy	368

Backpack Trail

Map	page 345	**Difficulty**	Easy
Length	0.46 miles	**Configuration**	One way
Trailhead	N/A	**Elev Gain/Loss**	21' / 124'

Start Coordinates N35.36171, W80.07848;   17 S 583720 3913547

There is a pit toilet located along this trail, between the marked campsites. The Backpack Trail is marked with white circles containing a hiker symbol.

Campground Trail

Map	page 346	**Difficulty**	Easy
Length	0.60 miles	**Configuration**	One way
Trailhead	N/A	**Elev Gain/Loss**	37' / 82'

Start Coordinates N35.37535, W80.07347;   17 S 584161 3915064

The Campground Trail runs from the beginning of the campground loop B intersection to the front of the poolhouse. The Campground Trail is marked with white triangles containing a hiker symbol.

Duck Blind Spur Trail

Map	page 347	**Difficulty**	Easy
Length	0.36 miles	**Configuration**	One way
Trailhead	N/A	**Elev Gain/Loss**	11' / 45'

Start Coordinates N35.35547, W80.07540;   17 S 584006 3912856

Duck Blind Spur follows an old road along a scenic creek. The name comes from two old duck blinds found at the cove at the end of the route. The trail markers on this trail feature a red circle containing a white horseback rider symbol.

Fall Mountain Trail

Map	page 348	**Difficulty**	Moderate
Length	4.02 miles	**Configuration**	Loop
Trailhead	Boat Ramp	**Elev Gain/Loss**	760' / 760'

Start Coordinates N35.38155, W80.06263;   17 S 585139 3915760

Fall Mountain Trail features a relatively long but moderate climb up and over Fall Mountain. At roughly 4 miles long, this is the longest hiking trail in the park. The name most likely comes from the waterfalls that used to exist at this point on the Yadkin River before Falls Dam was built. The trail markers feature an orange triangle containing a white hiker symbol.

Fall Mountain Trail starts at the norththern end of the Boat Ramp Trailhead parking lot along Lake Tillery. The trail switchbacks up and over the top of Fall Mountain. After traversing the long ridge top of this mountain, the trail descends the west end of the mountain and circles back to the lake. The trail ends at the southwest corner of the Boat Ramp parking lot.

Hattaway Mountain Trail

Map	page 350	**Difficulty**	Moderate
Length	2.07 miles	**Configuration**	Lollipop
Trailhead	Picnic Area	**Elev Gain/Loss**	555' / 555'

Start Coordinates N35.37690, W80.07253;   17 S 584245 3915235

The Hattaway Mountain Trail offers hikers a steep climb up to the top of Hattaway Mountain and back down the other side. The mountain is most likely named after former landowners in the area. The trail markers feature an orange square containing a white hiker symbol. The loop junction offers two different directions to hike this loop. Both routes involve steep climbs, but the recommended direction has you facing the lake on top of the mountain. Spotty views of Lake Tillery are available from this ridge during the summer.

The trail starts at the west end of the Picnic Area parking lot. After passing by the front of the poolhouse, the trail enters the woods and circles around to the backside of the pool. Turn right at the loop junction and follow the trail as it contours around the base of the mountain. You will notice plastic water valve boxes along this section of trail because it follows a waterline corridor.

On the northwest side of the mountain, the trail turns left and begins a steep climb to the ridgetop. Once on top, the trail curves left and follows the ridge over the summit of Hattaway Mountain. After traversing the ridgeline, the trail drops back down the mountain to the loop junction. There are occasional views of the lake and park on the way down. At the junction, turn right and follow the trail back to the parking lot.

Laurel Trail

Map	page 352	**Difficulty**	Easy
Length	0.64 miles	**Configuration**	Lollipop
Trailhead	Museum	**Elev Gain/Loss**	106' / 106'

Start Coordinates N35.37238, W80.07323;   17 S 584186 3914734

Laurel Trail is an self-guiding loop trail that leads past examples of common trees found in upland hardwood forests. An interpretive guide can be borrowed from the Park Office that details the numbered sites along this trail. The north end of the loop passes through an area that received heavy tree damage during Hurricane Fran in 1996. The trail markers feature a red hexagon containing a white hiker symbol.

Laurel Trail starts at the south end of the Office and Museum parking lot. The Morrow Mountain Trail shares the first part of this route. The trail descends gently to cross a small stream. Turn left at the loop junction just past a footbridge. A junction with the Morrow Mountain Trail is found near the confluence of two small creeks. Laurel Trail turns right and circles the vacation cabins. From here the trail drops down to the loop junction with itself. Turning left will take you back to the Museum parking lot.

Long Loop Trail

Map	page 354	**Difficulty**	Difficult
Length	10.15 miles	**Configuration**	Loop
Trailhead	Trail Parking	**Elev Gain/Loss**	1436' / 1436'

Start Coordinates N35.36520, W80.09217;   17 S 582472 3913921

The Long Loop Trail was called the "Outer Loop Trail" in the first edition of the Uwharrie Lakes Region Trail Guide. The name Outer Loop was an informal name used by park staff at that time. This route is one of the bridle trails in the park. The route markers or the Long Loop feature a red circle containing a white horseback rider symbol.

The Long Loop route makes a large loop around most of the developed area of the park. Parts of the route are shared with the Middle and Short Loop Trail routes.

Most of the Long Loop route follows service roads and old roadbeds. Some stretches of trail on the north side of the park and near the Trail Parking Trailhead follow newly built trail tread, built in 2012.

The Long Loop route starts at the south side of the Trail Parking parking area. The route crosses two small streams before circling southward around Morrow Mountain. The Short and Middle Loop routes split off from the Long Loop in the southern end of the park. Mountain Creek and Duck Blind Spur Trails are accessed from this route. The route passes near the backcountry campsites and the Family Campground, where it is joined by the Big Rocks Trail for a short distance.

After the Rocks Trail turns off to the right, the Long Loop route runs near the Quarry Trail and the Kron House exhibit. Beyond the Kron House, the route rejoins a gravel service road and eventually crosses the paved road at the main entrance to the park. The route leads past Staff quarters, and then turns onto new trail that leads back to the starting point at the parking lot.

Middle Loop Trail

Map	page 356	**Difficulty**	Moderate
Length	5.97 miles	**Configuration**	Lollipop
Trailhead	Trail Parking	**Elev Gain/Loss**	875' / 875'

Start Coordinates N35.36520, W80.09217;   17 S 582472 3913921

Part of the Middle Loop Trail route was called "Mountain Creek Trail" in the first edition of the Uwharrie Lakes Region Trail Guide. In the early 1990's, there were still some older wooden directional signs nailed to trees along this route that said "Mtn Creek". This route is one of the bridle trails in the park. The route markers for the Middle Loop feature a blue circle containing a white horseback rider symbol.

The Middle Loop route shares the first few miles of the Short and Long Loop routes. It splits off from the Long Loop route and stays in the southern half of the park before returning to the parking lot.

The route follows dirt and gravel service roads for most of its length. A beautiful new section of tread, built in 2012, switchbacks up the east side of and over the ridge between Morrow and Sugarloaf Mountains.

The Mountain Creek Spur Trail connects to the Middle/Long Loop Trail in the southeast corner of the park.

Morrow Mountain Trail

Map	page 358	**Difficulty**	Moderate
Length	2.42 miles	**Configuration**	One way
Trailhead	Museum	**Elev Gain/Loss**	863' / 419'

Start Coordinates N35.37238, W80.07323;   17 S 584186 3914734

Morrow Mountain Trail runs from the Museum Trailhead to the top of Morrow Mountain itself. Along the way it shares parts of two other trails: Laurel and Sugarloaf MountainTrails.

The trail markers for the Morrow Mountain Trail feature a blue triangle containing a white hiker symbol. There is a strenuous climb up the slopes of Morrow Mountain, but the views from the scenic overlooks at the top are worth the effort.

Mountain Creek Spur Trail

Map	page 347	**Difficulty**	Easy
Length	0.50 miles	**Configuration**	One way
Trailhead	N/A	**Elev Gain/Loss**	17' / 92'
Start Coordinates	N35.35021, W80.07551;	17 S 584001 3912273	

Mountain Creek Spur Trail follows an old road past an former home site and ends at the lakeshore, looking across the mouth of Mountain Creek. The trail markers on this trail feature a red circle containing a white horseback rider symbol.

In the first edition of Uwharrie Lakes Region Trail Guide, this trail was called the "Moonshine Spur Trail". The remains of a moonshine still were found near the shore at the end of this trail.

Mountain Loop Trail

Map	page 360	**Difficulty**	Easy
Length	0.60 miles	**Configuration**	Loop
Trailhead	Morrow Mountain	**Elev Gain/Loss**	181' / 181'
Start Coordinates	N35.35166, W80.09367;	17 S 582350 3912419	

The Mountain Loop Trail is marked with red squares.

Quarry Trail

Map	page 361	**Difficulty**	Easy
Length	0.61 miles	**Configuration**	Loop
Trailhead	Picnic Area	**Elev Gain/Loss**	109' / 106'
Start Coordinates	N35.37736, W80.07120;	17 S 584365 3915288	

The Quarry Trail is marked with blue diamonds.

Rocks Trail

Map	page 362	**Difficulty**	Moderate
Length	1.28 miles	**Configuration**	One way
Trailhead	N/A	**Elev Gain/Loss**	169' / 281'
Start Coordinates	N35.37098, W80.06839;	17 S 584627 3914583	

Rocks Trail leads from the Family Campground to a large outcropping of rock at the edge of Lake Tillery and the Pee Dee River. Various rock ledges offer outstanding views of Lake Tillery. The trail markers feature a blue square containing a white hiker symbol. The "2.5 miles" sign at the beginning of the Rocks Trail refers to the round trip mileage out and back to the starting point.

The trail starts at its junction with the Campground Trail. At first, the route follows a gated and graveled service road. The route then takes the left fork when the road splits.

Shortly after passing by a small block building, the route junctions with Long Loop bridle trail, turning left and following the bridle trail. The bridle trail markers feature a red circle containing a white horseback rider symbol.

After following the bridle trail for a quarter mile, the Rocks Trail splits off to the right and crosses over several small ridges before nearing the lake. The trail enters a thick stand of mountain laurel and then reaches the rocks of the outcropping above the water's edge.

Short Loop Trail

Map	page 364	**Difficulty**	Moderate
Length	4.38 miles	**Configuration**	Lollipop
Trailhead	Trail Parking	**Elev Gain/Loss**	663' / 663'

Start Coordinates N35.36520, W80.09217;   17 S 582472 3913921

The Short Loop route was called the "Inner Loop Trail" in the first edition of this guide. The route shares the first few miles of the Middle and Long Loop routes. It splits off and circles closely around Morrow Mountain before rejoining the Middle Loop route and returning to the parking lot. The Short Loop is marked with white circles containing a horseback rider symbol.

Sugarloaf Mountain Trail

Map	page 366	**Difficulty**	Moderate
Length	2.79 miles	**Configuration**	Lollipop
Trailhead	Trail Parking	**Elev Gain/Loss**	713' / 713'

Start Coordinates N35.36540, W80.09185;   17 S 582502 3913945

Sugarloaf Mountain Trail loops over and around Sugarloaf Mountain. Part of the route is shared with the Morrow Mountain Trail. Trail markers feature an orange diamond containing a white hiker symbol.

The route starts in the eastern corner of the Trail Parking lot. Shortly after leaving the lot, hikers come to the loop junction. The route follows the left fork and parallels the paved road for a while before finally crossing it and heading up the ridge of Sugarloaf Mountain. Along the ridge you can find scattered views of the lake and surrounding mountains.

After crossing the summit of the mountain, the trail drops to a junction with the Morrow Mountain Trail, which comes in from the left. Together the trails cross several small ridges before passing a junction with the Backcountry Campsite Trail. After the Morrow Mountain Trail leaves to the left, the Sugarloaf Mountain Trail climbs back over the ridge and returns to the parking lot.

Three Rivers Trail

Map	page 368	**Difficulty**	Easy
Length	0.73 miles	**Configuration**	Lollipop
Trailhead	Boat Ramp	**Elev Gain/Loss**	92' / 92'

Start Coordinates N35.38061, W80.06255;   17 S 585147 3915656

Three Rivers Trail is a fairly short nature trail located near the Boat Ramp. An interpretive guidebook can be borrowed from the Park Office that will provide details about the numbered stops along this trail. The trail markers feature a blue hexagon containing a white hiker symbol.

The trail starts at the southern end of the Boat Ramp parking lot, sharing the tread with the Fall Mountain Trail for a short distance. After crossing the paved road, the trail turns left at the loop junction.

Three Rivers Trail winds through a swampy woodland to the river's edge. A wildlife viewing blind is located at a small marsh. From the riverbank, the trail climbs up on a hill to offer wintertime views of the confluence of the Yadkin, Uwharrie, and Pee Dee Rivers, hence the name "Three Rivers Trail". The trail loops across the ridgetop before dropping back to the low area and the loop junction.

The trail ends back at the Boat Ramp parking lot.

Backpack Trail

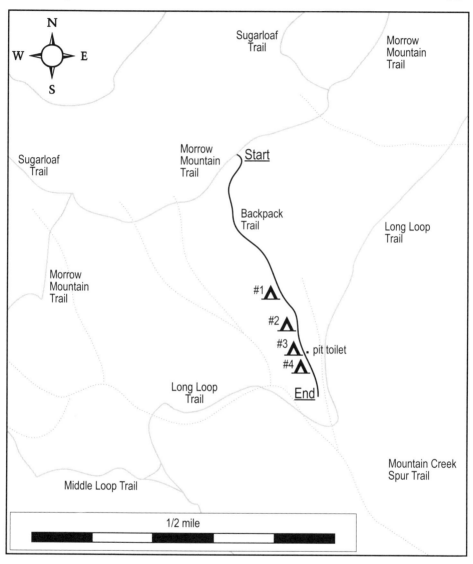

N
W E
S

Sugarloaf
Trail

Morrow
Mountain
Trail

Sugarloaf
Trail

Morrow
Mountain
Trail

Start

Backpack
Trail

Long Loop
Trail

Morrow
Mountain
Trail

#1

#2

#3 . pit toilet

#4

Long Loop
Trail

End

Mountain Creek
Spur Trail

Middle Loop Trail

1/2 mile

Campground Trail

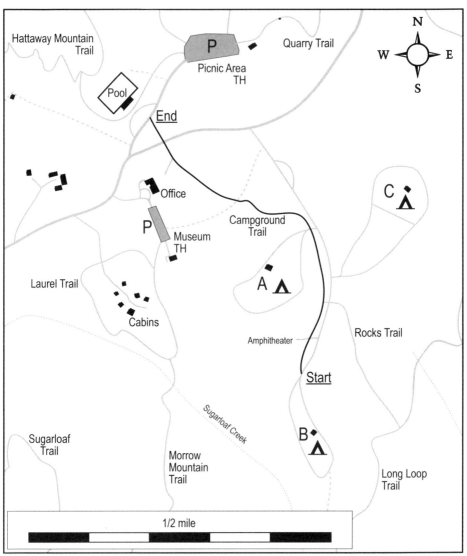

Hattaway Mountain Trail

P

Quarry Trail

Picnic Area
TH

Pool

End

N
W ◇ E
S

Office

C ⛺

P

Museum
TH

Campground
Trail

Laurel Trail

A ⛺

Cabins

Amphitheater

Rocks Trail

Start

Sugarloaf Creek

B ⛺

Sugarloaf
Trail

Morrow
Mountain
Trail

Long Loop
Trail

1/2 mile

Duck Blind, Mountain Creek Spurs

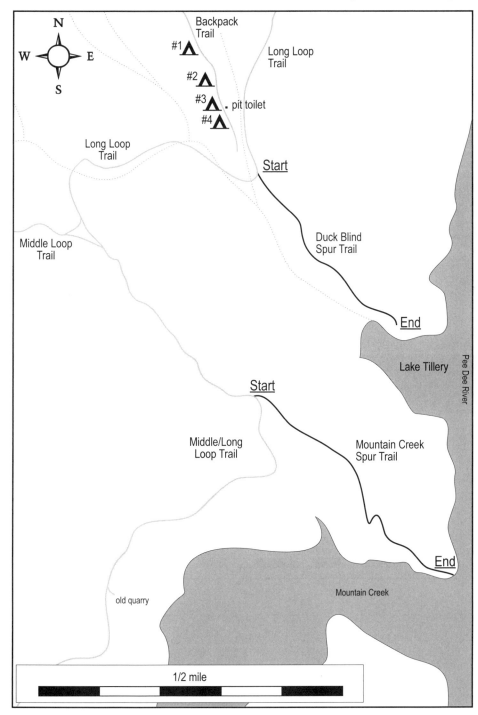

Fall Mountain Trail

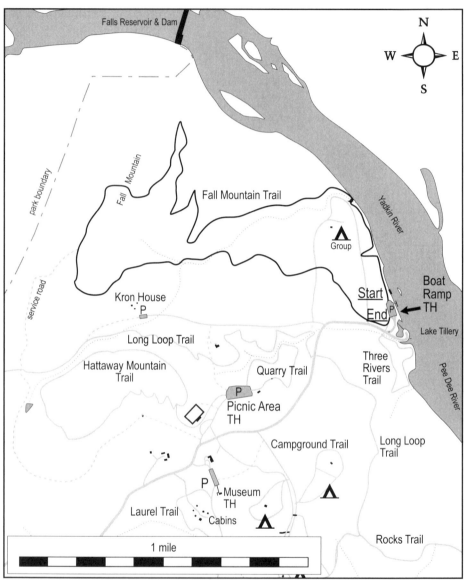

Elevation Profile: Fall Mountain Trail

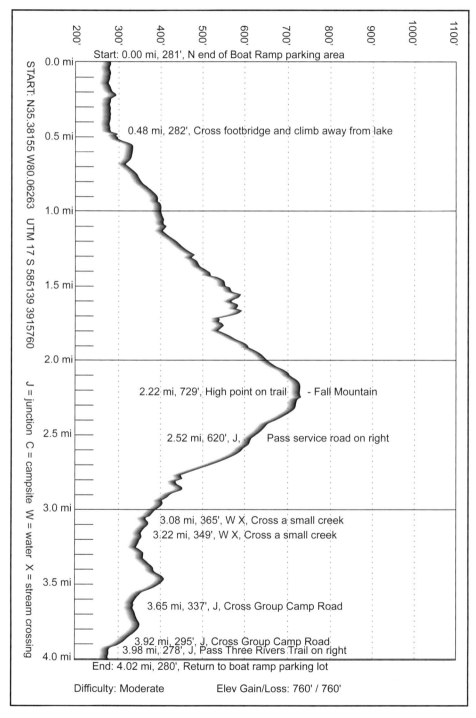

START: N35.38155 W80.06263   UTM 17 S 585139 3915760

J = junction C = campsite W = water X = stream crossing

Start: 0.00 mi, 281', N end of Boat Ramp parking area

0.48 mi, 282', Cross footbridge and climb away from lake

2.22 mi, 729', High point on trail - Fall Mountain

2.52 mi, 620', J,   Pass service road on right

3.08 mi, 365', W X, Cross a small creek
3.22 mi, 349', W X, Cross a small creek

3.65 mi, 337', J, Cross Group Camp Road

3.92 mi, 295', J, Cross Group Camp Road
3.98 mi, 278', J, Pass Three Rivers Trail on right

End: 4.02 mi, 280', Return to boat ramp parking lot

Difficulty: Moderate   Elev Gain/Loss: 760' / 760'

Hattaway Mountain Trail

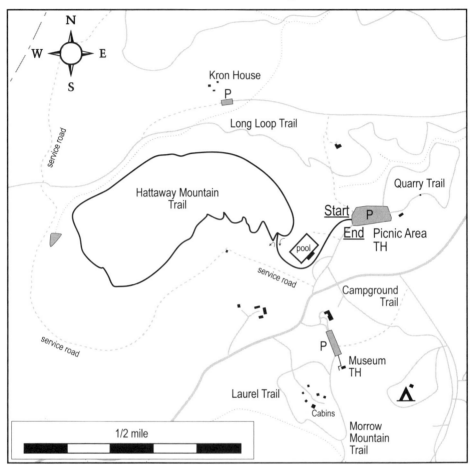

Elevation Profile: Hattway Mountain Trail

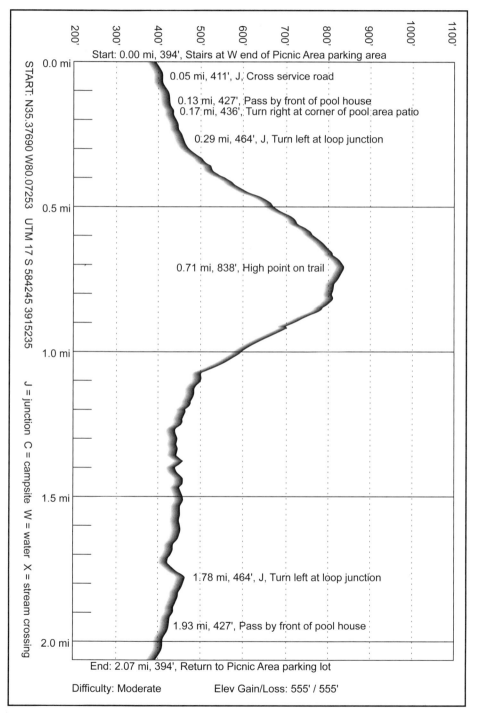

START: N35.37690 W80.07253 UTM 17 S 584245 3915235

J = junction C = campsite W = water X = stream crossing

Start: 0.00 mi, 394', Stairs at W end of Picnic Area parking area

0.05 mi, 411', J, Cross service road

0.13 mi, 427', Pass by front of pool house
0.17 mi, 436', Turn right at corner of pool area patio

0.29 mi, 464', J, Turn left at loop junction

0.71 mi, 838', High point on trail

1.78 mi, 464', J, Turn left at loop junction

1.93 mi, 427', Pass by front of pool house

End: 2.07 mi, 394', Return to Picnic Area parking lot

Difficulty: Moderate   Elev Gain/Loss: 555' / 555'

Laurel Trail

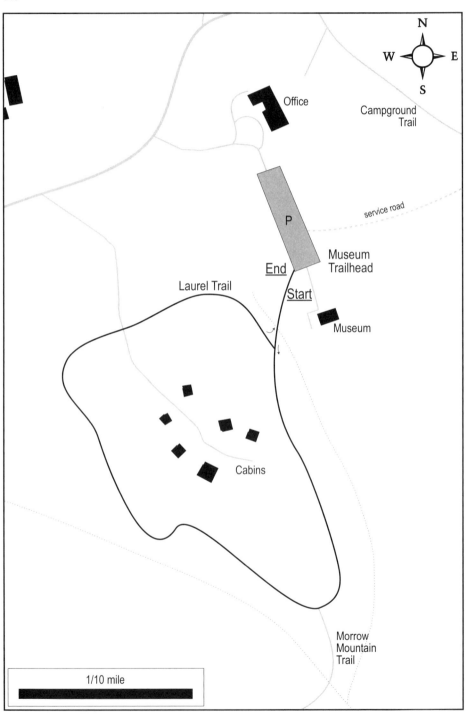

Elevation Profile: Laurel Trail

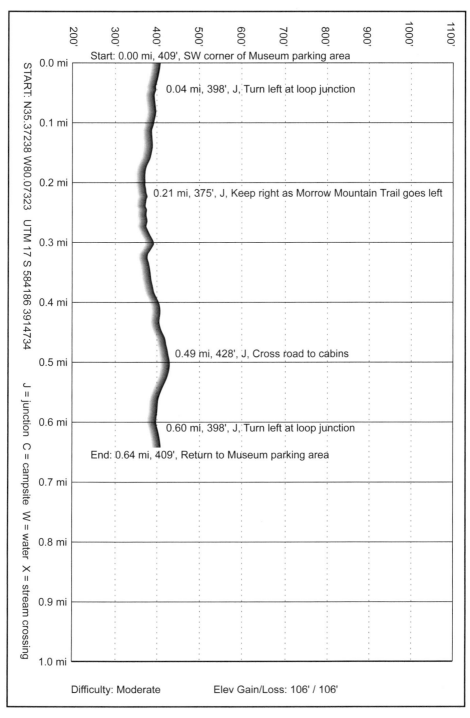

START: N35.37238 W80.07323   UTM 17 S 584186 3914734

J = junction C = campsite W = water X = stream crossing

Start: 0.00 mi, 409', SW corner of Museum parking area

0.04 mi, 398', J, Turn left at loop junction

0.21 mi, 375', J, Keep right as Morrow Mountain Trail goes left

0.49 mi, 428', J, Cross road to cabins

0.60 mi, 398', J, Turn left at loop junction

End: 0.64 mi, 409', Return to Museum parking area

Difficulty: Moderate   Elev Gain/Loss: 106' / 106'

Long Loop Trail

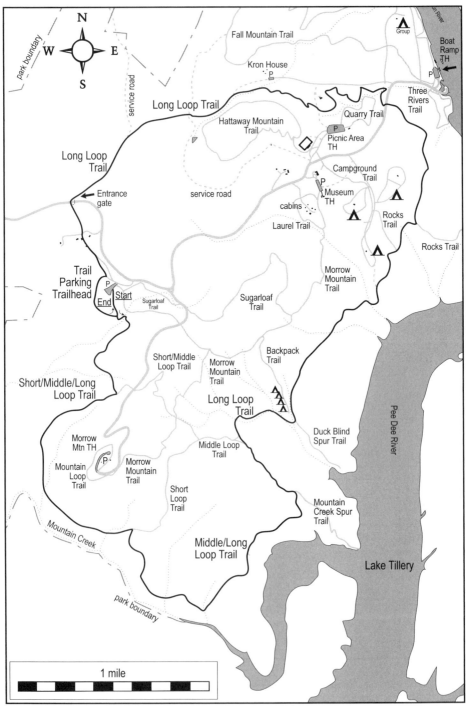

Elevation Profile: Long Loop Trail

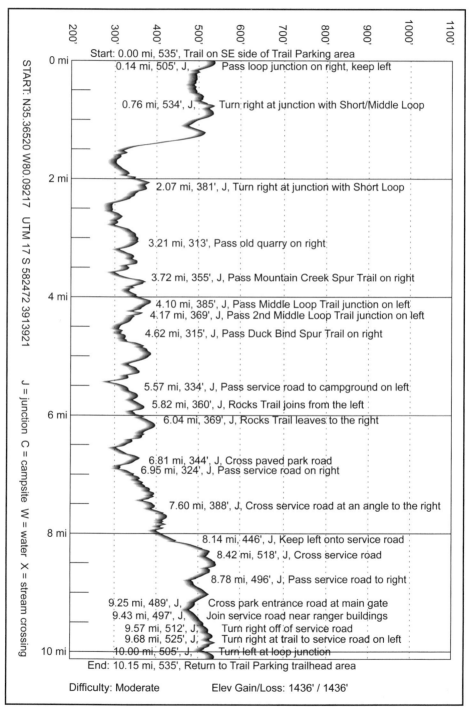

START: N35.36520 W80.09217 UTM 17 S 582472 3913921

J = junction C = campsite W = water X = stream crossing

200' 300' 400' 500' 600' 700' 800' 900' 1000' 1100'

0 mi — Start: 0.00 mi, 535', Trail on SE side of Trail Parking area
0.14 mi, 505', J, Pass loop junction on right, keep left
0.76 mi, 534', J, Turn right at junction with Short/Middle Loop

2 mi
2.07 mi, 381', J, Turn right at junction with Short Loop

3.21 mi, 313', Pass old quarry on right

3.72 mi, 355', J, Pass Mountain Creek Spur Trail on right

4 mi
4.10 mi, 385', J, Pass Middle Loop Trail junction on left
4.17 mi, 369', J, Pass 2nd Middle Loop Trail junction on left
4.62 mi, 315', J, Pass Duck Bind Spur Trail on right

5.57 mi, 334', J, Pass service road to campground on left
5.82 mi, 360', J, Rocks Trail joins from the left
6 mi
6.04 mi, 369', J, Rocks Trail leaves to the right

6.81 mi, 344', J, Cross paved park road
6.95 mi, 324', J, Pass service road on right

7.60 mi, 388', J, Cross service road at an angle to the right

8 mi
8.14 mi, 446', J, Keep left onto service road
8.42 mi, 518', J, Cross service road

8.78 mi, 496', J, Pass service road to right

9.25 mi, 489', J, Cross park entrance road at main gate
9.43 mi, 497', J, Join service road near ranger buildings
9.57 mi, 512', J, Turn right off of service road
9.68 mi, 525', J, Turn right at trail to service road on left
10 mi
10.00 mi, 505', J, Turn left at loop junction
End: 10.15 mi, 535', Return to Trail Parking trailhead area

Difficulty: Moderate   Elev Gain/Loss: 1436' / 1436'

Middle Loop Trail

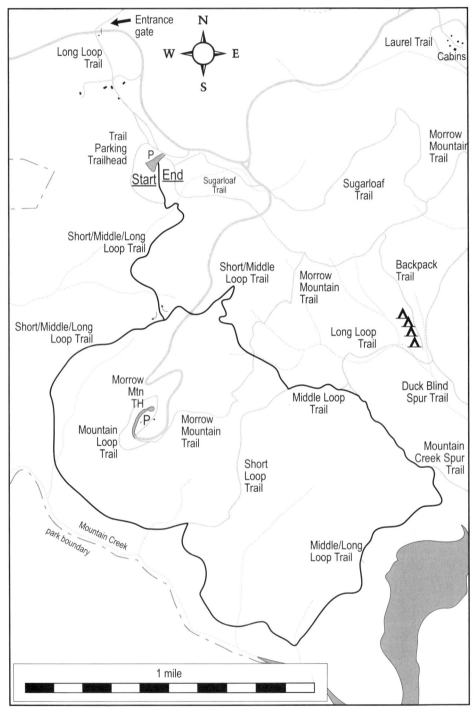

Entrance gate

N
W · E
S

Long Loop Trail

Laurel Trail

Cabins

Trail Parking Trailhead

P

Start | End

Morrow Mountain Trail

Sugarloaf Trail

Sugarloaf Trail

Short/Middle/Long Loop Trail

Short/Middle Loop Trail

Morrow Mountain Trail

Backpack Trail

Short/Middle/Long Loop Trail

Long Loop Trail

Morrow Mtn TH

P

Mountain Loop Trail

Morrow Mountain Trail

Middle Loop Trail

Duck Blind Spur Trail

Mountain Creek Spur Trail

Short Loop Trail

Mountain Creek

park boundary

Middle/Long Loop Trail

1 mile

Elevation Profile: Middle Loop Trail

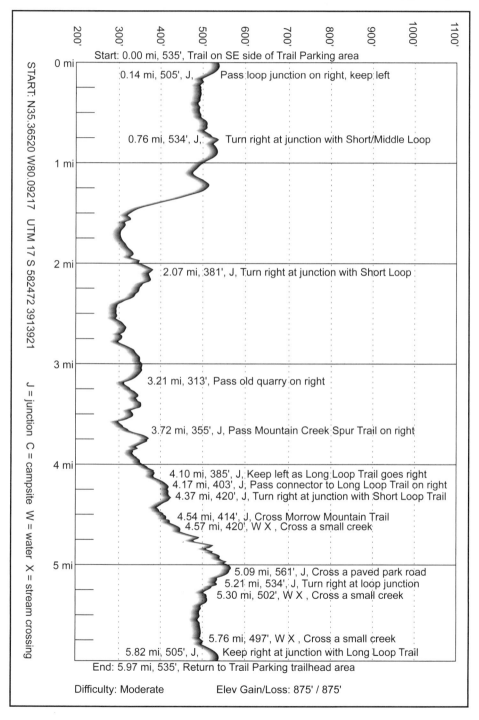

START: N35.36520 W80.09217 UTM 17 S 582472 3913921

J = junction C = campsite W = water X = stream crossing

200' 300' 400' 500' 600' 700' 800' 900' 1000' 1100'

Start: 0.00 mi, 535', Trail on SE side of Trail Parking area

0 mi

0.14 mi, 505', J,   Pass loop junction on right, keep left

0.76 mi, 534', J,   Turn right at junction with Short/Middle Loop

1 mi

2 mi

2.07 mi, 381', J, Turn right at junction with Short Loop

3 mi

3.21 mi, 313', Pass old quarry on right

3.72 mi, 355', J, Pass Mountain Creek Spur Trail on right

4 mi

4.10 mi, 385', J, Keep left as Long Loop Trail goes right
4.17 mi, 403', J, Pass connector to Long Loop Trail on right
4.37 mi, 420', J, Turn right at junction with Short Loop Trail

4.54 mi, 414', J, Cross Morrow Mountain Trail
4.57 mi, 420', W X , Cross a small creek

5 mi

5.09 mi, 561', J, Cross a paved park road
5.21 mi, 534', J, Turn right at loop junction
5.30 mi, 502', W X , Cross a small creek

5.76 mi, 497', W X , Cross a small creek
5.82 mi, 505', J,   Keep right at junction with Long Loop Trail

End: 5.97 mi, 535', Return to Trail Parking trailhead area

Difficulty: Moderate   Elev Gain/Loss: 875' / 875'

Morrow Mountain Trail

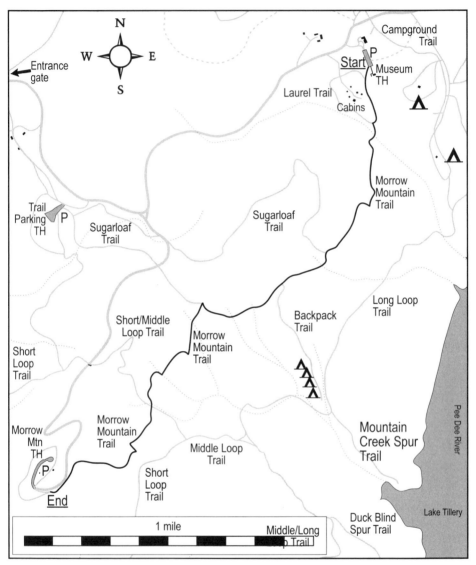

N
W E
S

Entrance gate

Campground Trail

Start
P
Museum TH

Laurel Trail

Cabins

Morrow Mountain Trail

Trail Parking TH
P

Sugarloaf Trail

Sugarloaf Trail

Long Loop Trail

Short/Middle Loop Trail

Backpack Trail

Morrow Mountain Trail

Short Loop Trail

Mountain Creek Spur Trail

Pee Dee River

Morrow Mtn TH
P

Morrow Mountain Trail

Middle Loop Trail

End

Short Loop Trail

1 mile

Middle/Long ...Trail

Duck Blind Spur Trail

Lake Tillery

Elevation Profile: Morrow Mountain Trail

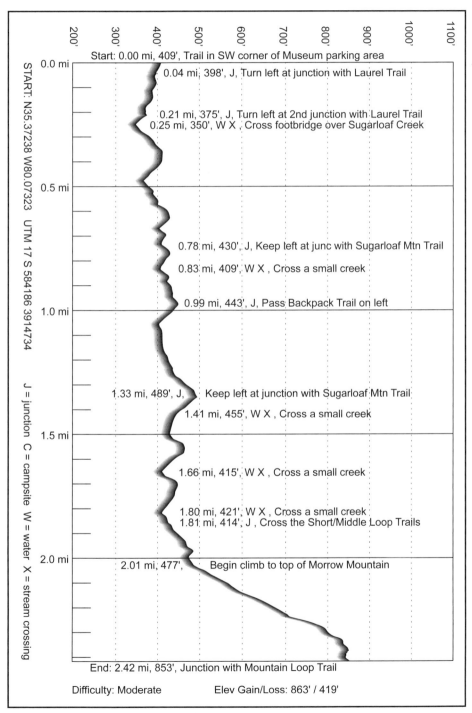

START: N35.37238 W80.07323   UTM 17 S 584186 3914734

J = junction C = campsite W = water X = stream crossing

200' 300' 400' 500' 600' 700' 800' 900' 1000' 1100'

Start: 0.00 mi, 409', Trail in SW corner of Museum parking area

0.0 mi

0.04 mi, 398', J, Turn left at junction with Laurel Trail

0.21 mi, 375', J, Turn left at 2nd junction with Laurel Trail
0.25 mi, 350', W X , Cross footbridge over Sugarloaf Creek

0.5 mi

0.78 mi, 430', J, Keep left at junc with Sugarloaf Mtn Trail

0.83 mi, 409', W X , Cross a small creek

0.99 mi, 443', J, Pass Backpack Trail on left

1.0 mi

1.33 mi, 489', J,   Keep left at junction with Sugarloaf Mtn Trail

1.41 mi, 455', W X , Cross a small creek

1.5 mi

1.66 mi, 415', W X , Cross a small creek

1.80 mi, 421', W X , Cross a small creek
1.81 mi, 414', J , Cross the Short/Middle Loop Trails

2.0 mi

2.01 mi, 477',   Begin climb to top of Morrow Mountain

End: 2.42 mi, 853', Junction with Mountain Loop Trail

Difficulty: Moderate   Elev Gain/Loss: 863' / 419'

Mountain Loop Trail

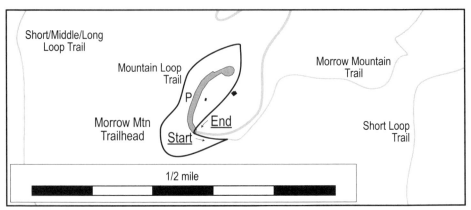

Short/Middle/Long Loop Trail

Mountain Loop Trail

Morrow Mountain Trail

P

End

Morrow Mtn Trailhead

Start

Short Loop Trail

1/2 mile

Elevation Profile: Mountain Loop Trail

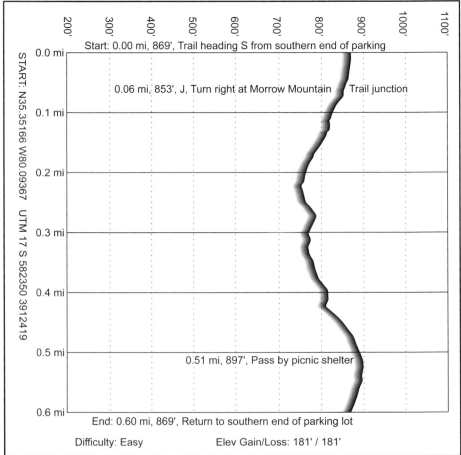

START: N35.35166 W80.09367 UTM 17 S 582350 3912419

Start: 0.00 mi, 869', Trail heading S from southern end of parking

0.06 mi, 853', J, Turn right at Morrow Mountain Trail junction

0.51 mi, 897', Pass by picnic shelter

End: 0.60 mi, 869', Return to southern end of parking lot

Difficulty: Easy   Elev Gain/Loss: 181' / 181'

Quarry Trail

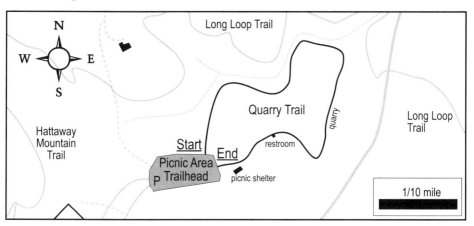

Elevation Profile: Quarry Trail

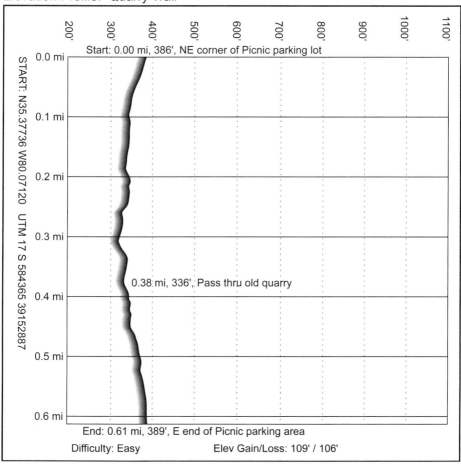

Rocks Trail

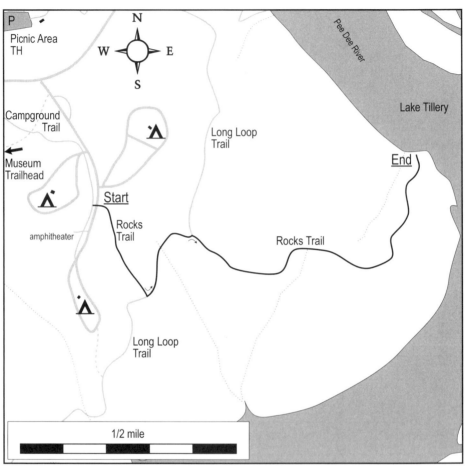

Elevation Profile: Rocks Trail

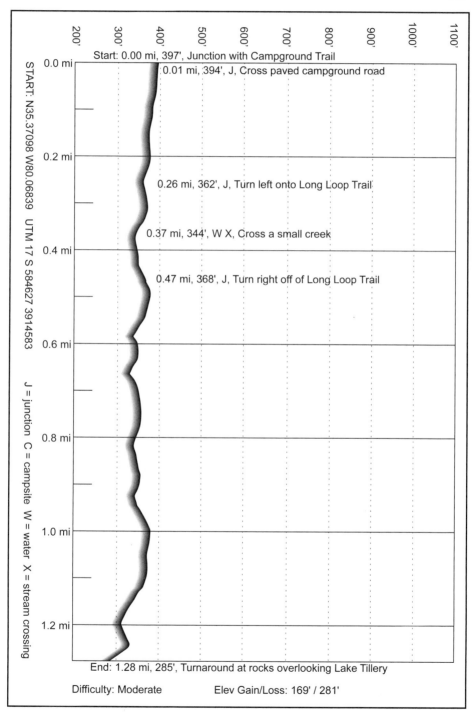

START: N35.37098 W80.06839 UTM 17 S 584627 3914583   J = junction C = campsite W = water X = stream crossing

Start: 0.00 mi, 397', Junction with Campground Trail

0.01 mi, 394', J, Cross paved campground road

0.26 mi, 362', J, Turn left onto Long Loop Trail

0.37 mi, 344', W X, Cross a small creek

0.47 mi, 368', J, Turn right off of Long Loop Trail

End: 1.28 mi, 285', Turnaround at rocks overlooking Lake Tillery

Difficulty: Moderate   Elev Gain/Loss: 169' / 281'

Short Loop Trail

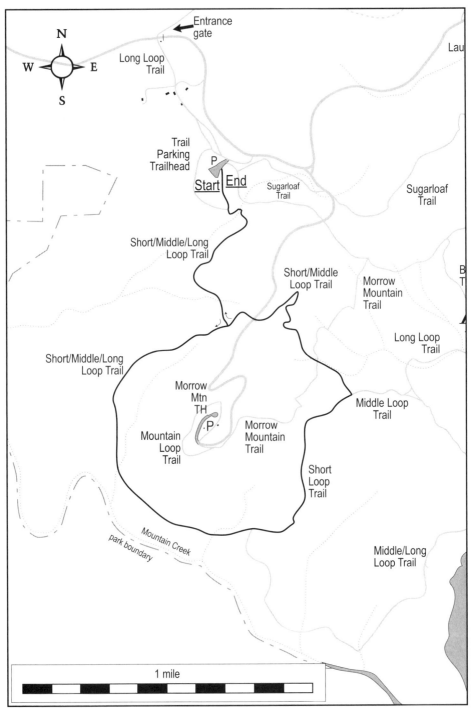

Elevation Profile: Short Loop Trail

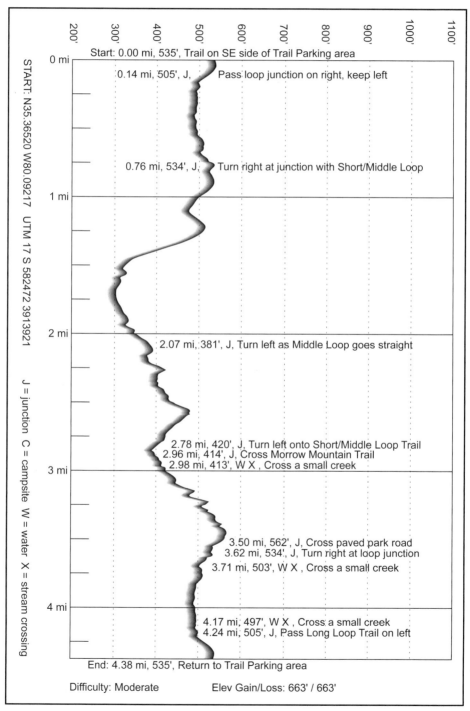

START: N35.36520 W80.09217 UTM 17 S 582472 3913921

J = junction C = campsite W = water X = stream crossing

Start: 0.00 mi, 535', Trail on SE side of Trail Parking area

0.14 mi, 505', J,   Pass loop junction on right, keep left

0.76 mi, 534', J,   Turn right at junction with Short/Middle Loop

2.07 mi, 381', J, Turn left as Middle Loop goes straight

2.78 mi, 420', J, Turn left onto Short/Middle Loop Trail
2.96 mi, 414', J, Cross Morrow Mountain Trail
2.98 mi, 413', W X , Cross a small creek

3.50 mi, 562', J, Cross paved park road
3.62 mi, 534', J, Turn right at loop junction
3.71 mi, 503', W X , Cross a small creek

4.17 mi, 497', W X , Cross a small creek
4.24 mi, 505', J, Pass Long Loop Trail on left

End: 4.38 mi, 535', Return to Trail Parking area

Difficulty: Moderate   Elev Gain/Loss: 663' / 663'

Sugarloaf Mountain Trail

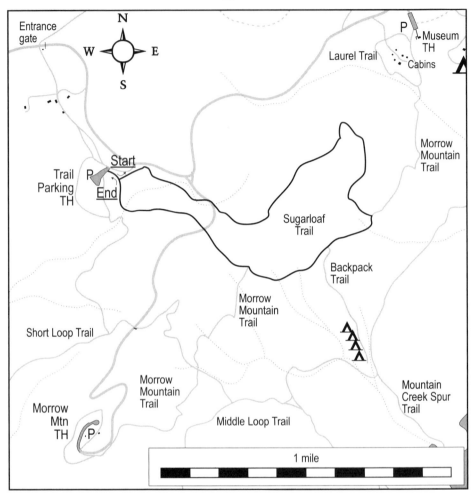

Elevation Profile: Sugarloaf Mountain Trail

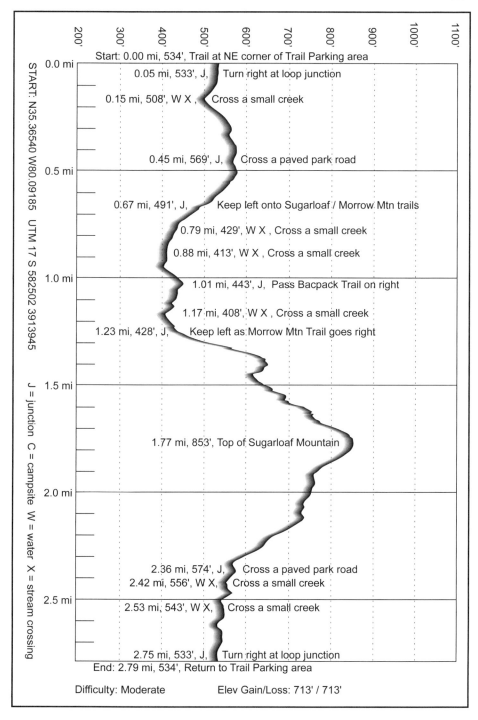

START: N35.36540 W80.09185   UTM 17 S 582502 3913945

J = junction C = campsite W = water X = stream crossing

Start: 0.00 mi, 534', Trail at NE corner of Trail Parking area
0.05 mi, 533', J, Turn right at loop junction
0.15 mi, 508', W X , Cross a small creek
0.45 mi, 569', J, Cross a paved park road
0.67 mi, 491', J, Keep left onto Sugarloaf / Morrow Mtn trails
0.79 mi, 429', W X , Cross a small creek
0.88 mi, 413', W X , Cross a small creek
1.01 mi, 443', J, Pass Bacpack Trail on right
1.17 mi, 408', W X , Cross a small creek
1.23 mi, 428', J, Keep left as Morrow Mtn Trail goes right
1.77 mi, 853', Top of Sugarloaf Mountain
2.36 mi, 574', J, Cross a paved park road
2.42 mi, 556', W X, Cross a small creek
2.53 mi, 543', W X, Cross a small creek
2.75 mi, 533', J, Turn right at loop junction
End: 2.79 mi, 534', Return to Trail Parking area

Difficulty: Moderate   Elev Gain/Loss: 713' / 713'

Three Rivers Trail

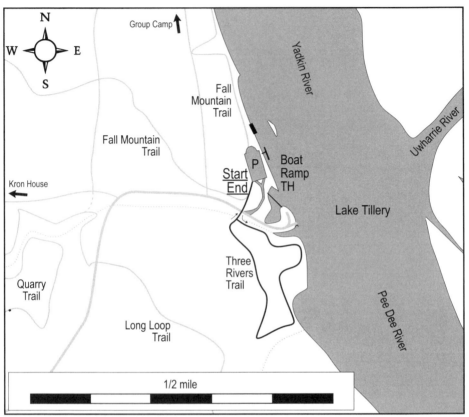

Elevation Profile: Three Rivers Trail

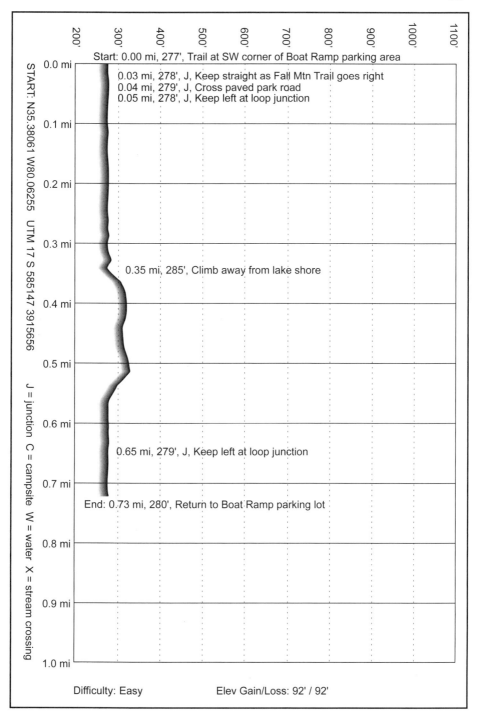

START: N35.38061 W80.06255 UTM 17 S 585147 3915656

J = junction C = campsite W = water X = stream crossing

200' 300' 400' 500' 600' 700' 800' 900' 1000' 1100'

Start: 0.00 mi, 277', Trail at SW corner of Boat Ramp parking area

0.03 mi, 278', J, Keep straight as Fall Mtn Trail goes right
0.04 mi, 279', J, Cross paved park road
0.05 mi, 278', J, Keep left at loop junction

0.35 mi, 285', Climb away from lake shore

0.65 mi, 279', J, Keep left at loop junction

End: 0.73 mi, 280', Return to Boat Ramp parking lot

0.0 mi
0.1 mi
0.2 mi
0.3 mi
0.4 mi
0.5 mi
0.6 mi
0.7 mi
0.8 mi
0.9 mi
1.0 mi

Difficulty: Easy   Elev Gain/Loss: 92' / 92'

Morrow Mountain State Park Trips

Trip	Use	Length (miles)	Elevation Gain/ Loss	Difficulty Rating	Page
MMSP Trip A	H	3.36	520' / 520'	Moderate	372
MMSP Trip B	H	4.11	681' / 681'	Moderate	374
MMSP Trip C	H	5.10	832' / 832'	Difficult	376
MMSP Trip D	H	5.57	1,618' / 1,618'	Difficult	378
MMSP Trip E	H	6.13	1,263' / 1,263'	Difficult	380
MMSP Trip F	H	9.79	1,889' / 1,889'	Difficult	382
MMSP Trip G	EH	4.38	663' / 663'	Moderate	364
MMSP Trip H	EH	5.97	875' / 875'	Moderate	356
MMSP Trip I	EH	10.15	1436' / 1436'	Difficult	354

Morrow Mountain Trip A

Map	page 372	**Difficulty**	Moderate
Length	3.36 miles	**Configuration**	Out and back
Trailhead	Museum	**Elev Gain/Loss**	520' / 520'

Start Coordinates N35.37274, W80.07304;   17 S 584203 3914775

Morrow Mountain Trip B

Map	page 374	**Difficulty**	Moderate
Length	4.11 miles	**Configuration**	Loop
Trailhead	Trail Parking	**Elev Gain/Loss**	681' / 681'

Start Coordinates N35.36520, W80.09217;   17 S 582472 3913921

Morrow Mountain Trip C

Map	page 376	**Difficulty**	Difficult
Length	5.10 miles	**Configuration**	Loop
Trailhead	Boat Ramp	**Elev Gain/Loss**	832' / 832'

Start Coordinates N35.38155, W80.06263;   17 S 585139 3915760

Morrow Mountain Trip D

Map	page 378	**Difficulty**	Difficult
Length	5.57 miles	**Configuration**	Combined
Trailhead	Trail Parking	**Elev Gain/Loss**	1,618' / 1,618'

Start Coordinates N35.36540, W80.09185;   17 S 582502 3913945

Morrow Mountain Trip E

Map	page 380	**Difficulty**	Difficult
Length	6.13 miles	**Configuration**	Loop
Trailhead	Museum	**Elev Gain/Loss**	1,263' / 1,263'

Start Coordinates N35.37238, W80.07323;   17 S 584186 3914734

Morrow Mountain Trip F

Map	page 382	**Difficulty**	Difficult
Length	9.79 miles	**Configuration**	Loop
Trailhead	Museum	**Elev Gain/Loss**	1,889' / 1,889'

Start Coordinates N35.37274, W80.07304;   17 S 584203 3914775

Morrow Mountain Trip G (see Short Loop Trail)

Morrow Mountain Trip H (see Middle Loop Trail)

Morrow Mountain Trip I (see Long Loop Trail)

MMSP Trip A

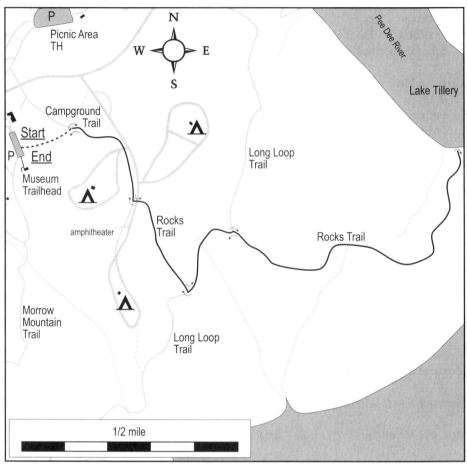

P

Picnic Area
TH

N
W ← ○ → E
S

Pee Dee River

Lake Tillery

Campground
Trail

Start

P   End

Museum
Trailhead

amphitheater

Long Loop
Trail

Rocks
Trail

Rocks Trail

Morrow
Mountain
Trail

Long Loop
Trail

1/2 mile

Elevation Profile: Morrow Mountain Trip A

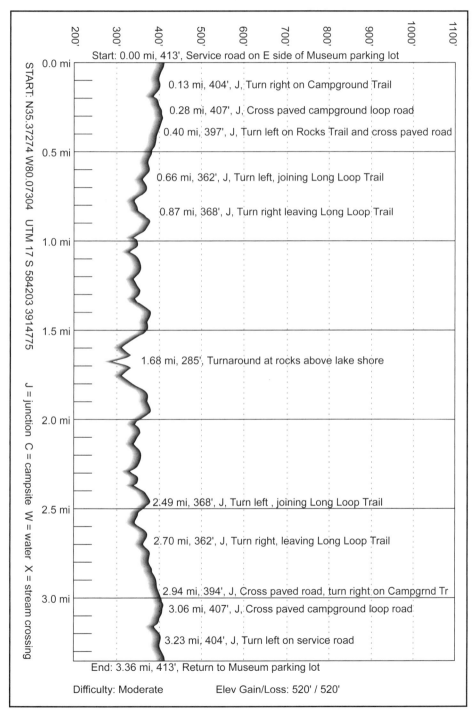

START: N35.37274 W80.07304 UTM 17 S 584203 3914775

J = junction C = campsite W = water X = stream crossing

Start: 0.00 mi, 413', Service road on E side of Museum parking lot

0.0 mi

0.13 mi, 404', J, Turn right on Campground Trail

0.28 mi, 407', J, Cross paved campground loop road

0.40 mi, 397', J, Turn left on Rocks Trail and cross paved road

0.5 mi

0.66 mi, 362', J, Turn left, joining Long Loop Trail

0.87 mi, 368', J, Turn right leaving Long Loop Trail

1.0 mi

1.5 mi

1.68 mi, 285', Turnaround at rocks above lake shore

2.0 mi

2.49 mi, 368', J, Turn left , joining Long Loop Trail

2.5 mi

2.70 mi, 362', J, Turn right, leaving Long Loop Trail

2.94 mi, 394', J, Cross paved road, turn right on Campgrnd Tr

3.0 mi

3.06 mi, 407', J, Cross paved campground loop road

3.23 mi, 404', J, Turn left on service road

End: 3.36 mi, 413', Return to Museum parking lot

Difficulty: Moderate   Elev Gain/Loss: 520' / 520'

MMSP Trip B

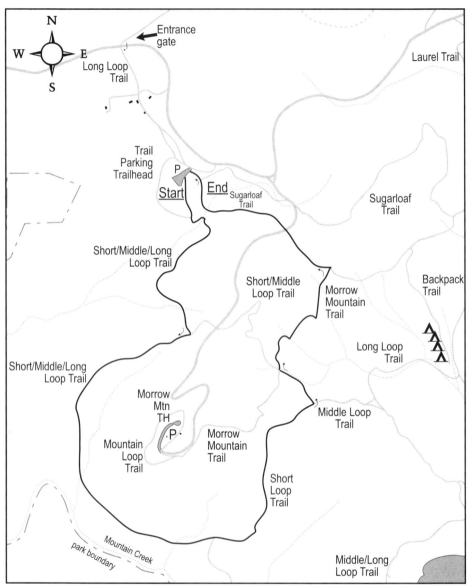

Elevation Profile: MMSP Trip B

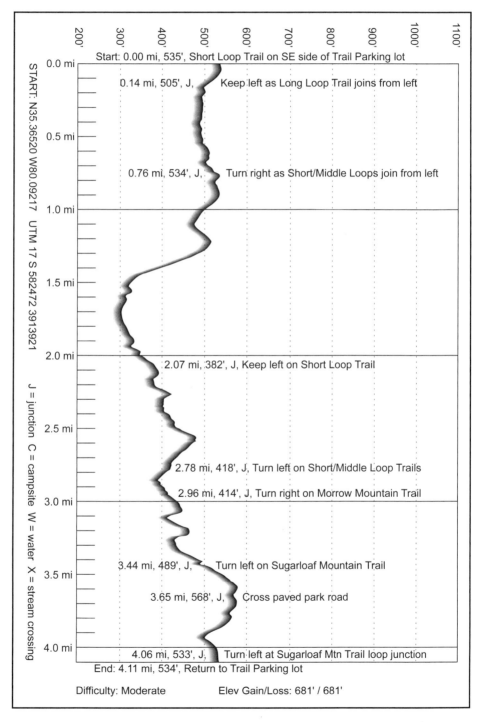

START: N35.36520 W80.09217 UTM 17 S 582472 3913921

J = junction C = campsite W = water X = stream crossing

Start: 0.00 mi, 535', Short Loop Trail on SE side of Trail Parking lot

0.14 mi, 505', J,   Keep left as Long Loop Trail joins from left

0.76 mi, 534', J,   Turn right as Short/Middle Loops join from left

2.07 mi, 382', J, Keep left on Short Loop Trail

2.78 mi, 418', J, Turn left on Short/Middle Loop Trails

2.96 mi, 414', J, Turn right on Morrow Mountain Trail

3.44 mi, 489', J,   Turn left on Sugarloaf Mountain Trail

3.65 mi, 568', J,   Cross paved park road

4.06 mi, 533', J,   Turn left at Sugarloaf Mtn Trail loop junction

End: 4.11 mi, 534', Return to Trail Parking lot

Difficulty: Moderate   Elev Gain/Loss: 681' / 681'

MMSP Trip C

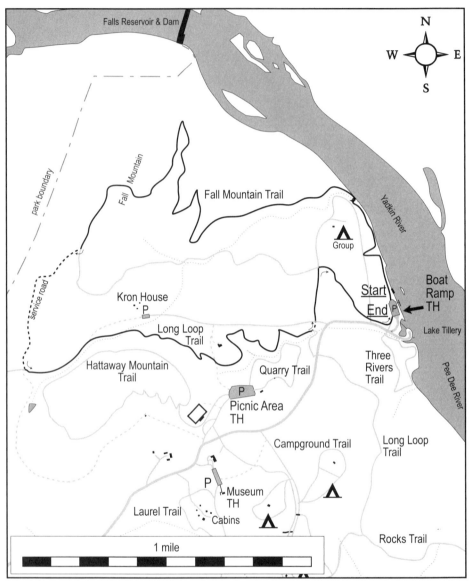

Falls Reservoir & Dam

N
W E
S

Fall Mountain

Fall Mountain Trail

Yadkin River

Group

Kron House
P

Start
End   Boat
Ramp
TH

Long Loop
Trail

Lake Tillery

Hattaway Mountain
Trail

Quarry Trail

Three
Rivers
Trail

Pee Dee River

P
Picnic Area
TH

Campground Trail

Long Loop
Trail

P
Museum
TH

Laurel Trail

Cabins

Rocks Trail

park boundary

service road

1 mile

Elevation Profile: MMSP Trip C

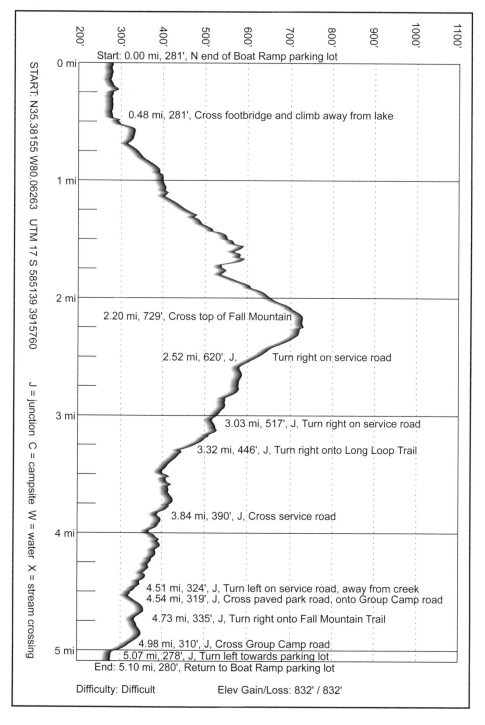

START: N35.38155 W80.06263   UTM 17 S 585139 3915760   J = junction C = campsite W = water X = stream crossing

Start: 0.00 mi, 281', N end of Boat Ramp parking lot

0.48 mi, 281', Cross footbridge and climb away from lake

2.20 mi, 729', Cross top of Fall Mountain

2.52 mi, 620', J,   Turn right on service road

3.03 mi, 517', J, Turn right on service road

3.32 mi, 446', J, Turn right onto Long Loop Trail

3.84 mi, 390', J, Cross service road

4.51 mi, 324', J, Turn left on service road, away from creek
4.54 mi, 319', J, Cross paved park road, onto Group Camp road

4.73 mi, 335', J, Turn right onto Fall Mountain Trail

4.98 mi, 310', J, Cross Group Camp road
5.07 mi, 278', J, Turn left towards parking lot
End: 5.10 mi, 280', Return to Boat Ramp parking lot

Difficulty: Difficult   Elev Gain/Loss: 832' / 832'

MMSP Trip D

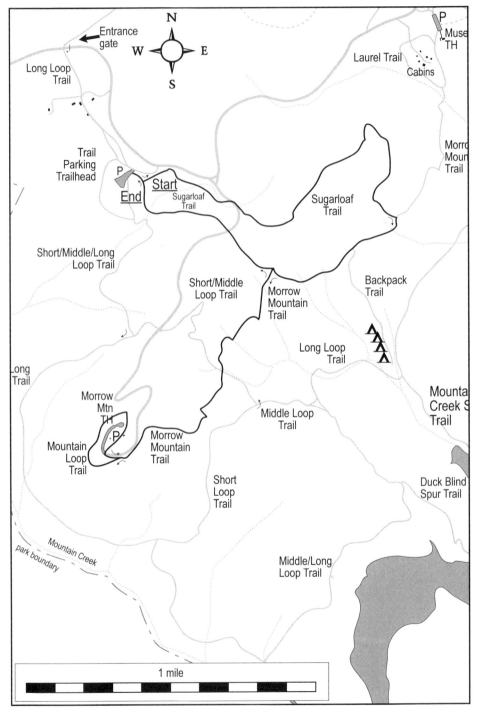

Elevation Profile: MMSP Trip D

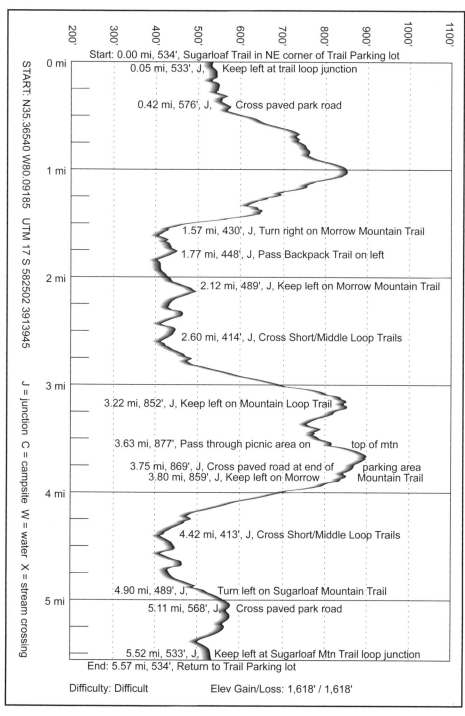

START: N35.36540 W80.09185   UTM 17 S 582502 3913945

J = junction C = campsite W = water X = stream crossing

Start: 0.00 mi, 534', Sugarloaf Trail in NE corner of Trail Parking lot

0.05 mi, 533', J, Keep left at trail loop junction

0.42 mi, 576', J, Cross paved park road

1.57 mi, 430', J, Turn right on Morrow Mountain Trail

1.77 mi, 448', J, Pass Backpack Trail on left

2.12 mi, 489', J, Keep left on Morrow Mountain Trail

2.60 mi, 414', J, Cross Short/Middle Loop Trails

3.22 mi, 852', J, Keep left on Mountain Loop Trail

3.63 mi, 877', Pass through picnic area on top of mtn

3.75 mi, 869', J, Cross paved road at end of parking area
3.80 mi, 859', J, Keep left on Morrow Mountain Trail

4.42 mi, 413', J, Cross Short/Middle Loop Trails

4.90 mi, 489', J, Turn left on Sugarloaf Mountain Trail

5.11 mi, 568', J, Cross paved park road

5.52 mi, 533', J, Keep left at Sugarloaf Mtn Trail loop junction

End: 5.57 mi, 534', Return to Trail Parking lot

Difficulty: Difficult   Elev Gain/Loss: 1,618' / 1,618'

MMSP Trip E

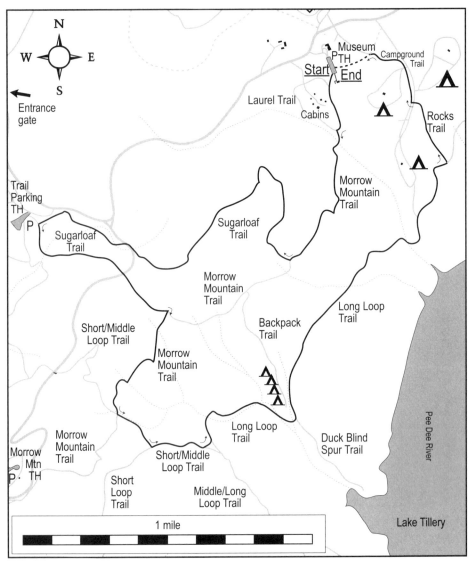

Elevation Profile: MMSP Trip E

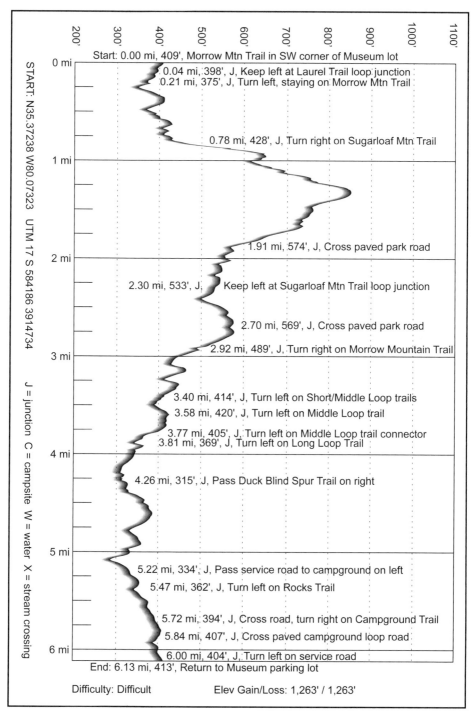

START: N35.37238 W80.07323 UTM 17 S 584186 3914734   J = junction C = campsite W = water X = stream crossing

Start: 0.00 mi, 409', Morrow Mtn Trail in SW corner of Museum lot

0.04 mi, 398', J, Keep left at Laurel Trail loop junction
0.21 mi, 375', J, Turn left, staying on Morrow Mtn Trail

0.78 mi, 428', J, Turn right on Sugarloaf Mtn Trail

1.91 mi, 574', J, Cross paved park road

2.30 mi, 533', J, Keep left at Sugarloaf Mtn Trail loop junction

2.70 mi, 569', J, Cross paved park road

2.92 mi, 489', J, Turn right on Morrow Mountain Trail

3.40 mi, 414', J, Turn left on Short/Middle Loop trails
3.58 mi, 420', J, Turn left on Middle Loop trail
3.77 mi, 405', J, Turn left on Middle Loop trail connector
3.81 mi, 369', J, Turn left on Long Loop Trail

4.26 mi, 315', J, Pass Duck Blind Spur Trail on right

5.22 mi, 334', J, Pass service road to campground on left
5.47 mi, 362', J, Turn left on Rocks Trail

5.72 mi, 394', J, Cross road, turn right on Campground Trail
5.84 mi, 407', J, Cross paved campground loop road

6.00 mi, 404', J, Turn left on service road
End: 6.13 mi, 413', Return to Museum parking lot

Difficulty: Difficult   Elev Gain/Loss: 1,263' / 1,263'

MMSP Trip F

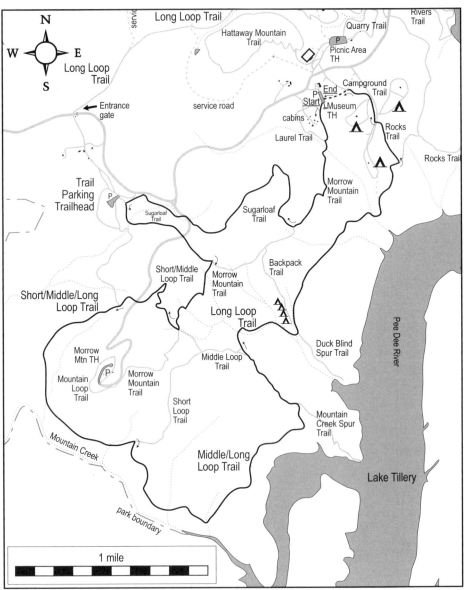

Elevation Profile: MMSP Trip F

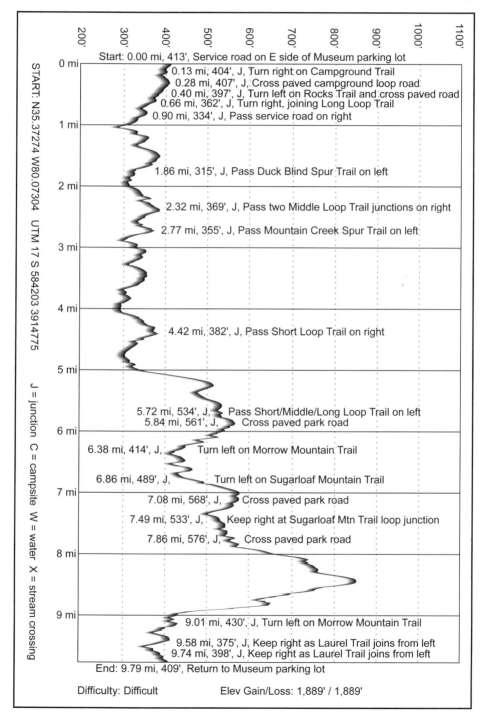

START: N35.37274 W80.07304 UTM 17 S 584203 3914775

J = junction C = campsite W = water X = stream crossing

Start: 0.00 mi, 413', Service road on E side of Museum parking lot

0.13 mi, 404', J, Turn right on Campground Trail
0.28 mi, 407', J, Cross paved campground loop road
0.40 mi, 397', J, Turn left on Rocks Trail and cross paved road
0.66 mi, 362', J, Turn right, joining Long Loop Trail
0.90 mi, 334', J, Pass service road on right

1.86 mi, 315', J, Pass Duck Blind Spur Trail on left

2.32 mi, 369', J, Pass two Middle Loop Trail junctions on right

2.77 mi, 355', J, Pass Mountain Creek Spur Trail on left

4.42 mi, 382', J, Pass Short Loop Trail on right

5.72 mi, 534', J, Pass Short/Middle/Long Loop Trail on left
5.84 mi, 561', J, Cross paved park road

6.38 mi, 414', J, Turn left on Morrow Mountain Trail

6.86 mi, 489', J, Turn left on Sugarloaf Mountain Trail

7.08 mi, 568', J, Cross paved park road

7.49 mi, 533', J, Keep right at Sugarloaf Mtn Trail loop junction

7.86 mi, 576', J, Cross paved park road

9.01 mi, 430', J, Turn left on Morrow Mountain Trail

9.58 mi, 375', J, Keep right as Laurel Trail joins from left
9.74 mi, 398', J, Keep right as Laurel Trail joins from left

End: 9.79 mi, 409', Return to Museum parking lot

Difficulty: Difficult   Elev Gain/Loss: 1,889' / 1,889'

NC Zoological Park

The NC Zoo has been working diligently over the past 10 years to include the Zoo and its partners in trail plans and programs that help recreational projects that conserve natural area, open up natural areas to public access, and encourage the sciences by mentoring the young. This effort is starting to pay off with actual linear feet of trail on the ground.

Trail development often happens when Eagle Scout candidates contact the Zoo and want to do projects. If you are interested in learning more about doing a project at the Zoo, contact the Volunteer Office at 336-879-7712.

The NC Zoo is developing hiking trails both on the property where the Zoo proper is located and on other significant natural heritage preserves the Zoo owns and manages. Although these are relatively short trails now, the Zoo has plans to expand the natural area trail network and connect it with future trails and greenways. The Zoo already features over 5 miles of trails inside the park that go in and around the animal exhibits.

NOTES OF INTEREST
The hiking trails at the Zoo itself are open from 6:30am to 7:00pm daily. Vehicular gates to the Park close at 7:30pm.

For more info on the Zoo Park itself, visit http://www.nczoo.org/

Anyone interested in performing volunteer work on the trails managed by the Zoo should contact the Volunteer Office at 336-879-7712 and ask to coordinate with the Curator of Horticulture. Be specific and wanting to do trail work, such as telling them you would like to do an Eagle Scout project on the Zoo's hiking trail.

ACCESS

Covered Bridge Trailhead
A small parking lot is located at the end of a short gravel drive that ends beside the Pisgah Covered Bridge. The Covered Bridge Loop Trail can be accessed at the bridge itself. The street address of this trailhead is 6900 Pisgah Covered Bridge Rd, Asheboro, NC.

UTM	17 S 600295 3933735
Lat/Lon	N35.54219 W79.89358

NC Zoo Park Area Map

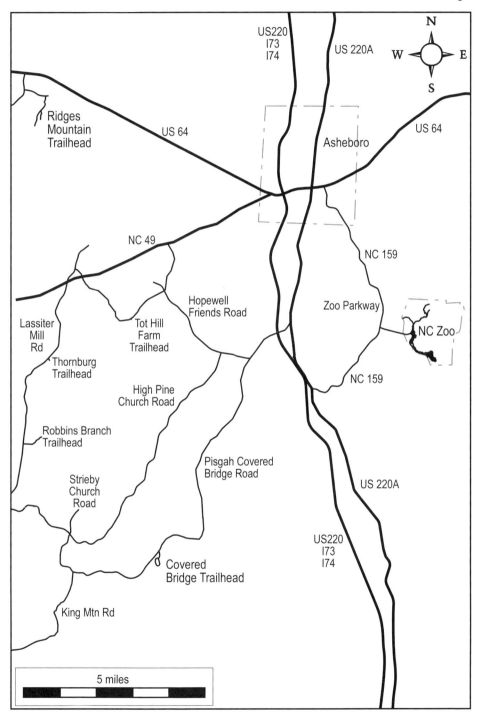

Ridges Mountain Trailhead

Space for several cars to park is located at the end of Summit Court. The Ridges Mountain Trail can be accessed from this trailhead. This trailhead is located at the Ridges Mountain Nature Preserve, not at the main Zoo Park. The street address of this trailhead is 504 Summit Ct, Asheboro, NC.

UTM	17 S 595195 3953654
Lat/Lon	N35.72226 W79.94747

Access is by appointment only. To schedule an outing please contact the N.C. Zoological Park at 336-879-7401 or the Piedmont Land Conservancy at 336-691-0088.

North America Trailhead

The North America parking lot is the first lot you come to as you enter the NC Zoo Park. This trailhead is located at the northern end of the parking lots and is tucked back in the corner near a zoo service road. Hikers can access the Purgatory Trail and Moonshine Run Trail from this trailhead. The Connector Trail can be accessed from the south end of the North America parking lots.

UTM	17 S 611704 3943820
Lat/Lon	N35.63188 W79.76635

NC Zoo Park

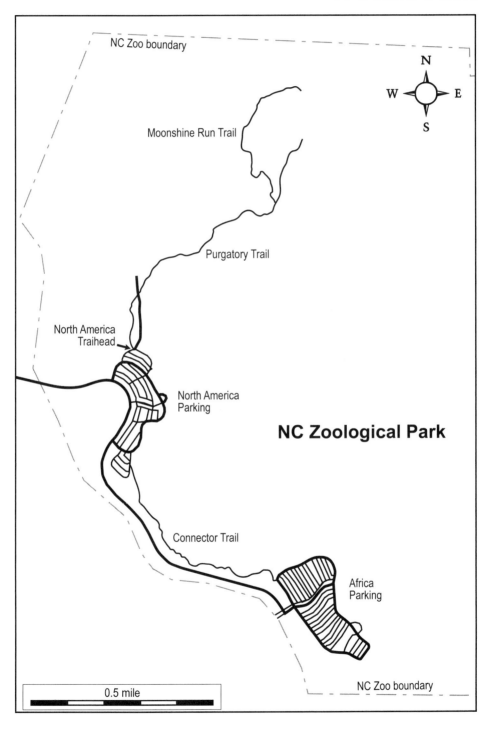

NC Zoo Park Trails

Trail Name	Length (miles)	Elevation Gain/Loss	Difficulty Rating	Map (page)
Connector	0.62	51' / 129'	Easy	392
Covered Bridge	0.15	15' / 15'	Easy	393
Moonshine Run	0.51	73' / 103'	Moderate	394
Purgatory	0.89	209' / 42'	Moderate	396
Ridges Mountain	0.79	161' / 28'	Easy	398

Connnector Trail

Map	page 392	**Difficulty**	Easy
Length	0.62 miles	**Configuration**	One Way
Trailhead	North America parking	**Elev Gain/Loss**	51' / 129'

Start Coordinates N35.62725, W79.76651;   17 S 611695 3943307

In 2009, the Zoo Connector Trail was built to tie together the parking areas for the North America and Africa sections of the Park. The north end of the trail starts near the southern end of the North America parking lots, on the sidewalk beside the Solar Pointe exhibit.

Covered Bridge Trail

Map	page 400	**Difficulty**	Easy
Length	0.15 miles	**Configuration**	Loop
Trailhead	Covered Bridge	**Elev Gain/Loss**	15' / 15'

Start Coordinates N35.54209, W79.89375;   17 S 600279 3933724

The Pisgah Covered Bridge is one of Randolph County's historical and cultural treasures. It is one of only two surviving covered bridges in the state and the only one easily accessible by the public.

Following the construction of a new road and bridge in the Pisgah community during the 1950s, the covered bridge fell into disrepair and was badly vandalized despite efforts by the DOT to maintain it. Recognizing the heritage of the bridge and its potential economic value to the community, Zoo Director Dr. Jones and the N.C. Zoo Society initiated an effort in April 1998 to refurbish the bridge and build an adjacent hiking trail along with picnic and parking areas. In 2003, the bridge was destroyed by a flash flood. Donations to the Zoo Society's fund permitted repairs to the bridge, the walkway and the small community park that serves tourists visiting the Pisgah Cover Bridge.

The Covered Bridge Trail is a short loop trail located at the historic Pisgah Covered Bridge, a small park in southeastern Randolph County.

Just downstream from the bridge is the Pisgah community baptismal pool, which is part of the walking trail at the site. The trail proceeds over a series of footbridges and returns over rougher landscape on the west side of the creek to create a circuit that includes the covered bridge itself.

Moonshine Run Trail

Map	page 394	**Difficulty**	Moderate
Length	0.51 miles	**Configuration**	One Way
Trailhead	n/a	**Elev Gain/Loss**	73' / 103'

Start Coordinates N35.63764, W79.75943;   17 S 612322 3944467

The Moonshine Run Trail is partially complete. This half mile trail starts at a junction with the Purgatory Trail and circles around the west and north sides of Purgatory Mountain. The trail currently ends at a turnaround on the north side of Purgatory Mountain. Numerous rock outcroppings, typical of Uwharrie mountains, are passed along the route.

Purgatory Trail

Map	page 396	**Difficulty**	Easy
Length	0.89 miles	**Configuration**	One Way
Trailhead	North America	**Elev Gain/Loss**	209' / 42'

Start Coordinates N35.63188, W79.76635;   17 S 611704 3943820

The Purgatory Trail to the top of Purgatory Mountain was opened in the Fall of 2012. This trail was initially developed as an Eagle Scout Project in 2002. Future plans include building a tree-top height observation tower on top of the mountain.

According to local legend, Purgatory Mountain gained its name during the U.S. Prohibition in the 1920s and early 1930s. As the story goes, there were so many whiskey stills built on the mountain at the time that their fires lit the area up at night like "purgatory."

Purgatory Mountain is the highest point on the entire zoo site. It's also part of the Uwharrie Mountain range, thought by geologists to be the oldest in North America. Hikers will enjoy seeing these biologically significant forests change from an oak hickory to a high-elevation chestnut forest at the top of the mountain.

Purgatory Trail is a relatively easy walk to a top of a typical Uwharrie mountain hosting a monadnock forest. The route passes by a federally rare sunflower restoration site, an unusual low elevation seep, remnants of old stills and cultural history, and climbs to an elevation of 928 feet. Several of these features are used by high school students in environmental education citizen science monitoring projects.

Despite being within 1 hour of most of NC's population, this trail allows one to experience the quiet of the deep woods without the intrusion of cars, traffic or sounds of the human world.

Ridges Mountain Trail

Map	page 398	**Difficulty**	Moderate
Length	0.79 miles	**Configuration**	One Way
Trailhead	Ridges Mountain	**Elev Gain/Loss**	161' / 28'

Start Coordinates N35.72224, W79.94742;   17 S 595199 3953652

Ridges Mountain Nature Preserve is located a few miles west of Asheboro in Randolph County. Access is by appointment only. To schedule an outing please contact the N.C. Zoological Park at 336-879-7401 or the Piedmont Land Conservancy at 336-691-0088.

The Natural Heritage Inventory of Randolph County lists Ridges Mountain as a "State" significant site (one of the best in the State) due to its high quality natural communities, significant rare species and large area of continuous habitat. Ridges Mountain is also historically significant as it was occupied by both Native Americans and early settlers.

The first part of the Ridges Mountain Trial follows an access road from the entrance gate, past a second gate, to a small clearing used for educational workshops. From this clearing, two signed trails lead southward along the ridge. The longer, western trail leads to the summit of Ridges Mountain, passing through an area of numerous rock outcroppings. The eastern trail passes by some historic stone works and heads southward towards the summit and the end of the western trail. The loop route to be formed by connecting these two trail legs was still incomplete in 2013. The first part of the trail at Ridges was built in 2005.

Future Trails

Hideaway Loop Trail - This trail will connect to the Moonshine Run Trail and loop all the way around Purgatory Mountain.

Woodell's Escape Trail - This trail is currently in the planning and development phase. This 1 mile trail is expected to be completed in 2015. The trail will start at a junction with the Moonshine Run Trail on the southwestern skirt of Purgatory Mountain. The trail route will then cross over Middle Mountain and eventually connect to a northern trail head off of Woodell Trail Road. The Zoo is currently fund raising for development of a 6 car parking lot at the new trail head, trail development using volunteers, and some wayfinding signage.

Hart's Run Trail - This trail is planned to start at a junction with the Hideaway Loop Trail on the east side of Purgatory Mountain and lead eastward from there.

The Batchelor Creek Trail is planned to start at the western side of the Africa parking area and lead to the west and south for over 2 miles.

Connector Trail

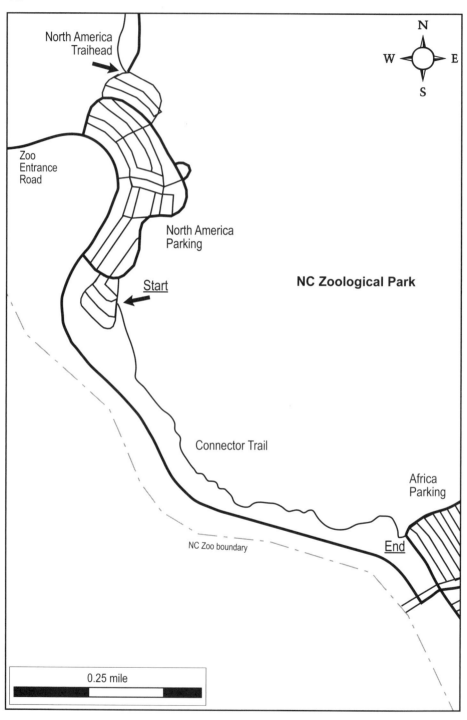

North America
Traihead

Zoo
Entrance
Road

North America
Parking

Start

NC Zoological Park

Connector Trail

Africa
Parking

End

NC Zoo boundary

0.25 mile

Covered Bridge Trail

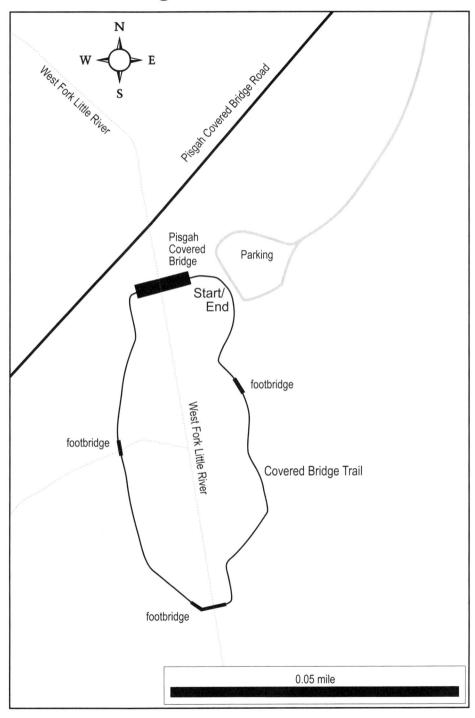

0.05 mile

Moonshine Run Trail

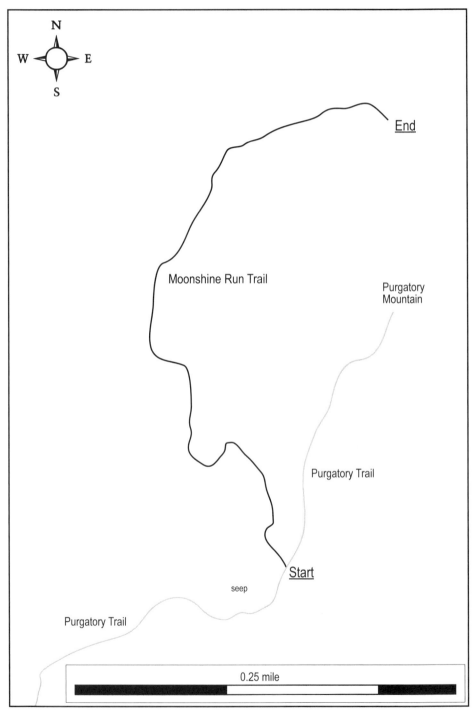

Elevation Profile: Moonshine Run Trail

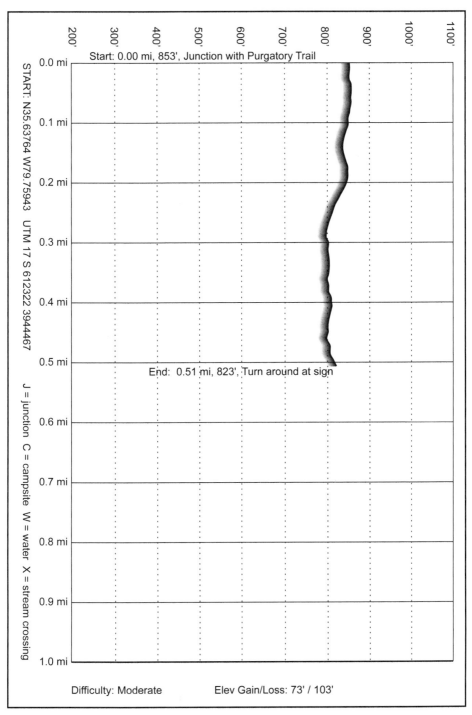

START: N35.63764 W79.75943 UTM 17 S 612322 3944467

J = junction C = campsite W = water X = stream crossing

Start: 0.00 mi, 853', Junction with Purgatory Trail

End: 0.51 mi, 823', Turn around at sign

Difficulty: Moderate   Elev Gain/Loss: 73' / 103'

Purgatory Trail

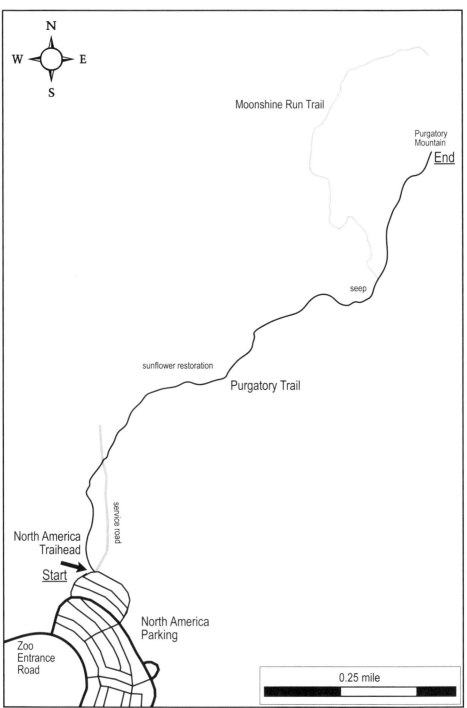

N
W — E
S

Moonshine Run Trail

Purgatory
Mountain

End

seep

sunflower restoration

Purgatory Trail

service road

North America
Traihead

Start

North America
Parking

Zoo
Entrance
Road

0.25 mile

Elevation Profile: Purgatory Trail

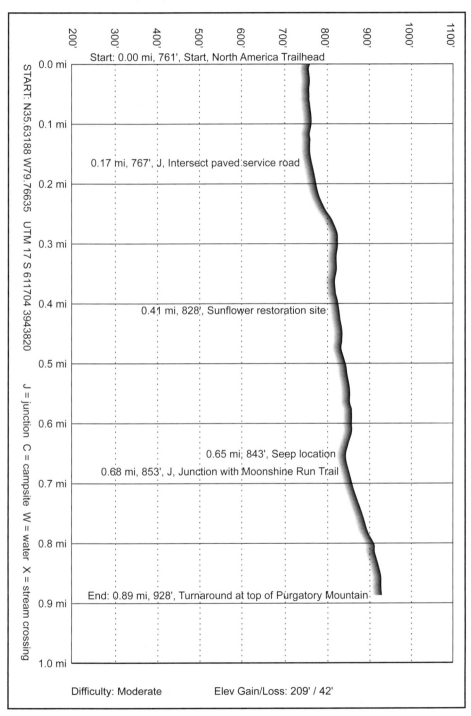

START: N35.63188 W79.76635   UTM 17 S 611704 3943820

J = junction   C = campsite   W = water   X = stream crossing

Start: 0.00 mi, 761', Start, North America Trailhead

0.17 mi, 767', J, Intersect paved service road

0.41 mi, 828', Sunflower restoration site

0.65 mi, 843', Seep location

0.68 mi, 853', J, Junction with Moonshine Run Trail

End: 0.89 mi, 928', Turnaround at top of Purgatory Mountain

Difficulty: Moderate   Elev Gain/Loss: 209' / 42'

Ridges Mountain Trail

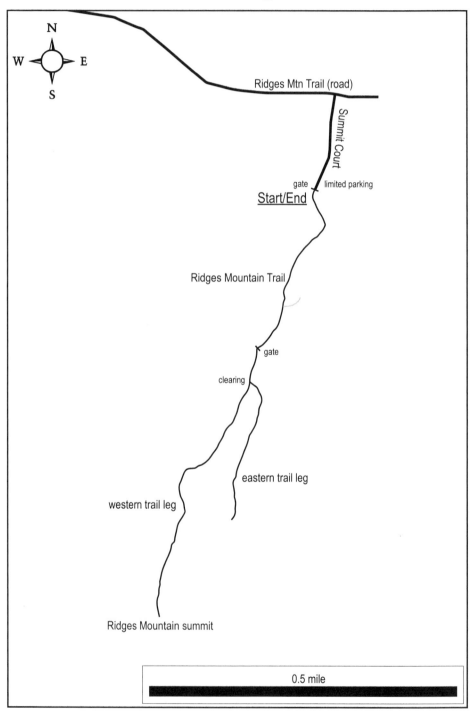

Elevation Profile: Ridges Mountain Trail

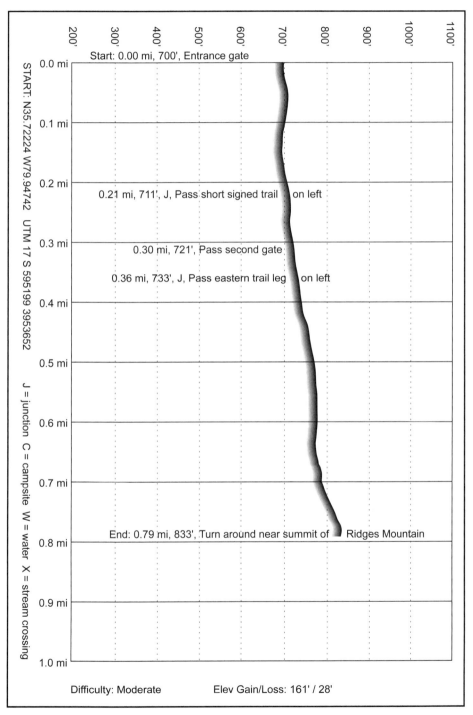

Start: 0.00 mi, 700', Entrance gate

0.21 mi, 711', J, Pass short signed trail on left

0.30 mi, 721', Pass second gate

0.36 mi, 733', J, Pass eastern trail leg on left

End: 0.79 mi, 833', Turn around near summit of Ridges Mountain

START: N35.72224 W79.94742 UTM 17 S 595199 3953652

J = junction C = campsite W = water X = stream crossing

Difficulty: Moderate   Elev Gain/Loss: 161' / 28'

Uwharrie Trail

The Uwharrie National Recreation Trail is probably the best known hiking trail in the Uwharrie Lakes Region. The Uwharrie Trail is USFS trail #276 now, but was previously #99. This number is sometime seen on maps, but not on signs along the trail. The Uwharrie Trail is marked with white paint blazes. There are wooden signs at most of the major road crossings and trail intersections. Other intersections are marked with brown carsonite posts.

At approximately 20 miles in length, the Uwharrie Trail is the longest hiking trail in the Uwharrie Lakes Region. But this 20 mile stretch of trail is just the southern half of the original Uwharrie Trail. Historically the Uwharrie Trail began much further north, near the Asheboro Municipal Airport.

In the late 1960's, Joe Moffitt started work on the Uwharrie Trail idea. Joe was the Scoutmaster for Troop 570 in Asheboro, NC. After taking his scouts to the southern Appalachian Mountains to get in a 50-mile hiking trip, he realized the Uwharrie Mountains where he lived could also be home to its own long hiking trail. Joe wanted to create a system of trails that could help teach young people proper values by reconnecting them to the land and our cultural history.

Moffit worked with the US Forest Service and private property owners to get "handshake" agreements for permission for a trail route to cross their property. The first sections of the trail route were put on the ground in 1968. Volunteers like Mike Chisholm, other Boy Scout troops, and USFS staff blazed and built the trail over the next few years.

Boy Scouts working on their Eagle Projects built many of the stone fireplaces found at the various campsites along the northern end of the route.

In 1972, construction of the southern portion of the route was begun by USFS staff and other Boy Scout troops. Robert Strider, USFS, flagged the route from 24-27 to 109 and the Scouts came behind him built the trail.

The Greater Uwharrie Mountains Preservation and Appreciation Committee (later renamed to the Uwharrie Trail Club) was founded in 1974 by Joe Moffitt and Mike Chisholm to help promote hiking as a healthy activity and to help maintain the trail.

Uwharrie Trail Corridor Map

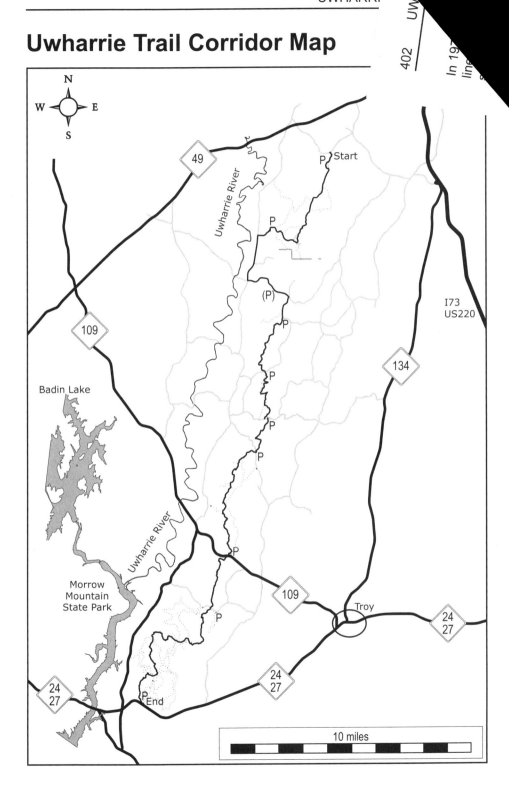

402

In 197
lin

UW

N
W E
S

49

Uwharrie River

P Start

P

(P)

P

P

P

P

I73
US220

134

Badin Lake

109

P

Uwharrie River

Morrow
Mountain
State Park

109

Troy

24
27

P

24
27

P

24
27

P End

10 miles

5, the section of trail just south of the Randolph and Montgomery County , was blazed, completing the full Uwharrie Trail route from Tot Hill Farm Road outhward to NC 24/27. Joe Moffitt and Troop 570 from Asheboro, Jerry Hancock and Troop 86 from Montgomery County, and other GUMPAC volunteers worked on this section. The route ran through a patchwork of privately owned and USFS owned properties. Some parts of the route followed public roads for a few miles.

An application for National Recreation Trail designation was submitted by USFS District Ranger Robert Carey on November 1, 1978. The application covered the southern end of the trail from NC 24/27 northward to Flint Hill Road, SR 1306. The section between Dusty Level Road and NC 109 was specifically left out due to a 160 foot long stretch of trail on private land. At the time, they only had verbal permission to cross this private land. The Chief of the USFS signed the final approval on February 1, 1980.

On June 19, 1984, the Birkhead Mountains Wilderness was created by the "North Carolina Wilderness Act of 1984". The Wilderness area included the Uwharrie Trail route from its north end at Tot Hill Farm Road to the boundary with privately owned property at the north end of Strieby Church Road. This 5.5 mile stretch of the trail was renamed the "Birkhead Mountain Trail".

Around 1997, Kelly Cagle, with the USFS Uwharrie District Ranger's office, filed an update to the National Recreation Trail application. This update declared the trail to be 20.5 miles long and included the section south of NC 109 that had been left out of the original application.

Access to the sections of trail that crossed private land was not guaranteed. A combination of factors, including changes in property ownership, logging activities, a lack of maintenance, and not being included on published trail maps, resulted in the trail sections on private property being "lost". Even the sections of trail on USFS property outside of the Wilderness area and the section designated as National Recreation Trail fell into disrepair over time and were essentially abandoned. The Uwharrie Trail Club also fell into a long period of dormancy. But many of the original white paint blazes remained out in the forest, waiting. A few people held on to the hope that the original trail could be reconnected and they promoted the idea where they could.

In 2006, a concerted effort began to acquire key properties and close the gap in the trail route. This effort ultimately involved more than 10 agencies. By 2011, a 370 acre tract in the heart of the Uwharries was permanently protected and placed into public ownership. This property filled a strategic gap in the historic Uwharrie Trail route, joining three otherwise disconnected Forest Service properties. This section of trail crosses over King Mountain, the highest peak in the Uwharrie National Forest proper.

In 2012, the LandTrust for Central North Carolina obtained seller-financing on another key property, Little Long Mountain. This property connects the King Mountain tract to USFS property adjoining the north end of the 20 mile National Recreation Trail section. This section of the trail route is the same as the last section of the original route, completed in 1975. The LandTrust will eventually transfer this property to USFS ownership.

In 2013, the NC Zoo purchased the 45 acre McArthur property along High Pine Church Road. This property adjoins the King Mountain property on the north side, connecting the trail corridor all the way to High Pine Church Road. The USFS and the NC Zoo are working on a land swap to place this property in USFS ownership.

On December 8, 2013, the trailhead on Thayer Road at the Randolph and Montgomery County line was dedicated as the Joe Moffitt Trailhead, honoring Mr. Moffitt for his contributions to the Uwharrie Trail. A stone monument and plaque are at the trailhead.

With these recent land acquisitions, the historic Uwharrie Trail route is within a few miles of being reconnected and protected for public access. Volunteers are hard at work re-opening the abandoned sections of trail on these properties.

In this chapter, the various sections of the historic Uwharrie Trail route are presented together. This approach is a little different from the area-based organization used for the rest of this guide. The sections begin at the northern end and progress southward. The Uwharrie Trail passes through two of the major geographic areas covered by this book: Wood Run and Morris Mountain.

The route is divided into sections of 2 to 4 miles in length, to allow more detail on the maps and charts. Each section ends at a major trail or road intersection. Some of the Hike Trip descriptions in other chapters include portions of the Uwharrie Trail.

Tree damage from storms has heavily influenced the routing and look of the Uwharrie Trail. Although volunteers and Forest Service crews opened the trails back up quickly, they are frequently bordered with fallen trees. In some places, the trail has simply been rerouted around piles of fallen trees. In September 1996, Hurricane Fran dealt a harsh blow to trees in the Uwharrie Lakes Region. Especially hard hit were several of the creek bottoms along this section of trail. Shallow root systems and soft soils couldn't stand up to winds funneled through the valleys. A major snowstorm in December 2000 brought down limbs and trees across the region. A "horizontal tornado" in June 2013 brought down numerous trees in the Wood Run Area.

ACCESS

Tot Hill Farm Trailhead

This trailhead is located on Tot Hill Farm Road (SR 1163), 2.1 miles south of NC 49. Tot Hill Farm Road forms a loop on the south side of NC 49. From the intersection at the eastern end of the loop (closer to Asheboro), the trailhead is 2.7

UTM	17 S 599179 3944169
Lat/Lon	N35.63636 W79.90460

miles from NC 49. From the western intersection, the trailhead is 2.0 miles from NC 49. Look for the brown and white Forest Service signs on NC 49 indicating the turn for the trailhead. There is a small parking lot for 10-15 cars and a map kiosk at this trailhead. The street address is approximately 3100 Tot Hill Farm Road, Asheboro, NC.

Robbins Branch Trailhead

This trailhead is located on Lassiter Mill Road, 1.9 miles north of the intersection with High Pine Church Road. At the end of the fairly long gravel USFS access road is a grassy parking area that can hold 20-30 vehicles. The entrance to the

UTM	17 S 595241 3939001
Lat/Lon	N35.59015 W79.94870

USFS driveway is located at street address 5527 Lassiter Mill Road, Asheboro, NC.

High Pine Church Road Trailhead (future)

This future trailhead is located on High Pine Church Road, 1.5 miles east of the intersection with Lassiter Mill Road and 0.7 miles west of Pisgah Covered Bridge Road. The street address is 6835 High Pine Church Road, Asheboro, NC.

UTM	17 S 595576 3935176
Lat/Lon	N35.55564 W79.94545

Pisgah Covered Bridge Road Trailhead

This historic trailhead is located on Pisgah Covered Bridge Road, 0.9 miles south of the intersection with High Pine Church Road, at a private road intersection. As the trail is extended northward from King Mountain, this trailhead will no longer be

UTM	17 S 596158 3933398
Lat/Lon	N35.53956 W79.93924

used. There is no official parking area at this trailhead, just a short gated USFS access road. The street address is 8753 Pisgah Covered Bridge Road, Asheboro, NC.

Joe Moffitt Trailhead

This trailhead is located on Thayer Road (SR 1305), 0.6 miles east of the intersection with Grissom Road and 2.3 miles south of Pisgah Covered Bridge Road along King Mountain Road (Randolph County) and then Thayer

| UTM | 17 S 594958 3929848 |
| Lat/Lon | N35.50767 W79.95289 |

Road (Montgomery County). The street address is 1030 Thayer Rd, Troy, NC. A monument was built here in 2013 to honor his vision and efforts on the Uwharrie Trail.

Jumping Off Rock Trailhead

This trailhead is located on Flint Hill Road (SR 1306), 1.6 miles east of Ophir Road and 2.1 miles west of Lovejoy Road. The trailhead was called the Dark Mountain Trailhead in the first edition of this guide.

| UTM | 17 S 595126 3926768 |
| Lat/Lon | N35.47989 W79.95141 |

There is a small parking lot for 6-8 vehicles, surrounded by a rail fence. A bulletin board is located beside the start of the Uwharrie Trail, which runs southward from this parking lot.

Horse Mountain Trailhead

Horse Mountain Trailhead is located on the unpaved portion of Tower Road (SR1134), 5.2 miles north of NC 109, and 1.6 miles south of Ophir Road. The trailhead is where the Uwharrie Trail crosses Tower Road. No provisions for

| UTM | 17 S 594375 3924546 |
| Lat/Lon | N35.45993 W79.95994 |

parking have been made at this trailhead, although a few vehicles might squeeze in along a gated Forest road on the east side of Tower Road. The street address is 2048 Tower Rd, Troy, NC.

109 Trailhead

This trailhead is located on NC 109, 6.0 miles north of the courthouse in Troy (by way of NC 109 Business) and 1.9 miles south of the River Road (SR 1150) intersection at Uwharrie. There is a

| UTM | 17 S 592467 3917730 |
| Lat/Lon | N35.39866 W79.98173 |

parking lot and bulletin board at this trailhead. There is room to park 10 or so vehicles here. The street address is 2545 North Carolina 109, Troy, NC.

Yates Place Trailhead

This trailhead is located on the north side of the Wood Run Area, along unpaved Dusty Level Road (SR 1146). There is a 10 car parking lot at Yates Place Camp along with several picnic tables and an

| UTM | 17 S 591852 3913997 |
| Lat/Lon | N35.36506 W79.98892 |

outhouse. Yates Place Trail leads westward from the gated road to the Uwharrie Trail. The Uwharrie Trail crosses

Dusty Level Road (SR 1146) 0.35 miles west of Yates Place Trailhead, but no provisions have been made for parking vehicles at that location. The street address is 590 Dusty Level Rd, Troy, NC.

Yates Place Trailhead is 5.3 miles from Uwharrie by way of NC 109. From Uwharrie, go south on 109 for 2.8 miles, turn right on Correll Road (SR 1147) and go 1.9 miles to the stop sign. Turn right onto unpaved Dusty Level Road (SR 1146) and go 0.6 miles and look for the sign.

Yates Place Trailhead is 5.2 miles from Uwharrie by way of River Road (SR 1150). From Uwharrie, go south on River Road for 2.6 miles, then turn left onto unpaved Dusty Level Road (SR 1146) and go another 2.6 miles to the trailhead.

24/27 Trailhead

Wood Run Trailhead is located on NC 24/27, 10.0 miles west of the courthouse in Troy. Coming from Albemarle on NC 24/27, the trailhead is 2.0 miles east of the Lake Tillery / Pee Dee River Bridge and 1.0 mile east of the River Road (SR

UTM	17 S 586968 3907920
Lat/Lon	N35.31071 W80.04333

1150) intersection. This trailhead was called the Wood Run Trailhead in the first edition of this guide, but I've changed it to match the name now used by the USFS.

A parking lot and information kiosk are located at the 24/27 Trailhead. Three trails start from this trailhead: the Uwharrie Trail, Dutchman's Creek Trail, and Wood Run Road which leads to the Wood Run Mountain Bike Trail System. About 20 vehicles can fit in the parking lot, and there is additional space along the driveway. Several campsites can be found within 0.3 miles on either hiking trail and a large flat grassy area is located beside the parking lot (within sight of NC 24/27). The street address is 4400 N Carolina 24, Mt Gilead, NC.

CAMPING

Camping is allowed anywhere on National Forest land, except in wildlife fields, at trailheads, and within 200 feet of creeks.

Part of the work done by the volunteers establishing the original Uwharrie Trail route included creating numbered "camps". These sites were usually located near a spring or creek. Rock fireplaces with steel cooking grills and a short chimney were built at several of these camps. The camps were often built as Eagle Scout projects. Several of the camps are marked with an aluminum plaque noting whose project it was, who worked on it, and when it was built. Although the location of some of these camps has been "lost", the information I've been able to find is included in the appropriate section descriptions.

MAPS

The local USFS District Ranger's office has produced simple maps/brochures over the years covering the entire length of the Uwharrie Trail. Most of these maps show trails, roads, streams, and USFS property boundaries. They generally do not include topo lines. Prior to the use of GPS mapping tools in the early 2000's, these brochure maps occasionally contained inaccurately drawn trail lines.

The latest version of the local USFS map is titled "Uwharrie Hiking Trails" and was updated 1/12/2012. This map covers the 20 miles of the Uwharrie National Recreation Trail on an 8.5" x 11" sheet of paper. This map is available online in PDF format.

The "Uwharrie National Forest" map produced by the USFS, also available online in PDF format, includes the Uwharrie Trail from NC 24/27 to Flint Hill Road. The scale of this map makes it more useful for car navigation than for trail hiking.

In 1983, G. Nicholas Hancock published a small guidebook and map covering the historic Uwharrie Trail route from Tot Hill Farm Road to NC 24-27. The book's title was *Guide To The Uwharrie Trail In The Uwharrie National Forest In Randolph And Montgomery Counties, North Carolina.*

The traditional USGS topographic quadrangle maps covering the Uwharrie Trail corridor are: Morrow Mountain, Troy, Lovejoy, and Eleazer. The 1994 revision shows the Uwharrie Trail and some of the old roads, but the trail location is approximate. The 2013 version of the new "US Topo" style topographic map does not show trail lines at all.

Gemini Maps of NC, Inc. last published a 1997 revision of its Uwharrie National Forest map. This large fold-out map includes the Uwharrie Trail. Although the map has topo lines, the trail lines are only a rough approximation of the trail locations.

Uwharrie Trail Sections

Trail Name	Length (miles)	Elevation Gain/Loss	Difficulty Rating	Map (page)
UT Section 1	4.67	757' / 777'	Moderate	426
UT Section 2	7.18	786' / 593'	Moderate	428
UT Section 3	3.15	641' / 674'	Moderate	430
UT Section 4	3.11	528' / 799'	Moderate	432
UT Section 5	2.01	564' / 319'	Moderate	434
UT Section 6	3.79	754' / 811'	Moderate	436
UT Section 7	2.47	531' / 490'	Moderate	438
UT Section 8	2.86	507' / 539'	Moderate	440
UT Section 9	3.36	598' / 619'	Moderate	442
UT Section 10	3.92	863' / 931'	Moderate	444
UT Section 11	2.04	312' / 397'	Moderate	446

Section 1: Tot Hill Farm Road to Hannah's Creek Trail

Map	page 426	**Difficulty**	Moderate
Length	4.67 miles	**Configuration**	One Way
Trailhead	Tot Hill Farm Road	**Elev Gain/Loss**	757' / 777'

Start Coordinates N35.63636, W79.90460;   17 S 599179 3944169

The original Uwharrie Trail route began at Tot Hill Farm Road just east of where Talbott's Branch crosses the road. There was no parking along Tot Hill Farm Road until after 2007, when the USFS acquired a small tract of land on the west side of the branch. There is now a small parking lot and kiosk at the trailhead.

Section 1 follows the Birkhead Mountain Trail for five miles from the Tot Hill Trailhead to the intersection with Hannah's Creek Trail.

From the trailhead, the trail drops immediately to cross Talbott's Branch. After a second crossing, on a footbridge, the route begins a slow ascent towards the top of Coolers Knob.

The route soon joins an old road bed. This old road is known as the Forrester Road. The Forrester family home place was located along this road. Their old sawmill site can be seen along the way.

As the route reaches a steeper section up the mountain, the trail route turns to the right, leaving the old road. The old road offers a more direct route up the mountain. The trail meanders to the west a short way before rejoining the old road further up the mountain.

Above the Forrester Road, the white-blazed trail again leaves the old road to the right. You'll have to pay attention in order to spot where the trail turns off the old road. The trail eventually rejoins the road, so the consequences of missing this junction are small.

The route follows the old road southward along the ridge. The junction of Birkhead Mountain Trail and Camp Three Trail is reached next. This junction is easily missed, as the Birkhead Mountain Trail turns right onto a footpath, leaving the old road. The Camp Three Trail starts at this junction and continues along the old road. It is easy to continue on the old road and not notice the trail turning off to the right.

The side trail to Camp 2 may be to the right near the junction of Birkhead Mountain Trail and Camp Three Trail.

A short distance south of the junction with Camp Three Trail, the trail passes through a saddle. Camp 1B is located on the right, beside the trail in this saddle. The faint side trail to Camp 1 and its seep spring can be found by dropping downhill to the west from the saddle. You'll have to search closely to spot the faint yellow blazes that mark the route. Hancock's guide refered to this as the Joe Moffitt Camp.

At Camp 1, the Scouts built a stone fireplace with a plaque on a nearby tree.

Continuing southward along the ridge, the trail passes a junction to the right with Robbins Branch Trail.

Further down the ridge the trail passes a junction to the left with the other end of Camp Three Trail. Camp 5 is located on the right side of the trail at this junction.

There is no water source at Camp 5. It was intended to be a dry campsite in order to help campers learn to deal with limited water supplies. Hancock's guide refered to this as Fairview Camp. A stone fireplace was built here. The plaque noting who built it has been stolen. If you have a picture of the plaque showing the wording, please contact the author of this guide.

From Camp 5, the trail begins dropping down the south end of Birkhead Mountain. Sharp-eyed hikers may spot the junction to the right with the side trail to Camp 4. This junction is located in a small saddle. This side trail hasn't been used or maintained in some time so your best clue is to spot the faint yellow blaze. If you reach a knoll with a well-used campsite area to the right of the trail, you've passed the saddle.

The side trail to Camp 4 can be followed by searching for the remaining yellow blazes. A small creek serves as a water source at Camp 4. The side trail passes through the camp area and connects to the Hannah's Creek Trail. See more details about Camp 4 in Section 2.

Christopher "Kit" Bingham's plantation was located in the area at the southern end of the Birkhead Mountain ridge. The Scouts erected a sign at this spot. An old road leads to the left from this junction. The old road heads south and intersects the side trail to Camp 6 near the Bingham Graveyard before continuing on to cross the North Prong of Hannah's Branch. According to Joe Moffitt, the old roadbed was once part of the Salisbury-Fayetteville Byway or Trail. He suspects that it was once traveled by the likes of Daniel Boone and Jesse and Frank James.

The trail eventually reaches a junction to the right with Hannah's Creek Trail. Section 1 ends at the junction of the Birkhead Mountain Trail and Hannah's Creek Trail.

A short distance beyond this junction is a four-way intersection. The Birkhead Mountain Trail continues to the right, leading to its end at the USFS property boundary. Straight ahead is a footpath that connects to the old road that runs past the Christopher Bingham plantation.

To the left is the yellow-blazed side trail to Camp 6. The Bingham Graveyard is located along this side trail. Camp 6 is located beside the North Prong of Hannah's Creek. Hancock's guie referred to this as Bingham Camp. A stone fireplace is located there. The plaque on the fireplace reads:

Section 2: Hannah's Creek Trail to FR 6520 (Seven Acre Road)

Map	page 428	**Difficulty**	Moderate
Length	7.18 miles	**Configuration**	One Way
Trailhead	n/a	**Elev Gain/Loss**	786' / 593'

Start Coordinates N35.58262, W79.92828;   17 S 597099 3938185

Section 2 is 7.18 miles long and follows the Hannah's Creek and Robbins Branch trails to the Robbins Branch Trailhead before leaving the woods to run along paved roads. At the end of 2013, the only legal route to connect Sections 1 and 3 includes 5.0 miles of hiking along paved roads. This is the route described in detail below.

The historic Uwharrie Trail route ran from the junction with Hannah's Creek Trail to the southern end of Birkhead Mountain Trail at the USFS property boundary. From the boundary, the route followed woods roads across private property to connect to Strieby Church Road. From Strieby Church, the route was a road walk to the end of Strieby Church Road, left on High Pine Church Road, right on Pisgah Covered Bridge Road and then to a gated USFS road.

As the efforts to secure a protected trail corridor from the Birkhead Mountains Wilderness southward continue, it is likely that this section will eventually be routed differently.

From the end of Section 1 at the junction with the Birkhead Mountain Trail, the Uwharrie Trail route heads west along Hannahs Creek Trail. Just past the first creek crossing, you may find a faint trail to the right leading along the creek to Camp 4. The camp is just 100' or so from Hannahs Creek Trail. Hancock's guide referred to this as the Chisholm Camp.

An old yellow-blazed side trail continues north from the Camp 4 location and climbs up to connect to the Birkhead Mountain Trail. This side trail hasn't been used in many years and can only be followed by looking for the remaining yellow blazes.

Just west of the Camp 4 creek is an old home place on the south side of the trail. The stone double-chimney stood for many years as the only reminder of this former residence. The effects of time and a very wet summer combined to bring the chimney down in July of 2013.

Continuing westward, the trail passes a junction to the right with an old road bed. This old road connects to the Birkhead Mountain Trail south of the southern junction with the Camp Three Trail.

The trail crosses Robbins Branch and begins an ascent up onto a ridge. Shortly after getting on the ridge, the trail passes a junction to the left with a faint unmarked foot trail. This trail is the Cooper Mountain Cemetery Trail. This junction is easier to spot when hiking Hannah's Creek Trail in the other direction (eastward).

Hannah's Creek Trail ends at the next junction. The Uwharrie Trail route continues to the left on Robbins Branch Trail. Robbins Branch Trail ends at the trailhead parking lot bearing the same name.

From the Robbins Branch Trailhead, the rest of the Uwharrie Trail route for this section is along roads. The route follows the gravel USFS access road from the parking lot to its end at paved Lassiter Mill Road. The route turns left on Lassiter Mill Road and goes 1.9 miles. The route then turns left on High Pine Church Road.

About 1.5 miles along High Pine Church Road there is a gated gravel drive on the right. The drive climbs steeply beyond the gate and a small stream flows under the drive just beyond the gate. This is the McArthur property and it will soon become a new trailhead and the end of Section 2. But for now the route continues another 0.7 miles along High Pine Church Road.

The route turns right at the intersection with Pisgah Covered Bridge Road and follows it for 0.9 miles to a private road on the right in a curve.

Section 2 ends along Pisgah Covered Bridge Road at this private road intersection.

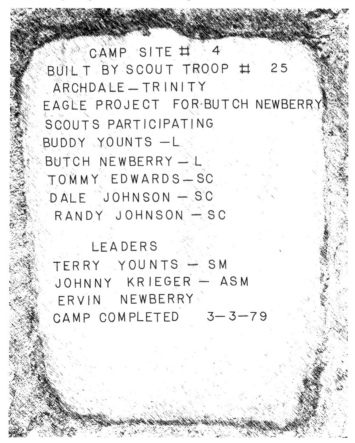

Section 3: FR 6520 (Seven Acre Road) to Thayer Road (SR1305)

Map	page 430	**Difficulty**	Moderate
Length	3.15 miles	**Configuration**	One Way
Trailhead	Pisgah Covered Bridge	**Elev Gain/Loss**	641' / 674'

Start Coordinates N35.53950, W79.93919;   17 S 596162 3933391

Section 3 currently begins at the intersection of a private road and Pisgah Covered Bridge Road, 0.9 miles south of High Pine Church Road. This location is the Pisgah Covered Bridge Road Trailhead. The section description that follows applies to the current route. Once the trail is developed from the new trailhead on High Pines Church Road southward, the first few miles of this section will be different.

This section of the trail has been abandoned for many years, but is being resurrected through efforts of the LandTrust of Central NC and the Greater Uwharrie Conservation Partnership. In 2011, ownership of the King Mountain property in the middle of this section was transferred to the USFS.

About 200' along the private road, there is a slightly overgrown road on the left. This overgrown road lies between a stand of trees on its left and a small field on its right. You may be able to see the USFS gate across this road near the far end of the field. This is USFS Road #6520, although there is no sign marking it as such. Some maps may label this road as Seven Acre Road.

The trail route follows FR 6520, which is even more overgrown beyond the gate. At about 1.0 mile from the gate, there is a white blazed foot trail leading to the left. There is a wide area, possibly the clearing at the end of FR 6520, about 100' beyond this trail intersection. This intersection of FR 6520 and the foot trail is most likely where the trail route from the new trailhead on High Pine Church Road will tie in.

The Uwharrie Trail route turns left onto the foot trail and continues southward.

After crossing over an unnamed mountain, the trail passes through a broad saddle. In this saddle, there is a wood signpost marking the intersection with the yellow-blazed side trail that leads to Camp 7. This side trail is about 0.2 miles long. Hancock's guide referred to this as Burnt Woods Camp. The plaque on the fireplace refers to it as Twin Springs Camp.

From the intersection with the Camp 7 side trail, the route climbs up onto King Mountain and traverses its three peaks. Near the lower middle peak, the trail passes by a large excavation left behind from a gold prospecting attempt. Not enough gold was found to make the operation successful so it was abandoned.

The southernmost peak of King Mountain is the highest. At just over 1,000 feet in elevation, King Mountain is the highest point on the Uwharrie Trail and the highest point in all of the Uwharrie National Forest. The name "King Mountain" is due to this distinction.

On the highest summit of King Mountain, the trail reaches an intersection of two old roads. The route turns right (westward) and soon veers left off the old road, heading into the woods following a white-blazed and orange-flagged trail.

The trail then descends steadily until it crosses a small creek. From the creek, the route stays low and winds southward until it intersects Thayer Road, a graveled state road.

Section 3 ends at the intersection with Thayer Road, which is the Joe Moffitt Trailhead.

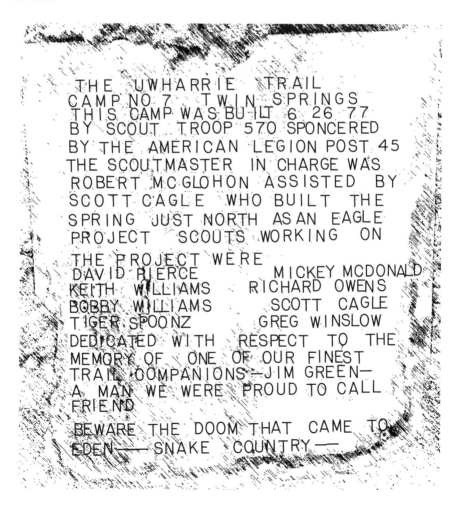

Section 4: Thayer Road (SR1305) to Jumping Off Rock Trailhead

Map	page 432	**Difficulty**	Moderate
Length	3.11 miles	**Configuration**	One Way
Trailhead	Joe Moffitt	**Elev Gain/Loss**	528' / 799'

Start Coordinates N35.50771, W79.95265;   17 S 594980 3929853

Section 4 of the Uwharrie Trail starts at its intersection with Thayer Road (SR 1305). About 60' west of the trail intersection, there is a gated road heading south from Thayer Road. There is parking for 2-3 cars beside the gate.

On December 8, 2013, The LandTrust for Central NC designated the trailhead at Thayer Road as the "Joe Moffitt Trailhead", to honor the original founder and visionary for the Uwharrie Trail.

The most notable feature in this section is a climb over Little Long Mountain. The top of this mountain is fairly open and offers the only 360 degree views along the Uwharrie Trail.

This section of the trail was the last to be built (blazed in 1975) but was mostly abandoned after the 1980's. Most of Little Long Mountain was privately owned. The original trail was not maintained and most of the trail blazes were lost due to age and timber operations.

In 2012, the LandTrust for Central NC purchased the private property and eventually plans to transfer ownership of this property to the USFS. New trail was being built by the LandTrust and volunteers over Little Long Mountain in 2013.

The summit of Little Long Mountain still offers mostly clear 360 degree views. Hancock's guide referred to a campsite on top called Camp Taloe.

After dropping off the southern slopes of Little Long Mountain, the route joins an old road bed. This old road is the same one that starts at the gate along Thayer Road at the beginning of this section.

The route then descends on the road to Poison Fork. The road junctions with another old road that runs along Poison Fork. The route turns right, heading downstream. The old road eventually crosses Poison Fork.

Just after crossing Poison Fork, the old road junctions with another old road, called Poison Fork Road. To the right, Poison Fork Road leads southward along its namesake, eventually ending at a USFS gate along paved Flint Hill Road. Just across the road, Poison Fork comes flows into Barnes Creek. There is a large swimming hole in Barnes Creek just above the confluence of these two creeks.

To the left, the old road bed climbs up a hill. Not far up this road is a lonely grave marker belonging to 10 year old Dania L. Woodell. At the time she passed in 1911, a small community was just starting to develop at this location. But plans for a church and cemetery were never realized. Little Dania's grave is all that remains here of a once hopeful family and town.

The trail crosses Poison Fork Road and climbs up onto a broad ridgeline on the southern end of Long Mountain. At a notable rock outcropping near the un-notable crest of the ridge, a yellow-blazed side trail leads to the right (southward) to Camp 8B. A plaque on the fireplace at Camp 8B reads:

From the side trail intersection, the route heads southward along the ridgeline. Eventually the trail overlooks Barnes Creek and follows it to an intersection with paved Flint Hill Road (SR 1306). This road is one of North Carolina's Scenic Byways and is known as the "Flint Hill Ramble".

At the paved road, the route turns left and crosses Barnes Creek on the road bridge. Just past the bridge is the parking lot for Jumping Off Rock Trailhead. Section 4 ends at the Jumping Off Rock Trailhead parking area.

```
       U. T. CAMP H 8-B
    BUILT BY SCOUT TROOP NO 111
    SPONSERD BY SCOUTS OF
    FAIRVIEW METHODIST MEN
    THOMASVILLE N·C· AUG·1981
    BUILT WITH GLENN IMBLER
    IN CHARGE FOR HIS EAGLE SCOUT
    PROJECT·
    HIS HELPERS WERE·
       KENETH CRAVEN ·S·M·
       EDDIE CRAVEN ·A·S·M·
    RANDALL ASHMORE
       CLIFTON HICKS
    THE LAST RECORDED PEOPLE TO
    LIVE HERE WAS DORY LUTHER
    IN THE EARLY 1900·S· BUT
    JUST WHO SETTELED HERE FIRST
    REMAINS A MISTERY· ONLY
    THE OLD OAK STANDING NEAR BY
    IS OLD ENOUGH TO REMEMBER THE
    HAPPENINGS AROUND THIS
       MISTERY ·HOMESTED
```

ping Off Rock Trailhead to Tower Road (SR 1134)

page 434		**Difficulty**	Moderate
2.01 miles		**Configuration**	One Way
Trailhead Jumping Off Rock		**Elev Gain/Loss**	564' / 319'

Start Coordinates N35.47989, W79.95141;   17 S 595126 3926768

Section 5 of the Uwharrie Trail starts at the Jumping Off Rock Trailhead on Flint Hill Road (SR 1306) and heads southward over Dark Mountain. This section of the Uwharrie Trail is the northern end of the part designated as a National Recreation Trail in 1980. From this point southward, the route is marked with white blazes and has been consistently used and somewhat maintained since it was built in the 1970's.

In the first edition of this guide, the Jumping Off Rock Trailhead was called the Dark Mountain Trailhead. This edition has been updated to match the name now used by the USFS on their signs and maps.

A quarter mile east of the trailhead on Flint Hill Road (SR 1306) is a pull-off beside a large rock outcropping called Jumping Off Rock. This is the namesake of the trailhead. The top of this rock is about 35 feet above Barnes Creek. The water at the bottom doesn't look quite deep enough for me to jump off, but I suppose someone has done it.

One local ghost tale describes how two brothers were hiding their family's gold beneath a rock outcropping on the mountain north of Barnes Creek. One of the boys was overtaken by greed and impulsively killed his brother, burying his body with the gold. The guilt soon drove him insane and the gold's location was lost. It's said that if you start digging around at the base of the right rock outcropping, a terrible wind will kick up and drive you away.

On a 2013 thru hike of the historic Uwharrie Trail route, our group camped at this trailhead and went up to Jumping Off Rock. The legend says you can look out and see the location of the buried gold on the far ridge. One of our group dug around a bit near the rock. Thunder boomed and we were soon driven back to our tents and spent the night listening to a wicked thunderstorm that thrashed the area. Was that the ghost of the slain brother still protecting his family's gold?

East of the trailhead, just before the first bridge, an unpaved road leads to the south. This road climbs up the ridge and passes several camping spots before being joined by the Uwharrie Trail. These campsites are likely the location of Camp 9. Hancock's guide referred to this as Liquor Spring Camp. The spring is located in a ravine SSE of the road. The road soon dwindles in size to a footpath and then continues on as the Uwharrie Trail.

From the trailhead parking lot, the Uwharrie Trail route begins a steep ascent up and over the Dark Mountain ridge. The trail climbs to a saddle and turns right to traverse over the lower southwestern peak of Dark Mountain.

An unmarked side trail once led SSE around the south and southeast sides of the northern peak of Dark Mountain to Painted Rock, Outlaw Cave, Liquor Spring. The northern peak of Dark Mountain is on privately owned land.

Dark Mountain is the most prominent geographical feature in this section. The mountain rises 953 feet above sea level, the highest point in Montgomery County. This imposing mountain has several interesting stories to go along with it.

Local legends tell of confederate deserters who were caught and killed on Dark Mountain itself. Painted Rock supposedly bears the blood stains from one of these unlucky deserters. The legend says you can wash off the stains, but they will reappear overnight.

Another story describes a bootlegger who escaped from revenuers and hid out on the mountain. He dug a cave in which to live, now known as Outlaw Cave, and continued to make whiskey at Liquor Spring.

You may not encounter any of the spirits of Dark Mountain when you visit, but they might liven up the conversation around the campfire. More details about these stories can be found in Joe Moffitt's *An Afternoon Hike Into The Past* and Fred Morgan's *Ghost Tales of the Uwharries and Haunted Uwharries*.

After descending down the south slope of Dark Mountain, the trail crosses gentle terrain. Camp 10 is thought to be located east of the trail in this area. Hancock's guide referred to a camp in this location as Dusty Level Camp. However, his guide also mistakenly identified the road at the end of this section as "Dusty Level Road", so he might have called it something else if he had caught his mistake.

Section 5 ends at the intersection with Tower Road (SR 1134). This intersection is the Horse Mountain Trailhead.

Section 6: Tower Road (SR 1134) to Morris Mtn Road (FR 6652)

Map	page 436	**Difficulty**	Moderate
Length	3.79 miles	**Configuration**	One Way
Trailhead	Horse Mountain	**Elev Gain/Loss**	754' / 811'

Start Coordinates N35.45993, W79.95994;   17 S 594375 3924546

Section 6 of the Uwharrie Trail starts at the intersection with Tower Road and runs southward through the Morris Mountain Area to end at a remote intersection with Morris Mountain Road, a gated USFS road.

This start location is the Horse Mountain Trailhead, named after the mountain just south of Tower Road. There is room to park 2-3 vehicles beside the USFS gate on the north side of Tower Road.

The trail skirts around the upper slopes of 855' high Horse Mountain. Once around this mountain, the trail descends and crosses Panther Branch Road, a gated USFS road.

A little farther on, the trail crosses Panther Branch. You should find a well established campsite beside this small creek. This is most likely the location of Camp 11.

From Panther Branch, the trail climbs up onto a long ridge west of Morris Mountain. Along the ridgeline, the route intersects graveled Barnes Creek Overlook Road.

Section 6 ends at a nondescript intersection with Morris Mountain Road, a gated USFS road. At this intersection, Morris Mountain Road is just an old dirt woods road. To the left, the road leads to a timber landing and is graveled from there to Tower Road. To the right, the road continues a short distance to a junction with Camp Road, a gated USFS road that connects to the West Morris Mountain Hunt Camp.

Section 7: Morris Mountain Road (FR 6652) to NC 109

Map	page 438	**Difficulty**	Moderate
Length	2.47 miles	**Configuration**	One Way
Trailhead	109	**Elev Gain/Loss**	531' / 490'

Start Coordinates N35.42467, W79.98460; 17 S 592177 3920612

Section 7 of the Uwharrie Trail starts at a remote intersection with Morris Mountain Road, a gated USFS road, and heads south to highway NC 109.

Descending from the start intersection, the route eventually joins with Camp Road for a short distance before splitting off to the right. To the right, Camp Road will take you to the West Morris Mountain Hunt Camp in 0.8 miles.

A few yellow blazes from the now-abandoned West Morris Mountain Trail may still be seen where the Uwharrie Trail leaves Camp Road. At one time, this side trail connected the Uwharrie Trail to the West Morris Mountain Hunt Camp. The route offered an alternative route to using Camp Road. It was probably built in the early 1980's, but has not been maintained for a number of years. Part of the route passes through a very overgrown area and other parts have been obliterated by timber operations.

To the left, after they split apart, both Camp Road and the Uwharrie Trail soon meet again at the footbridge over Spencer Creek. The existing bridge was built in 1991 through a cooperative effort between USFS employees and a crew from the Youth Conservation Corps. The new bridge replaced an older, smaller one.

The flat terrain along Spencer Creek in this area is heavily used for camping. The Camp 12 location is in this area. Hancock's guide referred to this as Spencer Creek Camp.

After crossing Spencer Creek and a small tributary stream, the trail climbs over an undulating ridge and then drops to cross Cattail Creek. Camp 13 is located near this creek crossing. From Cattail Creek, the trail climbs up onto a broad ridge.

Section 7 ends at the NC 109 Trailhead.

Section 8: NC 109 Trailhead to Dusty Level Road (SR 1146)

Map	page 440	**Difficulty**	Moderate
Length	2.86 miles	**Configuration**	One Way
Trailhead	NC 109	**Elev Gain/Loss**	507' / 539'

Start Coordinates N35.39866, W79.98173;   17 S 592467 3917730

Section 8 of the Uwharrie Trail starts at the NC 109 Trailhead and heads southward to Dusty Level Road, a graveled state road. The NC 109 Trailhead features a shaded gravel parking area that can hold a dozen vehicles.

This section of the Uwharrie Trail route connects the Wood Run Area to the Morris Mountain Area.

From the trailhead, the trail crosses highway NC 109. A few hundred yards into the woods, the trail crosses a very old road bed that is now overgrown. This road was once the main highway leading from Troy to Uwharrie and is notable for the hand laid stonework that still remains around the culverts and holds up the banked curves.

The route crosses a small stream, Cedar Branch, before climbing over a small ridge. The trail then passes a large rock outcropping as it descends to Watery Branch. The route parallels Watery Branch for about half a mile and passes a well-used campsite before climbing away from the branch. This campsite is likely the location of Camp 14.

The trail drops into one more small valley before climbing to the intersection with Dusty Level Road (SR 1146), a graveled state-maintained road. There is no parking at this road intersection, but the USFS Yates Place Camp is located 0.35 miles east along Dust Level Road. There are parking, picnic tables, and a vault toilet at the Camp, but no water source. The Camp is the location of the Yates Place Camp Trailhead.

Section 8 of the Uwharrie Trail ends at the intersection with Dusty Level Road (SR 1146).

Section 9: Dusty Level Road (SR 1146) to Dutchman's Creek Trail

Map	page 442	**Difficulty**	Moderate
Length	3.36 miles	**Configuration**	One Way
Trailhead	n/a	**Elev Gain/Loss**	598' / 619'

Start Coordinates N35.36800, W79.99379;   17 S 591407 3914318

Section 9 of the Uwharrie Trail starts at the intersection with Dusty Level Road and runs to a remote intersection with the Dutchman's Creek Trail.

A short distance south of the beginning of this section is a junction with the Yates Place Trail. This short trail provides a more scenic alternative to hiking along Dusty Level Road to reach Yates Place Camp. The shallow valley where this junction is located is most likely the location of Camp 15.

The route passes the end of Dutchman's Creek Trail at a junction on top of a small ridgeline. From here, the route works its way southward, crossing three small creeks and several ridges before crossing Dutchman's Creek. The open area around Dutchman's Creek is likely the location of Camp 16.

From Dutchman's Creek, the trail climbs again and crosses a couple of small streams. On top of a large ridge the trail intersects an old road. This road is the Dutchman's Creek Road (FR 6678), a gated USFS road. There are no signs at this intersection.

The trail descends gently down the far side of the ridge and crosses another unmarked old road (FR 6680). A short distance beyond the road intersection is the intersection with Dutchman's Creek Trail. This intersection marks the middle of the "figure 8" formed by the Uwharrie Trail and the Dutchman's Creek Trail. The 19.9 mile "figure 8" route is a popular trip for backpackers.

An out-and-back side trail, called the Pond Camp Trail, once connected to the Uwharrie Trail just north of the intersection with the Dutchman's Creek Trail. The sign post (no sign) and a few faded paint blazes were all that remained of this trail in 1997. Timber thinning and controlled burns in this area in prior years helped obliterate the trail. The tread was too indistinct to locate when I tried to follow it during my field research in the 1990's.

I found the half-rotten "Pond Camp Trail" sign a few years later, several miles away from this spot. The "pond" it was named after is likely a small pond at the headwaters of Clark's Creek. This "camp" does not appear to be one of the original series of numbered camps along the Uwharrie Trail route, but it was mentioned in Hancock's guide.

Section 9 of the Uwharrie Trail ends at the intersection with Dutchman's Creek Trail.

Section 10: Dutchman's Creek Trail to Keyauwee Trail

Map	page 444	**Difficulty**	Moderate
Length	3.92 miles	**Configuration**	One Way
Trailhead	n/a	**Elev Gain/Loss**	863' / 931'

Start Coordinates N35.34772, W80.01801;   17 S 589229 3912048

Section 10 of the Uwharrie Trail starts at a remote intersection with the Dutchman's Creek Trail and ends at a remote intersection with the Keyauwee Trail. This section of the trail parallels Big Island Creek and Upper Wood Run for much of its length, with a climb over the top of Dennis Mountain to cross from one creek valley to the other.

As you hike along the creeks, you'll notice many signs of the gold mining activity that took place here in the late 1800's. Rough roads were pushed into the hollows to get miners and their equipment to the gold. Numerous small pits can be seen along the creek bottoms where miners dug up the sediments to sift out gold flakes.

Shortly after leaving the start at the intersection with Dutchman's Creek Trail, the route crosses graveled Wood Run Road (FR 517). Descending from here, the trail soon reaches and follows Big Island Creek. There are several well-used campsites along Big Island Creek. One of these is the location of Camp 17, the last of the numbered campsites from the original Uwharrie Trail route.

The last crossing of Big Island Creek is 380 feet in elevation. This creek crossing is the lowest point on the Uwharrie Trail.

After leaving Big Island Creek, the trail climbs over Dennis Mountain, topping out at about 730 feet in elevation. Nice views were once found on top of the mountain, but trees have now obscured the vistas. A steep descent down the south side of Dennis Mountain leads you to Upper Wood Run.

The route follows Upper Wood Run, crossing the creek several times. There are numerous spots along the creek that can be used for camping.

The route leaves Upper Wood Run at a campsite within sight of Wood Run Road. The trail climbs onto a broad ridge and passes a junction with a signed side trail that leads to Wood Run Camp. This "camp" is located along Wood Run Road and features a vault toilet and a small grassy field for camping. Vehicles can be driven in on Wood Run Road to the camp, but the road is gated beyond it.

A short distance beyond the side trail is the intersection with Keyauwee Trail, one of the trails in the Wood Run Mountain Bike Trail System.

Section 10 of the Uwharrie Trail ends at this trail intersection.

Section 11: Keyauwee Trail to NC 24/27 Trailhead

Map	page 446	**Difficulty**	Moderate
Length	2.04 miles	**Configuration**	One Way
Trailhead	n/a	**Elev Gain/Loss**	312' / 397'

Start Coordinates N35.32754, W80.03574;   17 S 587640 3909793

Section 11, the southernmost section of the Uwharrie Trail, starts at a remote intersection with the Keyauwee Trail and ends at the 24/27 Trailhead. Following the Keyauwee Trail to the left leads 0.2 mile to Wood Run Camp.

From its start, this section of the trail descends gradually to cross a small stream. A climb over a small ridge is followed by a crossing of Wood Run. In June of 2013, a severe storm brought down numerous large trees in the Wood Run area. Although damage was seen as far north on the trail as Yates Place, the small ridge between these two creek crossings was hit especially hard. The tree debris in this area will be visible beside the trail for years to come.

The route heads upstream along Wood Run, but at times climbs far enough away from the creek to be out of sight. The trail does come back to the edge of the creek at a well-used campsite just before passing under some large power lines. An old logging road crosses the creek and the Uwharrie Trail at this campsite.

After passing under the power lines, the route crosses one small creek and then begins its final ascent to end at the NC 24/27 Trailhead.

There is room to park 30-40 vehicles in the graveled parking lot at the trailhead and under the power lines along NC 24/27. There is no water source or toilet facilities at this trailhead. Wood Run Road and the Dutchman's Creek Trail also connect to the trailhead parking lot.

Section 11 ends at the NC24/27 Trailhead.

Uwharrie Trail: Section 1

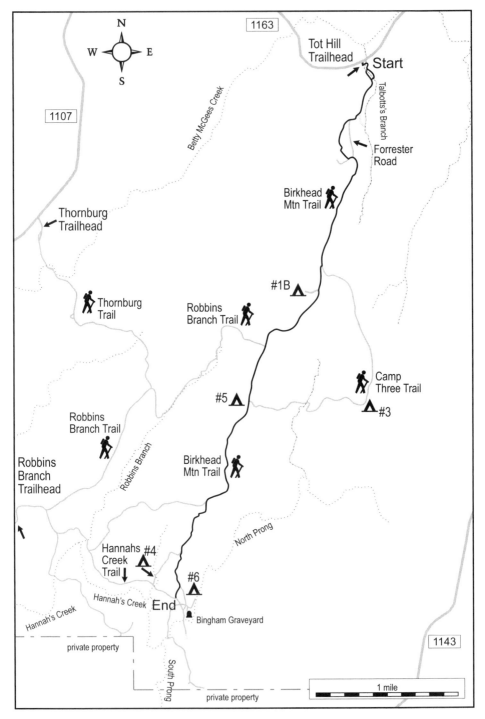

Elevation Profile: Uwharrie Trail: Section 1

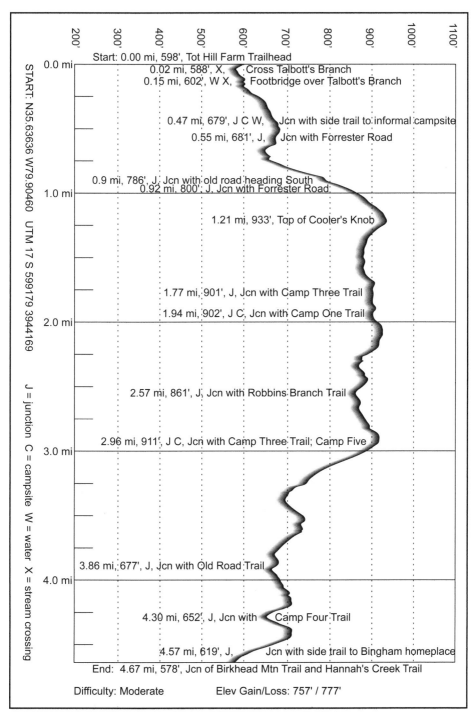

START: N35.63636 W79.90460 UTM 17 S 599179 3944169

J = junction C = campsite W = water X = stream crossing

Start: 0.00 mi, 598', Tot Hill Farm Trailhead
0.02 mi, 588', X, Cross Talbott's Branch
0.15 mi, 602', W X, Footbridge over Talbott's Branch

0.47 mi, 679', J C W, Jcn with side trail to informal campsite
0.55 mi, 681', J, Jcn with Forrester Road

0.9 mi, 786', J, Jcn with old road heading South
0.92 mi, 800', J, Jcn with Forrester Road

1.21 mi, 933', Top of Cooler's Knob

1.77 mi, 901', J, Jcn with Camp Three Trail
1.94 mi, 902', J C, Jcn with Camp One Trail

2.57 mi, 861', J, Jcn with Robbins Branch Trail

2.96 mi, 911', J C, Jcn with Camp Three Trail; Camp Five

3.86 mi, 677', J, Jcn with Old Road Trail

4.30 mi, 652', J, Jcn with Camp Four Trail

4.57 mi, 619', J, Jcn with side trail to Bingham homeplace
End: 4.67 mi, 578', Jcn of Birkhead Mtn Trail and Hannah's Creek Trail

Difficulty: Moderate   Elev Gain/Loss: 757' / 777'

Uwharrie Trail: Section 2

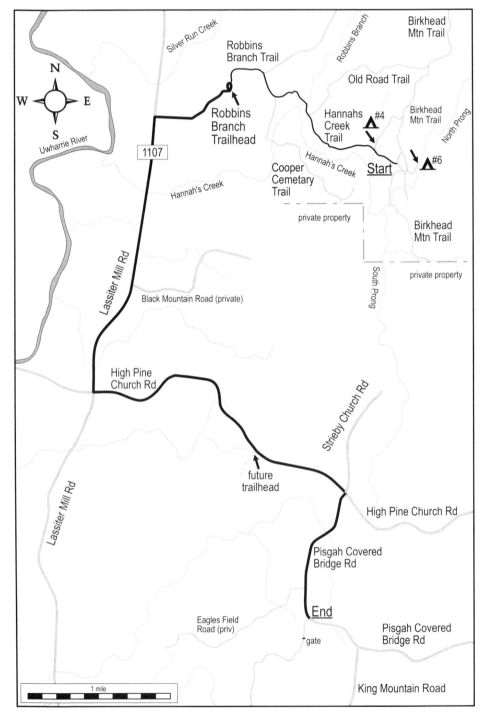

Elevation Profile: Uwharrie Trail: Section 2

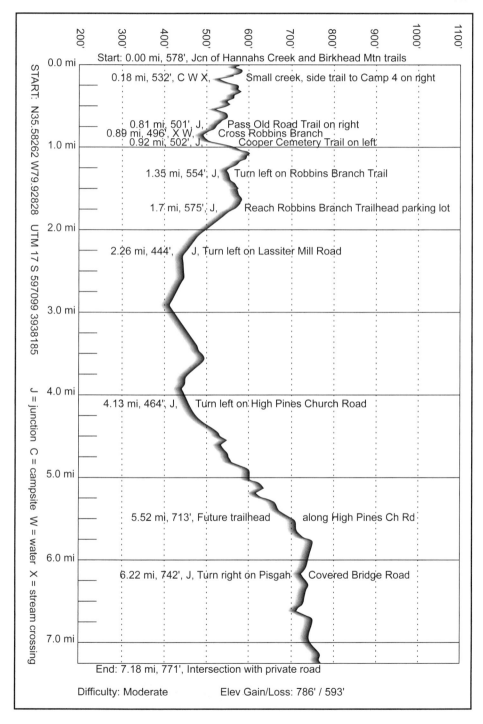

START: N35.58262 W79.92828 UTM 17 S 597099 3938185

J = junction C = campsite W = water X = stream crossing

200' 300' 400' 500' 600' 700' 800' 900' 1000' 1100'

0.0 mi — Start: 0.00 mi, 578', Jcn of Hannahs Creek and Birkhead Mtn trails

0.18 mi, 532', C W X,   Small creek, side trail to Camp 4 on right

0.81 mi, 501', J,   Pass Old Road Trail on right
0.89 mi, 496', X W,   Cross Robbins Branch
1.0 mi — 0.92 mi, 502', J,   Cooper Cemetery Trail on left

1.35 mi, 554', J,   Turn left on Robbins Branch Trail

1.7 mi, 575', J,   Reach Robbins Branch Trailhead parking lot

2.0 mi

2.26 mi, 444',   J, Turn left on Lassiter Mill Road

3.0 mi

4.0 mi

4.13 mi, 464', J,   Turn left on High Pines Church Road

5.0 mi

5.52 mi, 713', Future trailhead   along High Pines Ch Rd

6.0 mi

6.22 mi, 742', J, Turn right on Pisgah   Covered Bridge Road

7.0 mi

End: 7.18 mi, 771', Intersection with private road

Difficulty: Moderate   Elev Gain/Loss: 786' / 593'

Uwharrie Trail: Section 3

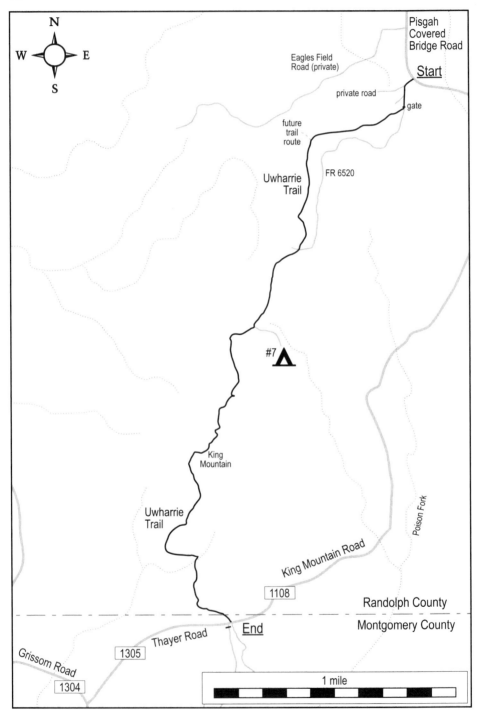

Elevation Profile: Uwharrie Trail: Section 3

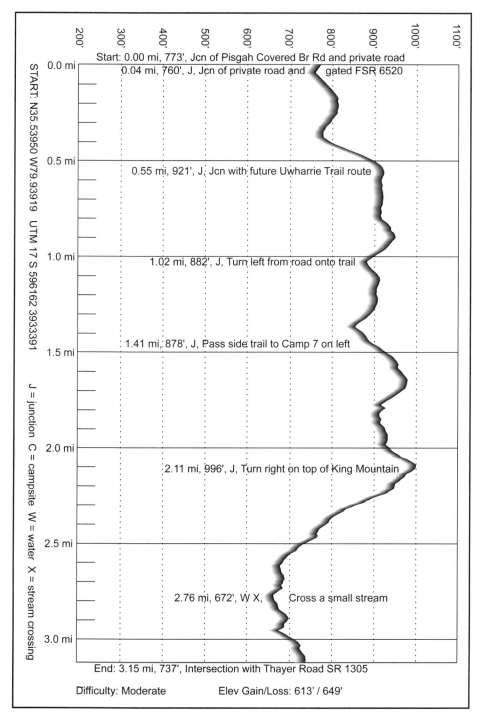

START: N35.53950 W79.93919 UTM 17 S 596162 3933391

J = junction C = campsite W = water X = stream crossing

Start: 0.00 mi, 773', Jcn of Pisgah Covered Br Rd and private road

0.04 mi, 760', J, Jcn of private road and gated FSR 6520

0.55 mi, 921', J, Jcn with future Uwharrie Trail route

1.02 mi, 882', J, Turn left from road onto trail

1.41 mi, 878', J, Pass side trail to Camp 7 on left

2.11 mi, 996', J, Turn right on top of King Mountain

2.76 mi, 672', W X, Cross a small stream

End: 3.15 mi, 737', Intersection with Thayer Road SR 1305

Difficulty: Moderate   Elev Gain/Loss: 613' / 649'

Uwharrie Trail: Section 4

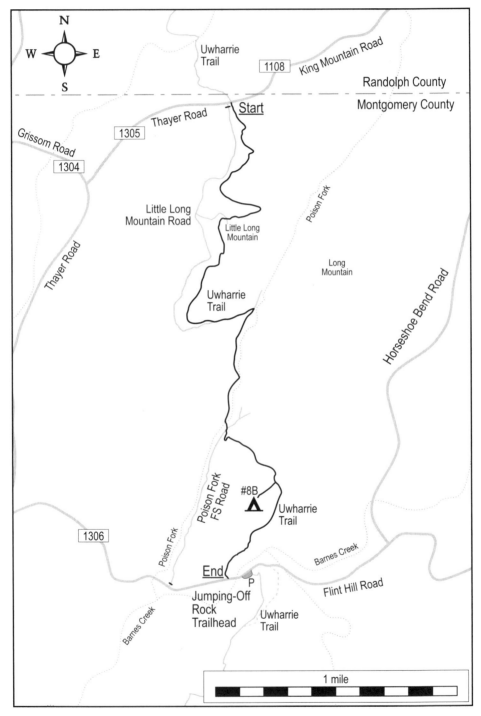

Elevation Profile: Uwharrie Trail: Section 4

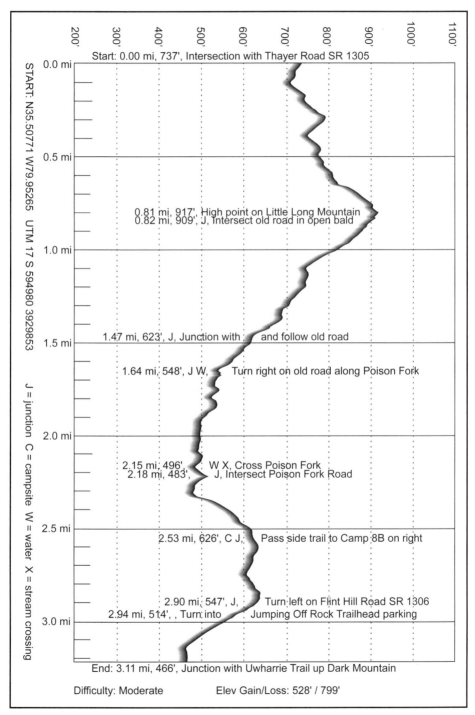

START: N35.50771 W79.95265 UTM 17 S 594980 3929853

J = junction C = campsite W = water X = stream crossing

Start: 0.00 mi, 737', Intersection with Thayer Road SR 1305

0.81 mi, 917', High point on Little Long Mountain
0.82 mi, 909', J, Intersect old road in open bald

1.47 mi, 623', J, Junction with   and follow old road

1.64 mi, 548', J W,   Turn right on old road along Poison Fork

2.15 mi, 496',   W X, Cross Poison Fork
2.18 mi, 483',   J, Intersect Poison Fork Road

2.53 mi, 626', C J,   Pass side trail to Camp 8B on right

2.90 mi, 547', J,   Turn left on Flint Hill Road SR 1306
2.94 mi, 514', , Turn into   Jumping Off Rock Trailhead parking

End: 3.11 mi, 466', Junction with Uwharrie Trail up Dark Mountain

Difficulty: Moderate   Elev Gain/Loss: 528' / 799'

Uwharrie Trail: Section 5

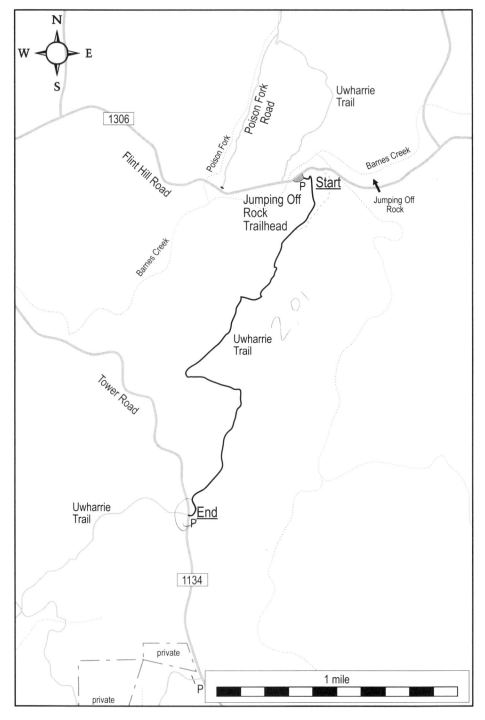

Elevation Profile: Uwharrie Trail: Section 5

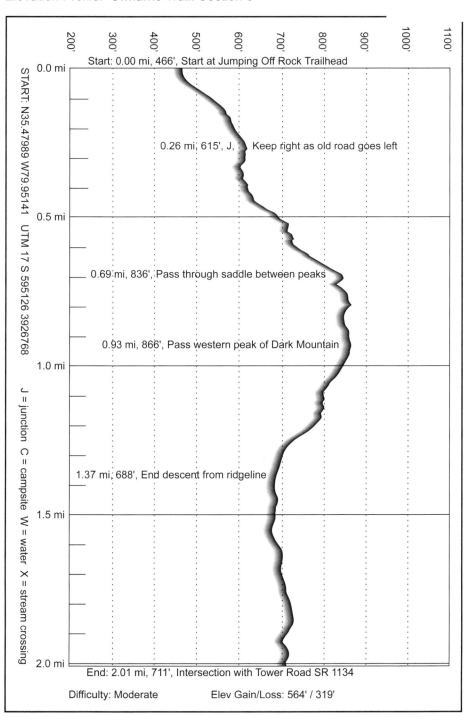

START: N35.47989 W79.95141 UTM 17 S 595126 3926768

J = junction C = campsite W = water X = stream crossing

Start: 0.00 mi, 466', Start at Jumping Off Rock Trailhead

0.26 mi, 615', J, Keep right as old road goes left

0.69 mi, 836', Pass through saddle between peaks

0.93 mi, 866', Pass western peak of Dark Mountain

1.37 mi, 688', End descent from ridgeline

End: 2.01 mi, 711', Intersection with Tower Road SR 1134

Difficulty: Moderate   Elev Gain/Loss: 564' / 319'

Uwharrie Trail: Section 6

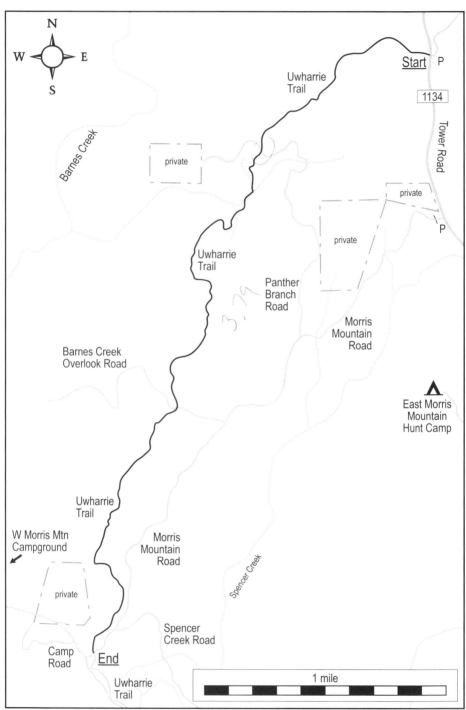

N
W E
S

Uwharrie
Trail

Start P

1134

Tower Road

Barnes Creek

private

Uwharrie
Trail

Panther
Branch
Road

private

private

3.79

Morris
Mountain
Road

Barnes Creek
Overlook Road

East Morris
Mountain
Hunt Camp

Uwharrie
Trail

W Morris Mtn
Campground

Morris
Mountain
Road

Spencer Creek

private

Camp
Road

End

Spencer
Creek Road

Uwharrie
Trail

1 mile

Elevation Profile: Uwharrie Trail: Section 6

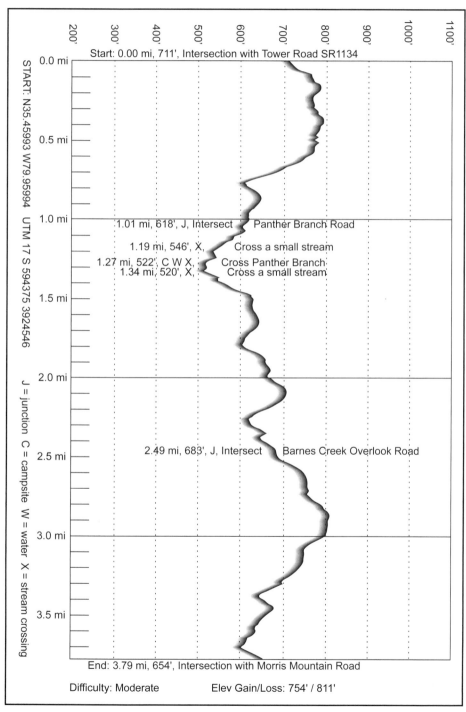

Start: 0.00 mi, 711', Intersection with Tower Road SR1134

START: N35.45993 W79.95994   UTM 17 S 594375 3924546

J = junction C = campsite W = water X = stream crossing

1.01 mi, 618', J, Intersect   Panther Branch Road
1.19 mi, 546', X,   Cross a small stream
1.27 mi, 522', C W X,   Cross Panther Branch
1.34 mi, 520', X,   Cross a small stream

2.49 mi, 683', J, Intersect   Barnes Creek Overlook Road

End: 3.79 mi, 654', Intersection with Morris Mountain Road

Difficulty: Moderate   Elev Gain/Loss: 754' / 811'

Uwharrie Trail: Section 7

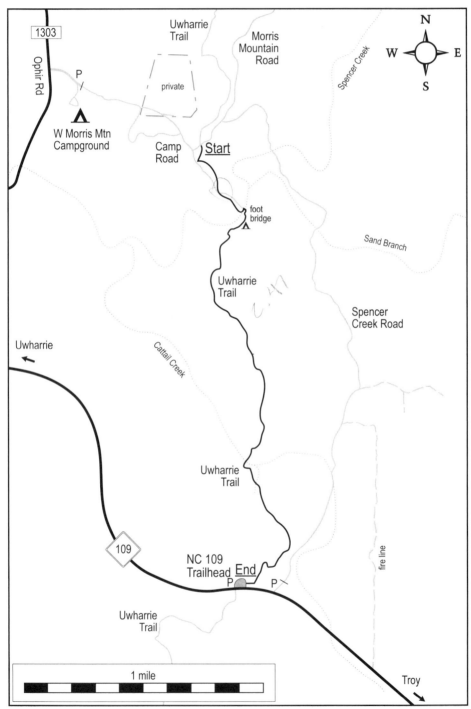

Elevation Profile: Uwharrie Trail: Section 7

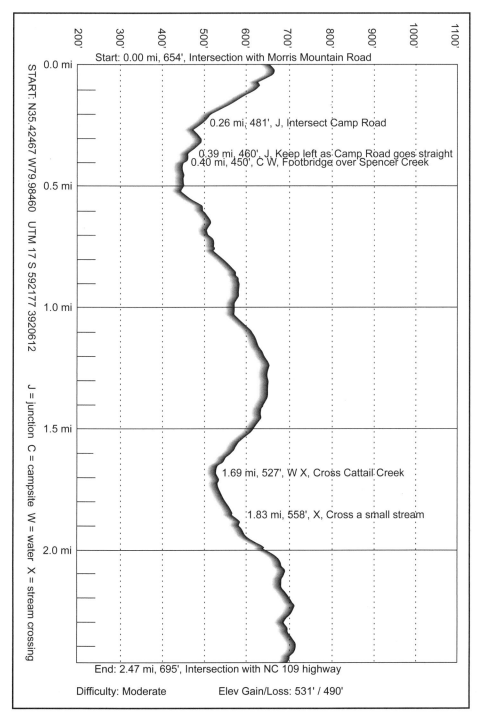

Start: 0.00 mi, 654', Intersection with Morris Mountain Road

0.26 mi, 481', J, Intersect Camp Road

0.39 mi, 460', J, Keep left as Camp Road goes straight
0.40 mi, 450', C W, Footbridge over Spencer Creek

1.69 mi, 527', W X, Cross Cattail Creek

1.83 mi, 558', X, Cross a small stream

START: N35.42467 W79.98460 UTM 17 S 592177 3920612

J = junction C = campsite W = water X = stream crossing

End: 2.47 mi, 695', Intersection with NC 109 highway

Difficulty: Moderate   Elev Gain/Loss: 531' / 490'

Uwharrie Trail: Section 8

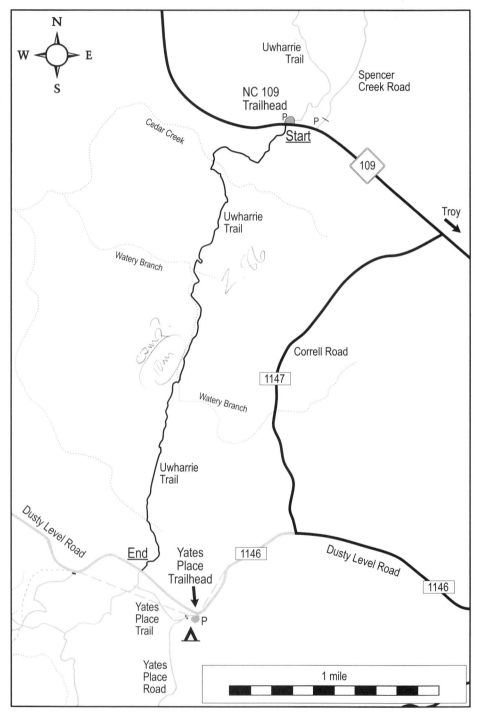

Elevation Profile: Uwharrie Trail: Section 8

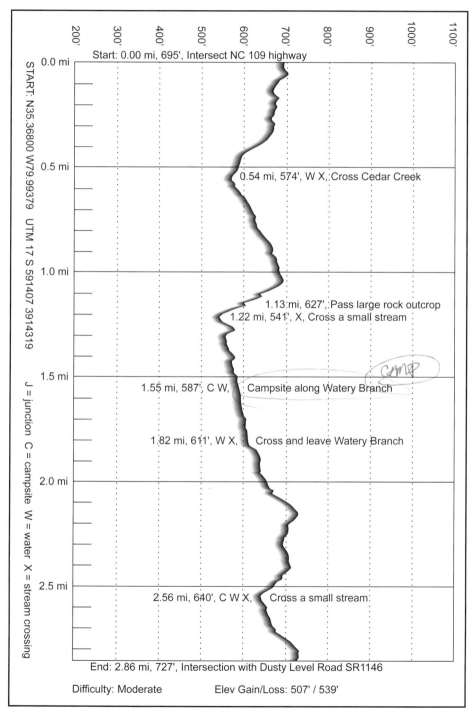

START: N35.36800 W79.99379 UTM 17 S 591407 3914319

J = junction C = campsite W = water X = stream crossing

Start: 0.00 mi, 695', Intersect NC 109 highway

0.54 mi, 574', W X, Cross Cedar Creek

1.13 mi, 627', Pass large rock outcrop

1.22 mi, 541', X, Cross a small stream

1.55 mi, 587', C W, Campsite along Watery Branch

1.82 mi, 611', W X, Cross and leave Watery Branch

2.56 mi, 640', C W X, Cross a small stream

End: 2.86 mi, 727', Intersection with Dusty Level Road SR1146

Difficulty: Moderate   Elev Gain/Loss: 507' / 539'

Uwharrie Trail: Section 9

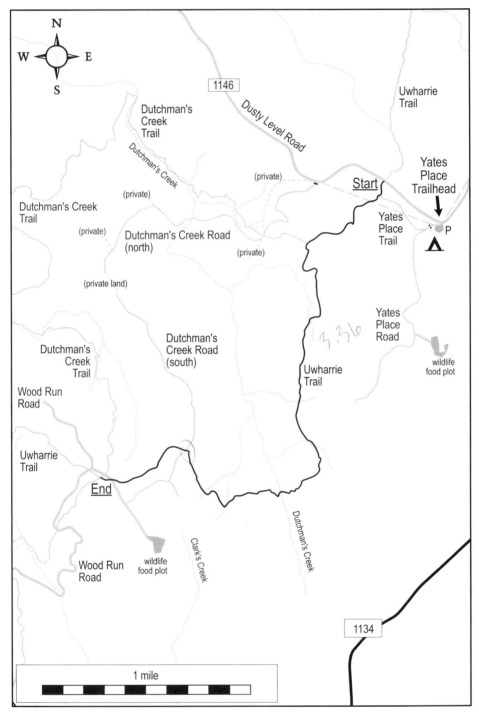

Elevation Profile: Uwharrie Trail: Section 9

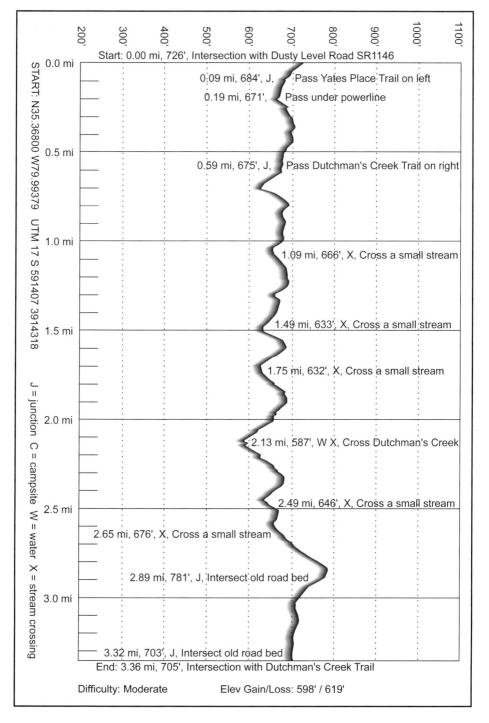

Start: 0.00 mi, 726', Intersection with Dusty Level Road SR1146

START: N35.36800 W79.99379 UTM 17 S 591407 3914318

J = junction C = campsite W = water X = stream crossing

0.09 mi, 684', J, Pass Yates Place Trail on left

0.19 mi, 671', Pass under powerline

0.59 mi, 675', J, Pass Dutchman's Creek Trail on right

1.09 mi, 666', X, Cross a small stream

1.49 mi, 633', X, Cross a small stream

1.75 mi, 632', X, Cross a small stream

2.13 mi, 587', W X, Cross Dutchman's Creek

2.49 mi, 646', X, Cross a small stream

2.65 mi, 676', X, Cross a small stream

2.89 mi, 781', J, Intersect old road bed

3.32 mi, 703', J, Intersect old road bed

End: 3.36 mi, 705', Intersection with Dutchman's Creek Trail

Difficulty: Moderate   Elev Gain/Loss: 598' / 619'

Uwharrie Trail: Section 10

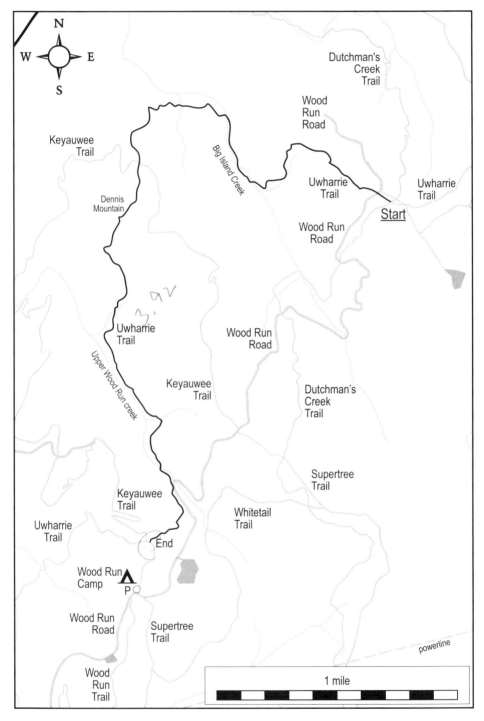

Elevation Profile: Uwharrie Trail: Section 10

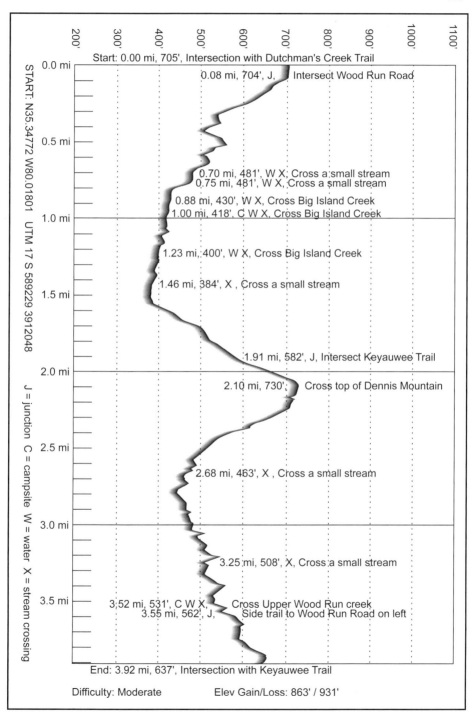

START: N35.34772 W80.01801 UTM 17 S 589229 3912048

J = junction C = campsite W = water X = stream crossing

Start: 0.00 mi, 705', Intersection with Dutchman's Creek Trail

0.08 mi, 704', J,   Intersect Wood Run Road

0.70 mi, 481', W X, Cross a small stream
0.75 mi, 481', W X, Cross a small stream
0.88 mi, 430', W X, Cross Big Island Creek
1.00 mi, 418', C W X, Cross Big Island Creek

1.23 mi, 400', W X, Cross Big Island Creek

1.46 mi, 384', X , Cross a small stream

1.91 mi, 582', J, Intersect Keyauwee Trail

2.10 mi, 730',   Cross top of Dennis Mountain

2.68 mi, 463', X , Cross a small stream

3.25 mi, 508', X, Cross a small stream

3.52 mi, 531', C W X,   Cross Upper Wood Run creek
3.55 mi, 562', J,   Side trail to Wood Run Road on left

End: 3.92 mi, 637', Intersection with Keyauwee Trail

Difficulty: Moderate   Elev Gain/Loss: 863' / 931'

Uwharrie Trail: Section 11

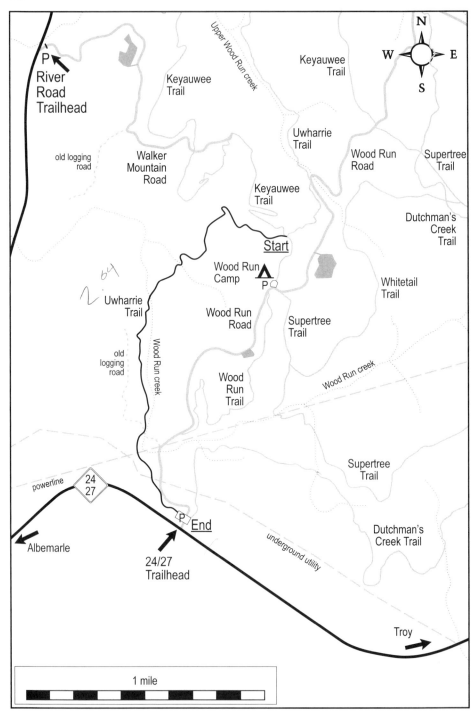

Elevation Profile: Uwharrie Trail: Section 11

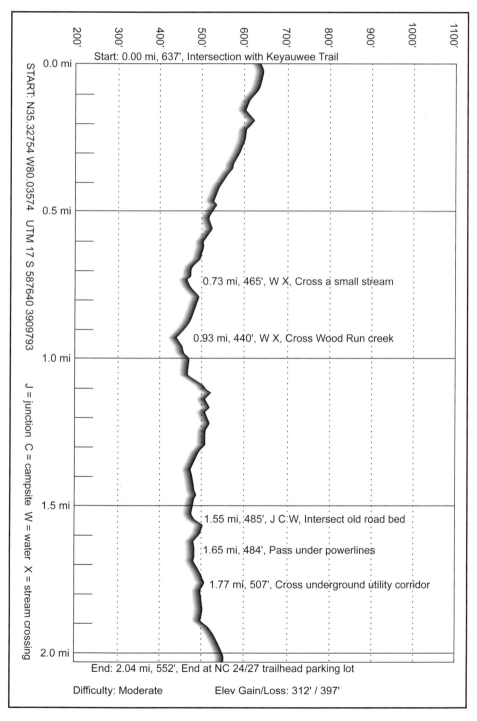

START: N35.32754 W80.03574 UTM 17 S 587640 3909793

J = junction C = campsite W = water X = stream crossing

Start: 0.00 mi, 637', Intersection with Keyauwee Trail

0.73 mi, 465', W X, Cross a small stream

0.93 mi, 440', W X, Cross Wood Run creek

1.55 mi, 485', J C W, Intersect old road bed

1.65 mi, 484', Pass under powerlines

1.77 mi, 507', Cross underground utility corridor

End: 2.04 mi, 552', End at NC 24/27 trailhead parking lot

Difficulty: Moderate   Elev Gain/Loss: 312' / 397'

Wood Run Area

The trail-rich Wood Run Area is one of my favorite parts of the Uwharrie Lakes Region. With terrain ranging from steep hills to long flat ridges, and scenery varying from laurel shrouded creeks to long range vistas, this destination is sure to win the heart of any outdoor enthusiast.

If you are a hiker, this area offers the most flexibility for customizing your own trip route. For mountain bikers, this is where you'll find the Wood Run Mountain Bike Trail System. When completed, this system will be the largest set of interconnected trails open to mountain bikes in central or eastern North Carolina. In addition to the bike trails, which are also open to hikers, these 6,000 acres include two major hiking-only trails and numerous old mining and logging roads.

With all these pathways crisscrossing the area, you can see the potential for planning out your own customized trip. When I chose which trips to include in this guide, I only picked the most obvious ones. There are still many other options, especially if your navigation skills are sharp enough to let you bushwhack from one trail to another.

ACCESS

24/27 Trailhead
The main access into the Wood Run Area is from its south side. 24/27 Trailhead is located on NC 24/27, 10.0 miles west of the courthouse in Troy. Coming from Albemarle on NC 24/27, the trailhead is 2.0 miles east of the Lake Tillery / Pee

UTM	17 S 586968 3907920
Lat/Lon	N35.31071 W80.04333

Dee River Bridge and 1.0 mile east of the River Road (SR 1150) intersection. This trailhead was called the Wood Run Trailhead in the first edition of this guide, but I've changed it to match the name now shown on the USFS maps.

A parking lot and information kiosk are located at the 24/27 Trailhead. Three trails start from this trailhead: the Uwharrie Trail, Dutchman's Creek Trail, and Wood Run Road which leads to the Wood Run Mountain Bike Trails. About 20 vehicles can fit in the parking lot, and there is additional space along the driveway. Several campsites can be found within 0.3 miles on either hiking trail and a large flat grassy area is beside the parking lot (within sight of NC 24/27).

Wood Run Area

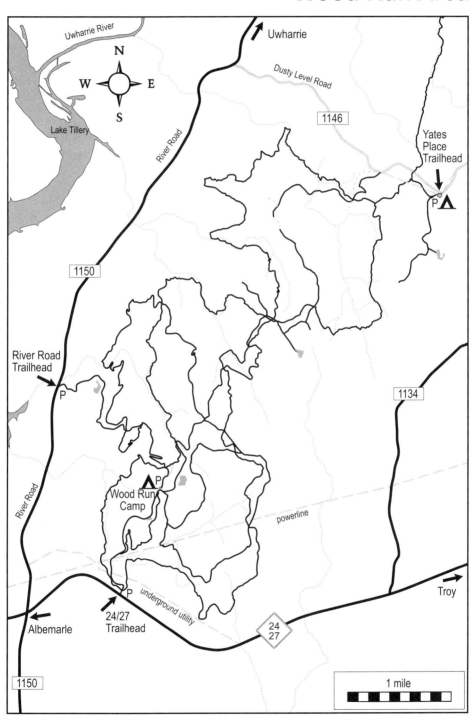

River Road Trailhead

River Road Trailhead is located on the west side of the Wood Run Area, on River Road (SR 1150). The trailhead is 2.5 miles north of NC 24/27 and 6.0 miles south of Uwharrie. River Road (SR 1150) crosses NC 24/27, 1.0 mile east of the Tillery Bridges.

UTM	17 S 585931 3911001
Lat/Lon	N35.33858 W80.05441

Walker Mountain Road, a gated and graveled Forest System road, starts at the gate and climbs up and around Walker Mountain, connecting to the Keyauwee Trail. There is room for 3 or 4 vehicles to park along the gravel road leading to the gate. No other facilities are found at this trailhead.

Yates Place Trailhead

A third access point is located on the north side of the Wood Run Area, along unpaved Dusty Level Road (SR 1146). Yates Place Trailhead consists of a small camping area and a gated Forest Service road.

UTM	17 S 591852 3913997
Lat/Lon	N35.36506 W79.98892

Yates Place Trailhead is 5.3 miles from Uwharrie by way of NC 109. From Uwharrie, go south on 109 for 2.8 miles, turn right on Correll Road (SR 1147) and go 1.9 miles to the stop sign. Turn right onto unpaved Dusty Level Road (SR 1146) and go 0.6 miles and look for the sign.

Yates Place Trailhead is 5.2 miles from Uwharrie by way of River Road (SR 1150). From Uwharrie, go south on River Road for 2.6 miles, then turn left onto unpaved Dusty Level Road (SR 1146) and go another 2.6 miles to the trailhead.

There is a 10 car parking lot at Yates Place Camp along with several picnic tables and an outhouse. From here you can follow gated Yates Place Road to its end. Yates Place Trail leads westward from the gated road to the Uwharrie Trail.

The Uwharrie Trail crosses Dusty Level Road (SR 1146) 0.35 miles west of Yates Place Trailhead, but no provisions have been made for parking vehicles at that location. The gate at Dutchman's Creek Road is 0.7 miles west of the trailhead and has room for 2-3 vehicles to park in front of the gate.

NOTES OF INTEREST

Four different creek systems wind their way among the maze of mountains in the Wood Run Area. Many of the mountains rise above 750 feet in elevation. In contrast, the creeks drain out at about 350 feet in elevation. The combination of numerous pathways and convoluted terrain make this piece of backcountry an ideal recreation destination for both beginning and experienced trail users.

Wood Run and Upper Wood Run are two of the creeks flowing among these mountains. "Run" means the same thing as "creek" or "stream". Saying Wood Run Creek is redundant. This book includes the uncapitalized word "creek" after these names for the benefit of those not familiar with the term "Run".

Many of the rocky creeks are lined with mountain laurel, remnants of a time when the Uwharries were a significant mountain range. Over 700 species of plants have been identified in the Uwharrie Lakes Region, including more than 100 species of trees. The forest covering these mountains today is mostly a mix of hardwoods and pines with a fairly open understory. For more adventurous travelers, this permits relatively easy cross-country foot travel.

Trail users will often see deer and turkey, as well as many other small creatures. Hunters use this part of the Forest extensively during deer hunting season in the fall.

Yates Place Camp is located at the north end of the Wood Run Area but is connected to it by only a few narrow tracts of public land. The Uwharrie and Dutchman's Creek Trails (hiking only) follow these corridors to reach Yates Place Camp. There are no roadbeds on these strips of public land that connect to the main parcel of land in the Wood Run Area.

Gold can still be found in some of the creeks in the Wood Run Area. Shallow pits found along the creeks are signs of past placer mining activity. Miners dug into the silt deposits along the creek bottoms to sift out the gold flakes and small nuggets. A few hand-dug mine shafts still exist where miners followed a productive vein of gold into the mountainside. Most of the nuggets are gone now, but recreational panners still find flakes of gold in these streams.

After the mining industry declined in importance to the regional economy, timber became the prominent treasure of the Uwharries. The importance of the timber industry continues to this day. Until the mid 1900's, sawmills were built where the trees grew and timber was sawn into boards on the spot. The timbermen built roads to truck lumber to market. Today these old sawmill roads are trail-users' treasures, adding to the network of pathways we can follow to enjoy the Forest.

The town of Lawrenceville, built in the early 1800's, was located near the 24/27 Trailhead. Lawrenceville was the county seat for the region, which at that time consisted of present-day Montgomery and Stanly Counties. The town even had an institution of higher learning, the Lawrenceville Academy. It was one of the first state accredited schools in the region. In 1841, a couple of fellows torched the courthouse to destroy some incriminating evidence. Shortly afterwards the county was divided into the two current counties. Lawrenceville was eventually abandoned and all that remains today are a few rocks from some of the house foundations.

There was another treasure that came out of the hills of the Wood Run Area. Moonshiners found the secluded hollows and creeks perfect for their operations. Old moonshine still sites can still be found along some of the creeks tucked back in hidden valleys. The moonshiners didn't build roads to their stills - they wanted to stay as hidden as possible. If you come across one of these old sites, you can just imagine the excitement they must have felt as they worked in secret to make their liquor.

CAMPING
There are numerous semi-established campsites along the hiking trails in the Wood Run Area, most of them located near creeks. Since camping is allowed anywhere in the Forest, I would suggest to backpackers with good Leave No Trace skills that you consider some of the flat-topped ridges a short distance away from the trails. These sites provide more solitude and a less abused setting, along with an escape from the cooler air that settles into the creek bottoms at night.

The only named camping site within this area is Wood Run Camp. It can be found 1.4 miles in from the Wood Run Trailhead on Wood Run Road (FR 517), a gated and graveled Forest System road. It can also be reached by turning right off the Uwharrie Trail at the first Keyauwee Trail intersection (see map). The site consists of a small field and a pit toilet. The portion of Wood Run Road leading to Wood Run Camp is often open to public vehicle traffic. Wood Run Road is gated just past Wood Run Camp.

Yates Place Camp is located on Dusty Level Road (SR 1146), at the north end of the Wood Run Area. This camp features picnic tables and an outhouse. Yates Place Trail (hiking only) leads from this site to the Uwharrie Trail.

MAPS
The local USFS District Ranger's office produces simple maps covering the the Wood Run Area and the entire length of the Uwharrie Trail. One of these maps is titled the Wood Run Mountain Bike Trail System. The bike trail lines are drawn over a map showing major streams and property lines. USFS owned property is shaded green. The trail lines are fairly accurate but do not show the relocations completed in late 2011, and this map does not show the hiking trails in the Wood Run Area.

In January 2012, the USFS updated an 8.5" x14" map titled Uwharrie Biking Trails. This map is similar to the one described above, but it does include the hiking trails.

Another 2012 map produced by the USFS is titled Uwharrie Hiking Trails. This map covers the Uwharrie Trail from NC 24/27 northward to SR 1306 at Jumping Off Rock Trailhead. This map shows State and FS roads, and the hiking-only trails, but does not show the Wood Run Mountain Bike trails.

The trail lines on one version of the USFS map produced in the 1980's, titled "Uwharrie Area Trail Map", were drawn incorrectly, showing Wood Run Road (FR 517) on the wrong side of the Uwharrie and Dutchman's Creek Trail intersection. This particular version, which has confused more than one hiker, was printed on 8 1/2" by 14" paper and did not have topo lines.

Another USFS-produced map, also called the "Uwharrie Area Trail Map" but printed on 11" by 17" paper, included topo lines. It was printed around 1985. This map was missing sections of the Uwharrie and Dutchman's Creek trails in the area south of Dusty Level Road (SR 1146).

USGS topographic quadrangle maps covering this area are: Morrow Mountain and Troy. The 1981-83 revisions do not show trails. A 1994 revision shows the Uwharrie and Dutchman's Creek hiking trails as well as some of the roads used in the Wood Run Bike Trail system.

The 1997 Uwharrie National Forest fold out map by Gemini Maps of NC, Inc. includes the Wood Run Area. Although the map has topo lines, the trail lines are only a rough approximation of the trail locations. The Uwharrie Trail line in the Wood Run Area is significantly incorrect in two spots: the map shows the trail on the west side of the mountain just north of Wood Run Camp instead of on the east side, and it shows the trail on the west side of Dennis Mountain instead of crossing the top. The Dutchman's Creek Trail line is drawn well south of Little Island Creek, instead of along the creek. The Gemini map also shows the currently open sections of the Wood Run Mountain Bike Trail System, but the lines are only a rough approximation of the trail locations.

Wood Run Area Trails

Trail Name	Length (miles)	Elevation Gain/Loss	Difficulty Rating	Map (page)
Dutchman's Creek Road N	1.10	202' / 115'	Moderate	462
Dutchman's Creek Road S	1.35	155' / 165'	Moderate	462
Dutchman's Creek	11.27	2,388' / 2,267'	Difficult	464
Keyauwee	6.01	1,080' / 1,038'	Moderate	466
Supertree	3.49	404' / 448'	Moderate	468
Walker Mountain Road	1.56	452' / 147'	Moderate	470
Whitetail	1.60	170' / 318'	Moderate	472
Wood Run Road	4.79	660' / 597'	Moderate	474
Wood Run Trail	1.27	222' / 132'	Moderate	476
Yates Place Road	1.19	107' / 103'	Easy	478
Yats Place Trail	0.32	11' / 105'	Easy	480

Uwharrie Trail

The sections of the Uwharrie Trail that pass through the Wood Run Area are covered in detail in the Uwharrie Trail chapter.

Dutchman's Creek Road (north)

Map	page 462	**Difficulty**	Moderate
Length	1.50 miles	**Configuration**	One Way
Trailhead	N/A	**Elev Gain/Loss**	193' / 253'

Start Coordinates N35.36790, W79.99948;   17 S 590890 3914302

Dutchman's Creek Road (north) is a gated USFS road (FR 6678). It begins at a brown Forest Service gate along Dusty Level Road (SR 1146), 0.7 miles west of Yates Place Trailhead, and drops down to cross Dutchman's Creek before climbing up to end at the edge of private property.

The first portion of the road is usually somewhat overgrown and rarely used. A well-used private road joins this Forest Service road for a short distance and is used by the private landowners who access their property further from Dusty Level Road.

There were a few decent views looking out over the surrounding mountains along the second section of this road, but these will disappear as the surrounding forest grows higher.

Crossing Dutchman's Creek can be tricky. The streambed is about 20 feet across and is covered with loose rocks. The water normally runs 6 to 8 inches deep.

Dutchman's Creek Road (north) ends at the private property line marked with no trespassing signs.

The map shows this roadbed continuing on the south side of the private property. Providing this information is not intended to imply that you have permission to follow the road bed across the privately owned property.

Dutchman's Creek Road (south)

Map	page 462	**Difficulty**	Moderate
Length	1.34 miles	**Configuration**	One Way
Trailhead	N/A	**Elev Gain/Loss**	172' / 180'

Start Coordinates N35.34829, W80.01881;   17 S 589156 3912110

As described in this guide, the Dutchman's Creek Road (south) route actually follows parts of three unsigned old roads that have different USFS numbers.

The route starts at a junction with Wood Run Road (FR 517), just north of the intersection with the Uwharrie Trail, and follows FR 6680 eastward. The road soon intersects both the Dutchman's Creek and Uwharrie Trails. At the first road junction, the route turns left onto FR 6680 and follows it to the next road junction. At this road junction, the route turns left again onto FR 6678 and follows it to end at the boundary with private property. The other road options at these two junctions lead to dead ends or to other private property boundaries.

The further this route gets from Wood Run Road, the less used and more overgrown the roadbed becomes. There are also some prescribed burn fire-lines that resemble roads crossing the real roads. These factors can make following this route more difficult.

The map shows the southern section of this road and how it connects to Wood Run Road. Providing this information is not intended to imply that you have permission to follow the road across the privately owned property.

Dutchman's Creek Trail

Map	page 464	**Difficulty**	Difficult
Length	11.27 miles	**Configuration**	One Way
Trailhead	24-27	**Elev Gain/Loss**	2,388' / 2,267'

Start Coordinates N35.31075, W80.04316;   17 S 586983 3907924

In the mid 1970's, Dutchman's Creek Trail (hiking only) was built to complement the Uwharrie hiking trail in the Wood Run Area. Local volunteers and Forest Service personnel worked together to build this trail. Dutchman's Creek Trail is named after a creek that runs across the northern end of the Wood Run Area. The trail follows this creek for a short distance. Dutchman's Creek Trail is designated as Trail #98 in the USFS system.

In September 1996, Hurricane Fran dealt a harsh blow to trees in the Uwharrie Lakes Region. Especially hard hit were several of the creek bottoms in the Wood Run Area. Shallow root systems and soft soils couldn't stand up to the winds that funneled through the valleys. Although volunteers and Forest Service crews opened the trails back up, they are frequently bordered with fallen trees.

Dutchman's Creek Trail is marked with yellow paint blazes. The trail begins at the Wood Run Trailhead, leaving from the east end of the parking lot beside the gate for Wood Run Road.

The Uwharrie hiking trail and the Dutchman's Creek Trail cross in the Wood Run Area to form a figure 8, offering hikers a choice of several possible loop trips. Dutchman's Creek Trail tends to run more on ridgelines than along creeks as it works its way through the area. As a consequence, fewer camping spots near water sources will be found along this trail. There are established sites at Big Island Creek and along Little Island and Dutchman's Creeks.

Dutchman's Creek Trail offers steeper climbs than the Uwharrie Trail. Climbing out of the Little Island Creek valley is memorable because the route passes over an extensive rock outcropping. The trail ends where it meets the Uwharrie Trail about half a mile south of Dusty Level Road (SR 1146).

Keyauwee Trail

Map	page 466	**Difficulty**	Moɑᴄ.
Length	6.01 miles	**Configuration**	One Way
Trailhead	Wood Run Camp	**Elev Gain/Loss**	1,080' / 1,038'

Start Coordinates N35.32464, W80.03652; 17 S 587572 3909472

The Keyauwee (key-YAH-wee) Trail was the second route opened up and signed for mountain bikes in 1996 by volunteers with the Uwharrie Mountain Bike Association (UMBA). At that time the trail was an out-and-back route starting across from the northern end of Supertree Trail. It was just 1.3 miles to the turnaround point. This original section followed an old logging road that ran up and over Keyauwee Mountain and ended in a saddle on the east side of Dennis Mountain. Keyauwee Trail is designated as trail #395A in the USFS system.

UMBA received a 1997 Adopt-A-Trail Grant from the state to fund part of the archaeological surveys required before the connecting sections of the Keyauwee Loop could be built. USFS District Ranger Tom Horner gave approval for UMBA to proceed with trail construction in December of 1997. Volunteers completed the connecting sections of the Keyauwee Trail in 1998, bringing the route around Dennis Mountain, tying into Walker Mountain Road, and ending at Wood Run Camp. This trail formed the first loop on the western side of the Wood Run Mountain Bike Trail System.

In the 2000's, UMBA was transitioned into a chapter of the Southern Off Road Bicycle Association (SORBA). Volunteers worked with the International Mountain Bicycling Association to raise funds and obtain grants to perform upgrades on the Wood Run Trails. Several miles of Keyauwee Trail were relocated and professionally constructed by Trail Dynamics, a company that specializes in trail construction. The portion of Keyauwee Trail that originally followed Walker Mountain Road was changed so that it just crosses the road. These relocations were completed in the Fall of 2011.

"Keyauwee" was the name of the last known band of native Americans to live in the Uwharrie Lakes Region. Men of the Keyauwee tribe were unusual because they were bearded, unlike most native Americans. Records mention them in the area as late as the early 1800's. Like many of the native tribes in NC, details about what eventually happened to them were never recorded and have probably been lost forever.

Several old moonshine still sites can be found along the creeks on the western portions of the trail.

There are several great views looking west from open spots on Walker Mountain. When the trail was first opened, the section climbing up from the end of Walker Mountain Road passed through an open field. Today the "field" is a stand of trees.

he route along the high side of this "field" still offers a few glimpses of the best view from any trail in the Uwharrie Lakes Region, encompassing the mountains of Morrow Mountain State Park, the Badin Lake Area, and the Lake Tillery Basin.

Like other trails in the Wood Run Mountain Bike Trail System, Keyauwee is marked with brown carsonite posts and/or wooden signs at intersections. Some of the signs bear the unique symbol of UMBA and the Wood Run Trail System, as well as a directional arrow. The trail is blazed with a vertical bar blue paint blaze.

Supertree Trail

Map	page 468	**Difficulty**	Moderate
Length	3.49 miles	**Configuration**	One Way
Trailhead	N/A	**Elev Gain/Loss**	404' / 448'
Start Coordinates N35.33403, W80.02923;		17 S 588224 3910519	

Supertree Trail was the first route cleared and signed by volunteers from the Uwharrie Mountain Bike Association. It was officially dedicated on National Trails Day in June of 1996, with approval from USFS District Ranger Tammy Malone. Combined with part of Wood Run Road, this trail created the first loop ride in the Wood Run Mountain Bike Trail System.

Supertree Trail is named for a stand of Loblolly Pine trees located along the route. The trees were planted in the 1960's by the NC Forest Service as part of an experiment to develop a new 'supertree' species. Supertree is designated as trail #395 in the USFS system.

When UMBA's volunteers began working on Supertree, the first and last sections of the route followed existing USFS logging roads. Both of these roads had been stabilized with gravel. The middle section of the route ran through a tract of private land that was not acquired by the USFS until the early 1990's. After they bought the property, the USFS plowed this roadbed and planted it in grass to prevent erosion. Most of the reseeded section lies under heavy forest cover, therefore the grass never established itself well. Numerous rocks pulled up during the plowing operation now lie loose on the surface of the ground, adding to the challenge of the route.

In 2011, SORBA volunteers and Trail Dynamics rerouted a portion of Supertree to move it away from an often-wet location under the powerlines.

When riding into the area on Wood Run Road, bikers encounter the end of Supertree Trail first, at the Wood Run Camp. Many riders turn up Supertree at this point instead of continuing up Wood Run Road to the start of Supertree. I generally prefer to climb up the graded and graveled Wood Run Road and then enjoy the downhill on Supertree's tighter singletrack-like sections.

Overall, Supertree is a moderately easy trail to ride. The only two significant climbs are near the beginning and just after crossing Wood Run creek, but they are both fairly short. The rest of the route is fairly smooth and would be rated an Easy difficulty level.

Like other trails in the Wood Run Mountain Bike Trail System, the Supertree route is marked with brown carsonite posts and wood signs at major intersections. The signs bear the unique symbol of UMBA and the Wood Run Trail System, as well as a directional arrow. The trail is marked with blue vertical bar paint blazes.

The sections of the Uwharrie Trail that pass through the Wood Run Area are covered in detail in the Uwharrie Trail chapter.

Walker Mountain Road

Map	page 470	**Difficulty**	Moderate
Length	1.56 miles	**Configuration**	One Way
Trailhead	River Road	**Elev Gain/Loss**	452' / 147'
Start Coordinates N35.33858, W80.05441; 17 S 585931 3911001			

Walker Mountain Road is a gated and graveled Forest system road. The route starts at River Road Trailhead, just south of where Upper Wood Run creek crosses under River Road. The road generally follows the creek upstream for almost 3/4 of a mile. The Keyauwee Trail used to follow the upper half of Walker Mountain Road, but it was relocated off of the road in 2011. The road crosses Keyauwee Trail once and ends at a junction with Keyauwee Trail.

As the road winds its way around the upper portion of the mountain, there are a few nice spots to enjoy the views looking westward. The views are the highlight of this route. You can see Lake Tillery and the mountains of Morrow Mountain State Park off to the west, as well as some of the neighboring mountains in the Wood Run Area.

Whitetail Trail

Map	page 472	**Difficulty**	Moderate
Length	1.60 miles	**Configuration**	One Way
Trailhead	N/A	**Elev Gain/Loss**	170' / 318'

Start Coordinates N35.32960, W80.02290;   17 S 588804 3910033

Whitetail Trail follows old road beds as it generally bisects the loop formed by Supertree Trail and Wood Run Road.

Wood Run Road

Map	page 474	**Difficulty**	Moderate
Length	4.79 miles	**Configuration**	One Way
Trailhead	24-27	**Elev Gain/Loss**	660' / 597'

Start Coordinates N35.31071, W80.04333;   17 S 586968 3907920

Wood Run Road (FR 517) is a gated and graveled Forest System road. It serves as the primary access road into the Wood Run Area. It was partially relocated in the 1970's to its current location. Portions of the route date back to the early 1800's or earlier. The USFS maintains the road, occasionally adding gravel and trimming back brush along the sides. There are no blazes along the route.

Wood Run Road forms the backbone of the Wood Run Mountain Bike Trail System. Starting at the 24-27 Trailhead, the road runs generally north-northeast across the area before ending above Little Island Creek. Future plans for the Wood Run Mountain Bike Trail System envision three loop trails leading out to either side. All of the bike and hiking trails in this area connect to or cross Wood Run Road. Wood Run Road is designated as trail #396 in the USFS system.

Most of Wood Run Road's length is graveled and well-used, providing a quick way for bikers to get into or out of the backcountry. There are a few significant hills along the route, but overall it provides smooth, fast double-track most of the way. The final half mile is more overgrown and less graveled and the double-track isn't worn in as well.

Wood Run Camp is located 1.2 miles in from NC 24-27. The "Camp" consists of an small open field and a vault toilet. Wood Run Road is gated and closed to vehicles beyond this point. The gate at the 24-27 Trailhead is usually left open and the public is allowed to drive to the Camp.

Wood Run Trail

Map	page 476	**Difficulty**	Moderate
Length	1.27 miles	**Configuration**	One Way
Trailhead	N/A	**Elev Gain/Loss**	222' / 132'
Start Coordinates	N35.31580, W80.04355;	17 S 586942 3908484	

Wood Run Trail follows new trail location as it provides an alternative to riding Wood Run Road all the way from the 24/27 Trailhead to Wood Run Camp. This trail is numbered 396 by the USFS.

Wood Run Trail was designed and built in 2011 by Trail Dynamics, Inc and volunteers as part of a grant project.

The start of the trail is on the right side of Wood Run Road just north of the big powerlines.

The route takes advantage of some small rock formations and the undulating terrain as it winds its way around some small ridges to the Wood Run Camp.

Yates Place Road

Map	page 478	**Difficulty**	Easy
Length	1.19 miles	**Configuration**	One Way
Trailhead	Yates Place	**Elev Gain/Loss**	107' / 103'
Start Coordinates	N35.36506, W79.98892;	17 S 591852 3913997	

Yates Place Road (FS 6746) is a gated USFS road that starts at the Yates Place Camp and runs southward. The road ends at a private property boundary.

Yates Place Trail

Map	page 480	**Difficulty**	Easy
Length	0.32 miles	**Configuration**	One Way
Trailhead	Yates Place	**Elev Gain/Loss**	11' / 105'
Start Coordinates	N35.36466, W79.99034;	17 S 591724 3913951	

The Yates Place Trail is a short footpath that connects Yates Place Camp to the Uwharrie Trail. This trail provides a more scenic alternative between these two points rather than simply hiking along Dusty Level Road, which parallels the route.

The Yates Place Trail begins on the right side of Yates Place Road, just beyond the gate on the southwest side of the camp area.

Dutchman's Creek Road

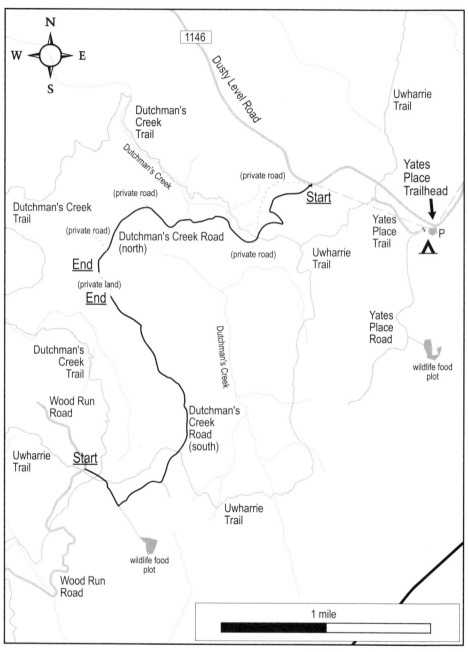

WOOD RUN AREA TRAILS

Elevation Profile: Dutchman's Creek Road

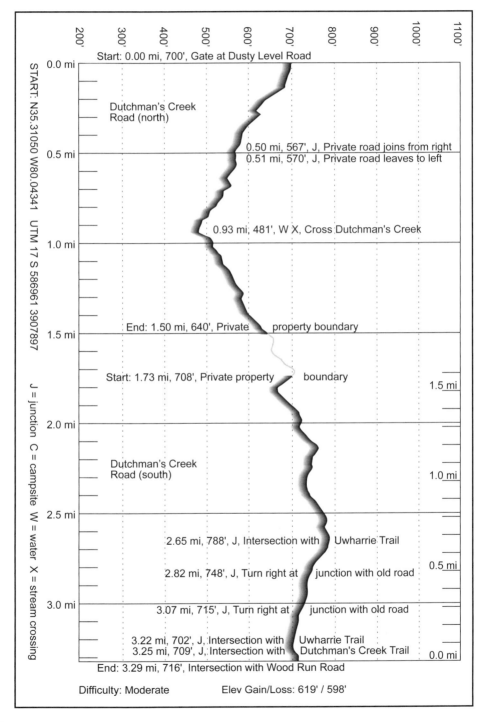

START: N35.31050 W80.04341   UTM 17 S 586961 3907897

J = junction C = campsite W = water X = stream crossing

Start: 0.00 mi, 700', Gate at Dusty Level Road

200' 300' 400' 500' 600' 700' 800' 900' 1000' 1100'

0.0 mi

Dutchman's Creek
Road (north)

0.5 mi

0.50 mi, 567', J, Private road joins from right
0.51 mi, 570', J, Private road leaves to left

0.93 mi, 481', W X, Cross Dutchman's Creek

1.0 mi

End: 1.50 mi, 640', Private   property boundary

1.5 mi

Start: 1.73 mi, 708', Private property   boundary

1.5 mi

2.0 mi

Dutchman's Creek
Road (south)

1.0 mi

2.5 mi

2.65 mi, 788', J, Intersection with   Uwharrie Trail

2.82 mi, 748', J, Turn right at   junction with old road

0.5 mi

3.0 mi

3.07 mi, 715', J, Turn right at   junction with old road

3.22 mi, 702', J, Intersection with   Uwharrie Trail
3.25 mi, 709', J, Intersection with   Dutchman's Creek Trail

0.0 mi

End: 3.29 mi, 716', Intersection with Wood Run Road

Difficulty: Moderate   Elev Gain/Loss: 619' / 598'

Dutchman's Creek Trail

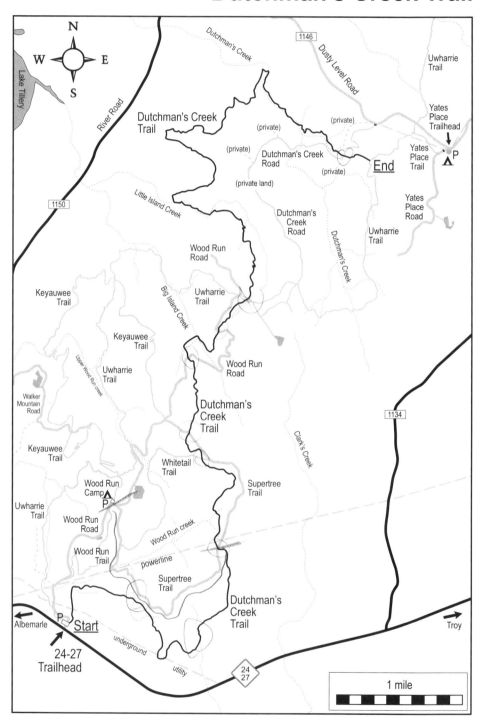

Elevation Profile: Dutchman's Creek Trail

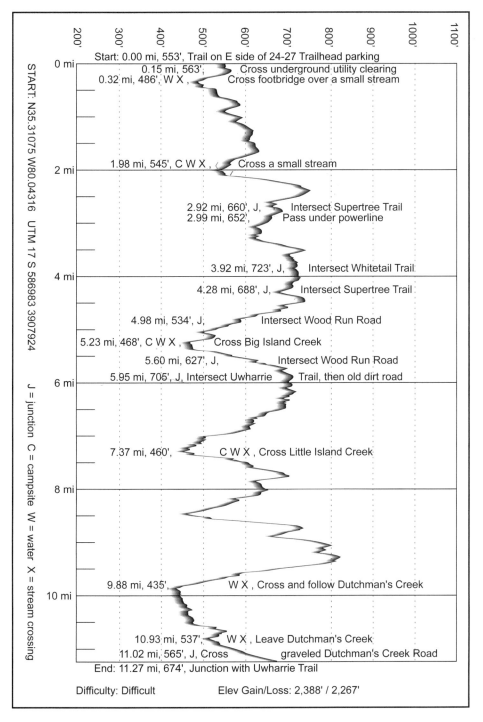

START: N35.31075 W80.04316   UTM 17 S 586983 3907924

J = junction C = campsite W = water X = stream crossing

200' 300' 400' 500' 600' 700' 800' 900' 1000' 1100'

0 mi
2 mi
4 mi
6 mi
8 mi
10 mi

Start: 0.00 mi, 553', Trail on E side of 24-27 Trailhead parking
0.15 mi, 563', Cross underground utility clearing
0.32 mi, 486', W X , Cross footbridge over a small stream
1.98 mi, 545', C W X , Cross a small stream
2.92 mi, 660', J, Intersect Supertree Trail
2.99 mi, 652', Pass under powerline
3.92 mi, 723', J, Intersect Whitetail Trail
4.28 mi, 688', J, Intersect Supertree Trail
4.98 mi, 534', J, Intersect Wood Run Road
5.23 mi, 468', C W X , Cross Big Island Creek
5.60 mi, 627', J, Intersect Wood Run Road
5.95 mi, 705', J, Intersect Uwharrie Trail, then old dirt road
7.37 mi, 460', C W X , Cross Little Island Creek
9.88 mi, 435', W X , Cross and follow Dutchman's Creek
10.93 mi, 537', W X , Leave Dutchman's Creek
11.02 mi, 565', J, Cross graveled Dutchman's Creek Road
End: 11.27 mi, 674', Junction with Uwharrie Trail

Difficulty: Difficult   Elev Gain/Loss: 2,388' / 2,267'

Keyauwee Trail

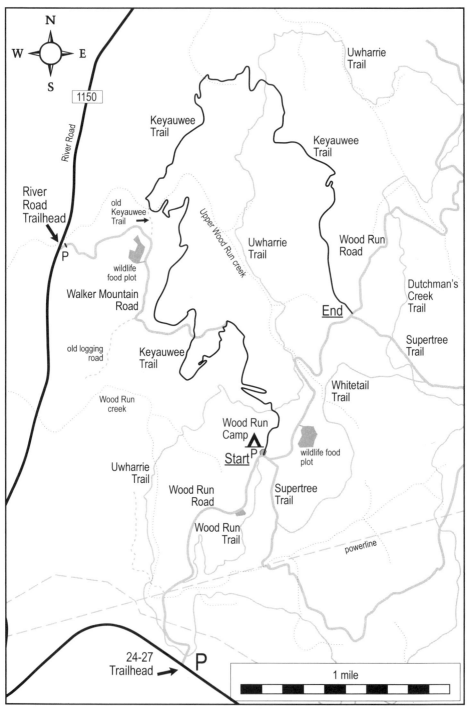

Elevation Profile: Keyauwee Trail

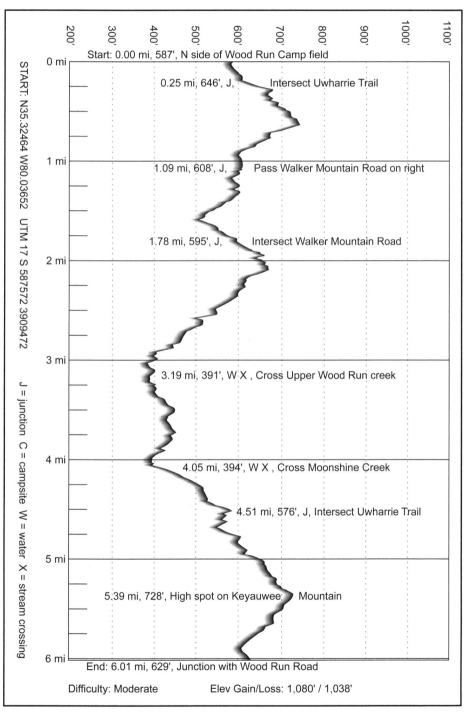

START: N35.32464 W80.03652   UTM 17 S 587572 3909472   J = junction C = campsite W = water X = stream crossing

Start: 0.00 mi, 587', N side of Wood Run Camp field

0.25 mi, 646', J,   Intersect Uwharrie Trail

1.09 mi, 608', J,   Pass Walker Mountain Road on right

1.78 mi, 595', J,   Intersect Walker Mountain Road

3.19 mi, 391', W X , Cross Upper Wood Run creek

4.05 mi, 394', W X , Cross Moonshine Creek

4.51 mi, 576', J, Intersect Uwharrie Trail

5.39 mi, 728', High spot on Keyauwee Mountain

End: 6.01 mi, 629', Junction with Wood Run Road

Difficulty: Moderate   Elev Gain/Loss: 1,080' / 1,038'

Supertree Trail

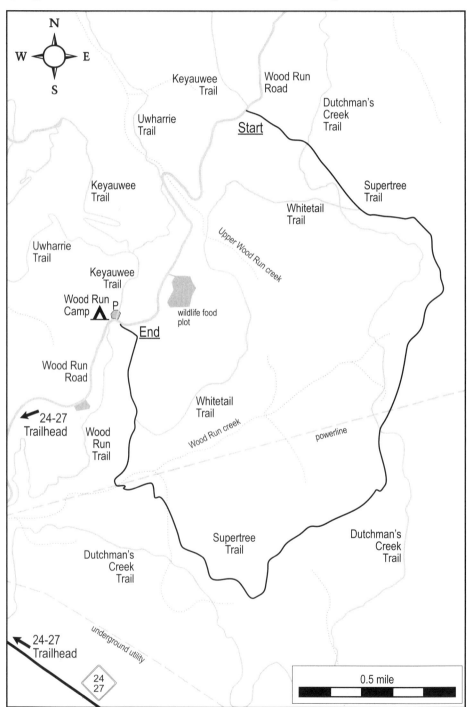

Elevation Profile: Supertree Trail

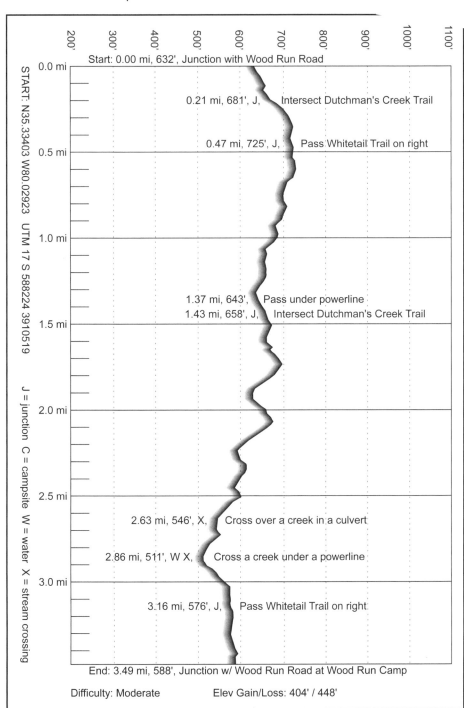

START: N35.33403 W80.02923 UTM 17 S 588224 3910519

J = junction C = campsite W = water X = stream crossing

Start: 0.00 mi, 632', Junction with Wood Run Road

0.21 mi, 681', J, Intersect Dutchman's Creek Trail

0.47 mi, 725', J, Pass Whitetail Trail on right

1.37 mi, 643', Pass under powerline
1.43 mi, 658', J, Intersect Dutchman's Creek Trail

2.63 mi, 546', X, Cross over a creek in a culvert

2.86 mi, 511', W X, Cross a creek under a powerline

3.16 mi, 576', J, Pass Whitetail Trail on right

End: 3.49 mi, 588', Junction w/ Wood Run Road at Wood Run Camp

Difficulty: Moderate   Elev Gain/Loss: 404' / 448'

Walker Mountain Road

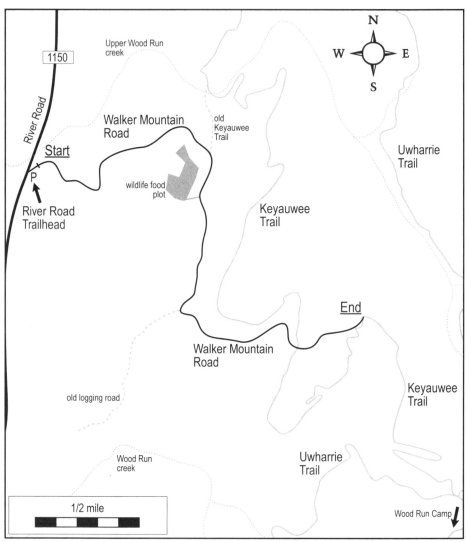

Elevation Profile: Walker Mountain Road

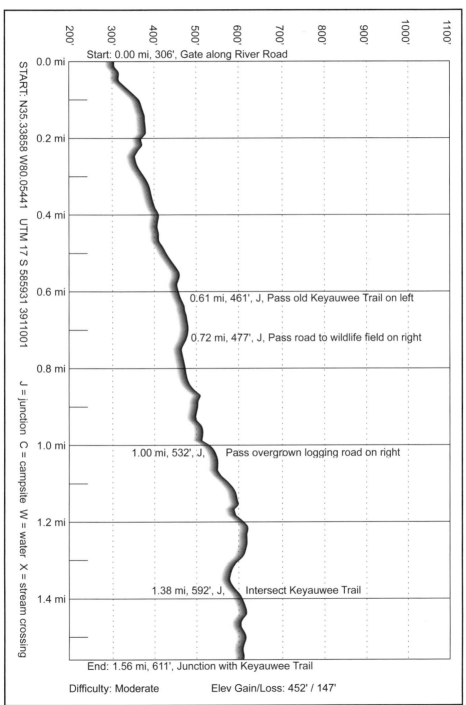

START: N35.33858 W80.05441 UTM 17 S 585931 3911001

J = junction C = campsite W = water X = stream crossing

Start: 0.00 mi, 306', Gate along River Road

0.61 mi, 461', J, Pass old Keyauwee Trail on left

0.72 mi, 477', J, Pass road to wildlife field on right

1.00 mi, 532', J,   Pass overgrown logging road on right

1.38 mi, 592', J,   Intersect Keyauwee Trail

End: 1.56 mi, 611', Junction with Keyauwee Trail

Difficulty: Moderate   Elev Gain/Loss: 452' / 147'

Whitetail Trail

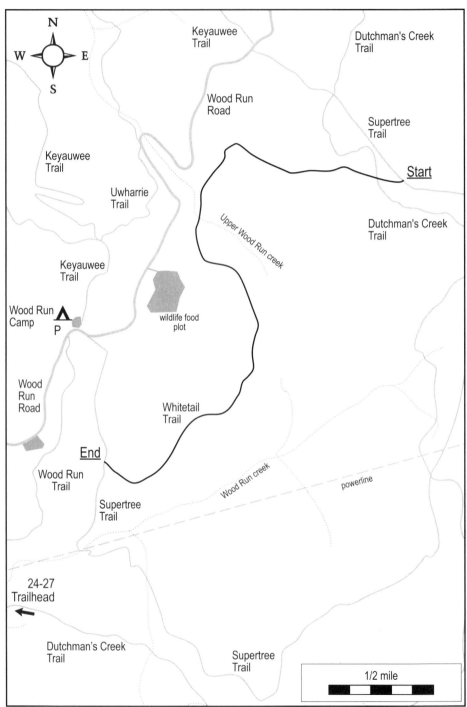

Elevation Profile: Whitetail Trail

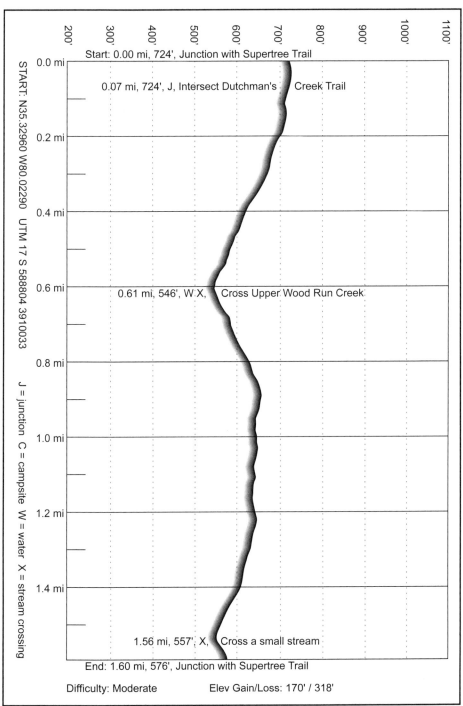

START: N35.32960 W80.02290 UTM 17 S 588804 3910033

J = junction C = campsite W = water X = stream crossing

Start: 0.00 mi, 724', Junction with Supertree Trail

0.07 mi, 724', J, Intersect Dutchman's Creek Trail

0.61 mi, 546', W, X, Cross Upper Wood Run Creek

1.56 mi, 557', X, Cross a small stream

End: 1.60 mi, 576', Junction with Supertree Trail

Difficulty: Moderate   Elev Gain/Loss: 170' / 318'

Wood Run Road

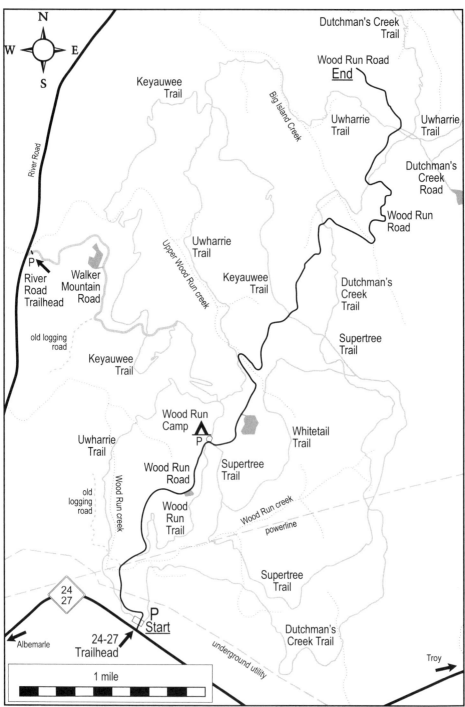

Dutchman's Creek Trail

Wood Run Road
End

Keyauwee Trail

Big Island Creek

Uwharrie Trail

Uwharrie Trail

Dutchman's Creek Road

Wood Run Road

River Road

P
River Road Trailhead

Walker Mountain Road

Upper Wood Run creek

Uwharrie Trail

Keyauwee Trail

Dutchman's Creek Trail

Supertree Trail

old logging road

Keyauwee Trail

Wood Run Camp

P

Uwharrie Trail

Wood Run creek

old logging road

Wood Run Road

Supertree Trail

Whitetail Trail

Wood Run Trail

Wood Run creek

powerline

Supertree Trail

24 27

Albemarle

P
Start

24-27 Trailhead

underground utility

Dutchman's Creek Trail

Troy

N W E S

1 mile

Elevation Profile: Wood Run Road

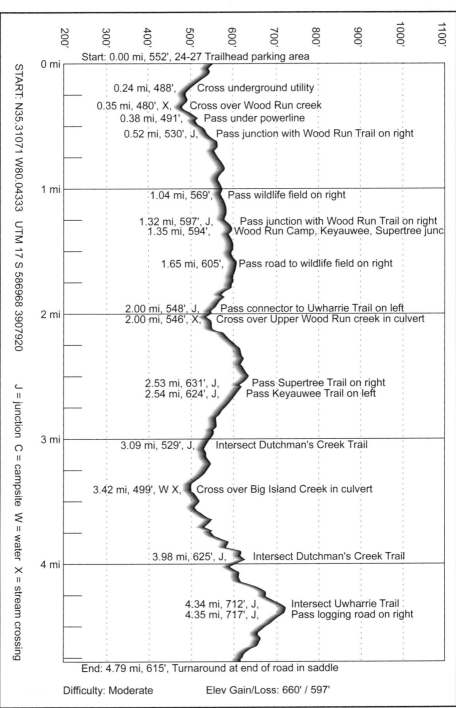

START: N35.31071 W80.04333 UTM 17 S 586968 3907920   J = junction C = campsite W = water X = stream crossing

| | 200' | 300' | 400' | 500' | 600' | 700' | 800' | 900' | 1000' | 1100' |

Start: 0.00 mi, 552', 24-27 Trailhead parking area

0 mi

0.24 mi, 488',   Cross underground utility
0.35 mi, 480', X,   Cross over Wood Run creek
0.38 mi, 491',   Pass under powerline
0.52 mi, 530', J,   Pass junction with Wood Run Trail on right

1 mi

1.04 mi, 569',   Pass wildlife field on right

1.32 mi, 597', J,   Pass junction with Wood Run Trail on right
1.35 mi, 594',   Wood Run Camp, Keyauwee, Supertree junc

1.65 mi, 605',   Pass road to wildlife field on right

2.00 mi, 548', J,   Pass connector to Uwharrie Trail on left
2 mi
2.00 mi, 546', X,   Cross over Upper Wood Run creek in culvert

2.53 mi, 631', J,   Pass Supertree Trail on right
2.54 mi, 624', J,   Pass Keyauwee Trail on left

3 mi

3.09 mi, 529', J,   Intersect Dutchman's Creek Trail

3.42 mi, 499', W X,   Cross over Big Island Creek in culvert

3.98 mi, 625', J,   Intersect Dutchman's Creek Trail
4 mi

4.34 mi, 712', J,   Intersect Uwharrie Trail
4.35 mi, 717', J,   Pass logging road on right

End: 4.79 mi, 615', Turnaround at end of road in saddle

Difficulty: Moderate   Elev Gain/Loss: 660' / 597'

Wood Run Trail

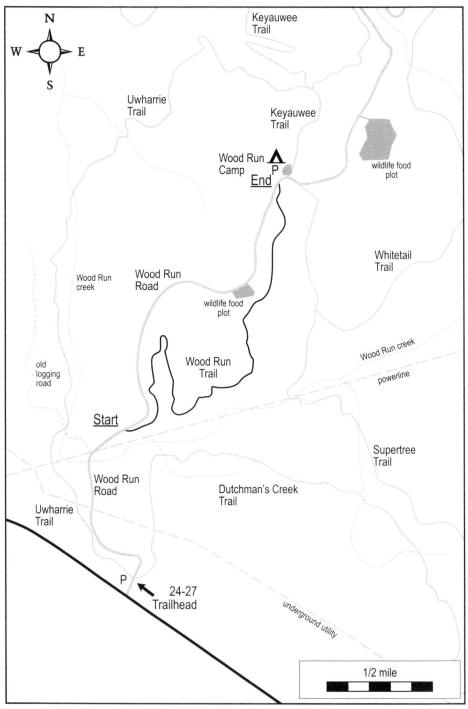

Elevation Profile: Wood Run Trail

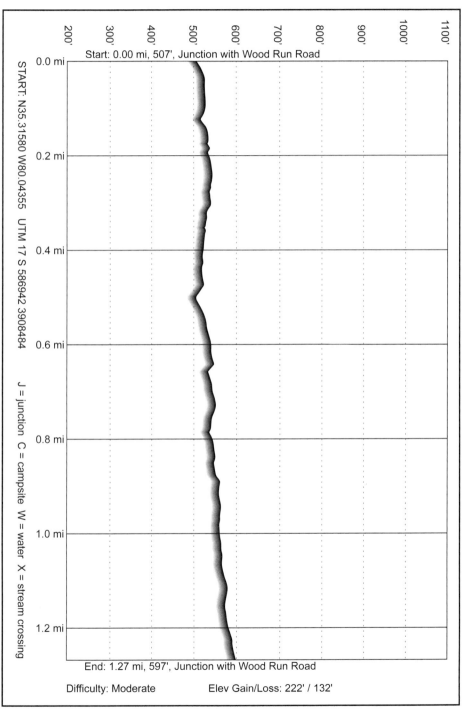

Start: 0.00 mi, 507', Junction with Wood Run Road

START: N35.31580 W80.04355 UTM 17 S 586942 3908484   J = junction C = campsite W = water X = stream crossing

End: 1.27 mi, 597', Junction with Wood Run Road

Difficulty: Moderate   Elev Gain/Loss: 222' / 132'

Yates Place Road

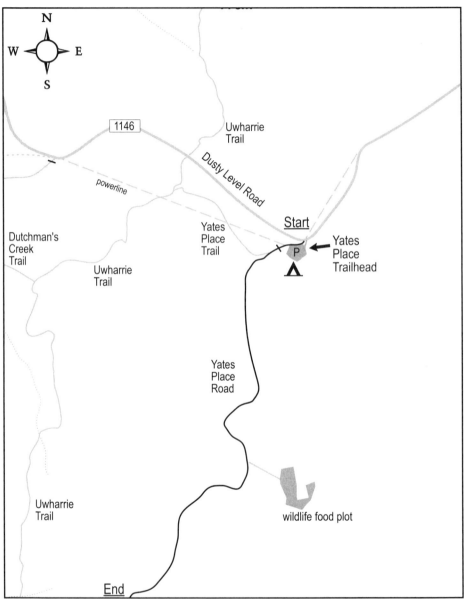

Elevation Profile: Yates Place Road

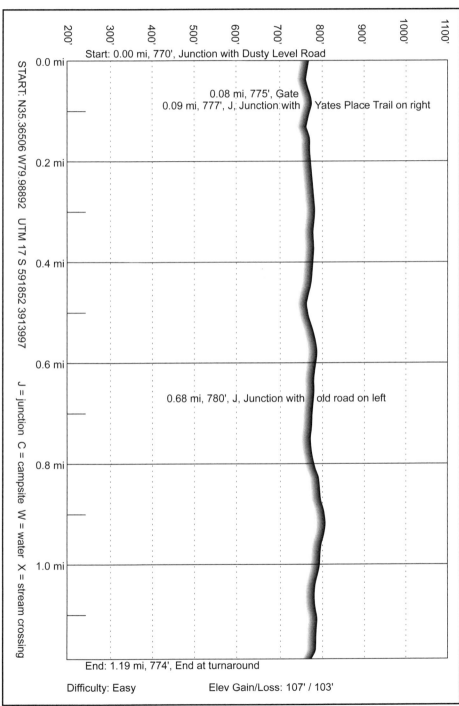

START: N35.36506 W79.98892 UTM 17 S 591852 3913997

J = junction C = campsite W = water X = stream crossing

Start: 0.00 mi, 770', Junction with Dusty Level Road

0.08 mi, 775', Gate
0.09 mi, 777', J, Junction with Yates Place Trail on right

0.68 mi, 780', J, Junction with old road on left

End: 1.19 mi, 774', End at turnaround

Difficulty: Easy

Elev Gain/Loss: 107' / 103'

Yates Place Trail

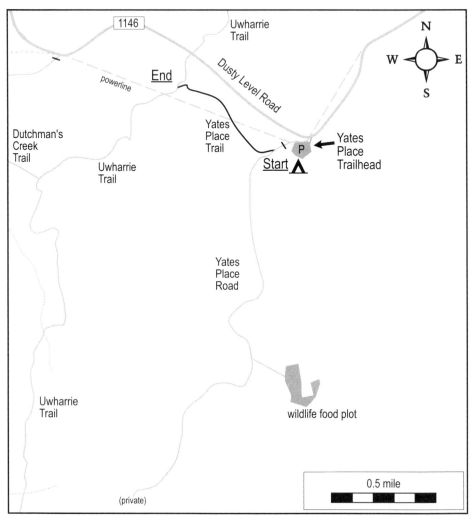

Elevation Profile: Yates Place Trail

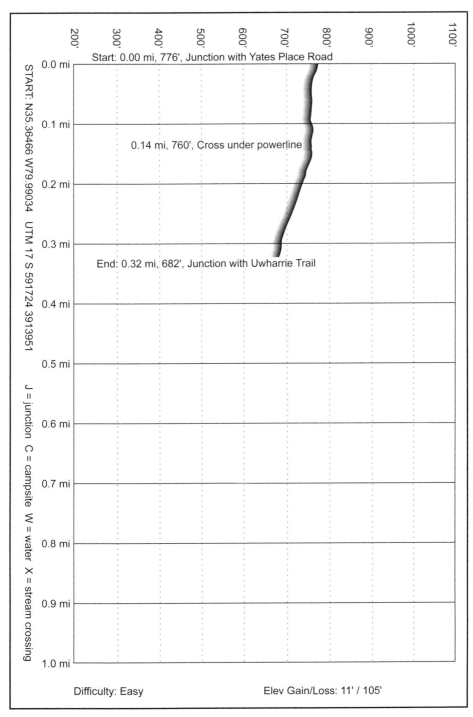

START: N35.36466 W79.99034 UTM 17 S 591724 3913951

J = junction C = campsite W = water X = stream crossing

Start: 0.00 mi, 776', Junction with Yates Place Road

0.14 mi, 760', Cross under powerline

End: 0.32 mi, 682', Junction with Uwharrie Trail

Difficulty: Easy   Elev Gain/Loss: 11' / 105'

Wood Run Area Trips

Trip	Use	Length (miles)	Elevation Gain/Loss	Difficulty Rating	Page
WRA Trip A	H	4.05	637' / 637'	Moderate	484
WRA Trip B	H	7.40	1,165' / 1,165'	Moderate	486
WRA Trip C	H	10.33	1,950' / 1,950'	Difficult	488
WRA Trip D	H	11.80	2,237' / 2,237'	Difficult	490
WRA Trip E	H	19.87	4,063' / 4,063'	Difficult	492
WRA Trip F	H	9.67	2,065' / 2,065'	Moderate	494
WRA Trip G	BH	8.24	1,051' / 1,051'	Moderate	496
WRA Trip H	BH	10.78	1,686' / 1,686'	Difficult	498
WRA Trip I	BH	13.14	1,995' / 1,995'	Difficult	500
WRA Trip J	BH	17.68	2,706' / 2,706'	Difficult	502

Wood Run Trip A

Map   page 484   **Difficulty**   Moderate
Length   4.05 miles   **Configuration**   Loop
Trailhead   24/27   **Elev Gain/Loss**   637' / 637'
Start Coordinates N35.31071, W80.04333;   17 S 586968 3907920

Wood Run Trip B

Map   page 486   **Difficulty**   Moderate
Length   7.40 miles   **Configuration**   Loop
Trailhead   24/27   **Elev Gain/Loss**   1,165' / 1,165'
Start Coordinates N35.31071, W80.04333;   17 S 586968 3907920

Wood Run Trip C

Map   page 488   **Difficulty**   Difficult
Length   10.33 miles   **Configuration**   Loop
Trailhead   24/27   **Elev Gain/Loss**   1,950' / 1,950'
Start Coordinates N35.31071, W80.04333;   17 S 586968 3907920

Wood Run Trip D

Map	page 490	**Difficulty**	Difficult
Length	11.80 miles	**Configuration**	Loop
Trailhead	24/27	**Elev Gain/Loss**	2,237' / 2,237'

Start Coordinates N35.31071, W80.04333;   17 S 586968 3907920

Wood Run Trip E

Map	page 492	**Difficulty**	Difficult
Length	19.87 miles	**Configuration**	Figure 8
Trailhead	24/27	**Elev Gain/Loss**	4,063' / 4,063'

Start Coordinates N35.31071, W80.04333;   17 S 586968 3907920

Wood Run Trip F

Map	page 494	**Difficulty**	Moderate
Length	9.67 miles	**Configuration**	Lollipop
Trailhead	Yates Place	**Elev Gain/Loss**	2,065' / 2,065'

Start Coordinates N35.36466, W79.99034;   17 S 591724 3913951

Wood Run Trip G

Map	page 496	**Difficulty**	Moderate
Length	8.24 miles	**Configuration**	Lollipop
Trailhead	24/27	**Elev Gain/Loss**	1,051' / 1,051'

Start Coordinates N35.31071, W80.04333;   17 S 586968 3907920

Wood Run Trip H

Map	page 498	**Difficulty**	Difficult
Length	10.78 miles	**Configuration**	Lollipop
Trailhead	24/27	**Elev Gain/Loss**	1,686' / 1,686'

Start Coordinates N35.31071, W80.04333;   17 S 586968 3907920

Wood Run Trip I

Map	page 500	**Difficulty**	Difficult
Length	13.14 miles	**Configuration**	Lollipop
Trailhead	24/27	**Elev Gain/Loss**	1,995' / 1,995'

Start Coordinates N35.31071, W80.04333;   17 S 586968 3907920

Wood Run Trip J

Map	page 502	**Difficulty**	Difficult
Length	17.68 miles	**Configuration**	Lollipop
Trailhead	24/27	**Elev Gain/Loss**	2,706' / 2,706'

Start Coordinates N35.31071, W80.04333;   17 S 586968 3907920

Wood Run Area Trip A

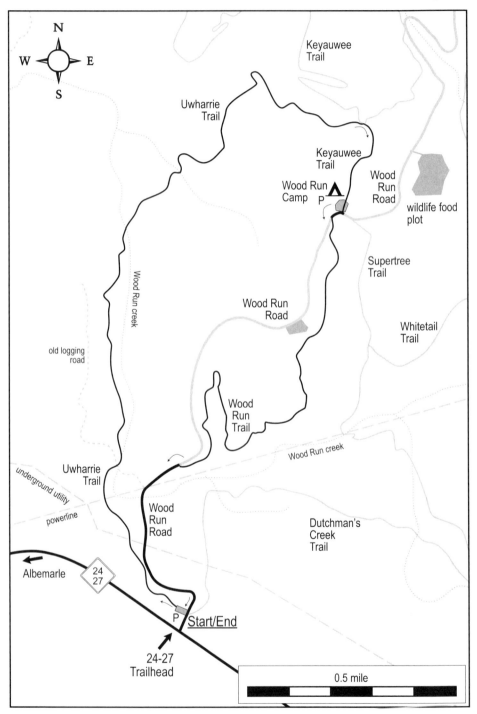

Keyauwee Trail

N
W E
S

Uwharrie Trail

Keyauwee Trail

Wood Run Camp

Wood Run Road

wildlife food plot

Wood Run creek

Supertree Trail

Wood Run Road

Whitetail Trail

old logging road

Wood Run Trail

Uwharrie Trail

Wood Run creek

underground utility

powerline

Wood Run Road

Dutchman's Creek Trail

Albemarle

24 27

P Start/End

24-27 Trailhead

0.5 mile

Elevation Profile: WRA Trip A

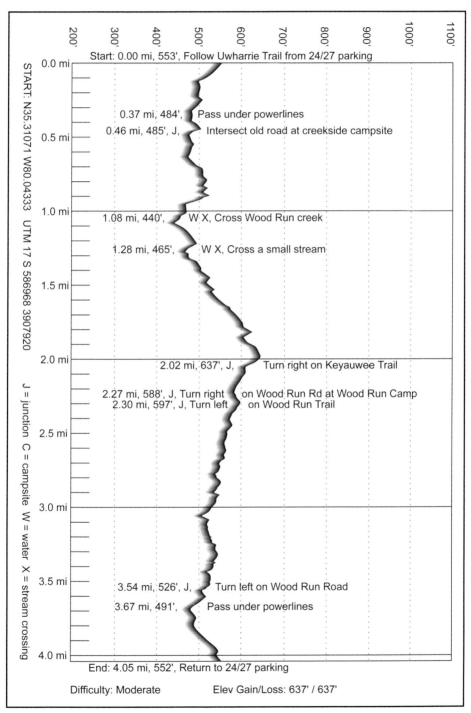

START: N35.31071 W80.04333 UTM 17 S 586968 3907920

J = junction C = campsite W = water X = stream crossing

Start: 0.00 mi, 553', Follow Uwharrie Trail from 24/27 parking

0.37 mi, 484',   Pass under powerlines
0.46 mi, 485', J,   Intersect old road at creekside campsite

1.08 mi, 440',   W X, Cross Wood Run creek

1.28 mi, 465',   W X, Cross a small stream

2.02 mi, 637', J,   Turn right on Keyauwee Trail

2.27 mi, 588', J, Turn right   on Wood Run Rd at Wood Run Camp
2.30 mi, 597', J, Turn left   on Wood Run Trail

3.54 mi, 526', J,   Turn left on Wood Run Road

3.67 mi, 491',   Pass under powerlines

End: 4.05 mi, 552', Return to 24/27 parking

Difficulty: Moderate   Elev Gain/Loss: 637' / 637'

Wood Run Area Trip B

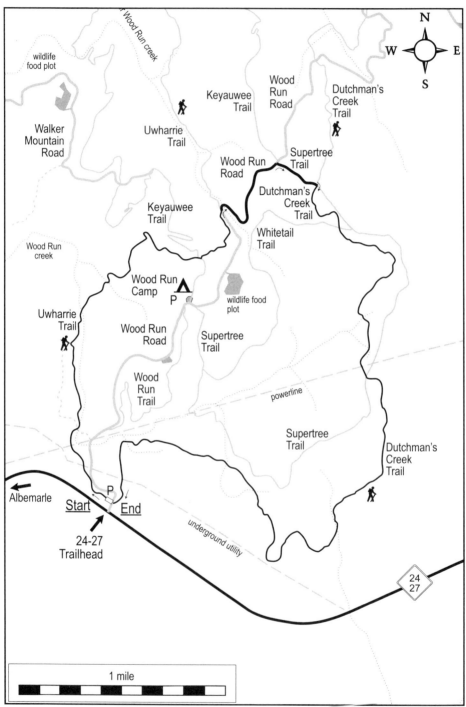

Elevation Profile: WRA Trip B

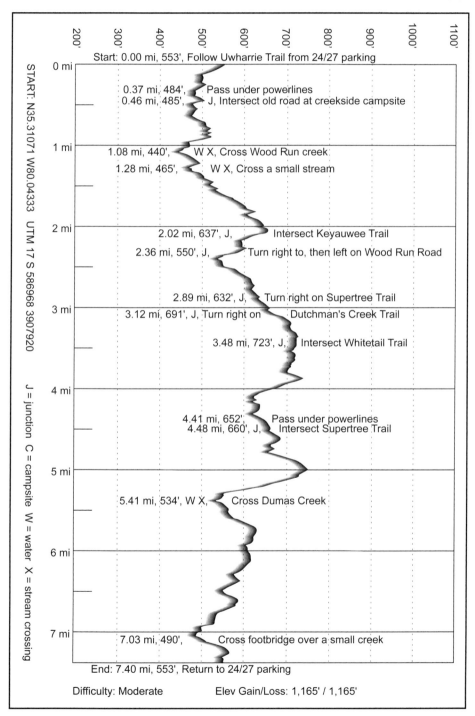

START: N35.31071 W80.04333 UTM 17 S 586968 3907920

J = junction C = campsite W = water X = stream crossing

Start: 0.00 mi, 553', Follow Uwharrie Trail from 24/27 parking

0.37 mi, 484', Pass under powerlines
0.46 mi, 485', J, Intersect old road at creekside campsite

1.08 mi, 440', W X, Cross Wood Run creek
1.28 mi, 465', W X, Cross a small stream

2.02 mi, 637', J, Intersect Keyauwee Trail
2.36 mi, 550', J, Turn right to, then left on Wood Run Road

2.89 mi, 632', J, Turn right on Supertree Trail
3.12 mi, 691', J, Turn right on Dutchman's Creek Trail
3.48 mi, 723', J, Intersect Whitetail Trail

4.41 mi, 652', Pass under powerlines
4.48 mi, 660', J, Intersect Supertree Trail

5.41 mi, 534', W X, Cross Dumas Creek

7.03 mi, 490', Cross footbridge over a small creek

End: 7.40 mi, 553', Return to 24/27 parking

Difficulty: Moderate   Elev Gain/Loss: 1,165' / 1,165'

Wood Run Area Trip C

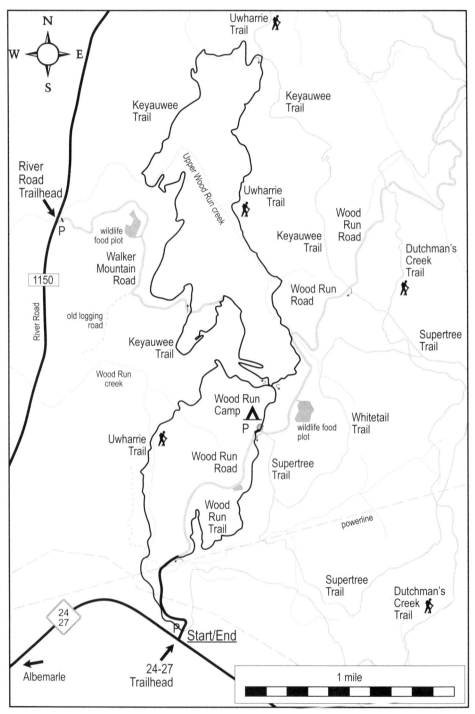

Elevation Profile: WRA Trip C

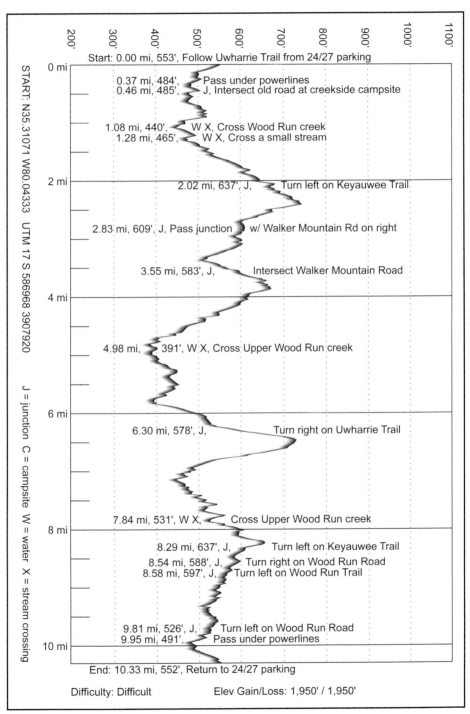

START: N35.31071 W80.04333 UTM 17 S 586968 3907920

J = junction C = campsite W = water X = stream crossing

200' 300' 400' 500' 600' 700' 800' 900' 1000' 1100'

Start: 0.00 mi, 553', Follow Uwharrie Trail from 24/27 parking

0 mi

0.37 mi, 484',   Pass under powerlines
0.46 mi, 485',   J, Intersect old road at creekside campsite

1.08 mi, 440',   W X, Cross Wood Run creek
1.28 mi, 465',   W X, Cross a small stream

2 mi

2.02 mi, 637', J,   Turn left on Keyauwee Trail

2.83 mi, 609', J, Pass junction   w/ Walker Mountain Rd on right

3.55 mi, 583', J,   Intersect Walker Mountain Road

4 mi

4.98 mi,   391', W X, Cross Upper Wood Run creek

6 mi

6.30 mi, 578', J,   Turn right on Uwharrie Trail

7.84 mi, 531', W X,   Cross Upper Wood Run creek

8 mi

8.29 mi, 637', J,   Turn left on Keyauwee Trail
8.54 mi, 588', J,   Turn right on Wood Run Road
8.58 mi, 597', J,   Turn left on Wood Run Trail

9.81 mi, 526', J,   Turn left on Wood Run Road
9.95 mi, 491',   Pass under powerlines

10 mi

End: 10.33 mi, 552', Return to 24/27 parking

Difficulty: Difficult   Elev Gain/Loss: 1,950' / 1,950'

Wood Run Area Trip D

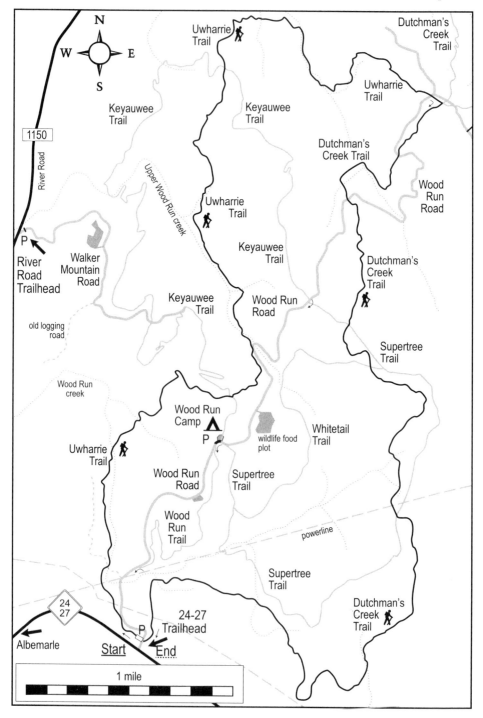

Elevation Profile: WRA Trip D

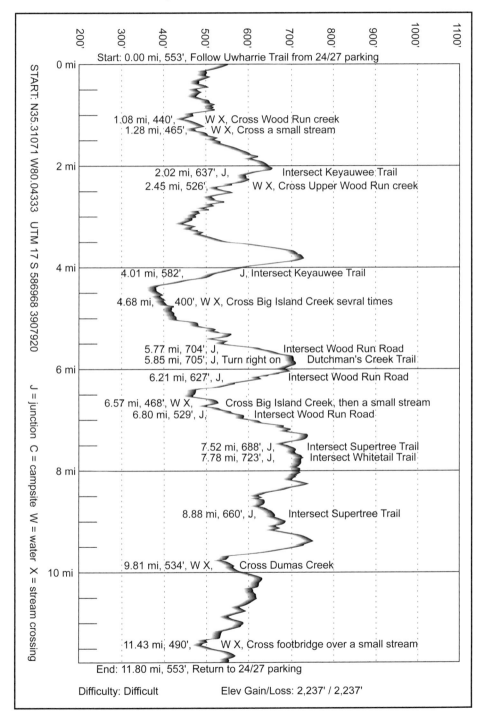

START: N35.31071 W80.04333   UTM 17 S 586968 3907920

J = junction C = campsite W = water X = stream crossing

200' 300' 400' 500' 600' 700' 800' 900' 1000' 1100'

0 mi — Start: 0.00 mi, 553', Follow Uwharrie Trail from 24/27 parking

1.08 mi, 440', W X, Cross Wood Run creek
1.28 mi, 465', W X, Cross a small stream

2 mi
2.02 mi, 637', J, Intersect Keyauwee Trail
2.45 mi, 526', W X, Cross Upper Wood Run creek

4 mi
4.01 mi, 582', J, Intersect Keyauwee Trail

4.68 mi, 400', W X, Cross Big Island Creek sevral times

5.77 mi, 704', J, Intersect Wood Run Road
5.85 mi, 705', J, Turn right on Dutchman's Creek Trail

6 mi
6.21 mi, 627', J, Intersect Wood Run Road
6.57 mi, 468', W X, Cross Big Island Creek, then a small stream
6.80 mi, 529', J, Intersect Wood Run Road

7.52 mi, 688', J, Intersect Supertree Trail
7.78 mi, 723', J, Intersect Whitetail Trail

8 mi

8.88 mi, 660', J, Intersect Supertree Trail

9.81 mi, 534', W X, Cross Dumas Creek

10 mi

11.43 mi, 490', W X, Cross footbridge over a small stream

End: 11.80 mi, 553', Return to 24/27 parking

Difficulty: Difficult   Elev Gain/Loss: 2,237' / 2,237'

Wood Run Area Trip E

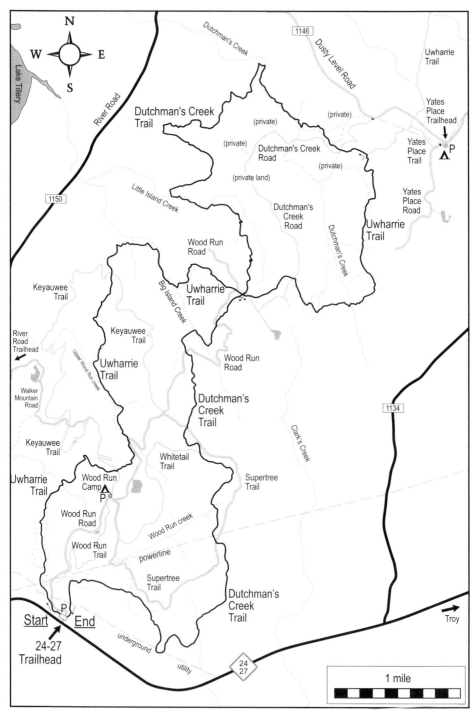

N
W   E
S

Lake Tillery

Dutchman's Creek

River Road

1146

Dusty Level Road

Uwharrie Trail

Dutchman's Creek Trail

(private)

(private)

Yates Place Trailhead

(private)

Dutchman's Creek Road

(private)

Yates Place Trail

P

1150

Little Island Creek

(private land)

Dutchman's Creek Road

Yates Place Road

Wood Run Road

Dutchman's Creek

Uwharrie Trail

Keyauwee Trail

Big Island Creek

Uwharrie Trail

River Road Trailhead

Keyauwee Trail

Upper Wood Run creek

Wood Run Road

Walker Mountain Road

Uwharrie Trail

1134

Dutchman's Creek Trail

Keyauwee Trail

Whitetail Trail

Clark's Creek

Uwharrie Trail

Wood Run Camp

P

Supertree Trail

Wood Run Road

Wood Run creek

Wood Run Trail

powerline

Supertree Trail

Dutchman's Creek Trail

Troy

Start   End

P

underground

24 27 Trailhead

utility

24 27

1 mile

Elevation Profile: WRA Trip E

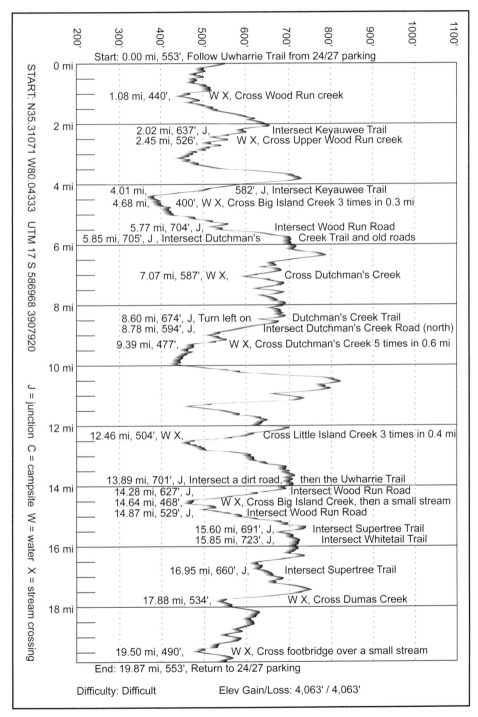

200' 300' 400' 500' 600' 700' 800' 900' 1000' 1100'

START: N35.31071 W80.04433   UTM 17 S 5869968 3907920

J = junction C = campsite W = water X = stream crossing

Start: 0.00 mi, 553', Follow Uwharrie Trail from 24/27 parking

0 mi

1.08 mi, 440', — W X, Cross Wood Run creek

2 mi

2.02 mi, 637', J, — Intersect Keyauwee Trail
2.45 mi, 526', — W X, Cross Upper Wood Run creek

4 mi

4.01 mi, — 582', J, Intersect Keyauwee Trail
4.68 mi, — 400', W X, Cross Big Island Creek 3 times in 0.3 mi

5.77 mi, 704', J, — Intersect Wood Run Road
5.85 mi, 705', J , Intersect Dutchman's — Creek Trail and old roads

6 mi

7.07 mi, 587', W X, — Cross Dutchman's Creek

8 mi

8.60 mi, 674', J, Turn left on — Dutchman's Creek Trail
8.78 mi, 594', J, — Intersect Dutchman's Creek Road (north)
9.39 mi, 477', — W X, Cross Dutchman's Creek 5 times in 0.6 mi

10 mi

12 mi

12.46 mi, 504', W X, — Cross Little Island Creek 3 times in 0.4 mi

13.89 mi, 701', J, Intersect a dirt road, — then the Uwharrie Trail

14 mi

14.28 mi, 627', J, — Intersect Wood Run Road
14.64 mi, 468', — W X, Cross Big Island Creek, then a small stream
14.87 mi, 529', J, — Intersect Wood Run Road

15.60 mi, 691', J, — Intersect Supertree Trail
15.85 mi, 723', J, — Intersect Whitetail Trail

16 mi

16.95 mi, 660', J, — Intersect Supertree Trail

17.88 mi, 534', — W X, Cross Dumas Creek

18 mi

19.50 mi, 490', — W X, Cross footbridge over a small stream

End: 19.87 mi, 553', Return to 24/27 parking

Difficulty: Difficult   Elev Gain/Loss: 4,063' / 4,063'

Wood Run Area Trip F

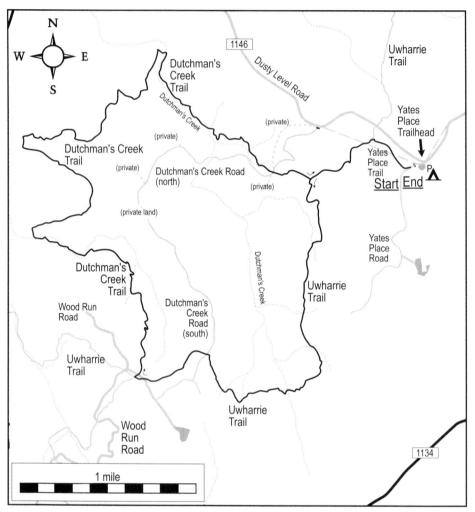

Elevation Profile: WRA Trip F

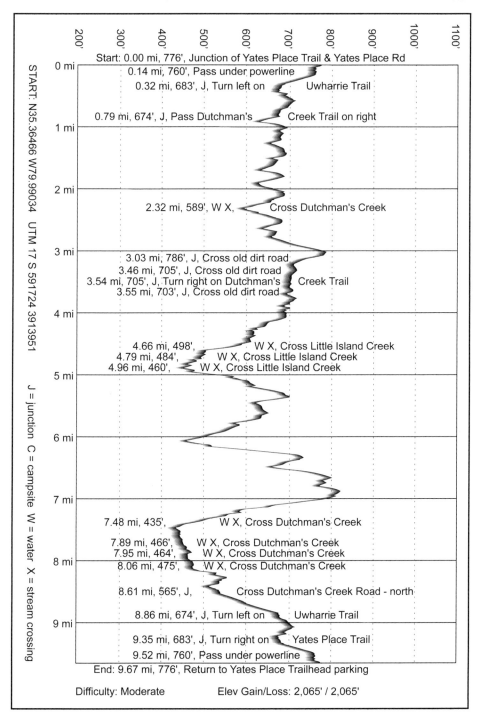

START: N35.36466 W79.99034 UTM 17 S 591724 3913951

J = junction C = campsite W = water X = stream crossing

Start: 0.00 mi, 776', Junction of Yates Place Trail & Yates Place Rd

0.14 mi, 760', Pass under powerline

0.32 mi, 683', J, Turn left on Uwharrie Trail

0.79 mi, 674', J, Pass Dutchman's Creek Trail on right

2.32 mi, 589', W X, Cross Dutchman's Creek

3.03 mi, 786', J, Cross old dirt road
3.46 mi, 705', J, Cross old dirt road
3.54 mi, 705', J, Turn right on Dutchman's Creek Trail
3.55 mi, 703', J, Cross old dirt road

4.66 mi, 498', W X, Cross Little Island Creek
4.79 mi, 484', W X, Cross Little Island Creek
4.96 mi, 460', W X, Cross Little Island Creek

7.48 mi, 435', W X, Cross Dutchman's Creek

7.89 mi, 466', W X, Cross Dutchman's Creek
7.95 mi, 464', W X, Cross Dutchman's Creek
8.06 mi, 475', W X, Cross Dutchman's Creek

8.61 mi, 565', J, Cross Dutchman's Creek Road - north

8.86 mi, 674', J, Turn left on Uwharrie Trail

9.35 mi, 683', J, Turn right on Yates Place Trail
9.52 mi, 760', Pass under powerline

End: 9.67 mi, 776', Return to Yates Place Trailhead parking

Difficulty: Moderate   Elev Gain/Loss: 2,065' / 2,065'

Wood Run Area Trip G

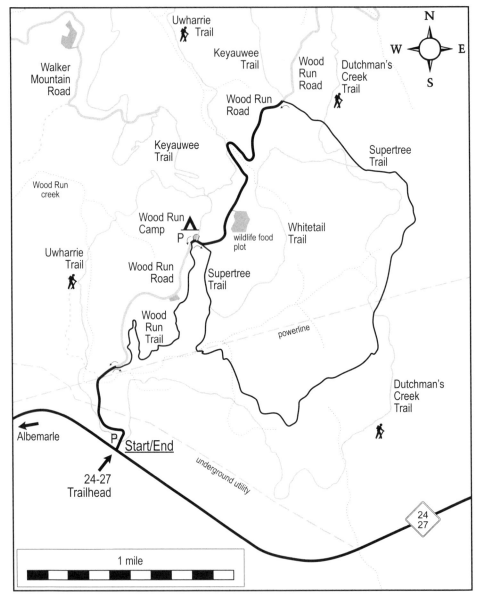

Elevation Profile: WRA Trip G

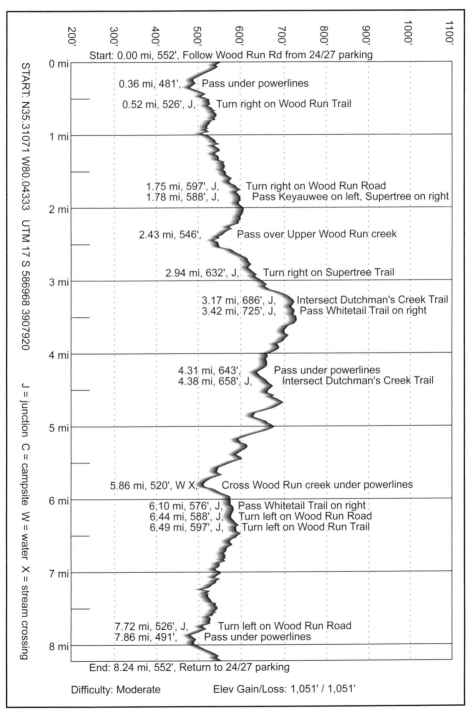

START: N35.31071 W80.04333 UTM 17 S 589968 3907920   J = junction C = campsite W = water X = stream crossing

Start: 0.00 mi, 552', Follow Wood Run Rd from 24/27 parking

0 mi

0.36 mi, 481', Pass under powerlines

0.52 mi, 526', J, Turn right on Wood Run Trail

1 mi

1.75 mi, 597', J, Turn right on Wood Run Road
1.78 mi, 588', J, Pass Keyauwee on left, Supertree on right

2 mi

2.43 mi, 546', Pass over Upper Wood Run creek

2.94 mi, 632', J, Turn right on Supertree Trail

3 mi

3.17 mi, 686', J, Intersect Dutchman's Creek Trail
3.42 mi, 725', J, Pass Whitetail Trail on right

4 mi

4.31 mi, 643' Pass under powerlines
4.38 mi, 658', J, Intersect Dutchman's Creek Trail

5 mi

5.86 mi, 520', W X, Cross Wood Run creek under powerlines

6 mi

6.10 mi, 576', J, Pass Whitetail Trail on right
6.44 mi, 588', J, Turn left on Wood Run Road
6.49 mi, 597', J, Turn left on Wood Run Trail

7 mi

7.72 mi, 526', J, Turn left on Wood Run Road
7.86 mi, 491', Pass under powerlines

8 mi

End: 8.24 mi, 552', Return to 24/27 parking

Difficulty: Moderate   Elev Gain/Loss: 1,051' / 1,051'

Wood Run Area Trip H

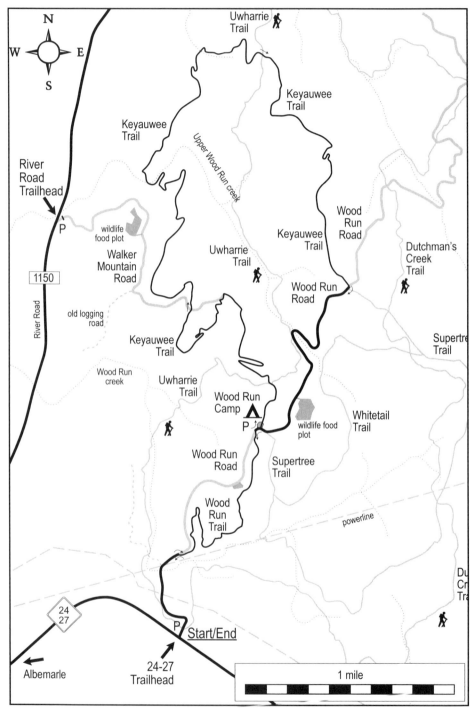

N
W E
S

Uwharrie
Trail

Keyauwee
Trail

Keyauwee
Trail

Upper Wood Run creek

River
Road
Trailhead

P

wildlife
food plot

Walker
Mountain
Road

1150

River Road

old logging
road

Keyauwee
Trail

Wood Run
creek

Uwharrie
Trail

Uwharrie
Trail

Keyauwee
Trail

Wood Run
Road

Wood
Run
Road

Dutchman's
Creek
Trail

Supertree
Trail

Wood Run
Camp

P

wildlife food
plot

Whitetail
Trail

Wood Run
Road

Supertree
Trail

Wood
Run
Trail

powerline

Du
Cr
Tra

24
27

P Start/End

Albemarle

24-27
Trailhead

1 mile

Elevation Profile: WRA Trip H

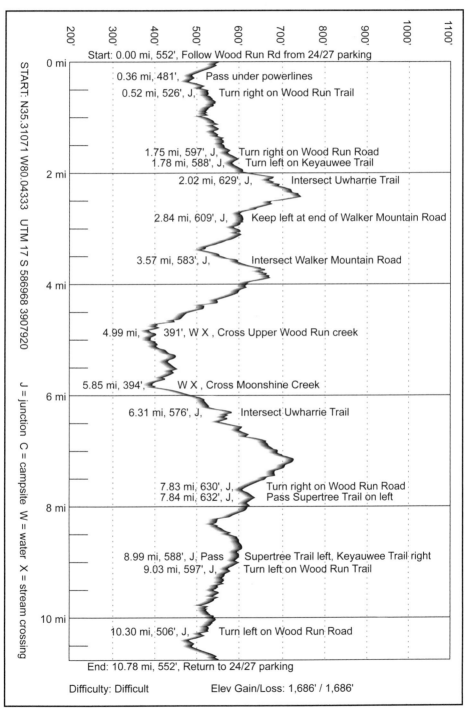

START: N35.31071 W80.04333 UTM 17 S 586968 3907920

J = junction C = campsite W = water X = stream crossing

200' 300' 400' 500' 600' 700' 800' 900' 1000' 1100'

0 mi — Start: 0.00 mi, 552', Follow Wood Run Rd from 24/27 parking

0.36 mi, 481', Pass under powerlines
0.52 mi, 526', J, Turn right on Wood Run Trail

1.75 mi, 597', J, Turn right on Wood Run Road
1.78 mi, 588', J, Turn left on Keyauwee Trail

2 mi — 2.02 mi, 629', J, Intersect Uwharrie Trail

2.84 mi, 609', J, Keep left at end of Walker Mountain Road

3.57 mi, 583', J, Intersect Walker Mountain Road

4 mi

4.99 mi, 391', W X , Cross Upper Wood Run creek

5.85 mi, 394', W X , Cross Moonshine Creek

6 mi — 6.31 mi, 576', J, Intersect Uwharrie Trail

7.83 mi, 630', J, Turn right on Wood Run Road
7.84 mi, 632', J, Pass Supertree Trail on left

8 mi

8.99 mi, 588', J, Pass Supertree Trail left, Keyauwee Trail right
9.03 mi, 597', J, Turn left on Wood Run Trail

10 mi

10.30 mi, 506', J, Turn left on Wood Run Road

End: 10.78 mi, 552', Return to 24/27 parking

Difficulty: Difficult   Elev Gain/Loss: 1,686' / 1,686'

Wood Run Area Trip I

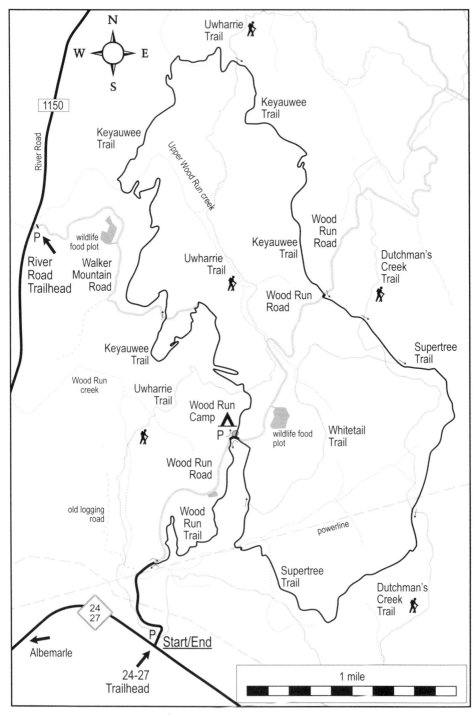

Elevation Profile: WRA Trip I

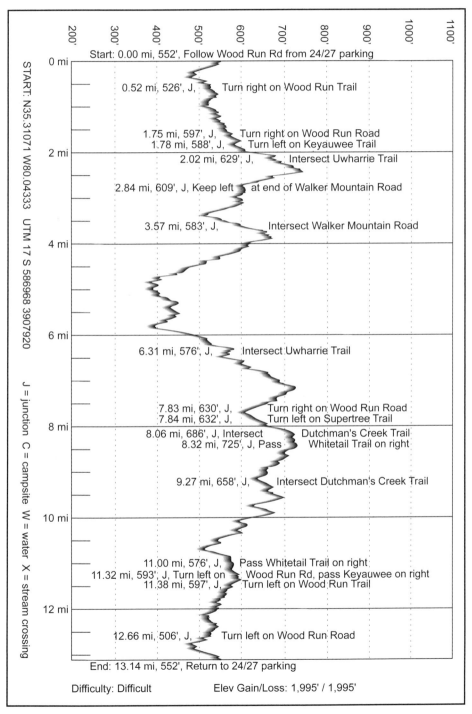

200' 300' 400' 500' 600' 700' 800' 900' 1000' 1100'

Start: 0.00 mi, 552', Follow Wood Run Rd from 24/27 parking

0 mi

0.52 mi, 526', J,   Turn right on Wood Run Trail

1.75 mi, 597', J,   Turn right on Wood Run Road
1.78 mi, 588', J,   Turn left on Keyauwee Trail
2 mi
2.02 mi, 629', J,   Intersect Uwharrie Trail

2.84 mi, 609', J, Keep left   at end of Walker Mountain Road

3.57 mi, 583', J,   Intersect Walker Mountain Road

4 mi

6 mi

6.31 mi, 576', J,   Intersect Uwharrie Trail

7.83 mi, 630', J,   Turn right on Wood Run Road
7.84 mi, 632', J,   Turn left on Supertree Trail
8 mi
8.06 mi, 686', J, Intersect   Dutchman's Creek Trail
8.32 mi, 725', J, Pass   Whitetail Trail on right

9.27 mi, 658', J,   Intersect Dutchman's Creek Trail

10 mi

11.00 mi, 576', J,   Pass Whitetail Trail on right
11.32 mi, 593', J, Turn left on   Wood Run Rd, pass Keyauwee on right
11.38 mi, 597', J,   Turn left on Wood Run Trail

12 mi

12.66 mi, 506', J,   Turn left on Wood Run Road

End: 13.14 mi, 552', Return to 24/27 parking

Difficulty: Difficult   Elev Gain/Loss: 1,995' / 1,995'

START: N35.31071 W80.04333 UTM 17 S 586968 3907920

J = junction C = campsite W = water X = stream crossing

Wood Run Area Trip J

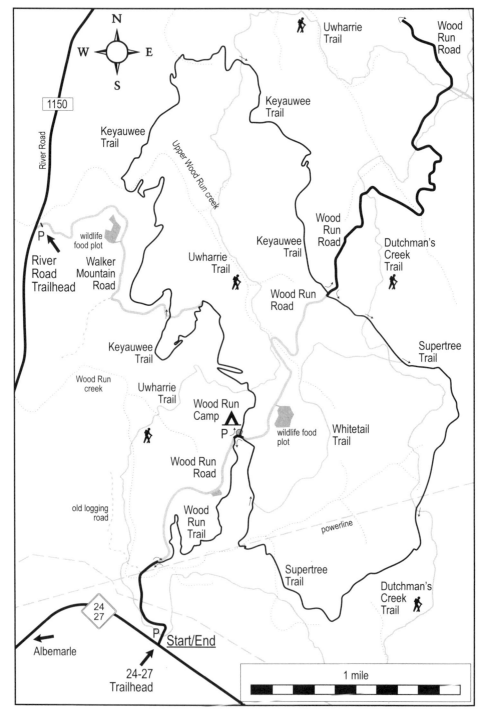

Elevation Profile: WRA Trip J

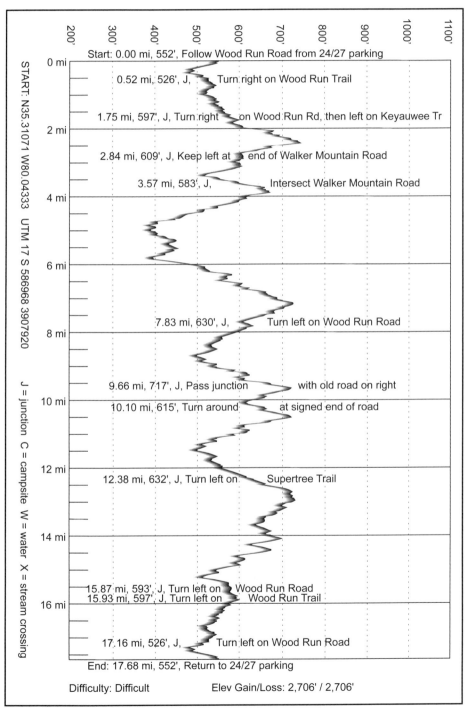

START: N35.31071 W80.04333 UTM 17 S 586968 3907920

J = junction C = campsite W = water X = stream crossing

Start: 0.00 mi, 552', Follow Wood Run Road from 24/27 parking

0.52 mi, 526', J,   Turn right on Wood Run Trail

1.75 mi, 597', J, Turn right   on Wood Run Rd, then left on Keyauwee Tr

2.84 mi, 609', J, Keep left at   end of Walker Mountain Road

3.57 mi, 583', J,   Intersect Walker Mountain Road

7.83 mi, 630', J,   Turn left on Wood Run Road

9.66 mi, 717', J, Pass junction   with old road on right

10.10 mi, 615', Turn around   at signed end of road

12.38 mi, 632', J, Turn left on   Supertree Trail

15.87 mi, 593', J, Turn left on   Wood Run Road
15.93 mi, 597', J, Turn left on   Wood Run Trail

17.16 mi, 526', J,   Turn left on Wood Run Road

End: 17.68 mi, 552', Return to 24/27 parking

Difficulty: Difficult   Elev Gain/Loss: 2,706' / 2,706'

Volunteer Opportunities

A number of trails in the Uwharrie Lakes Region exist, at least in part, thanks to the efforts of individuals who have freely given their time and efforts to build and maintain these public trails. The shrinking budgets of trail managing agencies and increasing numbers of trail users combine to make trail volunteers more important than ever before. Aside from the noble aspects of giving something back to the trails you enjoy, volunteering your time to help work on trails can simply be lots of fun. Joining up with an organization of trail volunteers lets you meet and spend time with other people who share your enjoyment of the backcountry. It's also a great way to meet new hiking and biking partners. The best part may be that it gives you another excuse to get out on the trails.

The organizations described below have all been involved in some way or another with trails in the Uwharrie Lakes Region. Contact them if you would like more information about getting involved with trail maintenance.

Uwharrie Mountain Bicycle Association / SORBA / Tarheel Trailblazers
Don Childrey, a trails enthusiast living in Montgomery County, began efforts in late 1995 to start a mountain bike organization. Brett Russell, a mountain biker and native of Troy, soon joined him and they started organizing a group to develop more trails for mountain bikes in the Uwharrie National Forest. Having first met by way of the Internet, these two men were able to attract volunteers from across the state who were also interested in helping create more mountain bike trails.

The Uwharrie Mountain Bicycle Association, or UMBA, was formed in 1996 and immediately began exploring and making plans for a system of trails to be used by mountain bikers and hikers. The Wood Run Area was chosen as the best site for this system because of its geography and numerous old roadbeds. The trail system they proposed combines these old mining and logging roads with new trail segments to create a system of six or seven interconnected loop trails.

Wood Run Road (FR 517), a graveled Forest System road nearly 5 miles long, formed the backbone of the system. The Supertree Trail and a 1.3 mile section of the Keyauwee Trail were opened and signed for mountain bikes in 1996 as part of the Wood Run Trails system. The assistance of USFS District Planner Kathy Ludlow and approval from USFS District Ranger Tammy Malone helped get this trail system off to a good start.

UMBA applied for and received a NC Adopt-A-Trail Grant in 1996-97 to build a new bulletin board at the 24/27 trailhead and fund required archaeological surveys in order to gain approval to build the Keyauwee Trail, a second loop in the system. Work on completing the rest of the Keyauwee Trail loop began in the fall of 1997 and was completed soon afterwards.

Over the next ten years or so, a few key local volunteers like Tommy Taylor, Chris Green, and Brian Bristol kept the trails maintained and rideable. These guys are still active today.

In the mid 2000's, Brian Bristol helped transition UMBA into a chapter of the Southern Off Road Bicycle Association (SORBA). SORBA then joined forces with the International Mountain Bicycling Association (IMBA). One of the next trail projects, conducted with assistance and expertise from the Tarheel Trailblazers club out of Charlotte, was construction of the Wood Run Trail, which provided an alternative to riding Wood Run Road all the way in to the trailheads.

With assistance from the regional and national level resources of SORBA/IMBA, the group was successful in obtaining grants of nearly $95,000 to perform much-needed work on the trails. USFS District Ranger Deborah Walker approved this trail project in September 2009. A contract was awarded to Trail Dynamics, a company specializing in trail building. Ed Sutton and his crew rerouted and built 5 new miles of tread on the Keyauwee Trail and rerouted part of Supertree away from a wet area under the power lines. This trail work was completed in September 2011.

In June 2013, a major storm felled trees on the majority of the Wood Run Area. Through the efforts of numerous volunteers, including trail groups from the equestrian and OHV communities, the clean-up progressed through the Fall of 2013.

For more information about upcoming trail maintenance plans and activities:

Tarheel Trailblazers   http://www.tarheeltrailblazers.com/
SORBA Uwharrie   http://www.sorbauwharrie.org/
                       http://www.uwharrietrails.org/
IMBA   http://www.imba.com/

Uwharrie Trail Partnership

In 1997 David Craft, a trail enthusiast from Greensboro, began an effort to reconnect the southern Uwharrie Trail section to the Birkhead Mountains Wilderness Area. He brought together several interested people and various organizations to meet and discuss the available options. Among the notable participants in this effort were Joe Moffitt, who started the original Uwharrie Trail, Tom Homer and Jake Cebula with the USFS, Jeff Michael of the LandTrust for Central North Carolina, and Alex Cousins with the Yadkin-Pee Dee Lakes Project.

The group met several times during 1997 and participants met individually with land owners and others in the proposed corridor. Possibilities for securing a trail route include land purchases, land swaps, rights of way, and easements.

In the late 2000's and early 2010's, efforts by the key volunteers in this group brought together numerous organizations. Together they were successful in protecting several key properties needed to reopen the original route of the Uwharrie Trail. The LandTrust for Central NC and the NC Zoo were two key organizations involved with land purchases or swaps needed to put the trail corridor into public ownership.

Find more information about how you can get involved or support the efforts of this group, through their Facebook group:

https://www.facebook.com/groups/116969541757588/

Uwharrie Trail Club

The Uwharrie Trail Club is based out of Asheboro, NC. The organization was originally named GUMPAC, for Greater Uwharrie Mountains Preservation and Appreciation Committee. Joe Moffitt and Mike Chisholm, who worked together to mark the original Uwharrie Trail, founded the club in 1974 with help from members of PATH, Piedmont Appalachian Trail Hikers, a volunteer trail maintenance organization from the Triad area. The name was later changed to the current name, Uwharrie Trail Club.

In 1996, Club volunteers built the Thornburg Trail, providing an additional access route into the Birkhead Mountains Wilderness.

The UTC holds occasional trail maintenance activities as well as recreational activities for members and friends. Outings include hiking, mountain biking, and canoeing trips.

For more information about the Uwharrie Trail Club:

http://uwharrietrailclub.org/

Friends of Uwharrie

The Friends Of Uwharrie represents the interests of all recreationists in the greater Uwharrie area which include, but are not limited to, hunting, fishing, boating, kayaking, gold panning, horseback riding, hiking, OHV riding and mountain biking.

For more information about the Friends of Uwharrie:

http://www.friendsofuwharrie.org/

PATH, Piedmont Appalachian Trail Hikers

PATH is a volunteer organization whose primary purpose is to maintain a 50 mile section of the Appalachian National Scenic Trail in southwest Virignia. PATH was founded in 1965 by several Triad area conservationists, one of whom was Louise Chatfield. Mrs. Chatfield was also involved in starting the Uwharrie Trail Club in the mid 1970's. A shelter along the Appalachian Trail was renamed the Chatfield Shelter in her honor in 1986. PATH has about 300 members who are spread out across North Carolina and southern Virginia.

Activities of PATH include a monthly work weekend on the AT and various hiking and backpacking trips. The organization also participates in outreach programs to educate the public about hiking opportunities and proper use of the backcountry.

For more information about PATH:

http://www.path-at.org/

Uwharrie Packrats

The Uwharrie Packrats was a hiking club active in the 1970's that also helped maintain the southern section of the Uwharrie Trail.

Yadkin-Pee Dee Lakes Project / Central Park NC

In early 1992, the NC Department of Commerce, Division of Community Assistance, approached the citizens of Anson, Davidson, Montgomery, Randolph, Richmond, Rowan and Stanly counties to gauge local interest in a joint strategic planning process. Despite common borders and cultural heritage, these rural counties had never collaborated together on a regional basis. From this time through March 1994, over 400 residents, state and local leaders, and representatives from the private sector participated in the regional effort, thus the birth of the Yadkin-Pee Dee Lakes Project, Inc.

The Yadkin-Pee Dee Lakes Project was a strategic planning initiative which initially served seven rural counties within the Yadkin-Pee Dee River Basin and its chain of six reservoirs. The Yadkin-Pee Dee Lakes Project's mission was to "promote and support efforts to balance economic development and environmental management throughout the Uwharrie Lakes Region".

In 2000, the Project published *A Strategy for North Carolina's "Central Park.* This document served as a blueprint for the development of a new economy for the region. The new economy was to be based on heritage and cultural tourism development and outdoor recreation opportunities. The region was expanded to included Moore County.

In the strategy document, it was noted that many were starting to refer to the Uwharrie Lakes Region as North Carolina's "Central Park". The organization eventually changed its name to Central Park NC to emphasize this concept.

The Central Park strategy continues to focus on small businesses development complementary to heritage and cultural tourism, and also developing the regional infrastructure for increasing overnight tourism. According to studies conducted by Appalachian State University and the Belk College of Business at UNC Charlotte, the implementation of this strategy will result in a doubling of overnight visitation to the region from 20% to 40% by focusing on scenic natural areas, driving/ sightseeing, nature walks, historic sites, and zoos/wildlife observation, and will create an additional 25,000 jobs above the benchmark forecast and an incremental positive net economic impact of $2.1 billion per year.

In 2005, Central Park NC began STARworks Center for Creative Enterprise in a former hosiery mill in the small town of Star. STARworks is home to several for profit and not for profit businesses, focusing on renewable energy, sustainable agriculture, and creative arts-related businesses.

For further information about Central Park NC please visit:

Central Park NC
100 Russell Drive
Star, NC 27356
910.428.9001
http://www.centralparknc.org/

Land Managing Agencies
You can contact the land managing agencies to find out more about opportunities to volunteer your time and efforts to improve or maintain the trails in the Uwharrie Lakes Region. There are many projects that individuals or small groups can complete or assist with.

Albemarle City Lake Park
815 Concord Road
Albemarle, NC 28001
Albemarle Parks & Recreation   704.984.9560
http://www.ci.albemarle.nc.us/

Boone's Cave Park
3552 Boone's Cave Road
Lexington, NC 27292
Davidson County Parks and Recreation Department 336-242-2285
Outdoor Recreation Specialist, Shelia Zuccaro 336-752-2322
http://www.co.davidson.nc.us/ParksAndRecreation/
Boone%60sCaveParkInformation.aspx

The LandTrust for Central North Carolina
204 East Innes Street, Suite 280
Salisbury, NC 28144
704-647-0302
landtrust@landtrustcnc.org
http://landtrustcnc.org/

Morrow Mountain State Park
49104 Morrow Mountain Road
Albemarle, NC 28001
704-982-4402
morrow.mountain@ncparks.gov
http://www.ncparks.gov/Visit/parks/momo/main.php

NC Zoological Park
4401 Zoo Parkway
Asheboro, NC 27205
1-800-488-0444 or 336-879-7000
Volunteer Coordinator 336-879-7712
http://www.nczoo.org/

Town of Troy Nature Preserve
Okeewemee Road
Troy, NC 27371
Troy Town Hall 910-572-3661
http://troy.nc.us/

Uwharrie Ranger District, USFS
USFS District Ranger Deborah Walker
USFS District Recreation Staff Supervisor Terry Savery
789 NC 24/27 East
Troy, NC 27371
910-576-6391
uwharrie@fs.fed.us
http://www.fs.usda.gov/main/nfsnc/home

Regional Information

When to visit
Weather in the Uwharrie Lakes Region is similar to the rest of Piedmont North Carolina. We're usually a few degrees warmer than Charlotte or Greensboro. In winter, we're much warmer than the western NC mountains, giving you a chance to hike or ride without worrying about extreme cold.

In summer, well, this is the South. Expect to sweat and swat. Spring and Fall would be the best times to catch the most comfortable weather in the Uwharrie Lakes Region.

Uwharrie Lakes Region Climate Data

	Average Minimum Temp	Average Maximum Temp	Average Temp	Average Rainfall	Average Snow
Jan	(F)	(F)	(F)	(in)	(in)
Feb	28.5	49.1	38.8	3.5	2.5
Mar	31.0	53.0	42.0	3.6	2.4
Apr	38.8	62.4	50.6	4.1	1.2
May	47.1	71.7	59.4	2.8	0.0
Jun	56.0	78.8	67.4	3.8	0.0
Jul	64.3	85.3	74.8	3.8	0.0
Aug	68.5	88.4	78.4	4.6	0.0
Sep	67.6	87.1	77.3	4.4	0.0
Oct	61.0	81.5	71.3	3.8	0.0
Nov	48.4	71.8	60.1	3.2	0.0
Dec	32.0	52.8	42.4	3.4	0.7
Annual	48.6	70.4	59.5	44.1	6.8

Note: This data is a composite of National Weather Service data from Charlotte, Greensboro, and Fayetteville weather stations.

Where to stay

Uwharrie National Forest
Primitive camping is allowed most anywhere on USFS lands. Four campground facilities in the Badin Lake Area (Arrowhead Campground, Badin Lake Campground, Badin Lake Group Camp, and Canebrake Horse Camp) require fees and/or reservations. The USFS also has several non-fee campsites available; more complete descriptions can be found in the chapter for each area.

There are no backcountry areas in the National Forest that prohibit campfires, but campers should follow Leave No Trace practices when building fires.

Morrow Mountain State Park
Camping in Morrow Mountain State Park is limited to the cabins, campground sites, group camps, and four backcountry sites. Refer to the Morrow Mountain State Park chapter for more details.

Other lodging
http://www.uwharriecabinrentals.com/
reservations@uwharriecabinrentals.com
800-516-2309

http://www.uwharriemountainrentals.com/
relax@adventureure.com
704/985-8372

http://www.4bfarm.net/
4bfarm@gmail.com
336-461-3276

Hotels and restaurants
There are hotels and restaurants available in the larger towns in the region, such as Albemarle and Asheboro. Larger towns will have a greater variety to choose from.

The Eldorado Outpost, a country convenience store located on NC 109 in Montgomery County about a mile north of the Uwharrie River, has a short order grill as well as convenience store fare. They also have a fair supply of camping, hunting and fishing items, as well as items for horseback riders and OHV enthusiasts.

Biking supplies
There are no bike shops closer than a 45 minute drive from the trail areas. It is wise to bring spare tubes and tools if you can use them to keep from having to cut your trip short due to minor breakdowns.

Other activities in the area

Canoeing

Visitors wishing to spend some time on the water can paddle on any of the lakes along the Yadkin and Pee Dee Rivers, although you should be aware that skiers and jetskis use the lakes heavily during the summer.

The Yadkin River Trail follows its namesake from near Lenoir, NC to Interstate 40 at High Rock Lake between Rowan and Davidson Counties, in the northern end of the Uwharrie Lakes Region .

Other options for paddlers include the Uwharrie River, which can be paddled from NC 49 near Asheboro to its mouth at Lake Tillery. The Uwharrie River offers 36 miles of Class I and II water through generally remote and wild scenery. The water quality is fair with some sediment but little obvious pollution.

The Rocky River, which runs along the southern edge of Stanly County, offers 46 miles of Class I and II water through a mix of remote and pastoral scenery. Water quality is good with only slight sedimentation.

The river information above comes from Benner and McCloud's *A Paddler's Guide to Eastern North Carolina, 1987*. This book provides additional details about the Uwharrie and Rocky Rivers, as well as others in the region such as the South Yadkin River.

Boating and fishing

The lakes and rivers in the Uwharrie Lakes Region provide many opportunities for boating and fishing. There are numerous public boat landings, including the ones at Morrow Mountain State Park and the Cove Boat Ramp in the Badin Lake Area. Visit the Wildlife Resources Commission website for fishing regulation information. http://www.ncwildlife.org/

Hunting

In addition to the 50,000+ acres of the Uwharrie National Forest, there are additional tracts of land open to the public through the Wildlife Resource Commission's Game Lands program.

For additional information about current hunting and fishing regulations visit http://www.ncwildlife.org/

Quick Reference Tables

Legend Tables

Area Code	Name	Page
ACLP	Albemarle City Lake Park	33
BLRA	Badin Lake Recreation Area	46
BMWA	Birkhead Mountains Wilderness Area	203
BCP	Boone's Cave Park	246
DCA	Denson's Creek Area	282
MMA	Morris Mountain Area	304
MMSP	Morrow Mountain State Park	330
NCZP	NC Zoological Park	384
UT	Uwharrie Trail	400
WRA	Wood Run Area	448

Use Code	Description
H	Hike
BH	Bike, Hike
EBH	Equestrian, Bike, Hike
OEBH	OHV, Equestrian, Bike, Hike

OHV Trips

Trip	Use	Length (miles)	Elevation Gain/Loss	Difficulty	Page
BLRA Trip M	OEBH	5.39	371' / 645'	Difficult +	190
BLRA Trip I	OEBH	6.75	1,288' / 1,288'	Moderate	182
BLRA Trip J	OEBH	6.75	1,170' / 1,170'	Moderate	184
BLRA Trip O	OEBH	6.86	1,169' / 1,169'	Moderate	196
BLRA Trip K	OEBH	9.24	1,972' / 1,972'	Difficult	186
BLRA Trip L	OEBH	11.02	2,600' / 2,600'	Difficult	188

Equestrian Trips

Trip	Use	Length (miles)	Elevation Gain/Loss	Difficulty	Page
MMSP Trip G	EH	4.38	663' / 663'	Moderate	364
BLRA Trip D	EBH	4.72	844' / 844'	Easy	138
BLRA Trip C	EBH	5.30	948' / 942'	Easy	136
BLRA Trip M	OEBH	5.39	371' / 645'	Difficult +	190
MMSP Trip H	EH	5.97	875' / 875'	Moderate	356
BLRA Trip E	EBH	6.10	1,038' / 1,044'	Easy	140
BLRA Trip N	EBH	6.56	1,220' / 1,220'	Moderate	194
BLRA Trip I	OEBH	6.75	1,288' / 1,288'	Moderate	182
BLRA Trip J	OEBH	6.75	1,170' / 1,170'	Moderate	184
BLRA Trip O	OEBH	6.86	1,169' / 1,169'	Moderate	196
BLRA Trip P	EBH	8.79	1,646' / 1,646'	Difficult	198
BLRA Trip K	OEBH	9.24	1,972' / 1,972'	Difficult	186
BLRA Trip F	EBH	9.43	1,698' / 1,698'	Moderate	142
MMSP Trip I	EH	10.15	1436' / 1436'	Difficult	354
BLRA Trip G	EBH	10.58	1,890' / 1,890'	Moderate	144
BLRA Trip H	EBH	10.87	2,189' / 2,183'	Difficult	146
BLRA Trip L	OEBH	11.02	2,600' / 2,600'	Difficult	188
BLRA Trip Q	EBH	16.16	2,907' / 2,907'	Difficult +	200

Bike Trips

Trip	Use	Length (miles)	Elevation Gain/Loss	Difficulty	Page
BLRA Trip D	EBH	4.72	844' / 844'	Easy	138
BLRA Trip C	EBH	5.30	948' / 942'	Easy	136
BLRA Trip M	OEBH	5.39	371' / 645'	Difficult +	190
BLRA Trip E	EBH	6.10	1,038' / 1,044'	Easy	140
BLRA Trip N	EBH	6.56	1,220' / 1,220'	Moderate	194
BLRA Trip I	OEBH	6.75	1,288' / 1,288'	Moderate	182
BLRA Trip J	OEBH	6.75	1,170' / 1,170'	Moderate	184
BLRA Trip O	OEBH	6.86	1,169' / 1,169'	Moderate	196
WRA Trip G	BH	8.24	1,051' / 1,051'	Moderate	496
BLRA Trip P	EBH	8.79	1,646' / 1,646'	Difficult	198
BLRA Trip K	OEBH	9.24	1,972' / 1,972'	Difficult	186
BLRA Trip F	EBH	9.43	1,698' / 1,698'	Moderate	142
BLRA Trip G	EBH	10.58	1,890' / 1,890'	Moderate	144
WRA Trip H	BH	10.78	1,686' / 1,686'	Difficult	498
BLRA Trip H	EBH	10.87	2,189' / 2,183'	Difficult	146
BLRA Trip L	OEBH	11.02	2,600' / 2,600'	Difficult	188
WRA Trip I	BH	13.14	1,995' / 1,995'	Difficult	500
BLRA Trip Q	EBH	16.16	2,907' / 2,907'	Difficult +	200
WRA Trip J	BH	17.68	2,706' / 2,706'	Difficult	502

Hike Trips

Trip	Use	Length (miles)	Elevation Gain/Loss	Difficulty	Page
DCA Trip A	H	0.97	131' / 131'	Easy	298
BCP Trip A	H	1.00	298' / 298'	Moderate	276
BCP Trip B	H	1.22	249' / 203'	Moderate	278
BLRA Trip A	H	1.86	248' / 221'	Easy	58
BCP Trip C	H	2.68	573' / 571'	Moderate	280
DCA Trip B	H	3.31	549' / 549'	Moderate	300
MMSP Trip A	H	3.36	520' / 520'	Moderate	372
WRA Trip A	H	4.05	637' / 637'	Moderate	484
MMSP Trip B	H	4.11	681' / 681'	Moderate	374
MMSP Trip G	EBH	4.38	663' / 663'	Moderate	364
BLRA Trip D	EBH	4.72	844' / 844'	Easy	138
MMSP Trip C	H	5.10	832' / 832'	Difficult	376
MMA Trip A	H	5.28	944' / 944'	Moderate	324
BLRA Trip C	EBH	5.30	948' / 942'	Easy	136
BLRA Trip M	OEBH	5.39	371' / 645'	Very Difficult	190
MMSP Trip D	H	5.57	1,618' / 1,618'	Difficult	378
BLRA Trip B	H	5.64	651' / 624'	Easy	56
MMSP Trip H	EBH	5.97	875' / 875'	Moderate	356
BLRA Trip E	EBH	6.10	1,038' / 1,044'	Easy	140
MMSP Trip E	H	6.13	1,263' / 1,263'	Difficult	380
BLRA Trip N	EBH	6.56	1,220' / 1,220'	Moderate	194
BLRA Trip I	OEBH	6.75	1,288' / 1,288'	Moderate	182
BLRA Trip J	OEBH	6.75	1,170' / 1,170'	Moderate	184
BMWA Trip D	H	6.86	1140' / 1140'	Difficult	238
BLRA Trip O	OEBH	6.86	1,169' / 1,169'	Moderate	196
BMWA Trip G	H	6.91	1120' / 1120'	Difficult	244
MMA Trip B	H	7.30	1,342' / 1,342'	Difficult	326
WRA Trip B	H	7.40	1,165' / 1,165'	Moderate	486
WRA Trip G	BH	8.24	1,051' / 1,051'	Moderate	496
BLRA Trip P	EBH	8.79	1,646' / 1,646'	Difficult	198
BLRA Trip K	OEBH	9.24	1,972' / 1,972'	Difficult	186
BLRA Trip F	EBH	9.43	1,698' / 1,698'	Moderate	142
BMWA Trip E	H	9.44	1595' / 1595'	Difficult	240
BMWA Trip B	H	9.64	1595' / 1595'	Difficult	234
WRA Trip F	H	9.67	2,065' / 2,065'	Moderate	494
MMSP Trip F	H	9.79	1,889' / 1,889'	Difficult	382
BMWA Trip A	H	9.83	1605' / 1605'	Difficult	232

Hike Trips (continued)

Trip	Use	Length (miles)	Elevation Gain/Loss	Difficulty	Page
MMSP Trip I	EH	10.15	1436' / 1436'	Difficult	354
WRA Trip C	H	10.33	1,950' / 1,950'	Difficult	488
BLRA Trip G	EBH	10.58	1,890' / 1,890'	Moderate	144
WRA Trip H	BH	10.78	1,686' / 1,686'	Difficult	498
BLRA Trip H	EBH	10.87	2,189' / 2,183'	Difficult	146
BLRA Trip L	OEBH	11.02	2,600' / 2,600'	Difficult	188
DCA Trip C	H	11.37	1,387' / 1,387'	Difficult	302
WRA Trip D	H	11.80	2,237' / 2,237'	Difficult	490
BMWA Trip C	H	12.22	2050' / 2050'	Difficult+	236
BMWA Trip F	H	12.27	2130' / 2130'	Difficult+	242
MMA Trip C	H	12.33	2,248' / 2,248'	Difficult	328
WRA Trip I	BH	13.14	1,995' / 1,995'	Difficult	500
BLRA Trip Q	EBH	16.16	2,907' / 2,907'	Difficult +	200
WRA Trip J	BH	17.68	2,706' / 2,706'	Difficult	502
WRA Trip E	H	19.87	4,063' / 4,063'	Difficult	492

Index